S0-AVG-560

ROGER SESSIONS

FREDERIK PRAUSNITZ

ROGER SESSIONS

How a "Difficult" Composer Got That Way

OXFORD
UNIVERSITY PRESS
2002

OXFORD
UNIVERSITY PRESS

Oxford New York
Auckland Bangkok Buenos Aires Cape Town Chennai
Dar es Salaam Delhi Hong Kong Instanbul Karachi Kolkata
Kuala Lumpur Madrid Melbourne Mexico City Mumbai Nairobi
São Paulo Shanghai Singapore Taipei Tokyo Toronto

and an associated company in Berlin

Published by Oxford University Press, Inc.
198 Madison Avenue, New York, New York 10016

www.oup.com

Library of Congress Cataloging-in-Publication Data
Prausnitz, Frederik.
Roger Sessions: how a "difficult" composer got that way / Frederik Prausnitz.
p. cm.
Includes bibliographical references and index.
ISBN 0-19-510892-2
1. Sessions, Roger, 1896– 2. Composers—United States—Biography. I. Title.
ML410.S473 P73 2002
780'.92—dc21
[B] 2001036718

1 3 5 7 9 8 6 4 2
Printed in the United States of America
on acid-free paper

for
Elizabeth Phelps Pease
and in memory of
Sir William Glock

A distinguished composer and teacher,
whose work communicates
the loneliness of artistic experience.

—INSCRIPTION OF ROGER SESSIONS' HONORARY DOCTORATE DIPLOMA, HARVARD

PREFACE

Every composer whose music seems difficult to grasp is, as long as the difficulty persists, suspected or accused of composing with his brain rather than his heart—as if the one could function without the other.

—ROGER SESSIONS

Close to the halfway mark of the twentieth century and almost halfway into Roger Sessions' creative years as a composer—on January 8, 1950, to be precise—the *New York Times* published an article of his under the heading "How a 'Difficult' Composer Gets That Way." As the subtitle of this book, adjusted to the past tense, it affords a focus for the narrative of the composer's life and, given our own vantage point at the end of the century, a workable perspective in which to consider the "why?" and the "which way?" of *Difficult* and of *That Way*.

Sessions was well aware of being a "difficult" composer, although he assigned no particular merit or fault to that condition. He affirms that

> I have sometimes been told that my music is "difficult" for the listener. There are those who consider this as praise, those who consider it a reproach. For my part I cannot regard it as, in itself, either the one or the other. But as far as it is so, it is the way the music comes, the way it has to come . . .
>
> I would prefer by far to write music which has something fresh to reveal at each new hearing than music which is completely self-evident the first time, and though it may remain pleasing makes no essential contribution thereafter.

For the performer, Sessions' music presents difficult challenges that are not likely to diminish over time. The quotation marks, however, around the word *difficult* in the *New York Times* heading suggest "perceived as difficult" or "alleged to be difficult," clearly indicating the general listener's perception; and it is to this listener that Sessions' article is addressed. Somewhere in the minds of many listeners there exists a suspicion that certain twentieth-century composers decided one day to write "modern music" and that this music was to be incomprehensible, elitist, and in-your-face. Abetted by a vocal faction within the musical establishment itself, this notion became a mighty barrier in the way new music was heard, even by listeners with—in Sessions' favorite phrase—"willing ears." In a market-oriented economy, such a barrier discouraged performance. And yet the works were written. Edgar Varese, Arnold Schoenberg, Anton Webern, Elliott Carter, Roger Sessions, Luigi Dallapiccola, Karlheinz Stockhausen, and many others were "difficult" composers indeed. But their work exists.

Composers do not work in a social vacuum, and the rapidly changing, troublesome times in which Sessions wrote his music played their part. "E nato difficile [born difficult]," shrugged Italian composer and friend Alfredo Casella when his young colleague asked his advice on how to make the "unplayable" Violin Concerto easier. Nearly a quarter-century passed before the mature Sessions fully realized that "it is the way the music comes, the way it had to come." That way had involved a long and often difficult process of discovery. To trace that process, ultimately embedded in the narrative of the composer's life, is the aim of this book.

As was Sessions' own practice in discussing his work, specialized musical terminology has been kept to a minimum. To this end, this narrative of his life is interrupted at three points by chapters on the *Musical Idea*, a concept with specific relevance to Sessions' own musical experience, as will be shown. No technical background in music theory is required to follow the argument in the three chapters that deal with the development of Sessions' musical thinking. as such. But for readers interested primarily in Sessions' life and times, it would be entirely possible to omit these chapters altogether, without losing the continuity of the general narrative. They are essential, however, to addressing the question of how Roger Sessions, composer, got that way.

Some twenty-five years ago, William Glock retired as Controller of Music for the British Broadcasting Corporation and became Sir William Glock, in recognition of contributions to the musical life of Great Britain that were unique even in a time of unparalleled cultural renaissance after the Second World War. He accepted the job of music editor for Eulenburg Music Books, in addition to serving in six other, equally demanding assignments, ranging from service on London's Orchestra Board to the directorship of the Bath Music Festival. To serve the music of his time continued to be his overriding priority as he rounded out a long and often controversial career as a musical administrator. It seemed natural for him to commission a number of books on twentieth-century composers, as a first assignment in his job as a music editor. After a delay of nearly two decades—almost entirely on my part—this book finally joins the other biographies that owed their inception to his resolve.

When Sir William asked me to write this book, my principal contact with Roger Sessions had been that of a conductor with a composer whose works he performed. I went to see Sessions. I knew very little about his life, but I was intrigued by the incongruity of his commanding position in the musical world at the time in stark contrast to the sparse performances his works received. When I told him of the still tentative project, Sessions immediately took it for granted that I would accept the job. He seemed pleased but warned me at once that "you need to have some facts first." For our next meeting I provided him with what we came to call fact sheets, dated forms in annual sequence, on which he could list events, people in his life, and works. He also presented me with a copy of his mother's autobiography, a helpful source of information regarding family background and another point of departure for evaluating some of his recollections of childhood and early years as a student.

After some years of refreshing his recollections in subsequent interviews, Sessions agreed to provide a second set of fact sheets. This turned out to be longer but covered the same ground, with almost identical information. Appendix 1, "Overview," represents a composite of these two files, with some additions and corrections as indicated. Interviews began in 1981 and took place at first in New

Roger Sessions — Facts — (1)

DATE	ADDRESS	WORKPLACE	TRIPS	PEOPLE	WORKS BEGUN	WORKS COMPLETED
	Full address if available, otherwise city	Main place of employment, study, or writing.	Personal or professional, itinerary and available dates.	Family, friends, teachers, colleagues, students.*		
1896	— 417 Washington Ave Brooklyn N.Y.	RS Born December 28		Father: Archibald Lowery Sessions Mother Ruth Huntington (Sessions) Sister, Hannah Sergeant S. born Feb. 16, 1889		
1897						
1898						
1899			Brother, John Archibald S— born May 21st	1899 or 1900 {first remembered events taken to Concert in Brooklyn or N.Y. — first signs of inclination for music		

*) Family: dates, important meetings (e.g.Aunt Addie), shared trips

Friends: when met, seen again

Teachers: subject, school, .

Colleagues, students: see below

1923

N.B.: Please include the following: Babbit, Berenson, Berg, Bloch, Boulanger, Carter, Casella, Cone, Dallapiccola, Davies (Max), Diamond, Drew, Ginastera, Glock, Harris, Imbrie, Kim, Kirchner, Klemperer, Krenek, Mennin, Milhaud, Parker (Horatio), Persichetti, Petrassi, Schnabel, Schoenberg, Schubart, Schuman, Shifrin, Spender, Steinberg (Michael), Steuermann, Stiedry, Stravinsky, Wagner (S

N.B.2: Please add names that should be included as well, but which haven't come up yet in our talks (e.g. Copland, Thomson, others (particularly in association with places: Berlin, Florence, Berkeley

.../2

First "fact sheet" filled out by Roger Sessions

York, whenever our respective professional activities at Juilliard allowed a lengthy meeting, following lunch at one of his favorite restaurants on Broadway. Later on we met at his home in Princeton. Interviews usually began with prepared questions, but he would soon range freely over different aspects of his life and his work, while I scribbled notes. Almost invariably, these meetings were followed within twenty-four hours by a telephone call that began with, "I am not quite sure if I expressed myself clearly enough . . . ," and went over familiar ground once more. Thus, gradually, during the last four years of his life, an image of the man and the composer Roger Sessions evolved, which I have tried to capture in the narrative of this account.

His were the thoughts and remembered feelings, of course, of a man looking back at the end of a long life. They are not necessarily consonant with his immediate reactions to people and events earlier on, and a quite different picture emerges occasionally from letters he had written at the time of the actual events. I have made no attempt to resolve apparent contradictions but left it to the readers to draw their own conclusions. Once I had decided to attempt a story of Sessions' life as it related to and ultimately determined his work, it soon became clear that the best way to do that was to let the composer speak for himself. I am deeply indebted to Roger Sessions' daughter, Elizabeth Pease, for her generous help in letting me work with a very large collection of family letters, particularly those of the early years of her father's evolution into a "difficult" composer.

John Sessions, like his sister, Elizabeth, answered questions about life in the Sessions family, in long, carefully considered letters. A distinguished cellist and highly successful teacher, he provided a point of view in which the fused roles of son and young colleague shed a unique light on a famous father. John also went to great lengths to find a rare photograph of his mother, who, unaccountably, did not like to have her picture taken.

Among Sessions' students, I am indebted to Milton Babbitt and Earl Kim for long interviews that provided yet another perspective on events and recollections of his life. Among my own students, Louis Stewart, Brian Stone, and Nicolas Waldvogel gave freely of their time and expertise in hunting down references and recorded information. Jon Newsom of the Library of Congress in Washington placed the rich resources of its music division at my disposal. Loras Schissel, also of the library, was an enthusiastic researcher.

Iris Newsom of the Congressional Library's publications division enlivened my stalled writing of this book by commissioning an article on my New York performance of Sessions' opera *Montezuma*, which helped me to bridge my overlapping and sometimes inimical identities as Sessions' biographer and performer of his work. Among those whose encouragement refreshed and sometimes renewed my resolve, Mark Hirsch and Ken Slovick of the Smithsonian Institution in Washington and Michael Krausz of Bryn Mawr College are owed a special debt.

In the end, Sheldon Meyer of Oxford University Press accepted my manuscript with such kindness that I had to finish it. In the process of preparing my text for its eventual appearance in print, editors Jonathan Wiener, Maureen Buja, Ellen Welch, and Jessica Ryan earned not only my enormous respect for their craftsmanship but also great gratitude for their patience.

My daughter, Maja, an editor in her own right, read the manuscript in a variety of evolving redactions. She was probably the least patient among those who encouraged me, and I owe her abundant thanks. The deepest acknowledgment and my greatest regret go to my wife, Margaret, who lived with this work in progress as intimately as I but who did not live to see it done.

CONTENTS

ROGER SESSIONS

INTRODUCTION

After the death of Roger Sessions the editors of Perspectives of New Music *asked friends, colleagues, and former students of the composer to contribute recollections to a commemorative section in the Spring–Summer 1985 issue of the periodical. The following article was my contribution.*

Near the end of Roger Sessions' last summer, a visitor would walk along Nassau Street past fashionable stores and restaurants facing the Princeton University campus. He would turn right on Bayard Lane, whose broad, tree-lined sweep belies its modest title, and continue among old gardens, big houses and shady trees until he reached the blue gabled, spacious former home of the composer during his tenure as a Princeton professor. Almost directly opposite Stanworth Lane begins a U-shaped roadway traversing some large tracts of more modest university housing.

Homes on Stanworth Lane come in two or three serviceable styles, mostly small duplex ranches grouped around good-sized commons. Cars are large and, like some of their former owners, may well have lived formerly on Bayard Lane. Lawns are dotted with toys and tricycles. Here and there a determined sunbather tries to ignore the sounds of a children's quarrel coming through open windows behind her. This is an enclave of the old and the very young among university faculty. Here Roger Sessions has lived for nearly twenty years since his retirement, and here I found him during those sultry final days of the summer of 1984.

Roger's is a small single house. Through the screen door, outlined against the bright rectangle of a window at the back, one can see him seated at one side of his living room. Although my entrance is noisy, as always on these visits, he has not heard me. He has installed himself on a straight-backed kitchen chair. Over the top of horn-rimmed glasses which also hold his hearing aid he peers at a large open volume in his lap. In response to my loud, cheery hello he finally looks up. His wide grin bares a set of very even teeth, splitting his round, firmly boned head very nearly from one large ear to the other. "I've been expecting you!" Then he carefully replaces the book among a row of similar volumes in the bookcase behind him. He has been reading the *Encyclopaedia Britannica*.

"My study is such a mess," he says, "we must talk down here today." It is a game he has played ever since Lisl's death, but the announcement is received, as intended, as news. "I've been trying to find the letters you wanted. Did I send you anything from Dallapiccola? He was my dearest friend among Europeans. And Milhaud, of course. But I don't think I have any letters from Milhaud. He was very close to me in Berkeley. But Luigi—when you see his letters you'll understand. I suppose you have all of Dallapiccola's music. I wish I knew where I put those things. My study is such a mess."

My visit to Sessions is not as conductor of his music this time but as his biographer. For two years we have gone over notes and materials and letters and chronologies. There is much repetition and there are variations among the repetitions. But from his frequently retold recollections there emerges a growing sense of that very private, distinguished, lovable man. Because they demand time, before and after, most of our visits had to take place in the summers. We had no way of knowing that this one would be the last.

A forlorn look comes over his face. "I can't hear you with these stupid glasses. I'll see if I've got another battery." He gropes behind his left ear to remove the frames. "No wonder; there's no battery in here. Excuse me a moment." As he crosses the room to the stairs opposite, one cannot help noting the incongruities of what adds up to an oddly impressive appearance. In honor of my visit, or so it seems, Roger is wearing a wide wool-knit tie and a well-worn tweed jacket. More suitable in the lingering summer heat are his ancient khaki shorts from whose frayed bottoms project bony knees and thin brown legs in ankle socks and heavy brogues. For all his topheavy appearance, the octogenarian composer climbs the steps to the second floor and his "messy study" with surprising agility and, as for as long as I have known him, with unconscious but completely commanding dignity.

I first saw him at a reception in New York's Greenwich Village. I had arrived late, nervous about meeting Roger Sessions—and I barely past being a music student. There he was, at the center of the largest group in that very crowded place. He appeared to be demonstrating the fine qualities of something he was holding in his hand. Peering over the heads of my fellow guests, I recognized that object of his affectionate praise as a set of teeth, his new dentures. Not until many years later, in the preparation and performance of Sessions' works, did it occur to me that I had been given a significant clue to the essence of his music: like himself, it wants to be taken simply for what it is; and what may strike the conditioned intellect as arcane will be revealed more readily to the attentive ear and to the heart. For Sessions, music was a way of sharing, of permitting another's participation in his experience where verbal communication would be unsuitable or undesirable. He did not find it difficult to hold forth among strangers on the physical comfort of a new set of teeth but reserved more complex or more personal areas of his being for a musical metamorphosis, always genuine, not often easy, expressed "in the simplest terms possible—but not simpler."

"You've got most of the facts right." The papers he has brought down are chronological tables of biographical detail, based on our most recent chats and submitted for his approval. No further mention of the battery for his hearing aid. In any event, from here on he'll do most of the talking.

"But my Aunt Addie *was* a concert singer. She did *not* give up her career because of stage fright." I make a note ('wonder why this is so important to him?). "She adored my father, you see. It's funny how in our family there were always clear lines drawn about who liked whom best. I liked my father and he liked me. My mother liked my younger brother—and ruined his life. And she worshiped her own father, of course, the Bishop. He liked my older sister Hannah. And, of course, there was another sister in between, Mary, but she died. My mother romanticized Mary and Mary's death a lot. My mother was a very strange woman."

As the biographical framework of Sessions' life gradually emerged, one thing became strikingly apparent: the experiences and circumstances of the person and the development of the composer show an organic unity in which the first invariably served the second. As a composer, Sessions matured slowly and wrote sparingly for many years. At age twenty-six, when he embarked on a "wayfarer" decade, mostly spent in Europe, he had completed only one of the works he still acknowledged today, *The Black Maskers.* During the mostly European years from 1923 to 1933, he wrote two major works. Two decades following his return to the United States were devoted to teaching, to writing about music, and to a small output of works each one of which, albeit a masterpiece in itself, became a precarious stepping stone to the next. With the second string quartet in 1952 and the sonata for solo violin in 1953 he appears to have felt himself complete in terms of a musical language which would serve his ideas. Then, at age 57, Roger Sessions became a prolific composer.

I asked him about his late start and about his deliberate, very slow rate of composition for so many years. "You see," he said, "I was very shy. I had to find myself first and gain confidence. And coming back from Europe I found America a very strange place. Some of the musical life had become quite European with the arrival of so many distinguished musicians who had fled the Nazis. At the same time some American composers seemed determined to 'invent' American music by external means. I had to discover who I was and what my music was."

Thus, during his first tenure at Princeton (1935–1945) and his following years of teaching at Berkeley (1945–1952), Sessions underwent a second apprenticeship, with himself as the master teacher. His musical output after that reflects the assurance for which he had so patiently labored: Symphonies 3 - 9, the opera *Montezuma*, concertos, cantatas, chamber music, and solo works, in roughly the number of creative years of Mozart's life or of Schubert's—but late. Then silence fell once more, following the death of his wife, Lisl.

The old man who sits across from me now, on a kitchen chair in his living room (in which nothing has been moved since that tragic event more than two years before), is still a man in mourning. "It is very hard for me. I miss Lisl, you see. And time passes more slowly when one is old. I am lonely." How does time pass? Attempting to write again. He has a Library of Congress commission for a chamber work. "I have some ideas. I think I will put it together soon." Or poking around his "messy study" as he is now poking around in the mass of memories he is trying to organize. Or telephoning his friends, sometimes twice daily. Occasionally one suspects he may have forgotten his earlier call. "Hello? This is Roger Sessions. I'm afraid I've been neglecting you."

Roger and Lisl were not given to outward signs of affection, at least not in the company of others. But they complemented and augmented each other remarkably. I last saw Lisl, a few months before her death, after the New York premiere of Sessions' opera *Montezuma,* which I conducted. She had been confined to a wheelchair for some time, but Roger engaged a limousine and driver to take her to Juilliard so that she might share the event. After the final curtain he took his bow onstage with the cast, but he refused to wait for friends and admirers who would seek him out backstage. "I left Lisl up there in her chair. Let's go!" And so we went, followed along the way by an ever-growing procession of well-wishers, out into the house where the applause began again, until we found the lady in her wheelchair, handsome and aristocratic as ever, holding a court of her own. While the two groups, hers and ours, mingled around them—for all the world like followers at a meeting of two sovereigns—Roger bent down to kiss her. For a moment she looked very young and her eyes were shining: "Roger, that was fine."

Now, as I sit with my friend, in a room that still seems to hold her presence, I can almost hear Lisl's voice. It has been exactly three years since my first visit to the house on Stanworth Lane, in search of Roger's book. "Write it soon," she had said; "I know Roger wants to see it done," and he broke in eagerly: "You see, I've had such a wonderful life!"

CHAPTER 1 The Matriarch

"Roger," said Archibald Sessions, "if your mother were a man, she'd be Emperor of the United States."

"You mean president, Daddy."

"No, we wouldn't have presidents anymore, just an emperor."

There were strong women in Roger Sessions' family. His second wife, Elizabeth ("Lisl," mother of his children), was such a one, as were others, equally remarkable, in the long history of the clan in western Massachusetts. And most of them were named Elizabeth. But none of them was stronger or more remarkable than his mother, whose name was Ruth.

Ruth Gregson Huntington was a gifted pianist, a skilled writer, an indefatigable social advocate on the liberal left, and a formidable family matriarch. Until Roger married his own Elizabeth (Lisl) in 1936, his mother remained, for all his efforts at reprieve, the woman in his life. In that year she published her autobiography, *Sixty Odd,* a delightful read, though, according to her son, selectively unreliable (in any case, the lady was seventy-odd at the time of publication). For all that, and some personal accommodation notwithstanding, the book sheds a revealing light on circumstances that shaped the composer's early life and on personal values that informed his outlook for years to come.

The family background she describes reflects an odd blend of New England conservatism with a recurring strain of quite inconsonant radical leanings. It was a difficult heritage—too difficult to bear for some and uncomfortable to live with. For all his moral sensitivity and intellectual awareness, Roger's father, Archibald Lowery Sessions, could not cope. But mother Ruth made a fine life of it, as did the two men who meant most to her: her father, Frederic Huntington, Episcopal bishop of Central New York State, and her son Roger, composer.

For nearly three hundred years before his birth, Roger's forebears were farmers and clergymen, lawyers and soldiers, kin and neighbors in the heartland of New England. They came to western Massachusetts in the early years of the seventeenth century, the Phelps' and the Porters, the Sessions' and the Huntingtons. And as his parents were first cousins, they all appear on both sides of the family tree.

There was William Phelps, whose son Nathaniel, deacon, "founded the town of Northampton," to which, some two and a half centuries later, Sessions' mother, Ruth Huntington, would return with her young family, leaving her husband to pursue his literary fortunes in New York City.

Then there was Samuel Porter, who settled across the river in Hadley. In 1752, his grandson Moses Porter built a great house called Forty Acres. There, in 1770, in the "Long Room," his daughter Elizabeth married Charles Phelps and, on New Year's Day 1801, their daughter Elizabeth Whiting Phelps married Dan Huntington, whose granddaughter Ruth would marry cousin Archie Sessions ("the quiet one from Brooklyn"), also at Forty Acres, on November 16, 1887.

And there was the widow Margaret Huntington, who had brought her four-year-old son, Samuel, from England in 1633. Samuel's great-grandson William went to fight in the American Revolution, two years after the birth of his son Dan Huntington. Dan's marriage to Elizabeth Whiting Phelps not only connected the Phelps, Porter, and Huntington branches of the composer's family tree but also would link them, two generations later, with the Sessions side of Roger's ancestral stock.

Only four years after he had built Forty Acres, Moses Porter was killed in the French and Indian War. Captain Porter's wife and her eight-year-old daughter, both Elizabeth, looked after house and farm alone until, in 1770, Charles Phelps came to claim young Elizabeth to wife and to stay.

In 1817, their son Charles Porter Phelps would build another great house there, the Phelps House. But his sister, Elizabeth Whiting Phelps, who married Dan Huntington, was forced to leave the ancestral domain. Of Puritan stock, with deacons and ministers among her ancestors, Elizabeth was born to a way of life in which approved religious observance played a central role within the closely knit New England community but found the gentler message of Channing's Unitarian beliefs more congenial to her nature than the Calvinist creed of her forebears. And although she remained a loyal member of the religious confession of her parish, a delegation of deacons came to call at Forty Acres to examine her "heretical views." Having failed to convince her inquisitors that, the personal variety of her beliefs notwithstanding, she could still embrace the principles of her inherited faith and having resisted all efforts to reclaim her, unconditionally, for their more muscular Christianity, she accepted expulsion from

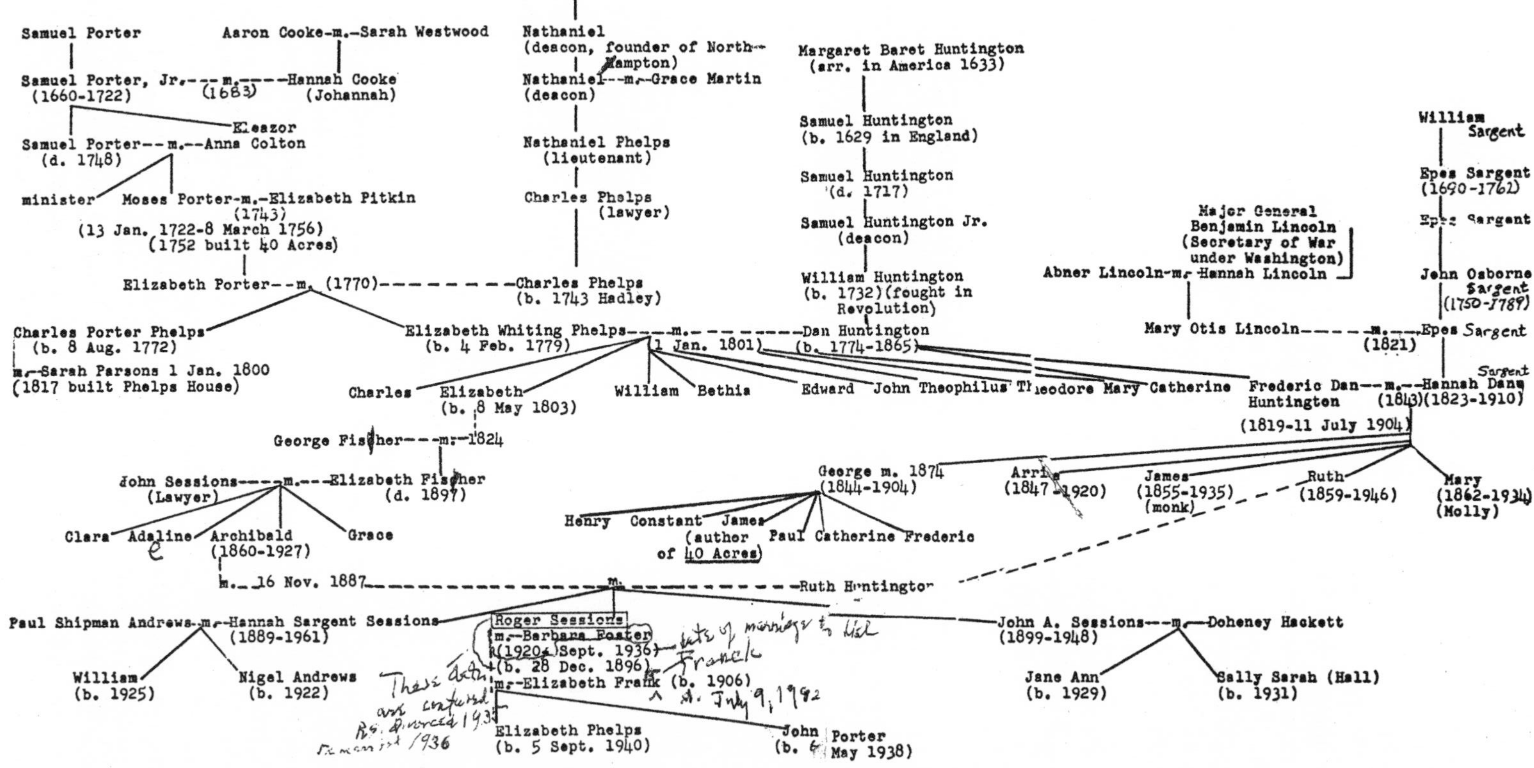

William Phelps
Nathaniel (deacon, founder of Northampton)
Nathaniel--m.--Grace Martin (deacon)
Nathaniel Phelps (lieutenant)
Charles Phelps (lawyer)
Samuel Porter
Aaron Cooke-m.-Sarah Westwood
Samuel Porter, Jr.---m.----Hannah Cooke (1660-1722) (1683) (Johannah)
Eleazor
Samuel Porter--m.--Anna Colton (d. 1748)
minister
Moses Porter-m.-Elizabeth Pitkin (1743) (13 Jan. 1722-8 March 1756) (1752 built 40 Acres)
Elizabeth Porter--m. (1770)--------Charles Phelps (b. 1743 Hadley)
Charles Porter Phelps (b. 8 Aug. 1772)
m.-Sarah Parsons 1 Jan. 1800 (1817 built Phelps House)
Elizabeth Whiting Phelps---m.---------Dan Huntington (b. 4 Feb. 1779) 1 Jan. 1801) (b. 1774-1865)
Margaret Baret Huntington (arr. in America 1633)
Samuel Huntington (b. 1629 in England)
Samuel Huntington (d. 1717)
Samuel Huntington Jr. (deacon)
William Huntington (b. 1732)(fought in Revolution)
Charles
Elizabeth (b. 8 May 1803)
William
Bethia
Edward
John Theophilus
Theodore
Mary
Catherine
Frederic Dan--m.--Hannah Dana Sargent Huntington (1843)(1823-1910) (1819-11 July 1904)
Major General Benjamin Lincoln (Secretary of War under Washington)
Abner Lincoln-m.-Hannah Lincoln
Mary Otis Lincoln-------m.---Epes Sargent (1821)
William Sargent
Epes Sargent (1690-1762)
Epes Sargent
John Osborne Sargent (1750-1789)
George Fischer---m.-1824
John Sessions-----m.---Elizabeth Fischer (Lawyer) (d. 1897)
Clara
Adaline
Archibald (1860-1927)
Grace
George m. 1874 (1844-1904)
Henry
Constant
James (author of 40 Acres)
Paul
Catherine
Frederic
Arria (1847-1920)
James (1855-1935) (monk)
Ruth (1859-1946)
Mary (1862-1934) (Molly)
m. 16 Nov. 1887-------m.---------Ruth Huntington
Paul Shipman Andrews-m.-Hannah Sargent Sessions (1889-1961)
William (b. 1925)
Nigel Andrews (b. 1922)
Roger Sessions
m.-Barbara Foster (1920-Sept. 1936)
(b. 28 Dec. 1896)
m.-Elizabeth Frank (b. 1906)
Elizabeth Phelps (b. 5 Sept. 1940)
John Porter (b. 6 May 1938)
John A. Sessions---m.--Doheney Hackett (1899-1948)
Jane Ann (b. 1929)
Sally Sarah (Hall) (b. 1931)

the congregation. Her husband, Dan Huntington, followed her into spiritual exile in Unitarian Cambridge.

The Huntingtons, Dan and Elizabeth, had eleven children. The youngest (by eighteen years), Frederic Dan Huntington, married Bostonian Hannah Sargent and became Ruth Huntington's father; while the second oldest, Elizabeth Fisher, had a daughter (the fifth Elizabeth in as many generations) who would marry New York lawyer John Sessions. On November 16, 1887, back in the Long Room at Forty Acres, their son Archibald was married to Ruth Huntington. Roger Huntington Sessions, composer, born on December 28, 1896, was the second of their three children.

Roger's mother, Ruth, born in Cambridge, grew up in Boston, far from her kin in western Massachusetts. It was her mother's folks, the Sargents, who were family in the big city. She tells the Sargent story as she heard it when she was a little girl:

> We had only one grandmother, Grandmother Sargent, who lived in Roxbury. She had told us stories of her young days, and we knew our Grandfather Sargent had been a sea captain who sailed his own merchant ships, and had traveled in Russia and other countries. Grandmother herself was the daughter of Abner Lincoln, a son of General Lincoln, Washington's aide-de-camp . . . Abner Lincoln kept a school at Hingham in which his daughter Mary taught. Epes Sargent, the young captain, was a widower with five children, who left his boys and girls at school while he went sailing. And they loved Mary so dearly that when Captain Sargent came back from his voyages and found them clinging to her, he came to love her too, so the story went, and married her. He gave up seafaring life, and when our mother and father became engaged the Sargents were living in a big hospitable Boston house.[1]

At the time when little Ruth first delighted in the romance of Capt. Epes Sargent and his Mary, her father was rector of Emmanuel Church in Boston. Frederic Huntington was a resourceful man of strong convictions. When Ruth was born, he had held the chair of Plummer Professor of Christian Morals at Harvard, but having experienced a crisis of faith with regard to the Unitarian confession he shared with his Cambridge colleagues, he embraced the Episcopal faith, a step that, like his mother's lapse from local orthodoxy, carried serious consequences. He was forced to resign his position at the university and took up his rectorship on the other side of the Charles River.

Daughter Ruth was too young to know or care why the family was forced to leave the house in Quincy Street where she was born, but as the mature woman of *Sixty Odd* she relates how "his intention of embracing the Episcopal faith was received [at Harvard] with active dismay. His many Unitarian friends felt hurt, puzzled, and some of them indignant. With many of his more intimate companions the relation was never quite the same."

Before the end of the decade, in 1868, Ruth's father was elected Episcopal

The Long Room at Forty Acres in Hadley, Massachusetts, where the first ancestral wedding was performed in 1770 and Sessions' parents were married in 1887. Photograph by Ruth Huntington Sessions.

bishop of Central New York State and moved to the diocesan headquarters in Syracuse, New York. From now on his family, including grandson Roger, would refer to Frederic Huntington as The Bishop.

The Bishop was a doer. His was not a ministry of social reform as such, but he addressed existing conditions in the diocese with paternal firmness and never hesitated to involve prominent families, including his own, in solving urban problems in Syracuse. In order to reduce mutual humiliation and occasional abuse when beggars knocked on doors, he started a citywide food stamp program. Families were encouraged to purchase tickets that a needy person could exchange for food and shelter at participating cheap restaurants and lodging homes. A room at the Bishop's residence was reserved for bundles of unwanted clothing to be dropped off daily for distribution among the poor. The entire Huntington family participated in sorting and mending the constant supply of contributions.

Ruth Huntington's oldest sister, Arria, was seconded to her father's program for the rehabilitation of women convicts, many of them "fallen" girls, whose release from prison offered them little hope for a better life. In the face of opposition from "certain political forces, hitherto the protectors of vice; wealthy patrons of the houses of prostitution which crowded certain sections of the city," she made this her life's work. Eventually she founded the Shelter, a school for young women, where first offenders could be sent.

Ruth herself, at age fourteen, worked as an assistant teacher in her father's new mission school in the largely German-populated northern part of the city.

She was to "do some scouting in the neighborhood, and then assist, under direction, with the teaching of a little Sunday class . . . Someone afterward gave us a melodeon on which I played hymns that we stenciled on cloth." Before long, she became the piano teacher for yet another mission school at the nearby Indian reservation of the Onandaga tribe. By her own account, she must have been quite a success: one of her students, a chieftain's daughter, eventually became the organist for Sunday services—on the melodeon.

But the social problems in which the Bishop and his family took an active interest were not confined to pastoral concerns for sinners, the poor, and the ethnically estranged of his community. In 1875, an event of general importance made a particularly powerful impression on sixteen-year-old Ruth: the American Women's Congress held its National Convention in Syracuse.

> We were tremendously enthusiastic when we heard that Louisa Alcott was coming, and would stay with our friends, the Mills . . . Miss Alcott's father, that quiet and completely unworldly Concord student, had held one of the interesting lecture discussions which he called "conversations" at our house, and justified the portrait she had painted of him in *Little Women*; and that book was then, as it has been ever since, a favorite story of growing girls. To see the author in person and hear her talk was a prospect which enlisted feminine interest, old and young, in the Congress itself.

Indeed, most of the agenda of the Women's Congress at Syracuse, which ranged far beyond *Little Women,* would not have been out of place at a comparable meeting a hundred years later. Among the speakers were Mary A. Livermore (on "superfluous women"); Elizabeth Stanton, equal suffrage proponent; Maria Mitchell, an astronomer who advised her students at Vassar to abstain from sewing in favor of science; Julia Ward Howe, author of "The Battle Hymn of the Republic"; and Phoebe Hanford, who reminded her listeners that in the seventeenth century the Quakers permitted their women to preach and pray in public, "mentioning the name of Lucretia Mott, at which the whole audience applauded." Ruth continues:

> Now sixteen, I had led far too easy a life to be conscious of the heroism which characterized those early days of Woman's struggle for independence. A typical product of the Victorian age, I believed that the destiny of woman was to rule over a domestic kingdom as queen and mistress; man's guiding star, a beneficent influence, a wise mother, a gifted teacher or writer or musician if possible, but at least, failing more striking achievements, a contented housewife.

As Ruth recounts her long life from the vantage point of *Sixty Odd,* it does not seem unlike the "typical product of the Victorian age" that the sixteen-year-old had believed appropriate. She would indeed rule over a domestic kingdom as queen and mistress and would try to be a wise mother. She was no less representative of contemporary proprieties in having to forego a professional life. Ruth was the musical one in the family. According to her son Roger, "She was

The old barn at Forty Acres. Photo annotated by Ruth Sessions, "as it was in our childhood."

not taken seriously, a sign of the times in the United States." As far as her own family was concerned, that was not entirely true. The Bishop took his daughter's musical aspirations seriously enough to present her, on her twenty-first birthday, with a two-year trip to Germany. She was to be a piano student in Leipzig.

Ruth's own recollections of her studies abroad read more like the account of a young woman intensely absorbed by social and political events in a foreign land than the memoirs of a serious music student. She did sign up for twice-weekly piano lessons with one Professor Coccius (dubbed by her fellow students "the Apostle of the Fourth Finger") and practiced conscientiously to develop the use of that digit "by putting extra tasks on it and building up its efficiency," but she also found that "music is no escape from the vicissitudes of life . . . You don't get terribly excited about it over here, you just go in for it."

The amount of music she had occasion to hear should have made as overwhelming an impression as, thirty years later, a wealth of first-rate performances in Boston would more than make up for the uninspired musical instruction her son Roger received at Harvard. But Ruth's accounts of Gewandhaus concerts by the Saxe-Meiningen Orchestra under Hans von Bülow or piano recitals by Clara Schumann—strong on amusing, extramusical detail and fulsome about the excellence of the performances—are oddly uncertain about what was actually being played: "The first movement of a Beethoven Symphony—the fifth I think."

Her political judgments, on the other hand, leave no doubt as to her having been there. One month after Ruth's arrival in Leipzig, the assassination of Czar

The Phelps House in Northhampton

Alexander II in Russia persuaded Prussian authorities to order the interrogation of "nihilists and other potential troublemakers." Passports of foreigners were collected and deposited in the Central Bureau of the police. Ruth witnessed a daylong procession of small one-horse carriages, "crowded with men who were to all appearances fugitives," bound for greater safety perhaps in rural districts. Ruth had no doubts about the merits of the government decree: "It was as if all the underground dens of criminality had disgorged their inhabitants . . . The nihilist ranks had been temporarily diminished, but there were disturbing elements in the population which must be suppressed." Her interest in social and political affairs would always be keen and her judgments quick, but as an often courageous champion of unpopular causes she still had some way to go.

She shows more sympathy toward social problems that her brother James reports from America. During her absence in Germany, James demonstrated once again the family penchant for accepting consequences of a strong personal belief at whatever cost to oneself or one's family. He intended to "join, or practically found, a monastic order, living in the slums of New York and devoting his life henceforth to poverty, celibacy and labor among the people of the tenement regions. It meant not only a parting which I knew would be agonizing to his father, but a change to the extreme Anglican position, and a reversion to primitive forms of doctrine and sacramental practice."

In the event, the Bishop was more understanding and generous than she had thought. He wrote to Ruth:

> How could I hold him back—knowing his heart, seeing what he has done for me, and fully believing that the church sorely needs both a standard of holy living in the ministry and a leaven of evangelicalization supplementing our miserable, half-secular parochial system . . . They live in poverty, chastity and obedience—with bare floors, no table cloths, scanty furniture, plain food, and seem content. I went and celebrated with them one morning, slept there on a cot, and we consecrated the different rooms with prayers . . . Pray for them.

"This was the [religious] transition of the third generation," Ruth observes. "Archie was the fourth." Young Archibald Lowery Sessions, grandson of the Bishop's older sister Elizabeth, had come to visit at Forty Acres in mid-August 1879, two years before Ruth's departure for Germany. The Huntington family used to spend their summers at the ancestral home for as long as Ruth could remember, and on this clear, bright morning, after an early thunderstorm, she had gone rowing with her cousin Ellen. When they got back, Ruth heard voices of strangers in the Long Room. She slipped upstairs to change into more suitable clothing than what she had worn on the river. Her little sister Molly followed her, bursting with the news:

> "Who do you suppose is here? [Cousins] Grace and Fred and Will, and a quiet one from Brooklyn, Cousin Lizzie Sessions' son. He's awfully good-looking but he doesn't say much."
>
> "I don't care about meeting him: he's his sister's pet. The others are jollier. Give me my brown gingham, Molly, will you? I suppose I'll have to go down."

Ruth goes on to say that "she set her feet in the stair-treads as firmly as if she had been Elizabeth Huntington going to meet the deacons. Behind the two nice Western [Massachusetts] boys stood a brown-eyed lad of nineteen. Yes, rather handsome, she said to herself."

A game of croquet followed, in which Ruth of the "unerring eye sent the ball flying from long range to hit that of her silent cousin, just in time to prevent him from carrying his partner to victory. Down went her square-toed shoe, and a hammer stroke dispatched his ball into exile."

She could hardly have foretold their future more perfectly. Meanwhile, on the following morning, the weather broke and the farm lay steaming under a thick blanket of rain:

> Exploring the attic was an appropriate pastime, and to this the boy and girl betook themselves, hunting out spinning wheels and trundle beds, looking out the window of the "prophet's chamber" across the rain-drenched meadow, finally squeezing into a tight little niche in the library to look at a black leather volume of Fox's *Book of Martyrs*, with its gruesome illustrations; it was a rather protracted session and amusing withal. Now and then they wandered off the subject of martyrs, and discussed mutual likings, one of which was music.

Frederic Dan Huntington, Episcopal Bishop of Central New York, "My grandfather F. D. H., the Old Man of the Tribe," reads Roger Sessions' note on the back of the photograph.

In the afternoon, Ruth took care to change into one of her most becoming gowns. Downstairs, she found Archie "deep in a rather faded book, of whose title she gained rather a fleeting glance. Newman's *Grammar of Assent;* most extraordinary reading for a college boy. Was he going to become a minister? . . . He put the book down when she came in."

Archie's visit stretched into an eventful week. On the day after Fox and Newman, the young people trudged along a muddy road to make a call on Cousin Ellen at the Phelps House. Ruth's foot slipped, and Archie caught her wrist to pull her to her feet. "His face was turned away; of a sudden a thrill passed from his finger-ends to her shoulder, a light but disturbing touch, such as she had never felt before . . . The east wind blew fine raindrops into their faces, and they fell into a rhythmic step, keeping pace with fresh energy."

A week of fine weather followed, toward the end of which the couple found themselves tucked up in a haymow:

> We went out to the barn for the ostensible purpose of letter-writing, and were a bit breathless and embarrassed as we sank into the soft, sun-warmed hay. The solitude, the familiar crackling of brittle haystalks, the chirp of a cricket, were momentous. The boy plunged at once into the faded *Grammar of Assent.*
>
> "Why do you read that? It can't be interesting."
>
> "Well when I went to college last year I was a comfortable Unitarian, but when I was sick, I began to think I was not satisfied. A man has to have some basis of faith if he is to accomplish anything, and know what he believes and why . . . I knew that my mother's grandmother had come over to Unitarianism from a more positive theology, and that my great-uncle [the Bishop] had changed his faith and gone into the Episcopal church. Mother was disappointed about that, but she is fond of your father, and thinks he is not bigoted. In the meantime, I have a friend who is a Catholic, and he lent me the *Grammar of Assent.* I wish you would read it . . . I wish you would tell me just what you do believe—what your faith rests on."

She does not record her answer, but he told her quite a lot about himself on that late-summer afternoon: about his plans to study law as his father wished and about plans to join his father's law firm, about his love of literature as a way of life, about his mother's and his uncles' education in France, and about his fondness for time spent by himself to think things out: "When it was finally time to descend from the hay-mow, Archie gave me his hand, and we slid over the edge of the mow and were still holding hands when we landed in the clover below . . . I was convinced the boy wanted help which I might give, and that I must try to meet his need. But the significance of that magic touch made the need a desire."

On Sunday, their last day, they shared a hymnal in the "little gray stone church" in Amherst, and

> there seemed to be divine intent in its words, and the message of the preacher was intensely significant in the light of our discussion the day before.
>
> In the afternoon Cousin Ellen shared our walk over the farm. There was a cardinal flower in bud beside the brook, and we stopped t admire it. I found it difficult to get an opportunity for something I wanted to say to Archie. I was carrying, out of sight, a worn copy of *The Imitation of Christ* which my older brother had given me years ago.
>
> "I want to lend you a book of mine," I said simply, when a chance came. "You see, I have absolutely no theology to fall back upon; I am ashamed to

Ruth Sessions in 1885. "Preparing to be married," reads her note on the back of the photo.

say that I never seemed to need it, with such a large supply in the family. But Thomas a Kempis is different. He's helped me to *live* what I couldn't understand. I believe that's the thing to do . . . When you feel you've got what you're looking for, just send this back some day. I'll know then that it proved to be what you wanted."

He took it and my hand with it. Molly's voice called from the woodshed arch near by: "Come on , you two! There's a wonderful Aurora; great streams of color going up." Half a dozen people stood together watching the north. The flickering waves of color reached almost to the zenith. A shaft of light shaped like a bird's wing moved above us. It was a supernatural seal on our unspoken pledge.

Eight years were to pass before the pledge was redeemed; and with only letters to sustain it during much of that time, the strain on their relationship was severe. Ruth's enthusiastic reports from Germany drew increasingly reserved replies until, in January 1882, a package arrived that contained the promised copy of Thomas a Kempis's *Imitation of Christ.* Archie had found his answer, but the accompanying letter expressing his gratitude bore his signature over a formal "affectionately yours." Ruth was dismayed:

> Could I be certain how much that mutual stirring of emotion four years ago had actually meant? But I glanced down at the old book, and opened it at a page which held a pressed four-leafed clover. Without doubt that was the leaf we had found at our feet on the last Sunday afternoon, walking with Cousin Ellen It lay between the leaves, and a passage had been marked by a line in the margin:
>
> *Nothing is sweeter than love, nothing more courageous, nothing fuller nor better in heaven or earth; because love is born of God, and cannot rest but in God, above all created things . . . Love oftentimes knoweth no bounds, but is fervent beyond all measure.*

They were married in 1887. The wedding was a grand affair: 1,500 invitations, the bride led to the altar on the arm of the Bishop, her father, the groom following with her mother, and her brothers—both priests—waiting at the altar. Ruth's account makes no mention of the groom's family.

CHAPTER 2

The Consort

A husband to be converted, what a delicious apple!

—BEAUDELAIRE/ISHERWOOD

The newlyweds spent the winter months of 1887–88 in a small flat in New York, three flights up, but with a splendid view over Central Park at 92d Street. In the spring they moved to a house in Englewood, New Jersey, then still a rural community a few miles north of New York City. Use of that pleasant place, for two years, had been one of their wedding gifts. It cannot have been convenient for a young lawyer to undertake a daily commute to his office in Pine Street, very nearly at the southern tip of Manhattan. The summer found Ruth at Forty Acres, where her husband was able to visit before their return to Englewood in the fall for the expected arrival of their first child, Hannah, born in January 1889.

Archibald Sessions never did become a very successful lawyer, but among his many qualities he soon revealed a quiet strength and wisdom in dealing with domestic crises. Ruth's background and upbringing had not prepared her for predictable financial uncertainties in the early stages of her self-employed husband's career and the young couple's frequent need to justify current expenses with an expectation of tomorrow's income. The Bishop's favorite daughter was appalled at her first experience of a month's unpaid grocery bills. It evoked memories of destitute Syracuse families, "who were able to shop only if they paid cash for every purchase."[1] Here was lost respectability, and in a climate of continuing financial concern that was more than she could bear. A stormy domestic scene blew over only when Archie offered to take over the paying of household bills and the preservation of the good name of Sessions among tradesmen. He was to play the same role of financial wise man without money during a more serious crisis in the early career of their son Roger.

In 1990, when the two-year wedding tenure on their house in Englewood had expired, the Sessions family moved back across the Hudson River again and settled in a small but comfortable apartment in Brooklyn. Archibald Sessions' heart was less than ever set on establishing a lucrative practice, and his active involvement in antiestablishment public politics, soon after their arrival in the city, did nothing to ease the long-term uncertainties of family income. But as an increasingly prominent member of the Young Men's Democratic Club of Brooklyn he played a leading role in the political reform movement against Tammany Hall rule in New York City.

The organization popularly known as Tammany and incorporated under the grand title of the Columbian Order of New York City had become a brawny and ruthlessly exercised power in civic affairs by the late 1880s. In establishing it a century before its founders had pledged "a society to promote the welfare and interests of the common man." By the mid-1800s, however, Tammany Hall had developed into a corrupt political machine, controlled by Democratic Party "bosses" and sustained by the votes of large numbers of needy urban dwellers, who cast their votes in exchange for material assistance. When Archibald brought his bride to New York in 1887, the infamous "Boss Tweed" had gone, but his organization retained firm control of the New York legislature and was now in an excellent position to consolidate its domination of the civil service. Conspicuous leverage over city government by persons not answerable to the electorate spurred demands for reform from within both political parties. The colorful Republican Theodore ("Teddy") Roosevelt, later president of the United States, was a prominent member of New York's Civil Service Board at the time and would be police commissioner from 1895 to 1897. He worked energetically for the cause of reform, with Tammany Hall and its influential supporters within the current power structure of the Democratic Party as chief local targets.

In the presidential election of 1884, Grover Cleveland had pledged to restore Jeffersonian ideals to the Democratic Party and to make civil service reform a major element of his national policy. The Young Men's Democratic Club, as an agency for reform within the party, was founded shortly after his election. Cleveland's defeat, however, by the Republican Benjamin Harrison in 1888 ("in the most corrupt campaign in U.S. history," according to Ruth's memoirs) came to be seen as a vindication of the Democratic right wing, a blow to the reform movement, and an obvious boost for the bruised political fortunes of the Tammany Society of New York City. The Young Men's Democratic Club took up the challenge.

According to Ruth, it was Archibald Sessions who came up with the idea of persuading Grover Cleveland to run again in the next presidential election. The time did not seem propitious. One David B. Hill, chairman of the regular Democratic Party, had already gathered seventy-two delegates to support his own nomination at the convention in Chicago. Frederick Hinrichs, president of the Young Men's Democratic Club of Brooklyn, thought Sessions' idea was "a heavy contract" but promised to try anyway. In the event, he managed to persuade the former president to run again. At a special convention in Syracuse, Cleveland was nominated as an Independent candidate, and he went on to win the election in 1892.

As a reward for his initiative, Hinrichs was appointed New York commissioner of tax arrears. Sessions became his deputy. To Ruth this "meant a good salary, a larger apartment, the settlement of debts and freedom from worry so long as that particular party remained in power." Unfortunately, the party lost its hold at the midterm elections two years later, and Sessions was forced to return to his long-neglected private law practice. He remained active in the Young Men's Democratic Club of Brooklyn, served twice as its president, and continued his work for municipal reform. But he never held political office again.

Ruth had not liked her husband's involvement in politics: "In the nineties, the whole field of political activity was seething with corruption, a slough in which few outsiders had ventured their feet." And while that knowledge might have provided some incentive to support Archie's political efforts for reform, she remained uneasily aware of the treacherous ground on which to found their family's future. But there was something else as well: she keenly resented that, as a woman, she was excluded from active participation in the political process: "Being a mere female, going to church societies and Girl's Friendly Meetings, writing articles, mending stockings, and making other people's clothes to fit my child and myself or trying out economical menus, seemed to offer so very little contribution to the community."

The exclusion of women from participation in politics was matched, of course, by the absence of career opportunities in the world of business, except on the lowest level of employment. Unlike women's suffrage, equal opportunity to compete for leadership in the workplace was not under discussion in any public forum at the time, but the conditions in which working women labored were beginning to attract general attention and organized efforts were being made to improve the quality of their working life. Here was a cause in which the Bishop's daughter found congenial employment. She was offered and accepted ("impetuously," she allowed) the presidency of the Consumers' League, Long Island Affiliate. The league's program called for public information on working conditions for women "in every branch of business or industry, from sweatshops to fashionable tailors' establishments and dry-goods stores." Unlike the league's well-established New York chapter, Ruth's Long Island branch was barely formed at the time, but it was formidable in potential size. She had no experience whatsoever in running this kind of organization, but she was "ready to set sail for unknown shores in a fog, without even studying a chart." Collecting and making public the often sensational information about working conditions for girls and older women in factories and shops gave her great satisfaction, albeit the response she achieved frequently fell short of her expectations:

> I addressed myself to rows of rolling gray and white coiffures, and gold-colored corseted busts . . . I made a point of reporting only what I had actually seen, and the tale was lurid enough; yet it seldom roused interest. After its completion there would almost always be some powerful dame who would rise majestically, saying, "Madam Chairman, will Mrs. Sessions tell us *why*, if conditions in stores and factories are what she describes them to be, it is impossible to get maids to work in families, where they can have every comfort and a perfectly good wage besides six dollars a week and room and board?"

Nor was Ruth's work confined to information gathering and brave talk before ladies' clubs. She relished any opportunity to speak at large public demonstrations. Her husband sometimes found her feisty public spirit unsuitable but provided dutiful escort whenever she felt the urge to rush into territory where ladies, Archie felt, should fear to tread.

As Ruth recalls it, the two of them attended one large gathering at which the president of Long Island's Municipal League was to speak and "found a crowd outside blocking the street, and two bands, one playing inside, the other out, with an impossible musical effect, also sellers of popcorn balls and peanuts, and distributors of flyers. It was a typical proletarian crowd, good-natured, enthusiastic, full of boosters and booers, the sort of audience with which I felt most at home." Her husband took one look at the high, narrow speakers' platform that faced the noisy crowd and declared, "You can't possibly throw your voice from that perch." When his wife persisted, he left the hall to pace the sidewalk outside, looking in now and then to see if all was well. According to Ruth, "The meeting went off very well, but whether it did any good I don't know."

Little more than a year after Archibald Sessions' forced return to private practice, he was offered and accepted a law partnership with a former college friend. Ruth had reservations about the young man, "whose talent and cleverness were unquestioned, but whose inherited fortune had been a handicap to solid work." Still, the new connections would now enable her family to maintain the comfortable lifestyle they had enjoyed during Archibald's brief tenure in political office and provide a more stable professional base than a position dependent on biannual election returns.

Reflecting their renewed confidence, they moved into an attractive little one-family house they had admired from their apartment windows in Brooklyn. For a while expenses would stretch their improved resources, but even Ruth had learned to "rob luxurious Peter, even if they could not always pay fact-facing Paul." Neighbors called 471 Washington Avenue the Bird House. Its fine backyard was shaded by a large peach tree. The front porch faced an old maple. There was a fireplace in the living room, and there was a nursery. They moved on the first of May 1896. A few weeks later Ruth announced that a second baby was on its way. As on other important occasions in his life, Roger Sessions, on arrival, would find himself in just the right place at just the right time.

Ruth was not well at the time. Because of "an impossible weakness and weariness" she was put to bed for much of her early pregnancy. In addition, there seems to have been a problem with her eyes. She was able to write "only on a cutting board at a level with my face, not seeing the letters, but keeping the lines straight somehow." But with her loss of an active outlet for her undiminished energies, writing had become a way to cope, and as with everything else that was important to her, she pursued her new craft with energy and almost instant success. She had stories published in the literary columns of the *New York Times* and the *New York Post*, received commissions for articles in women's and young people's magazines, and acted as volunteer editor for "a little paper for girls."

Nor was her literary activity confined to belles lettres or advice to the young: her most controversial article mounted a slashing attack on what she perceived as the Episcopal Church's institutional indifference to social abuses. She signed her piece with the pseudonym of Jacob Armitage, had it published in the *New York Standard*, and sent copies to every Episcopal bishop in the country and to many of the clergy. Among other replies published in the paper, her father's was warmly supportive. Ruth was thrilled, of course, but could not bring herself to reveal her authorship.

As the sultry spring of 1896 gave way to summer, Ruth and her daughter, Hannah ("Nan"), moved to Forty Acres, where Ruth's parents were already in residence. Archie could not get away from the city until October, by which time the Syracusans, except for the Bishop's large dog, Cleve, had left for upstate New York. The Sessionses spent "a glorious fortnight, cooking our meals over a wood fire in the long parlor . . . We roamed the woods, and drove over the hill roads, and brought back apples and pumpkins from upland farms."

When they finally returned to New York, Ruth had recovered her health and energy. Late autumn was exceptionally busy for both of them, with work and with preparations for the baby's arrival. Christmas stockings were filled, packages mailed, "and on the morning of the twenty-seventh [*sic*] just in time to be welcomed by daylight, our oldest son appeared; a funny little baby, all mouth, as the nurse observed, and with eyes as dark as the proverbial fruit of the blackthorn."

CHAPTER 3 Young Roger

Perhaps the half forgotten tune of some little song, sung a bit differently then, was the first musical idea of one's own; and this embryo, carefully nurtured by powers unknown, grew into a giant who devoured everything about him and changed it into his own flesh and blood.

—E. T. A. HOFFMANN

Ruth Sessions, matriarch in training, began by being an adoring mother, taking special delight in portents of her son's future that seemed to confirm her own most cherished hopes and ambitions. In hindsight of four decades on, and in the carefully polished prose of *Sixty Odd*, she writes as one who welcomed a promising composer to this world with all the care and special concern he might have wished; in turn, during the first months of his life baby Roger Huntington Sessions appears to have pleased his mother with a promising variety of fine infant responses to music.

Late on a certain cold winter evening he was awakened by the sound of an out-of-season hurdy-gurdy performance outside his window. It was duly noted that "his eyes opened wide, his face grew pink, his hands moved excitedly." The chronicle does not record whether this was in protest or approval, but Ruth opted for an interpretation of musical favor. Considering her son's later views on folksy music, let alone on disturbance of his privacy, she might have done better to argue the other way. However, he always wanted to be a conductor.

Ruth's own part in nurturing the baby's musical responses appears to have been both practical and therapeutic. Baby Roger exhibited a stubborn dread of the descending motion he felt as he was carried downstairs from the nursery. To solve this problem she would begin the daily ritual of his panicky descent by playing the piano while his father fetched him in his arms. A gavotte from one of Bach's French Suites matched Daddy's step and took Roger's mind off his panic. Before long, he would signal vigorously whenever he was ready for another musical ride.

Neighbors called him the singing baby. He sang in his carriage, in his bath, and in bed. According to his mother, he reproduced whatever tunes he heard with recognizable fidelity and sang long before he talked. He spoke his first word on hearing a military band. From a window that overlooked Fifth Avenue he and his nine-year-old sister, Nan, were allowed to watch a parade celebrating the end of the Spanish-American War. The military music and the cheers of the crowd fascinated him. Henceforth he added the syllable *wah* to his chanting, a credible contraction of *hurrah*.

On Whitsunday 1899, in midmorning, Baby Roger became a big brother. John Archibald, youngest of the Sessions children, received the names of his father and his father's father. Grandfather Sessions had passed away only a few months before, and with him the manifest family expectation that Archibald would someday fulfill his father's favorite dream by becoming an outstanding lawyer. Thus when, soon after young John's birth, Archie's law partner died unexpectedly, there seemed no longer to be a real or assumed obligation for Archie to continue in a profession he had entered out of a sense of filial obligation. It would have been difficult, in any case, for one man to run the office without someone to help with the court work, an expense the ever-precarious Sessions budget could not support. Finding another partner seemed an uncertain option, and a return to private practice was an even less tempting prospect for one who had tried, without conspicuous success, twice before. His heart had never been in it: he wanted something to do with books.

By a happy coincidence, an offer in the field of book publishing seemed to offer a perfect solution. In the hope that it might serve as a first step toward success in a more congenial field, Archie accepted a position with the publishers of a new edition of the *Encyclopaedia Britannica*. The salary, albeit rather less than the income the family had enjoyed during his years as a political appointee or as a law partner, would be regular and safe. And so it was decided that he should give up the practice of law. As it turned out, the immediate results were mixed. Archie enjoyed the work, but finances were badly strained. Fortuitously again, a small inheritance helped save the house on Brooklyn Heights, at least for another year.

With current cares at bay, the family limped into Hadley early that summer, Ruth quite literally, with "phlebitic trouble" that kept her on crutches for several weeks. But there was plenty of help: Huntingtons abounded. Ruth's parents and her older brother, George, with wife and five children had already arrived. Soon to follow were Ruth's sisters Arria and Molly; and to the children's delight the Bishop had brought the dog Cleve to accompany the boisterous comings and goings between Forty Acres and Phelps House.

These were restoring months, and the Sessions family deeply enjoyed their

Henshaw House, "a fine old mansion on Elm Street" in Northhampton, where Ruth Sessions served as house mother for off-campus students at Smith College, and where the boy Roger grew up.

last summer of the nineteenth century. Nan rowed with her cousins; baby John lay on a comforter spread over the grass; Roger practiced real words and tried to put them together. While Aunt Molly looked after the younger children, Arria was writing a book on the early history of Forty Acres; and in the evenings the Bishop would read aloud from Trollope's *Last Chronicle of Barset.*

In the autumn, back in New York, Roger discovered the piano. "He touched one note at a time," writes his proud mother, "prolonging it and listening to its last vibration, and then perhaps playing a chord, stretching his small fingers almost timidly, with a smile to himself. He never attempted tunes." He was taken to his first symphony concert at the Brooklyn Academy, a young people's matinee conducted by Walter Damrosch. Ruth had been given tickets for a proscenium box, dismissed some apprehensive thoughts about Roger's reaction to the sound of a full orchestra at close quarters, and was soon absorbed in the music. Damrosch was conducting the "Pilgrim's Chorus" from *Tannhäuser* when she became aware that people were staring at her box. Roger , resplendent in white kilts and with both arms in the air, had climbed on his chair and was trying to follow the conductor's gestures beat for beat. Wisely, no doubt, she did not try to interfere with such joyful participation. Roger kept up his efforts until the performance had ended and the applause begun.

Remembering this incident at first or second hand (and with variations), Sessions loved to recount it to the end of his life. But there was also an earlier childhood recollection, not nearly so pleasant, which he used to retell with a touch of lingering unease. "On Thanksgiving day in 1899, though it might have been Halloween," he was taken for a walk, with his brother's nurse pushing

John along in a pram. Suddenly, across a fence, Roger saw a larger-than-life monstrous face leering at him. The apparition turned out to be a boy in a mask, but Roger's terror was total. A feeling of impending doom far outlasted his initial shock, and he thought it likely, later on, that he might have overheard some mention of the awesome eschatological portents that tend to surface at the end of centuries. Certainly he understood words much better now than he was yet able to speak them, having worked hard all summer at matching their sound with their message.

As it happened, the world at large did not come to an end in the year 1900, but Roger's own world was about to break apart. The blow fell soon after the turn of the century. The Sessionses' economy had deteriorated so badly that giving up their beloved small house in the spring seemed inevitable. Archibald's salary proved increasingly inadequate for the support of a growing family, and various schemes for achieving additional savings or earnings had been discussed and rejected: move to the slums, move in with the family, start a dressmaking establishment at home. In the end, a sense of fated futility inhibited further initiative.

It happened at the end of a particularly bright and sunny day in early spring. Roger had just overcome a siege of whooping cough that had laid him low soon after his conducting debut at the Damrosch concert, but the afternoon had been warm enough for him to play outdoors again. With dinner ready and the baby put to bed, Archie was expected home at any moment. Ruth was keeping an eye on the garden gate. Thinking happily that little John seemed to have escaped infection with his brother's cough and that, no matter what troubles might have to be overcome in the coming weeks, another lovely summer would soon follow the distressing season in town, she saw her husband approach, and she "saw defeat in his face." His news was devastating. The publishers for whom he worked were closing their New York office, and the firm would continue its work in London. Sessions was offered employment there, but without any long-term assurance about his future in he job. The move, if they could afford it at all, would take them far outside home territory. With a very young family and their resources already strained, neither Archibald nor Ruth gave serious consideration to this prospect.

"It was then that a thought, *which had been coming into my mind with consistent appeal,* began to renew its claims on Ruth." The qualifying part of that statement (my emphasis) suggests that this latest chapter in her husband's professional crisis may not have been entirely unexpected or even unwelcome to Ruth. In terms of her own life and of her plans for the children's immediate future, she was ready to take charge. For that, she felt, a separation had to be faced. And perhaps, she reasoned, that might be the very opportunity her husband needed as well:

> It had dawned on me that if only I could make it possible for my husband to be free of all cares and goading expenses, and if he could have a year or

Ruth Sessions, 1901 with sons Roger (nearly 5) and John (18 months)

> more in which to buckle down and find his own level in the literary world . . . it would be the chance of his life; a chance he had never known before. If there were some way for me to make a home for the children and at the same time provide for the family expenses . . . I knew well that he could work out his destiny.

Archibald's reaction to her proposal is not recorded, but he acquiesced in short order. Ruth wrote to her father that they were giving up their house on the first of May, that she hoped her husband's Harvard training would qualify him to teach English in a college, and that she wished they might find something in New England. The Bishop, already in residence at Forty Acres for the spring planting, replied within twenty-four hours of receipt. He had discussed his daughter's problem with President Seeley of Smith College in Northampton. Seeley had no faculty opening for Archibald this late in the academic planning stage, of course, but there was a shortage of supervised off-campus living for the students. Would Ruth be willing to come to Northampton with the children to open an off-campus residence for girls? Ruth would.

Thus, at age four, Roger returned to the land of his forefathers, just across the river from the ancestral farm. His father helped the family move into their new home, an attractive house on the lower slope of Round Hill with a view of Mount Holyoke. In years to come, Archibald would continue his brief visits, and he would be a welcome and not infrequent guest during his family's summers at Forty Acres. But the determined long-range planning with which Ruth went to work and the considerable capital her parents soon invested in order to get her started in a permanent home of her own suggest that a temporary separation, just "for a year or more," was never considered.

Ruth cared for her husband with genuine affection, and the move she had undertaken must have been hard to face at first. But her decision, with Archibald's quiet sanction and her parents' financial support, made good sense in that it ensured a stable environment in which to bring up her children. Given the rigid gender roles of the times, an implication of failure on Archie's part would have been inevitable had she advanced his financial problems as her main consideration. For a devoted wife, however, to assume primary family responsibility in order to foster her husband's manifest literary talent seemed the right thing to do. In the event she embraced her solution with relish.

From the start, Ruth's enterprise was a success. There would be yet another move, two years later, to a much larger house in Northampton. Ruth's mother helped with a loan to purchase "the fine old mansion on Elm street," bordering the college grounds. It was to be Ruth's possession during her tenure as housemother for off-campus students and later that of Smith College. And it was the house in which the boy Roger grew up:

> The Henshaw House was built in a familiar old pattern, with large rooms, low-studded but airy, built around a huge chimney which furnished two fireplaces on each floor, and crowned its roof, another chimney giving similar fireplaces in the rear. The big front door, with its stately knocker, opened into a tiny hall between the two first floor drawing rooms, a staircase ascending crosswise, of fine woodwork with a picturesque railing. At the summit I had to make a slight change, cutting through a narrow hall beside the chimney, in order to connect the front of the house with the back hall, from which two very steep stairways, one up and one down, led to the dining room below and the third story. The latter extended over the ell, and we put four small bedrooms there, but kept that addition in conformity with the proportions of the main building.[1]

Across the river, at Forty Acres, the Bishop died on a beautiful summer day in 1904. After months of increasing weakness, loss of memory, and occasional lapses of consciousness, death came quietly "as the afternoon shadows lengthened under the windows of his room." Ruth's daughter, Nan, took charge of the younger children. Archibald had come up from New York when the end was near. Ruth's brother George was ill himself, in Hanover, but Brother James, the monk, was expected on the following day.

In the evening, Archie made his wife go back early to Phelps House. She had

Roger Sessions, age 5.

been up most of the night before and had already begun to cope with the business of informing relatives, handling the press, arranging for services, and preparing for the arrival of a large group of mourners. With her usual determination, she rose early the next morning to write a long letter to her brother George. Archie came into the room at seven, and she asked him to post the letter. He hesitated. Then he said, "I can't, dear," and put his arms around her. Three hours after his father's death, George had suffered a fatal heart attack. Their mother had found the telegram among messages of condolence at Forty Acres. This time Ruth collapsed.

In the autumn of 1906, nine-year-old Roger was sent to boarding school or, rather, a succession of boarding schools. He was far from ready. A bright little loner, he felt awkward and shy as a boy among boys. Whenever he could bring himself to take part in some forbidden escapade in the hope of being more fully accepted by his fellows, he seemed fated to end up as the one who got caught. His first such experience, at the Cloyne School in Newport, Rhode Island, was so great a shock that his parents were forced to withdraw him after a few months.

Cloyne enjoyed a fine reputation for academic excellence, but discipline was strict, and the days of a young boarder were ordered by a firm schedule and rigidly enforced rules. Boys who broke rules could expect not only punishment but also humiliation. Subjects of censure were made to wear yellow ribbons and were forbidden to speak to their schoolmates or be spoken to by other boys. To the end of his life, Sessions nursed an unforgiving venom about Cloyne, fueled by a number of tragic-comic recollections.

The final calamity began with a box of cookies from home. For once, to his delight, Roger found himself the instant center of his schoolmates' attention. That evening, after lights-out, he trudged happily across to a friend's bed to share his treasure with a boisterous gathering of munching little boys. The noise soon attracted the law, and at the first sound of approaching footsteps Roger's more experienced guests disappeared magically into their own beds. Terrified, Roger dived under his friend's blanket. He was caught, of course, and taken to the headmaster. Of the oration Roger had to endure he understood only that his had been "the worst offense a boy could commit." Fortunately, Christmas holidays were nearly at hand and, after parental consultation, his brief tenure at Cloyne School came to an end.

The Kingsley School at Essex Fells in New Jersey was next. Roger was happier here, although discipline was no less strict than at Cloyne. Kingsley was, in fact, a military academy where students wore uniforms and paraded with guns under the watchful eye of a former field officer in the Spanish-American War. During his stay at Kingsley, Roger saw quite a bit of his father. In the years since the family's separation Archibald's "work to do with books" had flourished. He was now an editor at Street & Smith, a publishing firm with offices on Seventh Avenue, and had made many friends in New York's literary and artistic circles. On his visits to Kingsley the elder Sessions lent a sympathetic ear to his son's tales of anxieties and achievements and helped him to cope with shyness toward fellow students and with inner conflicts in the face of authority.

How the child Roger really felt about his parents' separation is hard to know. The grown man denied any early sense of it. From contemporary letters and later conversation, however, one might guess that his relationship with both father and mother acquired an exceptional intensity as a result. His passionate attachment to a father who became a much-longed-for visitor during the boy's year at Kingsley echoed in frequent reminiscences of episodes that a more normal childhood might have let him absorb without so frequent a need to recall and retell. One such memory dates from Kingsley. It seems that Archibald Sessions' exceptional good looks made him conspicuous in any surroundings; but for Roger's schoolmates Archibald's dark, swarthy coloring soon made him "the Spaniard," a pejorative term, born of a freshly remembered war and frequently used by the school's drillmaster, among others. To young Roger this casual slight of his hero by some of his fellows was a shameful affront; and the man, even the old man, Sessions never tired of the tale.

Archibald's sisters, Aunts Addie and Nettie, also lived near enough for occasional visits. Roger, whose charm for the ladies developed early (and lasted for life), endeared himself by sending his latest drawings and paintings as thank-you notes for various treats. A particularly close feeling drew him to Addie, a gifted singer who eventually had to forfeit a professional career, possibly because of stage fright.

The warmth and uncritical acceptance that drew Roger to his father and his father's sisters was not in his mother's nature. Ruth loved him fiercely but could never forgo an opportunity to teach, preach, or appear to put conditions on her love. She writes to her ten-year-old:

> You are not to bore other people by talking all the time about your stamp business: You know you do sometimes talk a good deal, and think a good deal, about things which are not directly interesting to others. We always have to use more or less self-control, & notice when people are bored, or ask us not to talk about things. I don't want you to run any chance of being laughed at for things you could avoid: but otherwise it is no matter.[2]

That last sentence must have appeared particularly unhelpful to poor Roger. He had in fact written to his mother about the teasing by his new schoolmates with regard to his "Spaniard" father. Though unavoidable, perhaps, it was hardly "no matter."

In Roger's next effort, he stays on neutral ground, but Ruth is relentless: "9 ½ for that letter—no, 9, for it was not very tidy or very newsy." Roger still did not understand that "newsy" meant matters of interest to the recipient of his report and must not include the subject of his beloved stamp collection. Ruth's next letter is an ultimatum:

> My dear boy, on Sunday I want you to send me a *nice letter*, as well written as you would write an exercise for school. I want you to tell me some of the things you have been doing and seeing, or studying. And see what a thoroughly pleasant and interesting one you can make. I read a letter the other day written by your cousin Roger F. to his grandmother, & it was such a nice one it made me ashamed of my son's letters. If you don't write me a well written letter, I shall give up writing you at all, except on Sundays.
>
> You must begin now to think of giving your mother pleasure instead of just sending notes about stamps. Don't write about stamps *at all* this time . . . Your grandfather [the Bishop] always wrote such beautiful letters that I want you to be like him. See how well you can do on Sunday.
>
> Lovingly, Mother.

Roger finally came through with the approved model, a useful exercise for the fastidious literary and musical craftsman to be, if not very rewarding for an unhappy little boy away from home. But having achieved her aim, his mother did not stint with judicious praise: "I read [your letter] out loud at the table, & everybody admired the classical and historical quotations! Now next time I will permit a little stamp discourse, not exceeding twenty-five words. You will find it very interesting to stay within a certain number of words when you have some special thing to say." If being a nag were the hallmark of fine teaching, Ruth Sessions would have ranked at the top of the profession. It is hardly surprising that Roger learned to avoid mentioning matters of real concern to him, a skill he would practice and perfect for all time. For now and for years to come, he would write to his mother faithfully, "newsy" letters in often amusing detail, while any personal concern he broached would risk an instant lecture in reply:

> I am *very* glad you are learning to dance. You must try very hard to become a good dancer, & keep time in your head & feet at the same time, so as to keep up with the music: for a man who cannot dance well always finds it hard to get partners at a dance, & it is bad luck to be "turned down" by too many girls! So I want you to take pains & see how nicely you can do. I fancy you could make a very good dancer if you try hard to learn, & particularly if you take pains to go with the music, & not get out of step.

From September of 1908 until the spring of 1911 Roger attended Kent School in northern Connecticut. Nestled in the wooded Litchfield hills, some fifty miles north of Hartford, the school's 1,500-acre campus borders on the Housatonic River, which is spanned at the town of Kent by one of the area's two covered bridges. It may well have been the most beautifully situated boarding school Roger attended, and it was very much his mother's territory. Supported by the Companionship of the Holy Cross, of which she was a member, it was an affiliate of the Anglican monastic order founded some forty years before by her brother James in New York. As with young Roger's other boarding schools, discipline was strict, but the shy child had by now, and by his own admission, become something of a rebel. He long remembered but apparently did not resent that his piano lessons were suspended as punishment for an irreverent remark about the director of the school. All in all, however, Roger felt more at home at Kent than he had either at Cloyne or at Kingsley. His own son, John, was to attend Kent, and in 1955 Sessions wrote a mass for unison chorus and organ, commissioned by the school.

Sessions' early musical studies were unremarkable. Like many a child of music-loving parents, he took piano lessons. Beginning in 1902, he studied with first one, then the other of two organists at the Episcopal church in Northampton, the Messrs. Edwards and Chase, and later with Ruth herself. Lessons were interrupted when Roger entered Cloyne, then resumed at Kingsley and Kent. Except for the disciplinary suspension of lessons at Kent, there is little mention of the subject, even by his mother. He himself, on later occasions, had only scorn for what he had been taught.

On a fine summer day, between his first and second year at Kent, Roger was riding his bicycle, whistling a tune, as he bumped along the familiar country roads at Hadley: "Suddenly I was aware that I was whistling tunes of my own concoction instead of tunes I had played. I enjoyed the sensation of 'composing' and decided to write down what I had sung."[3] In fact, he claimed later on, he suddenly knew that this would be his life's work, and he wasted no time in getting started. During the same summer, he was taken to performances of *Die Meistersinger* and of *Carmen* at Springfield. The Wagner opera in particular captured his imagination. He immediately cast about for a suitable operatic subject of his own, noting unhappily that Wagner had preempted much of his favorite mythological material. Nevertheless, he soon settled on *Lancelot and Elaine,* compiling his own libretto from Tennyson's *Idylls of the King.* At the end of the following year, the young author, just shy of his fourteenth birthday, proudly affixed the date of completion: "Act III finished December 23, 1910 at 12:28 AM." The final curtain falls with Elaine's lament:

> *"Sweet is true love tho' giv'n in vain, in vain,*
> *And sweet is death that puts an end to pain . . .*
> *O love, if death be sweeter, let me die.*[4]

His mother recollects "that he had made the Guinevere motive, as he told me with all the earnestness of a romantic twelve-year-old [*sic*], the most attractive of all but with less meaning, because, though beautiful, she has no soul." A remarkable judgment on the king's wayward wife, and a notable one as regards this "romantic twelve-year-old," who chose to make the king's other woman the heroine of his plot.

His father showed the manuscript to some distinguished composers in New York, among them Humperdinck, who was in town for the American premiere of his *Die Königskinder* at the Metropolitan Opera. Another scheduled appointment, with Puccini, was canceled by the composer at the last moment. Some forty years later, Sessions learned from his great friend and Italian colleague Luigi Dallapiccola that Puccini had once agonized about a meeting in New York, at which he was to have given his opinion on a young American composer's professional promise. He had failed to keep the appointment.

One wonders, of course, on what evidence these eminent composers might have based their advice. For a boy who had begun to write music barely two years before and whose exposure to professional instruction had been marginal at best, *Lancelot and Elaine* represented bold enthusiasm and quite remarkable determination—but hardly enough evidence on which to decide a career. As it happened, however, enthusiasm and determination prevailed over the odds. At the opening of the academic year 1911–12, Roger Sessions, American composer aged fourteen, matriculated as a music student at Harvard University, where his grandfather had once held the chair of Plummer Professor of Christian Morals.

CHAPTER 4

Letters from Harvard

I have already the germ of the music in mind.

—ROGER SESSIONS

On a sunny day in September 1911, with high hopes and with a composer's absolute confidence he would not savor again for many years to come, Harvard freshman Roger Sessions moved into lodgings at 41 Hawthorne Street in Cambridge, Massachusetts. Being very much younger than his fellow undergraduates, he was to live off campus during his first two years at the university; and in order to shield the lone fourteen-year-old from worldly temptations in his newly independent life, his older sister, Nan, newly graduated from Radcliffe (Harvard's then separate college for women), was installed in his apartment as well, "with an elderly maid to look after them both."

Shortly after their arrival, the young composer received an important invitation. He was to call on a longtime family friend, Mrs. Wilmerding, a lady of means with considerable influence in Boston's musical circles. Sister-in-law to the late Theodore Thomas, founder and first conductor of the Chicago Symphony and a major figure in turn-of-the-century American musical life, Mrs. Wilmerding would be delighted to meet and be of assistance to the musical grandson of a prominent former Bostonian. Roger was even more delighted. At the appointed hour, with his entire oeuvre tucked under his arm and convinced that he was about to make an important musical ally of this friendly patroness, he presented himself on Mrs. Wilmerding's doorstep.

Forty years later, in Florence, Sessions opened the first of seven Fulbright Lectures on musical life in America with a stinging account of that meeting:

> That lady asked him, a young student, to call on her, and, waving his compositions aside without bothering to look at them, begged him for his own good not to dream of a career as a composer. No American, she explained, could hope to achieve anything as a composer since he was not born into an atmosphere of composition and—as an American—probably did not even have music in his blood. She urged him to aim rather at being a conductor.[1]

So much for conductors! The draft for his Italian lectures seems to pause in deferred outrage at this point, as he continues on a fresh page: "I recall this story of course not for whatever biographical interest it may have . . . but [because] it illustrates very well an attitude that was extremely prevalent in the United States at the time."[2]

Sessions' disclaimer notwithstanding, the incident is of considerable biographical interest, of course, and it rankled for years to come. But the burden of his youthful encounter with prevalent notions about American music, in the person of a well-meaning Boston matron, was certainly shared by composers throughout the land. Their music must either copy superior European models or content itself with reflections of America's colonial or ethnic traditions. He would have to tangle with fashionable implications of both, as composer, writer, and teacher, before achieving, late in life, the creative ease and confidence of his own musical voice.

The story of Sessions' gradual discovery of a musical language appropriate to his inner vision of the "musical syntax of conscious emotion,"[3] is the story of an extraordinarily slow process. Its eventual success owed something to his flinty determination to master, first of all, whatever could be learned from others and as much again to a scrupulously selective inner ear and its tireless demands, with every new work, of a fresh adaptation of musical means to the particular requirements of a *prior musical image*. This need, in the face of lifelong misapprehensions by musical antagonists and some acolytes alike, was at the very heart of Sessions' approach to composition. Its eventual consummation against odds owes something to the dogged intransigence he inherited from his New England forebears but also, at crucial times in Sessions' life, to some exceptionally good luck.

His initial disappointment with well-meaning Mrs. Wilmerding and, eventually, with well-intentioned musical instruction at Harvard notwithstanding, Sessions was extraordinarily fortunate to find himself in Boston at this particular time. Fresh from the vast musical hinterland that was America at the beginning of the twentieth century, he needed to *hear* a lot of music. He knew it and he found it. Boston, in those final years before the outbreak of the Great War in Europe, certainly qualified as a perfect American city in which to experience first-rate performances of a wide range of symphonic and operatic repertory. Boston in 1911 was a very different place from the city in which the

Bishop's children had grown up half a century before. And nowhere was that change more evident than in the musical life of the community in which young Roger took his first, tentative steps toward becoming a musician.

The advent of the Boston Symphony Orchestra, a mere thirty years before, transformed the city's musical climate, and subsequent additions of very active operatic and chamber music organizations rounded out a generous variety of seasonal offerings in which indigenous forces performed on a level of musical proficiency easily matching that of their best European counterparts. It was all very new and wonderful, but its wide range of offerings and their exceptional level of performance would barely last through Sessions' undergraduate years at Harvard.

Like the newly arrived composition student on the Cambridge side of the Charles River, musical Boston in 1911 was very young indeed. Heir to a much older tradition of cultural development in other fields of arts and science, the "Athens of America" had suffered a slow start in music. Within a decade of the English immigrants' first landing in 1620 near what is now the town of Plymouth, settlers formed the Massachusetts Bay Colony at Boston. Within another ten years they had established Harvard College and a book press. But the future cultural capital of New England lagged behind other American communities in adopting a large-scale pattern of indigenous musical life because of the particular constraints of its early religious climate.

In their own way, Sessions' Puritan forebears brought some lively musical traditions to their new country. The practice of "Psalm singing," for instance, was not only a religious but also a practiced social activity in which all 150 Psalms, in various prose or rhymed translations, were sung to thirty-nine tunes borrowed from English, French, and Dutch Psalters. An improved version, based on a new rhymed translation by a convention of thirty clergymen, appeared in Boston as the *Bay Psalm Book* in 1640—the first American publication, in English, on any subject. The later practice of "lining out," in which the preceptor sang a line that would then be repeated by the congregation, allowed for general participation and offered some scope for flexible use of musical variants within a body of popular musical patrimony.

But secular (read: *sinful*) musical activities were not encouraged in Puritan Boston. Opera—any theatrical performance, for that matter—was strictly forbidden. Charleston, South Carolina, had something akin to the "ballad opera" of seventeenth-century British fashion during the early eighteenth century. New Orleans had an established season of French opera before the city was sold, as part of the Louisiana Purchase, to the young American republic. A little later, in 1815, it commissioned the building of a major opera house. In New York, Mozart's librettist Lorenzo da Ponte, while on the faculty of Columbia University, in 1825 participated in the founding of an opera theater, where celebrated artists performed in a wide range of repertory. Seventeen years later, the New York Philharmonic, oldest of America's major orchestras, was founded.

The severely Low Church community of Boston confined its public events to whatever local parishes were able to offer. A modest chamber music affair did take place in 1731, but it was not until the very end of the Colonial period, in 1771, that one Josiah Flagg was able to organize a musical event for large instrumental forces, using instrumentalists from the Sixty-fourth Regiment Band.

During the first half of the nineteenth century, a number of mostly amateur ensembles provided performances of orchestral music on a regular basis: the Boston Philo-Harmonic Society (1815–1824), the orchestra of the Boston Academy of Music (1833–1847), and the Musical Fund Society, a cooperative venture that included both musicians and music lovers (1847–1855). A sociological curiosity was the Fadette Ladies' Orchestra. Founded in the mid–nineteenth century by a group of six women, it grew into a successful ensemble of some forty players by the early 1900s, offering an opportunity to women instrumentalists banned by custom from membership in other orchestras. They provided a pit orchestra for musicals, toured the USA, and even played some early film scores. In 1920, after a number of Boston Symphony players went on an abortive strike and music director Pierre Monteux hired replacements, the Musicians' Union did manage to close down the "semiprofessional" Fadettes.

In 1849, a group of young musicians from Berlin had founded the Germania Musical Society (1849–1854), providing Boston with its first fully professional concert series. Three years after the orchestra disbanded, its flutist, Carl Zerrahn, organized a series of Philharmonic concerts, using once again a mixture of professional and amateur musicians until, in 1863, the Civil War put an end to this effort as well. After the war Zerrahn took over the direction of concerts under the auspices of the Harvard Musical Association. This alumni-sponsored organization was an offshoot of the undergraduate Pierian Society in which, many years later, young Roger Sessions would play a fairly indifferent oboe. That was the extent of public concert activity in Boston until a newly founded Boston Symphony Orchestra gave its first performance on September 22, 1881.

Like Roger's mother, Ruth, the Boston Symphony's founder, Maj. Henry Lee Higginson, had studied music in Europe. Impressed by a level of orchestral playing far superior to anything he had heard at home, he devoted most of his later life to creating "a full and permanent orchestra, offering the best music at low prices, such as may be found in all large European cities." Scion of a prominent Boston banking family, Major Higginson combined generous financial support of the Boston Symphony with autocratic control of all aspects of its fiscal and executive management. For forty years he led the organization as its undisputed ruler, until, in 1918, he was persuaded to turn over his powers to a board of trustees. In the words of a fellow Bostonian, Major Higginson controlled the orchestra's fortunes as firmly as did the ruling prince of any German city-state.

During the decade before Sessions' arrival in town, Boston had witnessed the construction of superb musical theaters and concert halls. Having threatened to stop his support for the symphony unless money could be raised to replace its original quarters, the old Music Hall, Major Higginson succeeded in having a splendid new home built for his orchestra. In 1900 the BSO moved into Symphony Hall, an acoustical marvel that also became the first concert hall in America owned by its resident orchestra.

Eight years later, the trustees of the New England Conservatory made a similar contribution to musical life in Boston. Attractive wood-paneled Jordan Hall, with its rich resonance and steeply raked banks of seats, favors the performance of chamber ensembles and solo works and rounds out available facilities for all kinds of musical performance. It was named after one of the conservatory's founders. His son, Eben D. Jordan Jr., started the Boston Opera Company, which opened its doors in 1909 in yet another fine new theater.

A young American could hardly have chosen a better place and time in which to discover music than Boston in 1911. Indeed, the city's musical resources came to mean much more to Roger Sessions than an agreeable complement to his formal musical instruction at Harvard. It did not take the new student very long to decide on which side of the Charles he would find treasure to be laid up for his future. "The only trouble with Harvard," confided Sessions to his former pupil, later Princeton colleague, and lifelong friend Edward T. Cone,

> was that in those days there was no thought of serious training for a professional musician. They were educating cultured gentlemen rather than musicians. I didn't know this. I simply took the courses, and didn't take them, I regret to say, too seriously. I heard a tremendous amount of music in those years. I spent a lot of my father's money going to concerts and buying scores and all that sort of thing. I heard the Boston Symphony every week—sometimes two or three times a week—and I went to many other concerts.[4]

During his undergraduate years at Harvard, Sessions wrote faithfully to his mother in Northampton and to his father in New York, increasingly informative letters, in which he reported on events, offered thoughts and reactions, frequently asked for advice, and freely shared a sense of his enthusiasms and disappointments. Some forty letters to his mother remain, beginning in 1912–13, his sophomore year.[5]

Not surprisingly, Sessions' first letters reveal an almost childish, lonely boy, young for his age and even younger within his new environment. It could not have been easy for him to feel at home with classmates, three or four years older, who rejoiced in their newfound collegiate freedom while he shared digs in town with his sister.

Even after he moved to campus in 1913–14, his letters do not express a particular sense of identification with his school environment. Given an already strong attachment to his mother, his early feelings of isolation within the college community found a measure of relief in those very confiding reports to her—about music, about religion, about "insincere" teachers and fellow students, and from time to time, about his shy ventures into friendship with some special girl. In view of his mother's own well-established need to maintain a controlling hold, it is hardly surprising that she insisted on receiving Roger's regular reports long after his own need to share had found other outlets.

Cambridge
Sept. 26, 1912

Dearest Mother,—

I got back safely and on time on Sunday, and everything began Monday. Among other things I began eating at Memorial on Monday noon. The food there is really better than at Boarding school, anyhow, although I wouldn't say that to any body else, of course.

My work in college has begun, and I am taking all the courses I had planned, except Psychology, which Mr. Moore thought would make too much for me. So my complete list for this year

Music 2a	—	Vocal Composition
" 5	—	Canon and Fugue
" 6	—	Orchestration
Physiology 1.		
German F	—	Conversation and Composition
History D	—	European History
English D	—	Composition

. . . I made two resolutions for this year. The first is to get all I can out of every one of my courses. The second is to keep looking spick and span. Those and my piano practicing and my being business like are my fads for this year. Another fad is to write to you twice a week, and to Daddy twice a week.

My darling mother,—

There is not much to tell you, as you were here yesterday. [Aunt] Addie came yesterday afternoon, and Sister met her. They arrived just as I finished arranging the bed, etc., which came from downtown.

I have decided to take a couple of oboe lessons, as it would probably do me an immense amount of good. I shall probably take lessons of the third symphony oboist.

We all went to church this morning and thought of John carrying the cross up the aisle in St. John's at home. I am extremely thankful that the cross is at least being used.

There is nothing more to say, except that I miss you awfully, and hope you can afford to surprise us again soon.

Perhaps I will be able to get to Northampton this fall. I hope so anyway. Give my love to John.

Your loving son
Roger

> *My darling Mother,—*
>
> Sister has asked me to send you this bill, which she just received today. She went to bed early to-night on account of a sick headache. I think she is pretty tired, but she is getting more or less rested. She paid her grocery and butter bills today.
>
> The first Pierian concert takes place on Tuesday evening the 19th. The program consists of two classes of music—Harvard marches, and concert selections . . . The classical concert comes the last part of the year . . .

On the defensive, Roger was ever a charmer, often with a wildly optimistic new idea to follow.

> November 18, 1912
>
> . . . I think that other fellows would consider themselves extremely fortunate if they had a mother like you. I certainly consider myself the most fortunate fellow in the world in that respect.

The bad news follows. Midyear grades in courses other than music were not wonderful: a C in History and a D in German and, yes, a B in Physiology. On the strength of that solitary B, he tries for the Sessions preemptive diversion: "As far as Physiology is concerned, I have sort of felt the need of having something to fall back upon, and, as there is nothing except music that I am more interested in, perhaps the study of medecin [*sic*] would be a very good thing for me. However, we will talk about it when I see you on Saturday and Sunday." Whatever may have been said on that weekend, there is no further mention of a medical career.

> I have tried to get Miss Sawyer this afternoon to apologize for the noise the other night. It was only about 11 o'clock, not between 12 and 1, however. But there was, of course, no excuse; I am willing to take the blame, and am going to Miss Sawyer when she gets home. I am awfully sorry, and I will, and I am sure Sister will try to keep quiet in the future.

Sister, in fact, was recalled home soon after, leaving Roger in sole possession of the flat in Hawthorne Street. There is little mention in his letters of everyday doings during his early years at Harvard. Small talk was never Roger's forte, nor would Ruth have encouraged it. But there are glimpses of undergraduate life and of the financial resources with which he provided for campus expenses and for concert tickets:

> I am having an awfully good time here. Albert has improved a lot since he has stopped drinking beer. I am a little "homesick" for Sister though.
>
> Well, good night. I am of course going to persuade Daddy to cut my allowance in half next year; if he refuses I shall save the extra $20 a month for clothes etc.

Homesick or not, Sister's well-established habit of control must have been a little hard to bear on her subsequent visits in Cambridge: "Sister was here Tuesday, and she and William Greene and I went to supper together with Miss Moffat and Evelyn Bolles . . . She took the maternal attitude towards me all the time, and when Miss Moffat offered me a second cup of Turkish coffee she tried to interfere and say I mustn't have it. But I did, and lived to tell the tale."

By far the most frequent topic in Sessions' reports from Harvard is his enthusiastic discovery of orchestral repertory in fine performances; at the same time, however, the reflected joy in his encounter with great music at first hand is balanced by reports of frustration with Harvard, particularly with an "insincere" attitude toward music on the part of faculty and students alike. In this respect, the fiercely caring thinker about music of later years is already in place:

My darling Mother,

Here is the check which Daddy sent me.

That was a lovely letter of yours. I suppose it is hard to keep from feeling the insincerity of others. I didn't mean to say that my courses aren't doing me any good; because I think they are, in the very fact that they show me what kind of people I will have to put up with. But when Mr. Spalding[6] can never say anything without trying to be funny, and Mr. Hill[7] can't stand anything except modern music, and has practically said so in so many words that good music should be like ragtime, no piece living more than fifteen years at most, there must be something wrong . . .

. . . I have also heard Brahms' second symphony at the concerts here, & am getting to like Brahms more and more. Have you heard any of his symphonies yet? . . . The first movement is calm and lovely; the second is intimate; the third is graceful; and the last movement is exuberant with an occasional slight touch of melancholy which Brahms never wholly avoided. There is sometimes some padding, which jars a little, but that is only a technical error.

I think that I agree with you about old and modern music. I think, however, that the inspiration of modern music is just as real, and in the case of Wagner just as uplifting as the older music . . . I don't think I ever appreciated Tristan till I heard it yesterday afternoon. It was undoubtedly a poor performance, but I was absolutely sorry to have the ship come in so soon. I enjoy that scene where Tristan is waiting for it so much . . .

Among Sessions' early problems within the musical community of the university, his conservative, not to say provincial, background in music added to his sense of isolation. He reveled in newfound musical riches but found it hard to cope with the fashionable surface of classroom exchanges among teachers and fellow students for whom Wagner was no longer "modern music."

Sessions' strength, then as later among the quarrelsome "schools" of composition of the mid-twentieth century, lay in the immediacy with which he experienced music, his own as well as others'. Assumptions based on musical fashion and the twisting professional consensus on who or what was in or out angered him even in his maturity. In 1913 they troubled him: "Last night was a lovely concert at the Symphony—Bach's suite in D major; Haydn's symphony in G; three quaint old German dances by Mozart, and Beethoven's second symphony. It is a relief to know that the great conductors are reactionary."[8] An odd last sentence, on the face of it. But it forecasts the hardheaded composer Sessions, who would reject musical "systems" and "schools" while admiring certain works of composers associated with them. The fifteen-year-old composer was not willing to accept prevailing, popularly new-music oriented views of the university establishment at a time when major works of the recent past were new and challenging to his musical empathy. As a composer and as a listener he held to an independent course of sorting out spontaneous musical experience, and he produced some impressive evidence of analytical and intellectual perspective based simply on what he heard and what he found in the score.[9]

My darling mother,—

. . . Thank you for the article on Schoenberg. As there is a great interest in any thing new here, I have heard some of his piano music—in fact, I bought one of his pieces myself. It is very interesting and may be really worth something; it is, however, much easier to make music of perpetual dissonance than really euphonious—at least so it seems to me. His "music," however, is not without effect on the hearer—it has a distinctly depressing effect upon the hearer: it reminds me of a picture of a "portrait bust" I saw in the Literary Digest—a triangular affair with terribly large eyes. If art was ever decadent, it was here. I think that Schoenberg's system of harmony might however be employed sometimes, say, in the course of a long piece, with wonderful effect; but a perpetual discord seems to be too much of a good thing . . .

. . . There is one function of music however against which my taste revolts, although I don't tell anybody so. There was a piece called "Max and Moritz" played by the Symphony last week, which was meant to describe the tricks of two little boys—common schoolboy tricks, you know, without poetry, absolutely. In one place, for instance, the music was supposed to describe how they put bugs into their uncle's bed. Perhaps I may be one of the hated reactionaries, but I think that such a composition degrades the whole purpose of music. And what was the musical content? Nothing but a technical and instrumental *tour de force*. Yet the piece is regarded around here as a remarkable piece of modern *serious* music . . . I give no opinions, however, to other people; I merely keep silent . . .

. . . Can't you and I go over some modern music this summer. You see, you have not had the opportunity to become acquainted with the works of Debussy and Strauss as I have. And my mind has changed in regard to Schoenberg, too. I think that *perhaps* he has discovered a new medium of

> beauty, and that just as Debussy, which seemed so complicated some years ago, sounds as child's play today, Schoenberg may sound beautiful in a few years. Strauss, moreover, has in his opera, *Electra,* made marvelous use of dissonance, yet the composer says that he never writes what to him sounds disagreeably dissonant or cacophonous. Although *Electra* was denounced by the critics when produced in America, it is certainly one of the most inspiring things written since Wagner; and the public showed their appreciation of it . . . I don't want to say, as I once did, that Schoenberg is crazy, mad, etc. But his dissonances do not seem nearly so bad as Wagner's and Strauss's when I first heard them.

On the face of it, the descriptive musical effects of *Max and Moritz* must surely have seemed comparable in kind to Strauss's orchestral illustrations for the adventures of *Don Quixote.* The difference would lie in "what was the musical content?"A mere tour de force in the former case, but what else in the latter? Roger's primary justification of Strauss's use of dissonance is an important clue: the composer did not *hear* these sounds as disagreeably cacophonous. The emphasis on hearing, on the inner ear as the a priori justification of a composer's choice of musical means, will be basic for Sessions' work to come. Moreover, his further reference to the *listener's* ear—his own, in this case—anticipates a notable distinction as his ideas about the respective musical experience of composer, performer, and listener will develop.[10]

The primacy of the intuitive inner ear, capable of producing active images as well as their eventual justifications in terms of musical craft, is illustrated in the next letter. Roger has just heard a performance of Schoenberg's *Five Pieces,* op. 16, and sends an example from the third movement, *Farben,* to his mother. Evidently he was not aware that the composer's originally published reference was to changing colors on a lake—which makes his own image appear the more strikingly close.

> To me it suggested a gray, misty horizon on the ocean. It is founded on this chord [Ex. 4.1], which is modified with constantly changed but precise color, but it remains grayish in suggestion.
>
> Friday night I heard *Don Giovanni,* by Mozart. It was a wonderful production, and was the second one of Mozart's operas I have heard. I think that Mozart's operas are as perfect in their way as Wagner's, though not nearly so lofty in conception. The more acquainted I get with *Tristan, Die Meistersinger* and *Götterdämmerung* the more I feel that each is the greatest of its kind. *Tristan* and *Die Meistersinger* appeal especially to me, however; the former on account of its mediaeval setting and its simplicity—especially the third act, with the wonderful harmonization of scene and music. *Die Meistersinger* I like also for its setting, but more for its beauty of melody. Harmonically this is the simplest of Wagner's operas; contrapun-

Example 4.1

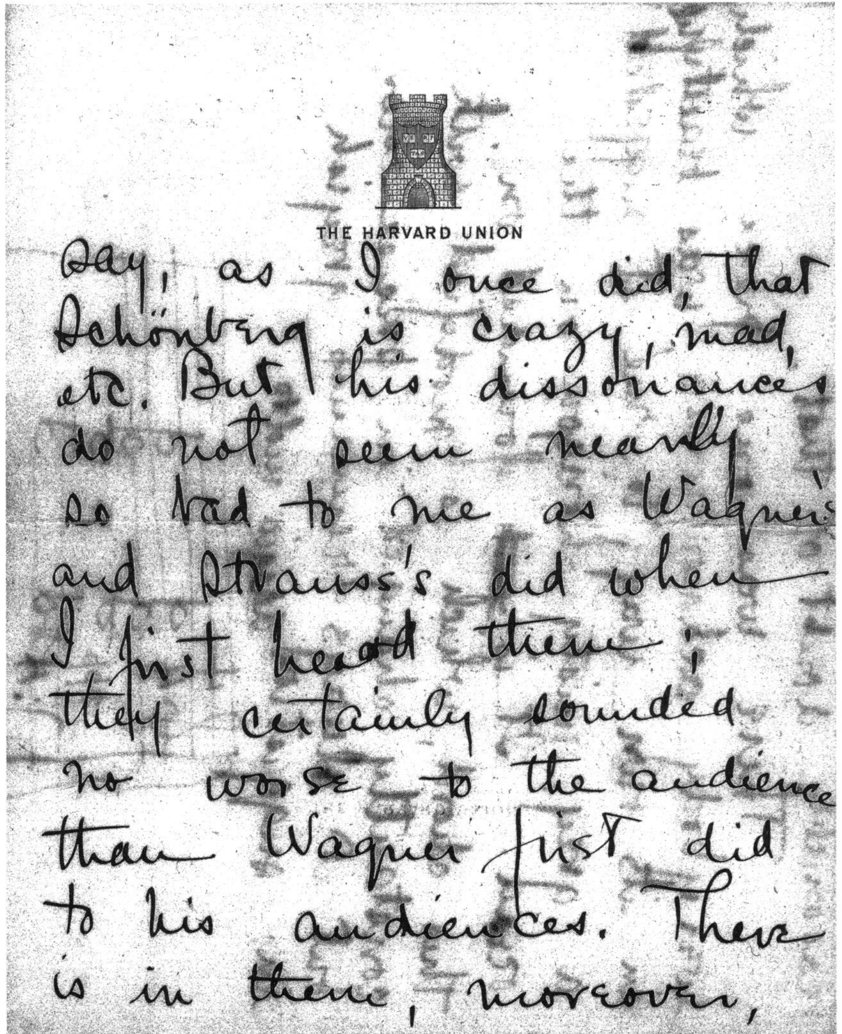
THE HARVARD UNION

say, as I once did, that Schönberg is crazy, mad, etc. But his dissonances do not seem nearly so bad to me as Wagner's and Strauss's did when I first heard them; they certainly sounded no worse to the audience than Wagner first did to his audiences. There is in them, moreover,

tally it is by far the most complicated, and the architecture is also marvelous.

. . . I hope I have not fatigued you with this, and am glad to have learned from sister that your attack was from causes which may be prevented in the future. B+ in orchestration. Love to John.

Your loving son

It is easy to understand how Sessions' real musical education and commitment during the Harvard years centered on the Boston side of the Charles River

reasonable doubt of that.
There was one piece which everybody acknowledged, was beautiful in its own way; to me it suggested a grey, misty horizon on the ocean. It is founded on this chord, which is modified with constantly changed in precise color, but it always remains greyish in suggestion. adagio molto

ppp

But this does not give ~~a~~ a ~~entirely~~ complete impression. It must be heard. I will bring home the score, and show it to you.

Ever your loving son
Roger.

and why his B+ in Orchestration rated only a bare mention at the end of a twelve-page letter. With afternoon performances of *Tristan,* followed by an evening at Symphony, the allure of Cambridge with its garrulous lectures on musical aesthetics offered no contest in capturing the imagination of a boy awed by the impact of musical listening and the very thrill of "being there."

Karl Muck, who had led the BSO from 1906 to 1908, returned as chief conductor in 1912 and remained there until 1918. Soon after America's entry into the First World War, however, popular hysteria led to the German conductor's internment as an enemy alien. Under his direction the orchestra performed a range of repertory, particularly the works of living composers, that was not matched again until the reign of Serge Koussevitzky, beginning in 1924.

In opera, Boston's offerings were no less remarkable. The Boston Opera Company had opened, in 1909, in a splendid new theater designed by Wallace Sabine of Harvard University, the same acoustician whose contribution made Symphony Hall into one of the world's great concert halls and the New England Conservatory's Jordan Hall an equally fine place for chamber music. The Boston Opera Company barely lasted through Sessions' years at Harvard. An extravagantly expensive tour to France in 1914 forced it into bankruptcy. But during its brief heyday it provided opera on a scale not equaled in Boston before or since.

Sessions mentions performances of works that stretched from Mozart to Strauss, not single productions once or twice repeated but a proper repertory season. Wagner appears to have been his particular favorite, and he was indeed fortunate to have had many opportunities to hear *Tristan, Die Meistersinger*, even *Parsifal.* And he really listened:

> On Friday night I went to the *Meistersinger,* but again started to write; the opera, however, lasted till after twelve, and again I was terribly tired . . . Gadski[11] again was Eva . . . But the Sachs, I think, carried off the honors of the evening. As I remember the Sachs we saw, he took Beckmesser rather seriously, didn't he? This one, however, did not take him at all seriously, especially in the first act. The scenery, also, was quite remarkable. It was more impressionistic, perhaps, than when we saw it here, but at the same time it gave just the right impression. When the curtain rose on the second act, the audience burst out clapping, in spite of the fact that there was music going on. That is saying a good deal in Boston, and even in the third act of *Tristan* I don't think that it has happened here before. As for the music, we know what that is like. I will only say that I can't think of another opera which is so interesting all the way through. I don't get bored a minute, and in spite of the fact that the second act is about an hour and a quarter long, I found it altogether too short.

When he writes that "I can't think of another opera which is so interesting all the way through" he speaks as a young composer: most listeners might have found it wonderful or moving. "Interesting all the way through" is a professional reaction.

From the fall of 1913 Sessions' letters leave the impression that, during his last two years at Harvard, he devoted much of his energy to literary efforts, essays on music as well as editorial work for an in-house monthly periodical produced by music students:

> I am trying for the new musical paper—the *Harvard Musical Review*. It takes a good deal of time, and if I can't get my more important work done I

shall drop it, of course. I have to try to get an article from Mr. Whiting next week.

My article, which, by the way, will come out this month, is directed against professional criticism. I think I have answered (whether effectively or not) any argument that can be made their favor. Only when I see a piece of first-rate criticism, do I begin to doubt myself. But the good criticisms are so few and far between that the person who has not heard the music cannot tell the good from the bad.

Dec. 5, 13.

Dear Mother—

I am awfully sorry I haven't written to you until now, but we have been quite busy getting the H.M.R.'s off. I sent you four yesterday. . . . In the criticism of the number which appeared in the *Crimson*, the reviewer quoted me against myself; that is, he made the statements that my editorial, with its what he called a "nervous, chip-on-the-shoulder, dustily contemptuous attitude," was just the sort of criticism I would object to; he praised my article more or less, saying that it was timely and suggestive, but that it went too far.

I am working especially hard for the *Review,* as I want, if possible, to get the presidency of it next year. I am not sure whether I should have the executive ability, though. But I shall do my best, certainly.

Personal considerations may well have played a part in the intensity and enthusiasm with which Sessions pursued an editorial post on the *Review*. His letters continue to reflect a sense of frustration with an academic environment in which music students neither shared nor valued his emotional absorption in music: "They seem to regard [music] as merely a pastime, while the real emotion in it does not appeal to them." Much of his writing for the *Review* reflects a missionary zeal, and in his avid pursuit of the editorial post he may have thought of it as a vantage point from which to smite the ungodly. But there was yet another aspect to his politicking, He was too shy, too young, too unsure of himself to assume an easy relationship with classmates—or to let them be. Elective office would provide status:

I am afraid my career at Harvard has been a failure. I would have done more, and should have, if I had the power. Please let me hear from you; I am ~~awf~~ [*sic*] pretty homesick.

[Undated; on *Musical Review* note paper, as are most of Sessions' letters during his remaining Harvard years.]

The *Musical Review* dinner was a success, and I got on well as toastmaster. I do not mind speaking so much now.

[Undated; shortly before
Christmas 1913]

I enclose an editorial which I wrote for the December number of the *Musical Review*, about the New York reception of Strauss's *Rosenkavalier*. The attitude of the critics was so rotten that I would have liked to express myself a little more strongly, but I did not think it advisable . . . I want to supplement my destructive article of the November number by a constructive article on criticism. That destructive article, by-the-way, has made a little impression in that it is provoking two replies from more or less prominent people in the January number—one *pro* and the other *con.* So you see that it was regarded as a matter of a little importance . . .

Good bye till Sunday. I don't want much for Christmas. Being home is good enough for me, you see.

It looks as if I must be the one to save this magazine, if indeed it is to be saved . . . I am sitting up all night (it is 3:40 A.M. now) to do some work on an article apropos of "Our attitude towards the ultra modern contemporary tendencies in music." Most people think that you must be either radical or conservative; but I see very good reasons for being neither. The extreme radical is no more harmful than the extreme conservative; but I think he is often less sincere as there is a certain romance in iconoclasm which everybody experiences sooner or later.

Just then, at the beginning of his last semester at Harvard, Sessions' extracurricular successes received respective dampers from home as well as from the university. With the mounting evidence of her son's absorbing literary avocation Ruth felt neglected. Her son attempts instant damage control:

Please don't think that I am not interested in everything you do. I look forward to every one of your letters, and read them over and over. I am longing to see you again, and hope to get to Northampton before long. But please tell me all about yourself; I truly have tried hard to write to you but have been at my wits end. But now the *Review* is all done and will be out at the end of the week.

But Ruth has already been in touch with the college administration. It appears that Roger was placed on probation, a fact not mentioned in any of his extant letters home to date. The dean replies to his mother's inquiry:

January 13, 1913

My dear Mrs. Sessions,

I thank you for your letter of January ninth in regard to Roger. I do not think that you need feel greatly disturbed over Roger's condition, although it is true that if he does not maintain a record, good in every way from now on, his probation may be closed without further warning. But Roger, I judge from the long and pleasant talk which I had with him, is a sensible as well as a brilliant boy, and will devote himself to his studies.

I believe that you were quite right in sending him to College, young as he was, for although he is boyish in some ways, he has shown himself mature enough to profit by College work . . . He *is* a musical genius, and I want to see that genius developed.

The boy took his punishment in such good spirit that I feel sure he will heed the warning and redeem himself. I am going to have him in again to talk with him about taking a degree with distinction.

Between the lines of his letters home you will, no doubt, read suggestions. Another reason why I am interested in him, is that I find we are far off cousins . . .

My dearest Mother:—

I had intended to write you more, but find that I have not time, for I am going to work every minute till the mid-years, so that I can get *good* marks then. I have read your letter several times, and I loved to get it; for I have been a good deal discouraged this week, and your letter came as a comfort and an inspiration. You may be sure that I determined before you wrote to go again to church regularly; and I have so far carried it out pretty well . . . [The dean] seems absolutely confident that I will be all right at the end of the year, and I know I will. So 1915 will be the greatest year of my life.

I haven't written much, nor made any promises; please expect instead *results*, which are forthcoming.

Your ever most loving son
Roger

. . . The Dean seemed to think I had been foolish, but not that I had done anything particularly disgraceful; he regards my probation as a severe *warning*, rather than a threat.

R.H.S.

Roger proved to be as good as his words. His probationary condition was removed before Easter. He took his degree with distinction. And he was elected editor and president of the *Harvard Musical Review* before the year was out.

The dean had not been wrong, however: Roger *was* young. The age difference between him and his classmates was bound to restrict shared confidences with his friends, and his budding romantic affinities are confided to his mother. There are touching references to an early romantic attachment, reminiscent of Ruth's own description of her first meetings with Roger's father:

We did not talk much—any more than usual, but I, at least, felt that we were perfectly congenial and that each knew what the other was feeling. When we wanted to speak, we spoke, otherwise not. But there was no con-

> straint at all, and we talked really more than we have before, for that reason. I think we are getting to know each other better, and I appreciate her more every time I see her. When she sends me back my book, I am going to write her if she alludes to it in her letter as if she is at all interested in the plays. I think she is, too, for she had already read the *Trojan Women* when I took her to *Hamlet*. So she must be reading more.

Angela, sister of Roger's friend Billy Richmond, remains a frequent topic in his final letters from Harvard: "I received a most grateful letter from Angela, which was certainly the best I ever got from a girl, and it made it quite evident that it was my violets she wore on the great occasion. I thought the poem was fine too." He persuades his mother to invite Angela to a house party in Northampton—more likely, in fact, the party was planned for that purpose. Nonetheless, the relationship does not appear to have developed beyond a shyly manipulative stage:

> I expect that Sister, Elmer, Billy Richmond and I will reach Northampton some time Saturday afternoon—at 5:12 in Northampton, if I am not mistaken—the 1:25 from Boston. Elmer is going to stay till Monday, Billy till Sunday. I would rather like to arrange a theater party for that evening—with supper beforehand at the house. But if you feel that you haven't the energy to arrange it, please don't. My not acknowledging those neckties may show that I don't deserve it. But it would be nice to take Angela, Sister, Billy, Elmer, and another girl to the theater after supper at our house.
>
> You are a *peach* to have been so patient about the h.p.
>
> Although I wrote Angela last Monday night, I have not yet heard from her. I suppose she has been too busy with her Prom., etc., to write me; but I ought to hear Monday. I will give you the money for the tickets at the h.p. I read over her last letter, and found that she really said all she could have said under the circumstances.

Whatever those circumstances, it appears that Angela decided not to attend the "h.p." in Northampton, and there is no further mention of her in Roger's correspondence.

Meanwhile, with an aggressiveness absent from his hapless affair of the heart, young Sessions, the musician, managed to storm one of the citadels of Boston's cultural establishment: the palatial home of Isabella Stewart (Mrs. Jack) Gardner:[12]

> The notorious Mrs. Jack! You can imagine my surprise mingled with consternation . . . I played much better than usual, and got through *Elektra* at a great rate. Whereupon and *worüber* Mrs. Jack began to enthuse, hinted that I was the best imitator of orchestral effects she had ever heard except Jean de Reske,[13] and made me promise to go to her palace on Friday evening . . .

and do the same by *Salome* . . . The first time she ever heard *Salome*, she told me airily, was when Strauss played it for her before it was finished. Jean de Reske taught her all the Wagner Operas.

I realize that to tell you all this will make you beside yourself with fear I will make an ass of yourself; but I am practicing *Salome* very diligently . . . This is more or less the chance of my life . . . please don't be horrified! I would much rather not have played for her in the first place, but since I evidently made a hit, why then it's Mrs. Gardner's bad taste rather than my good playing.

Well, Mother dearest, you may allay your anxiety completely about Mrs. J., for I played *Salome* only before a small and select company that heard *Elektra* in my "brilliant and altogether masterly" interpretation. And, as Salome is ten times as easy as *Elektra*, it sounded extremely well on what is reputed to be the best Steinway in the world. I was surprised to hear *my* playing sound so well.

What with his shy romance, his quest for elected office, his probation, and his social triumph during these final months at Harvard, it is small wonder that Sessions had also to undergo the kind of crisis of faith to which members of his family seem to have inclined. In this, however, his very youth may have averted more lasting distress—he was graduating from Harvard at age seventeen: "I am now having a terrible conflict about my attitude towards life and towards the whole world in which I live. Please pray for me, because I need help, and this is so vital and personal a thing that no one but God can help me, and I know I shall be led right if only I depend on Him to the utmost of my power."

Whatever the problem, God and Siegfried appear in reassuring contiguity in the very next letter:

I think we are all pragmatists at heart; but I should never dream of trying to justify religion in the pragmatic manner. To me, if it is necessary at all to justify religion, a very vital and lively form of the "ontological argument" is sufficient evidence of the existence of an omniscient, omnipotent, and good Being, Whom I can only approach through Christ.

Now, about *Siegfried*. Reserved seats are $3, and $2.50. The boxes are $40, $35, and $30, and seat six apiece. In a box I should, of course, pay for my own seat. But whatever we decide to do we should do as soon as possible.

An almost unbroken thread of musical information runs through the entire Harvard correspondence, revealing an increasingly detailed and authentic image of the young man as an artist. Oddly enough, there is very little mention of his own music, and mostly assigned class work at that:

I am sending you, or rather have sent you a song which I have just recently composed. It is the poem which you recommended to me. I am afraid I have paid more attention to the musical side of it than to the exact phrasing, etc., but it is much harder to write the words of a song than the recita-

Example 4.2

tive of an opera, as the vocal part must be musically interesting, whereas in the opera the interest is in the orchestra.

The song of mine in G flat I changed a little before handing it in—the ending, I mean. I will send you the "revised version" today [Ex. 4.2].[14]

Mr. Spalding's latest criticism of my fugue is that I modulate too much and that I have too many dissonances. I am going to keep quiet; but leave them as they are, as I don't want to get in the habit of giving in when it is merely a matter of taste. And besides, I had an inspiration for every measure.

Later he would declare that the music he wrote during that period and for some years to come did not represent him at all and that he had not yet learned to develop his ideas. But even then, he took it for granted that the musical idea came first. He employs the word *inspiration* in a straightforward, almost technical way, as a gauge of musical validity. It would not have been a term likely to persuade his teachers or likely to be in frequent use during classroom analysis or general discussion of music. But to him, then or later in life, it served as a genuine measure of musical worth.

We have seen how, in his earlier defense of "contemporary" music to his

mother (p. 43), he argued that "the inspiration of modern music is just as real, and in the case of Wagner just as uplifting as the older music." Just what inspiration meant for Sessions, as a practical experience, is first noted in the following letter extract: "At last I have found a subject for my Boott Prize Chorus. I have already *the germ of the music in mind* [my emphasis]. It is Dryden's 'Ode for St. Cecilia's Day'—a poem to which, when we read it over, music instinctively shapes itself. If I can carry my ideas out, it will be the best thing, by far, that I have done so far."

For Sessions, *the germ of the music in mind* would always be a spontaneous musical image of basic and ultimately encompassing material for a particular work. Even the technical means with which such an "inspiration" prefigured its own requirements would be contained in that germ and would vary from work to work; but this was something that the young composer had barely sensed, and there was none at Harvard to help him.

Sessions confided his need for real training as a composer to Edward Burlingham Hill, the one member of the faculty to whom he was beginning to feel close. Edward T. Cone records Sessions' account:

> [Burlingham Hill] took me for a walk and said to me, somewhat confidentially—or I assumed that it was: "I want to tell you that we are not in a po-

sition here to give you what you need. I won't go into the reasons why." And he urged me very strongly to go after I graduated to France to study with Ravel. . . .

This was the spring of 1914, and so I didn't go to study with Ravel. Obviously I couldn't have. And in some ways I don't regret it at all. In fact I'm sure it was much better that I didn't; because in the first place I was eighteen years old [*sic*], and I didn't know anything about the musical world except what I had gotten from going to concerts. I was quite shy—very shy, in fact—and I don't know at all how being precipitated into French musical life would have affected me.[15]

CHAPTER 5

Ernest Bloch

You'll have to work very hard for two years; and then you'll be able to do what you want.

—BLOCH TO SESSIONS,
NEW YORK, FALL OF 1919

My forces scattered themselves, and the work which I have always done for you is more than unworthy of what I could and should have done.

—SESSIONS TO BLOCH,
NEW HAMPSHIRE, AUGUST 27, 1921

In the fall of 1919, Roger Sessions first cracked the mold. Three centuries of New England were his birthright and his burden; a privileged upbringing and a first-class education had turned a bright and musically alert boy into an accomplished young musician; but an enduring notion that, for all his keen musical imagination and for all his dutifully acquired theoretical skills, some essential ingredient of compositional craft still eluded him drove him outside the inherited background in search of help. He needed a teacher. And with that search, undertaken on his own and for a purpose defined by himself, he took his first step toward personal and artistic independence. He found what he was looking for in the person of a wonderfully charismatic European Jew, recently arrived in New York and just then on the verge of his own meteoric American career.

Ernest Bloch, Swiss composer in his fortieth year, had fled the war-torn continent across the Atlantic two years before. Born in Geneva, trained in Frankfurt and Munich, and deeply conscious of his Hebraic roots, he had just completed what he would later call his Jewish Cycle of works, including the *Israel* Symphony and *Schelomo*. An earlier opera, *Macbeth*, had received performances at the Opéra Comique in Paris. A fine conductor, Bloch had been a candidate for the music directorship of the orchestra in Lausanne in 1910–1911 but was defeated for the post by one of his former pupils, Ernest Ansermet.

Between 1911 and 1915 he lectured on aesthetics at the conservatory in Geneva, but solid professional recognition as a composer did not come to him in his native Switzerland. Indeed, in order to provide a living for himself and for his young family he worked part-time in his father's clock business. By 1916, the war had effectively choked off any chance for a composer to develop his career elsewhere in Europe, and when Bloch got the chance to come to America as conductor of the Maud Allan dance company, he took it gratefully. New beginnings in New York were bewildering. The Maud Allan tour collapsed after six weeks, but Bloch's immense personal drive, the outgoing warmth of his personality, and, soon, an impressive public and critical response to his music led to a prosperous, if sometimes stormy, American career.

Throughout these hectic times, Bloch never stopped composing. On the last day of his first year in the United States, the Flonzaley Quartet in New York played his First String Quartet, begun in the Old World and completed in the New. Important performances of his works followed. At the invitation of Karl Muck, Bloch conducted his *Three Jewish Poems* with the Boston Symphony in March of 1917. The orchestra included the work on a guest appearance in New Haven, and it was on that occasion that Roger Sessions, then a student at Yale University, first heard the music of Ernest Bloch.

The young American, who would be Bloch's most famous pupil and a friend for life, was completing his academic tour of duty at Yale with a B. Mus. in the spring of that year. At graduation he was to receive the university's coveted Steinert Award (including a cash award of $100.00) for his *Symphonic Prelude*, the first movement of a projected symphony. Maurice Ravel, Sessions' hoped-for teacher after graduation from Harvard in 1915, was driving an ambulance behind the Western Front—by default: he had tried to enlist, but the French army had found the composer under regulation size. Thus Sessions had returned once more to his New England mold and enrolled in the composition class of Horatio Parker, a greatly respected composer, organist, and dean of Yale University's School of Music.

Parker himself had never broken the mold. His family background and the outward course of his formative years as a composer closely resembled Sessions' own: staunch New England heritage, composition with George Chadwick in Boston, three years at the *Hochschule* in Munich, and, soon after his return to the United States, a prestigious university appointment, the Battell Professorship at Yale, which he retained until his death in 1919. He had enjoyed a distinguished position on the American musical scene, with performances by the best orchestras and the premiere of his opera *Mona* at the Metropolitan Opera in New York, but his creative powers peaked early, years before the young century's new currents in musical composition swept past him and his work. When Sessions became his pupil, he found an immensely likable teacher, dispirited and old at fifty-two. He reports to his mother:

Nov. 17, 1915

> . . . Parker has been cordial to me, and I hope to call at his house early next week. Next week I am to conduct the Scherzo of the *Eroica* in class while another fellow plays it on the piano. It is really a very hard movement to conduct, as one has to keep beating very fast in perfect time, and that is a good deal harder than it sounds. Parker says he doesn't think that I can do it; but I do and hope to show him that I can.[1]

We do not know whether this odd exercise justified the student's confidence or bore out his teacher's misgivings. Certainly even Sessions' most devoted future admirers would be bound to admit that the composer's podium skills rarely rose above "terrible." Nevertheless, throughout his long and distinguished career as a composer Sessions' own faith in his effectiveness as conductor of his works remained unshaken.

Sessions' relationship with his new teacher was a complex one and would grow uncomfortable over time. He liked Parker from the start and was welcomed by him and his family as an attractive young man and a promising talent: "Wednesday night I went to the Parkers, had a very good time. P. greeted me at the door, and we had time for a nice talk about the Musical Review, etc., before Mrs. P. joined us. Mrs. P. is a buxom German lady—very nice. The daughters are cordial and attractive, but rather conventional society girls. It was very nice and informal, and P. asked me to drop in often."[2]

Sessions' Yale years were unproductive in terms of his musical development. He worked diligently at his assignments, but the results were inhibited by an odd conflict between his manifest personal fondness for his teacher and a persistent reluctance to risk showing him his work, for fear of receiving suggestions that might inhibit his own musical ideas. In his second year he writes to his mother: "I think you will like my symphony. Of course I have not begun it yet; but the plan is growing clearer, and I expect to really make something of it. The only thing I dread is having Parker see it periodically: for that will obscure my ideas and help to botch things generally. I am going to try and fix it so that I can work things out more or less by myself, however."[3]

A few months later, on March 4, 1917, he reports: "I am working very hard on my symphony just now, and having to dodge Parker; for I am anxious to preserve my independence . . . The music school students, I am told, are expecting me to get the Steinert prize of $100.00. As a matter of fact I think very little of that; but I am just living for my symphony now, and am *very* busy."

Sessions' life at Yale differed greatly from his carefree undergraduate years at Harvard. Money was tight, although he continued to receive an allowance from his father. He augmented his income by waiting tables at Commons, and ushering at New Haven Symphony concerts. At a time of acute worry about his father's health, he even sold whatever books he thought he might spare. His old preparatory school, Kent, engaged him to teach every second week, as director of the Glee Club and as instructor of a general music course, at a fee of five dollars per visit plus travel expenses.

He seems to have made his cheerful best of that situation, but a growing sense of being out of synch with the majority of his contemporaries troubled him greatly. Rather than the age difference that had set him apart at Harvard, it was the enthusiasm among Yale students in favor of active preparation for possible American participation in the war in Europe that troubled him. His own views had grown more determinately pacifist as martial fever gripped Yale's undergraduate population. On January 21, 1917, he wrote to his mother:

> The University voted 1102 to 286 in favor of compulsory military training on Thursday . . . I made a point of voting "No."
>
> . . . The spirit of militarism is everywhere down here just now, especially among fellows who have no conception of what it would mean. I was in Jamie's room last night, for instance; and he was gloating over the fact that if war came he would be an officer, because he has been in the Yale battery. I gave him a piece of my mind. . . . It has been interesting to follow the papers in connection with Wilson's peace work, and to note how shamelessly the Republican ones shift their ground and are determined to find some fault with Wilson at all cost. But it makes one terribly pessimistic.
>
> . . . The symphony is progressing slowly.

In his doubts about the wisdom of America's gradual political shift toward joining the war in Europe Sessions found firm support at home, but he was not at all certain what he might do if he should be called to serve:

> I haven't even now the slightest idea what position I should take. I remember you saying that you hoped that both John and I would have the courage to keep out of the war if it should come; and I sometimes think that non-resistance is the only consistent policy for one who believes as we do; yet I don't see how individuals could be effective as non-resistants in time of war. There certainly has to be something active mixed up in it; and, if war comes, and I could choose what I should like, I would prefer to work in some international organization like Rolland's *Agence Internationale des Prisonniers de Guerre*.[4]

A week later, he writes:

> A book of Bertrand Russell's which is just out, entitled *Why Men Fight*, has made a tremendous impression on me, Russell, you know, is the foremost of the conscientious objectors in England . . . You must read *Why Men Fight*; it is written in the most splendid spirit, and corresponds in English to Rolland's book in French, although he is even on a higher plane than Rolland, I think. This is perhaps due to the fact that *Why Men Fight* was written later, as [Rolland's] *Audessus de la Melée* [Above the battle] was written in the very first months of the war.[5]

During the last summer before America's entry into the war, he wrote to his mother from a holiday visit to the Cape:

The sea was calm and noiseless, except for the almost caressing delicacy of the waves upon the shore. The lights from Martha's Vinyard [*sic*] made an almost unbroken reflection across the waves—seven miles. But as I looked out to sea, I could not help thinking of an entirely different world, the world which the sea connects us with; and it made me feel strangely sad . . . I could not help praying that we should keep out of the war and not inflict more terrible wounds upon the face of the bleeding world than has been done already.[6]

His fellow students at Yale were not the only ones, however, who did not appreciate such sentiments. Roger had not confined his views on the war to darkling allusions to Matthew Arnold or reports to his mother on how Yale joined the war effort. The mills of government ground slowly, but in the summer of 1919 a federal agent called on Ruth seeking information about her son Roger, "a draft dodger and a seditious pacifist":

AGENT: "It seems, to begin with, that he signed a telegram which he sent to President Wilson, asking him not to declare war. That was a traitorous act; it was going against the government. He oughtn't to have done it; it made him liable . . ."

RUTH S: "What, *now?* The war is over. There isn't any war."

AGENT: "Yes, but there are just as many traitors. We're getting them right along; sending them to Leavenworth and other places. I hold my job till the fall, anyway."

RUTH S: "I'm glad you have steady employment."

The interview did not go well. At the mention of Harvard the investigator volunteered darkly that "they have a lot of radicals at that college." Inevitably the exchange turned to Ruth's own view on the war:

RUTH S: "I will say that it coincides with the point of view of the British Labor Party. That's very important, you know, and Great Britain is our foremost ally."

AGENT: "What is it? A union? We haven't any use for those fellers. I.W.W.'s make a lot of trouble; they shoot'em out West."

At that point, Ruth fetched her copy of the *Labor Manifesto* and made him go over it. "I never knew about that party," he allowed. "You are a right smart woman to find out about such things." Graciously she offered her own copy of *The British Labor Party Principles* to speed her parting guest (off to interview the president of Smith College, whence the historic trail of sedition by Roger Sessions is lost). But Ruth's offer was declined: "It wouldn't be the thing to be carrying [such] papers about."[7]

A quarter-century later, in an article written at the beginning of the Second World War, Sessions suggests that he had in fact changed his mind on pacifism during the last months of the Great War.[8] Subtitled "A Letter to an Imaginary Colleague," the article reflects Sessions' view of the artist's role and responsibility in the world situation in 1942. But it also contains so much autobiographical detail that it becomes difficult not to wonder if the "imaginary" young colleague, whom it claims to address, might not share a belated identity with the middle-aged composer's specter of his own uneasily remembered self of 1917, a specter perhaps in need of being exorcised.

Following his graduation from Yale in 1917, Sessions landed a job on home turf and soon received what seemed like a major encouragement as a composer. Engaged to teach some music courses at Smith College, he showed his prizewinning "Symphonic Prelude" to the head of his department, who promptly submitted it to Joseph Stransky, then conductor of the New York Philharmonic. Stransky promised a reading of the whole symphony upon its completion, "in Northampton, perhaps in New York." With that prospect, the young composer went to work, dutifully but without much pleasure.

The work did not prosper. He blamed his teachers at Harvard and Yale, who had shown him the tools with which other composers shaped their ideas into large musical structures but not a way of managing the materials of his own symphony: "You were taught how a Rondo is put together; then you wrote a Rondo. Nothing at all organic about it. That's why Bloch was such a revelation."[9]

Unremarkable though it may seem, and perfectly sensible at this point, to seek advice from a distinguished newcomer on the American scene, the decision came hard. Even toward the end of his life, Sessions owned to a nagging sense of having betrayed Parker when he decided to study with Bloch. He was fond of his old teacher at Yale and well aware of how, for all his distinguished professional achievements, Parker remained dissatisfied with himself as a composer.

When Sessions decided to turn for help to a composer whose background, personal style, and professional conduct were indeed worlds apart from that of the American establishment at the time, it was not so much Parker but a part of himself and of the world into which he was born that had to be denied. But that was the breaking of the mold.

The contrast of Parker's genteel withdrawal and Bloch's dynamic campaign for professional recognition in the United States could not have been more striking. In 1917 Bloch accepted a teaching post at Mannes College in New York, and from that base he began to move from strength to strength as a composer. The New York Society of Friends of Music sponsored a full program of his works, including *Schelomo* and *Psalms No. 22, 137,* and *114*, as well as the *Israel* Symphony and *Jewish Poems*. Bloch and Arthur Bodansky conducted. In the following year the Philadelphia Orchestra scheduled a similar concert, the composer again conducting. We have already mentioned his appearance with the Boston Symphony.

In 1919, the year Sessions wrote his letter asking for an appointment in New York, Bloch's Suite for Viola and Piano (or Orchestra) won the $1,000 prize for a new composition of chamber music offered by one of America's most remarkable musical benefactors, Elizabeth Sprague Coolidge, through the Library of Congress in Washington. Chamber music was Mrs. Coolidge's particular interest and found splendid fulfillment in the Berkshire chamber music festivals at South Mountain, Massachusetts, annual awards of an Elizabeth Sprague Coolidge Medal for "eminent services to chamber music," and, finally, the Elizabeth Sprague Coolidge Foundation, endowed by her in 1925, whose income supported performances in the Coolidge Auditorium at the Library of Congress in Washington. Over two hundred works by American and European composers were composed on Coolidge commissions. Ernest Bloch's American reputation as a composer had achieved major status by now.

The Sessions interview in New York started badly. Bloch asked him to play his symphony at the piano, took up a position behind Sessions' chair, and began, loudly, to chant the names of composers he "recognized" in the music. Embarrassed, but anxious to show that he was not unaware of musical reminiscences, Sessions joined in the clamor, anticipating Bloch's identifications in order to prevent that strident voice from doling out further humiliation. At last, Bloch called a halt. "It's no disgrace to show the influence of other composers. We all learn from someone. But there's an important composer missing in this music, Mr. Sessions—*you!* If you want to study with me, you'll have to make a hard decision: forget about this symphony for now. You'll have to work very hard for two years, and after that you'll be able to do what you want."[10]

Bloch then sat down at the piano and, for the next quarter of an hour, took apart the opening measures of Beethoven's piano sonata op. 2, no. 1, and put them together again. This was an entirely different kind of analysis from the kind Sessions had been made to practice in his theory classes at Harvard and at Yale. Bloch showed him that there was a purpose in what the composer had chosen to do and that every choice supported that purpose.

More than half a century later, as Sessions recalled the experience, some of the excitement and delight of the original discovery would still inform his remembering: "It was simple: 4 + 4 + 2 + 2 [measures] etc.—how the motifs got shorter and the musical rhythm got tighter and—with the harmony—oh yes, with the bass rising—all of it built up to the climax of the phrase. I learned more from that than I had in all the years of study before."[11]

So it began. Lessons in New York were agreed upon, as many as a young music teacher could afford. Years later, composition students of the mature Sessions would have found very familiar reminiscences in their teacher's story of his own lessons with Bloch: "It's a matter of using the *ear.* An ear, like every other part of the body, is not just a tool but an organism. If something gets stuck in the side of a wall, and I can pull it out with my fingers, two fingers can do many more things than a wrench. A wrench is stronger, but two fingers have a greater variety of possibilities—they are an organism. Like the ear!"[12]

The shift of emphasis from the grip of a system to the authority of the composer's ear was basic and profound, not only in making Bloch's pupil understand the nature of composition but also in its lasting impact on the work of the mature composer. Sessions' life would be a search for the connection between his inner vision and its appropriate means of musical expression. By no means, however, did Bloch's teaching neglect technical aspects of compositional craft in favor of developing the subjective sensibility of his student's inner ear. As in his initial interview, Bloch would use examples from four hundred years of musical literature for in-depth analysis—not only with regard to what the composer had done but also as to what musical result he had achieved in the doing. From his pupil's point of view, technical understanding evolved from relating a composer's way with musical materials to the effective use of available means in achieving results: "It was the same kind of teaching as in Schoenberg's *Harmonielehre.*[13] Whether you use a gradual modulation or an abrupt shift of tonality in reaching an harmonic goal, the intended musical effect must justify the means you employ."[14] Schoenberg put it this way in his harmony textbook: in writing about a robbery, you would have to have a very good reason for making the robbers more sympathetic or interesting than their victims or the detective who solves the case.

Bloch's historical frame of reference and his lively, hyperbolic enthusiasms reached further into the past than the mostly nineteenth-century common practice that had informed much of Sessions' studies to date. In a 1927 article, Sessions recalls Bloch's comment on a passage in the *De Profundis* of Orlando di Lasso: "I can conceive of a day when Beethoven will seem old-fashioned; even Bach may some day seem old-fashioned, while Wagner has begun to seem so already. But this can never grow old."[15]

Throughout his entire life, Sessions showed a remarkable talent for lasting friendships, and his brief tenure at Smith provided no exception. Among those who were to play important roles in his future were Senda and Bessie Berenson, sisters of the eminent art critic and collector Bernard Berenson, on whose estate near Florence Sessions spent the first two years of a future wayfarer decade in Europe. Roy Dickinson Welch, fellow instructor in the music department—"one of the few people I could really talk to at Smith"[16]—would invite Sessions, in 1933, to join the music faculty at Princeton University. And with Barbara Foster, student of art history and adroit violinist, he fell in love at around the time he began to study with Bloch. Roger and Barbara became engaged and married eighteen months later, in June 1920.

The wedding, at the home of the bride's parents in New Hampshire, brought out the Sessions clan in force: father, mother, aunts, brother John, and sister Nan. Ruth Sessions, very much taken with her "brilliant and fascinating" daughter-in-law, nevertheless had reservations: "Our young people were marrying with no more realistic idea of the implications of matrimony than their forbears had, and we elders wondered with some anxiety whether life would destroy or sublimate the romance and imaginative rapture which these temperamental children were bringing to their union."[17]

Well might they have wondered, although these tactful forebodings were only confided to Ruth's autobiography some sixteen years later—in the year of her son's *second* marriage. The first one, to Barbara Foster, was a disaster: "She did not understand what it is to be a creative artist . . . She had the approach of a musicologist—although she was not. She was an art-"ologist" . . . Her mother, a very stupid woman, wanted to oversee our lives. She resented the money I spent on lessons with Bloch."[18]

For all of Sessions' remembered frustration, it would not be difficult to imagine the different perspective of a gifted young woman, on the very point of entering into her own professional life and trying to put years of serious preparation in her own field to some use. Barbara had just graduated summa cum laude, and she was ill prepared for a full-time job of muse and handmaiden to a "creative artist," aka. Roger Sessions. Her new husband, much as he may have chafed at times under the enveloping care of his mother, had nevertheless come to find much-needed support in Ruth's single-minded participation in his professional concerns. From the start, he expected no less from the young woman "who understands me perfectly, yet believes in me." But even while he still thought of her role with regard to his career in much the same terms as that which his mother had filled, he found himself unprepared—by his own admission—to provide his young wife with a sense of active partnership in areas of her own concern. Nor—to complete a triangle that would become more rigid over time—is it hard to understand why Ruth, during the fifteen years of her son's ill-fated marriage, remained strong in defense of a daughter-in-law with whose efforts to safeguard an endangered professional identity of her own she could empathize—but who had *not*, after all, taken her place in Roger's life.

It remains difficult to see what kept the marriage together for fifteen years. They separated often, and both partners had extramarital affairs almost as soon as they left Smith. In his disingenuous way, following an inventory of Barbara's failings, Sessions would add, "I was not a very faithful husband. But I don't think that fidelity is necessary for love."

While wedding preparations and, for Barbara, final examinations at Smith College were in full swing, Ernest Bloch received an important job offer.[19] In a letter dated May 1, 1920, and signed by one Martha Sanders, he was asked to head the new Cleveland Institute of Music. The institute did not yet formally exist, but the letter informed Bloch that

> a group of men and women, desirous of establishing a conservatory upon the best and highest educational lines, [have] incorporated for profit, upon advice of the best obtainable legal counsel. We do not intend, however, to run the conservatory upon commercial principles, but we do expect to have it conducted upon a sound business basis . . .
>
> We have no endowment, no buildings, but we have a very good start in subscription to finance a period of three years and to secure opening the school next November.[20]

Bloch's reply is dated May 6:

> I should be extremely eager to undertake the directorship of a *real* School of Music, provided it be based on sound artistic and practical principles . . . I have come to the conclusion that most of the actual methods used in the ordinary Music Schools are no longer corresponding to the needs of our time . . . I have many ideas of my own that I would be very glad to put into practice on a larger scale, and thus help the musical development of this country.

A sampling of his ideas and requirements followed on May 13. There would have to be "a large room or hall for *choral singing* and *ensemble music,*" also "a selected musical library, containing the masterpieces of the literature and the most important books on music and a fund . . . for a certain number of scholarships." Then, "my own idea concerning teachers. They would have to be given a free hand in their teaching, provided they have a *real* and *true* individuality."

Furthermore:

> Personally, I would like to head the Department of all advanced branches of Composition, practical instrumentation, Analysis of the masterpieces, Critic [*sic*] etc., as well as instrumental ensemble-playing and choral singing, supervising of course all other courses . . . It is high time for this great country to provide for a real music-school, where soloists, *orchestral players,* singers, conductors, critics, composers, could be thoroughly educated and trained without always looking to Europe for help.

And finally: "Concerning my salary . . . I would hardly give up my actual situation in New York unless the salary equals about twenty thousand dollars a year."

Not surprisingly, this set of pronouncements and demands caused an uneasy flutter among Bloch's prospective employers. An interim letter to him explained that during the process of incorporation the board would have to reorganize and could not act on his appointment until it was able to vote on it. Meanwhile, would the maestro come to Cleveland to help sort things out?

The maestro would not. To the contrary, while he could "quite understand reasons for a possible year's delay," the maestro applied pressure for an early decision in view of his "commitments" in the near future (on the basis of available information these were as notional as his twenty thousand dollars' worth of "actual situation" in New York). Perhaps the new board's chairman, Dr. Briggs, could come to New York.

Dr. Briggs could not. The problem was that the entire "subscription to finance a period of three years" amounted to only $30,000 thus far, a matter about which an anxious board had chosen not to inform their prospective employee and an equally anxious employee had never asked.

A compromise agreement was worked out: Bloch was to be appointed artistic director, with a salary of $15,000, for "half-time" duties during a preliminary year of planning and organization. He would agree to establish residence in Cleveland but continue to spend alternate weeks in New York. Mrs. Sanders would hold the post of manager. Future responsibilities as full-time artistic director would be subject to a later agreement but would be compensated in any case at a salary of $20,000 as originally requested. Bloch signed the agreement on August 25, 1920.

Among the first to be offered a faculty position at the new conservatory was his student Roger Sessions, at a salary of $2,500, a princely increase for the new family man, who had been earning $1,500 at Smith College. Bloch tried to secure additional work for him at the university—as conductor of the orchestra. In the event, however, with a new teaching post at stake, Sessions' conductorial confidence appears to have yielded to prudence. Mrs. Sanders, charged with getting things ready for the official opening in the fall of 1921, reports: "I had a letter from Mr. Sessions in which he seemed more or less upset by my letter asking him whether he could consider the University School orchestra . . . If I remember rightly, you thought Mr. Sessions would be the proper person to undertake it."

Bloch's attempt to smooth ruffled feathers ran into a brusque artistic ego. "I am glad my letter to Mrs. Sanders amused you," Sessions replied on August 27, 1921. Evidently, the lady had already tried to mollify an angry young man, whose letter continues, not very attractively: "I shall answer her in my most oily manner! I really find these little feminine endearments rather amusing—except for the waste of time they involve." For all that, Bloch had already troubled Sanders to make housing arrangements for his fledgling assistant and wife: "Les Sessions se contenteraient, au besoin, d'une grande chambre meublée (avec bain)." A more engaging side of Sessions' manner at that time, and of the artless candor he never lost, prompted him—in the same letter—to inform his teacher and (as yet) prospective employer:

> The truth is that I am utterly without self-discipline, in my whole life; and this has thwarted me and frustrated me at every turn. To give one instance: the work that I have done for you has been *false,* simply because I have put so little energy into it—through sheer lack of will. When I started out with you I wanted with the utmost sincerity to do my work justice; but my forces scattered themselves, and the work which I have always done for you is more than unworthy of what I could and should have done.[21]

Self-doubt and a sense of guilt about his "scattered forces of concentration" plagued the young Sessions throughout his years of formal study with Bloch and well beyond. With the empathy of a great teacher, Bloch addressed the problem by allowing his student to share his own. In a letter to his mother, written sometime during the second year in Cleveland, Sessions reports:

> Saturday Barbara & I went with Bloch to a very picturesque German restaurant, and our conversation developed into a talk with Bloch which meant a very great deal to me. Somehow we got talking about my work, especially my work in composition, & Bloch gave me a great deal of advice and help. He has often had the same lack of confidence and the other difficulties which I have in my composing, and told me very freely about things that had helped him, and expressed his entire confidence that I would be

> able to do something really fine. It was so encouraging to have such a talk with him, and will really help me a great deal. Lack of self-confidence such as I have is an American disease; Bloch assured me that there was no reason for it in my case, & it did me no end of good to talk with him about it; for it is the worst disease that an artist can have, especially at the outset of his career, for there are millions of things to discourage him after the career is under way.[22]

Bloch assembled a young faculty. The composers, including Sessions, the Swiss Jean Binet, and New Englander Theodore ("Teddy") Chanler, spent happy evenings at their teacher's house. A shared sense of cultural alienation in a provincial midwestern city encouraged them to rely on one another's resources, and the cosmopolitan Ernest Bloch may well have felt most at ease with his bright disciples and their young families. Cleveland society welcomed them all with genuine hospitality but was not about to change its ways for a group of young people who did not care to follow a fine dinner with "silly games like the one where some one starts spelling a word and each person adds a letter, trying not to finish the word—until a very late hour," as Barbara writes in a bitter letter. "They can not make me try to make a social *monkey* of my husband—*I will not!*—I will try to do my best to help him with what he feels necessary for the Institute—but *nothing more!*"

At the conservatory, Bloch continued to set a heady pace getting his new school under way, organizing the staff, recruiting students and faculty, and, carefully but with a will, easing his enterprise into the existing cultural and musical fabric of the city. "Everything is very inspiring to see," Sessions wrote home two months after the opening. "Mr. Bloch is doing a very fine work in forcing the rival factions in Cleveland into friendliness and cooperation together."

In their second year, both Sessionses were working. Roger taught at the institute, "7 classes, 30 hours a week"; Barbara taught school and "was not so depressed as last year." As their chambre, meublée (avec bain) had not boasted kitchen facilities, meals except breakfast ("cooked on our various electrical appliances") had had to be taken at a nearby cafeteria. Now, on their combined income, they were able to move to a small apartment. And Roger bought a motorcycle. The friend who taught him to ride cautioned him not to take long trips until he had gained some experience. Nevertheless he embarked for western Massachusetts at once, had an accident on his return through Pennsylvania, but was fortunate to recover as a guest in the home of the Good Samaritan who found him in the road. The motorbike did not recover.

Cleveland remained uncongenial. Roger found the Cleveland Symphony impressively proficient, its conductor much less so. Barbara, on her first visit to the Art Museum, thought the building was beautifully designed for its purpose, "but nothing in it would make me want me to go back." Both of them missed the countryside. "It makes me more than a little homesick and extremely rebellious at being shut away from all the beautiful signs of coming fall," Barbara writes to

Ruth. "The leaves on Cleveland trees seem to dry and shrivel on the branches without any intervening moments of beauty." Being the main beneficiary of their available resources—interesting work, a small but lively circle of musical friends, and the ubiquitous redeeming, demanding presence of Ernest Bloch—Roger undoubtedly found life in Cleveland less stressful than did his wife.

From time to time there were visiting luminaries of the music world. Siegfried Wagner came with his wife, Winifred, and had lunch with Bloch and Sessions: "Strange to hear him talk about 'my father.'" Stravinsky was engaged to conduct a program of his own works with the Cleveland Symphony, and Bloch gave a dinner party in his honor. Sessions was introduced and fell into conversation with the visitor about the extent of a performer's musical initiative within the composer's score in performance. Stravinsky became so engrossed in the topic that he invited the young composer to attend the next concert of his music in Philadelphia, where they might continue their talk.

With borrowed money and brimming with ideas for their debate, Sessions arrived in Philadelphia only to find himself shy and tongue-tied when he called at the hotel. Stravinsky had other callers at the time but suggested that he and Sessions have lunch:

> Well, I was a young jerk, he was a great man. I just had lunch alone. I met him on the way out. Later he said to someone, "What a strange young man, he could have had lunch with me, but had it by himself." We met again, many years later, in New York. Stravinsky said, "I've some very nice Scotch." We talked about Schoenberg. Stravinsky said, "I don't know Schoenberg, but he is a very great composer. In ten years we'll have to admit it. So why not now?"[23]

Formal composition lessons were not resumed in Cleveland. Bloch was generous with advice but thought Sessions was ready to make his own way as a composer. "After two years, you'll be able to do what you want"—now that the time had come, this seemed more troublesome than he had thought. In the spring of 1922 he wrote to his mother:

> At present the great difficulty is to get anything *finished.* I have five—six compositions on hand now, including a symphony, a smaller orchestral work, and a piano sonata, together with three smaller movements, which may be incorporated in these or other longer ones. On one of the smaller ones I am working very hard in the hopes of finishing it before a recital here, to be held before the end of the year; but don't count too much on it too much [*sic*].

None of these projects survived. He worked hardest, it seems, at working: "At present I am working on my second symphony (really, of course, my first[24]) and think I can make a very fine work out of it. I also have some smaller things in mind, but don't know whether I can solve the problems involved in those until I have created a style, or at least a method of work, in something on a larger scale."

In the fall he reached the opposite conclusion:

> I intend to start the year with short things, like the one I did last summer; for I am convinced that it is still too soon for me to attempt to finish the longer works, until I have some more sheer facility in expressing myself. The effort of construction even on the smallest scale, at expressing myself simply, without strain and without mannerism, of finding the right form for one's ideas is harder in proportion to the worth of the ideas; and besides, everything tempts me to be anything but natural. I have some good ideas which I think will work out very well on a small scale; and so I propose to experiment constantly and without too much regard to the ultimate and intrinsic value of the result. In such a procedure the results are sure to be at least as valuable as those obtainable by the too tense and self-conscious method that I have pursued before.

One cannot help but admire the surefooted instinct that informed Bloch's decision to suspend regular lessons during this time. Sessions' long struggle to find his own voice as a composer was well under way by now. Neither the older man nor his newly independent pupil could have foreseen the mighty effort it would take to balance "facility of expressing himself vs. the right form for one's ideas." It would take him another twenty-five years, generating a relatively small number of remarkable works along the way, before the balance was achieved that produced a prodigious flow of creation during the mature years of the composer's life.

Meanwhile a project was already at hand that made it possible for Sessions to take a significant first step. Smith College commissioned him to compose incidental music for a play by Leonid Andreyev.[25] The work was to be performed on campus in 1923, two years after Sessions had resigned from its faculty to become Bloch's assistant at the Cleveland Institute of Music. *The Black Maskers* remains as his only acknowledged work of the Bloch period.

Some sixty years later, Sessions would look upon this music as a kind of halfway house toward his discovery of himself as a composer: a step forward toward independence from his teacher but not yet, in his own eyes, a step toward finding "the right form for one's ideas." He brooded that "after all, it was not pure music, it lacked inner coherence. I realized that I had written something real; but I still needed to learn to write without a program."[26] Reasonable reservations, coming from a mature composer who had labored long and hard to create the complex but increasingly *organic* musical structures that became a hallmark of his work. But it would have been remarkable indeed if he had been able to provide incidental music with "inner coherence" for a play built on incoherence as a dramatic device.

Andreyev's play revels in insider revelations of insanity, a dreamlike spread of episodes in the alternately personal or externally perceived experience of a thirteenth-century crusader knight who, upon his return home, discovers evidence of his ignoble birth and goes mad. At a masked ball, attractively disguised guests reveal themselves as his own personified failings. Then the uninvited Black

Maskers appear, frightful subhumans who storm the castle and overcome its inhabitants. As the master lies dead in the chapel, he stands over his own corpse, singing a song to Satan during a final revelry in which the Black Maskers are expelled while the place goes up in flames.

The extent to which Sessions had already loosened the strings that had strapped his earlier exercises to Bloch's own musical thinking caused some uneasiness on both parts. Bloch does not seem to have relished his disciple's musical independence beyond a certain point, while his young pupil discovered its heady allure:

> I began to be once more very much aware that there were other composers in the world besides Bloch. During the summer of 1922, the orchestral scores of *Petrouchka* and *Sacre du Printemps* were published, and I got to know them for the first time, though I had known the four-hand arrangements for nearly ten years . . . That had an enormous influence on me. Bloch didn't like it at all, for a number of reasons, some of which I understand very well—from a human point of view; I don't understand them from a musical point of view. Of course the fact that I had this big enthusiasm didn't help matters at all.[27]

Sessions dedicated *The Black Maskers* to his teacher. Bloch attended the first performance at Smith College and was impressed but disturbed. "I could not sleep all night after your *Black Maskers,*" he told his pupil, who thought it a great compliment.

The year of 1923 had begun full of professional promise for them all. The conservatory was thriving. "Committee offers me exclusive directorship," reads the day telegram of May 31 from Director Ernest Bloch to Lillian Rogers, a friend in New York. "Mrs. Sanders to be assistant director. Would you consider coming next year as general manager?" The boss was taking charge of the enterprise. Mrs. Rogers was engaged at a handsome salary of $6,000. It is doubtful if Bloch understood that, notwithstanding Mrs. Sanders' subordinate position within the administrative structure of the conservatory, as a board member of the corporation she represented his employers. She cannot have been pleased at being reassigned from a position of relatively independent fiscal and managerial responsibility to that of an executive secretary with a fancy title. Nor would she have taken kindly to Bloch's appointment of an outsider (and an attractive woman) to assume her own former responsibilities in an enterprise in which she had played a pivotal role from the start.

Bloch, who was busily negotiating for out-of-town engagements as conductor and as teacher of master classes at other music schools, had shuffled his cabinet in order to retain firm control over the conservatory's operation during his increasingly frequent and lengthy periods of absence. Nevertheless, as an outsider in the closely knit society that supported his enterprise in Cleveland he could scarcely afford to offend the one close administrative associate, whose connection with the board would make her a major player in any future dispute. He seems to have been so confident about the strength of his control within the conservatory and about the respect and esteem of Cleveland's musical establishment at large that his apparent carelessness came dangerously close to hubris at the time. Sessions wrote to his mother:

> I think [Mrs. Rogers] will do Bloch a great deal of good; she is the motherly type that can encourage him, and she has no illusions about him, besides being a very nice person. Bloch's situation is going to be a little more delicate this year than usual; unfortunately some quite unnecessary and indiscreet remarks of his apropos of the conductor of the orchestra, which he made in the presence of strangers, were repeated; and this, together with the fact that Sokoloff[28] is obviously a little afraid of his superior musicianship, has not enhanced any budding friendship there might be between the orchestra people and Bloch. Hence they are not going to play any of his works this year; and I fear he will have to be kept in good humor if the situation is to be improved. If he will keep his temper the situation will redound greatly to his advantage, undoubtedly; but he will have to be discreet and diplomatic. Therefore I hope Lillian Rogers can keep him calm; and I think that she can if anyone can.

In June came Sessions' premiere at Smith and a joyous report from his teacher to absent friends, including the composer's wife, who had missed the event in order to visit her ailing grandmother. Mrs. Sanders acknowledged Bloch's telegram by return: "I am enchanted that Mr. Sessions had such a success and that you find the music so splendid. I am placing the telegram on the Bulletin Board where all can see it tomorrow."

A few days later, Barbara reports to her mother-in-law:

> A letter from Roger came yesterday, and the tone of it showed him invigorated and enthusiastic, and I'm sure that the whole experience has been wonderfully good for him. He found a large enrollment for his [summer school] courses with several interesting pupils. Posted on the bulletin board was a telegram to Mrs. Sanders from "Ernie" saying: "Sessions music the most prodigious thing I have heard here. He is a great genius and America should be proud of him."

Sessions taught summer school. As Barbara had already reported, he found himself to be a teacher in popular demand. Sanders to Bloch, June 29: "Our enrollment today is 136. Roger Sessions has a fuller schedule than he has ever had before." On August 2 she had second thoughts: "We all felt so doubtful that he would have very much to do that we gave him two thirds of everything that came in, which proved to be very good for him and not very good for us." NB: Sessions' "very good two thirds of everything" came to a grand total of $329.

But the best was yet to come. In the fall, with financial help from his father, a pocketful of recommendations from Bloch, and a leave of absence from the conservatory, Sessions embarked on his first trip to Europe.

There is nothing to indicate that this grand tour produced or was intended to produce more tangible musical results than similar ones had yielded for Ruth Huntington or Horatio Parker before him. It may have been a final aspect of "the mold," a New England gentleman musician's rite of passage. But young Roger was not about to argue the custom. Indeed, from the early twenties a migration of young American composers, from different backgrounds and mostly with more serious intent, had been under way to the musical wellsprings of Europe, to study, to absorb, and to learn. To give him his due, he had just begun to outgrow his own European master, and whatever the intentions of his elders who made the trip possible, he was going abroad for the living pleasure of discovery and fun.

On Bloch's instruction, Sessions began by paying his respects to Nadia Boulanger, doyenne of young musical America in Paris. He made a fine impression but did not linger. As a cultural tourist, he continued on to London, then south to Geneva, Bloch's old city and Jean Binet's, and finally to Florence, "where I had such a good time that I ran out of money and had to abandon the trip I had planned to Rome."

The man who returned to Cleveland had every reason to look with confidence to his future: a fine first success as a composer, a sensibility of musical life abroad, and a settled, creditable teaching post under a great chief. He settled down to write music and reports to his mother:

> I am writing—I call it a "chamber concerto" for string quartet and piano. It isn't exactly a quintet, since the piano and the quartet are treated as quite separate entities which are played off against each other, rather than as parts of the same group. It is quite different from the *Black Maskers* but I believe this is a good thing—or will be when it is finished . . . This regular life brings me more back into my *Florentine* mood of last summer and gives me the encouraging conviction that it was a manner of life, fully as much as a place—beautiful as the place is—that put me in that mood in the first place . . . we can be really confident about my future.
>
> I must stop now as I have a class—Spring is beautiful on our road—meadowlarks, cardinal birds, and of course robins galore!

The year 1924–1925 promised to be a banner one for the school. Enrollment stood at 450. The conservatory had played host to a number of internationally celebrated guests on its recital series. Cleveland seemed content with its new musical center. Bloch gave master classes at the San Francisco Conservatory during the summer of 1924 and was scheduled to do the same at the Eastman School of Music in Rochester, New York, in January and February of 1925.

But not everyone was pleased with the absentee director. Martha Sanders wrote to "Ernest Bloch, director, c/o San Francisco Conservatory," June 23, 1924: "I have been somewhat disturbed at seeing in the Eastman School of Music advertising and in all the publicity sent from California that there is no mention of your connection with the Institute."

Two days later, a very formal Sanders informed Bloch that, "at the annual meeting of the stockholders and directors of the Cleveland Institute of Music you were reelected as Director of the Company for the coming year."

Sessions (left) and Bloch digging a hole in Cleveland. Photograph courtesy of the Library of Congress.

Bloch returned in the fall, the season proceeded smoothly, and he left again for his February engagement in Rochester, New York. His own team kept in very affectionate touch. Lillian Rogers, general manager, to Ernest Bloch, c/o the Eastman School of Music, on February 9, 1925:

> *Dearest Boss:*
>
> Your letter today made me so happy! I am so glad you are meeting with such success, *looking* at so many beautiful girls, and that you are feeling good. Keep it all up . . .

"Business" is good. Do not get so interested in Rochester that you will not come back. We all adore you too, miss you and want you.

Always and forever,

The blow fell without warning. At four o'clock on May 12, 1925, two board members, chairman Dr. Briggs and a Mr. Cary, waylaid Bloch outside the lecture hall where he had just completed a master class. They asked him to resign, effective September 1925, but refused to give a reason beyond the fact that "you are not popular among the community."[29] Clearly stunned, Bloch told them to go ahead and fire him, but he would not resign. They suggested that "it would be more advantageous" if he resigned.

Bloch's dismissal had been voted on at a board meeting on May 11. On May 12, he was asked to resign. On May 13, notwithstanding the board's plea to Bloch not to discuss the matter publicly until an agreement was achieved, Mrs. Sanders leaked the news to the faculty, while allegedly trying to make them sign their contracts.

Subsequent negotiations left all his questions unanswered. For ten days the standoff continued, until, in the end, Bloch resigned. His statement released to the press avoids any mention of his being forced out: "The Executive Committee now feels that the Institute can progress without me . . . I have been engaged to supervise the San Francisco Conservatory of Music during January and February of 1926."

Bloch's personal notes tell a very different story of an apparently perverse decision by the board, the brutal suddenness with which it was conveyed, the "stonewalling" by chairman Dr. Briggs and other members of the board's executive committee, and the enigmatic role of Mrs. Sanders, as well as reactions of conservatory faculty and staff. Bloch's own story unfolds in a series of dated notes, carefully written out in ink and now preserved in the Ernest Bloch archives of the Library of Congress in Washington. Relevant excerpts may be examined in appendix 3 of this book.

The conservatory faculty reacted with alarm. It was not hyperbole on Bloch's part when he wrote: "Institute = EB." But to those whose professional lives and livelihood were tied into his tenure, it might not have seemed as implausible as it did to "EB" that Bloch's aggressive drive, his disdainful import of an exclusive cultural elite (to say nothing of at least occasional disparagement of local talent), and his very foreigness had not completely won the hearts and minds of midwestern Cleveland.

Bloch himself had not yet spoken to the faculty. The board executive continued to feel strongly about the need to refrain from any public statements until the outcome of negotiations was settled. In the midst of rumor and confusion, Mrs. Sanders' apparent zeal to get faculty contracts signed was unhelpful. "Despair and disgust" on the part of some might well have been expected. In the end there were resignations to protest what was being done, among them that of Roger Sessions: "Cleveland with Ernest Bloch was bad enough. Without him it would have been impossible."[30]

Sessions never had any doubt about the reason for Bloch's dismissal: "He was caught *in flagrante.* His girl friend was . . . very indiscreet, very exuberant. Probably meant nothing to him, but he was fired. Furious!"[31] The board's ultimatum, following their "secret" executive committee meeting, would be understandable in such a case, as would be their stonewalling of Bloch's demand for an explanation. Even in the initial request for Bloch's resignation, the effective deadline of his actually leaving office was to be five months hence, while under pressure of an imminent scandal instant dismissal would have been unavoidable. Nevertheless, Bloch's own notes give every appearance of truly baffled personal anguish.[32]

During the following season, the San Francisco Conservatory engaged Ernest Bloch as its director for the academic year 1926–1927.

Sessions went to see his father in New York. Archibald Sessions was a sick man when his son came to visit. Their meeting in the spring of 1925 was to be their last. Sessions loved the telling of his father's final bit of advice:

"What do you want to do now?"
"Go to Italy."
"Then you should go."
"But I have no money."
"Then you must find some."

CHAPTER 6 Berenson

Young talent prospers in seclusion,
But genius needs the bustle of the world.
—GOETHE, *Torquato Tasso*

Nestled comfortably into the wooded hills above Florence, the village of Settignano served as the municipal hub for a number of large private estates with their villas and mansion houses, some newly built and fashionably ornate, others ancient but crumbling with style. The most notable of these was the Villa I Tatti, home of Bernard Berenson, eminent art critic, collector, connoisseur, and writer on Italian Renaissance painting and sculpture. Here, during the first quarter of the century, he housed his celebrated art collection, assembled a great library, and improved the imposing grounds. Upon his death in 1959 he would leave the villa and its fifty thousand books to his alma mater, Harvard University, as the nucleus of an institute of humanistic studies.

Born Bernhard Berenson in the Lithuanian village of Butrimonys in 1865 (the *h* in his first name was dropped during the First World War as too German), he was raised on the cultural and religious values of his grandfather's pious Jewish home, until his freethinking father emigrated to Boston and established himself in America. The family—mother, brother Bernhard, age ten, and a younger sister—followed. As a brilliant student at Boston Latin School young Berenson attracted the attention of well-placed Bostonians with whose financial help he was able to enroll at Harvard. As Sessions would twenty-five years later, Berenson contributed regularly to university publications, and in his senior year he became editor in chief of the *Harvard Monthly*. A generous grant from Isabella Stewart Gardner made it possible for him to travel in Europe for a year after graduation. And there he stayed, enthralled by the vast treasures of painting, sculpture, and architecture that were to provide the professional focus of his life.

He wrote prolifically on his subject, the art of the Italian Renaissance, and eventually, in his most ambitious undertaking, cataloged in two enormous volumes all Renaissance paintings then extant in Europe. But for all his distinguished scholarship, he claimed to be, first and foremost, a lover of art:

> It has been my life's work to live the work of art, to turn it over and over on my mental palate, to brood, to dream over it; and then in the hope of getting to understand it better I have written about it. As consumer of the art product I have the right to do all that. As I am neither figure artist, nor architect, nor musician, I have no certain right to speak of the producer.[1]
>
> [I am] concerned with the work of art as it affects the spectator, the listener, the enjoyer, and not its maker, unless he too becomes an enjoyer.[2]

Berenson did well with the enjoyers of art. As a very costly consultant in the high-stakes business of attribution and sale of major works on both sides of the Atlantic, he served the great merchant princes of the art world: Wildenstein, Glaezer, and Duveen among others, as well as most of the great private collectors of his time: Freer of Chicago, Frick of New York, Walters of Baltimore, Isabella Stewart Gardner of Boston, and Baron Edmond de Rothschild of Paris. And he amassed the fortune that created the Villa I Tatti.

The estate on the slopes overlooking Florence soon became a magnet for the rich and famous, for art dealers and the collectors, for serious students and for the merely curious. They came, they admired, and some of them stayed. The villa, spacious though it was, could not accommodate the rising tide of visitors. Small cottages, *villinos*, in and around Settignano were bought up or built to house the overflow and to give the master some peace to do his work.

Sessions had been Bernard Berenson's guest at I Tatti at the end of his "grand tour" in 1923 and from the fall of 1925 through the spring of 1928 lived and worked there as one of the permanent residents. "B.B.'s" Bostonian sisters, Senda and Bessie, had provided the connection. Graduates of Smith College, they remained at the school as teachers. Ruth Sessions recalled "the picture of Senda Berenson," head of the athletics department for years, "a slight graceful figure fascinating to her pupils, with a faculty for putting common sense into the heads of her countless adorers, and a charmer among her colleagues and drawing-room followers." In 1911 Senda had married a colleague, Prof. Herbert Abbott, whose family, prominent in the Connecticut Valley, long enjoyed friendly relations with the Huntingtons of Forty Acres. B.B. sent a wedding present of $2,500 and invited the young couple to spend their honeymoon in Settignano. Senda had liked Roger Sessions while they both taught at Smith, and it was on her initiative that he had been invited to spend the final weeks of his 1923

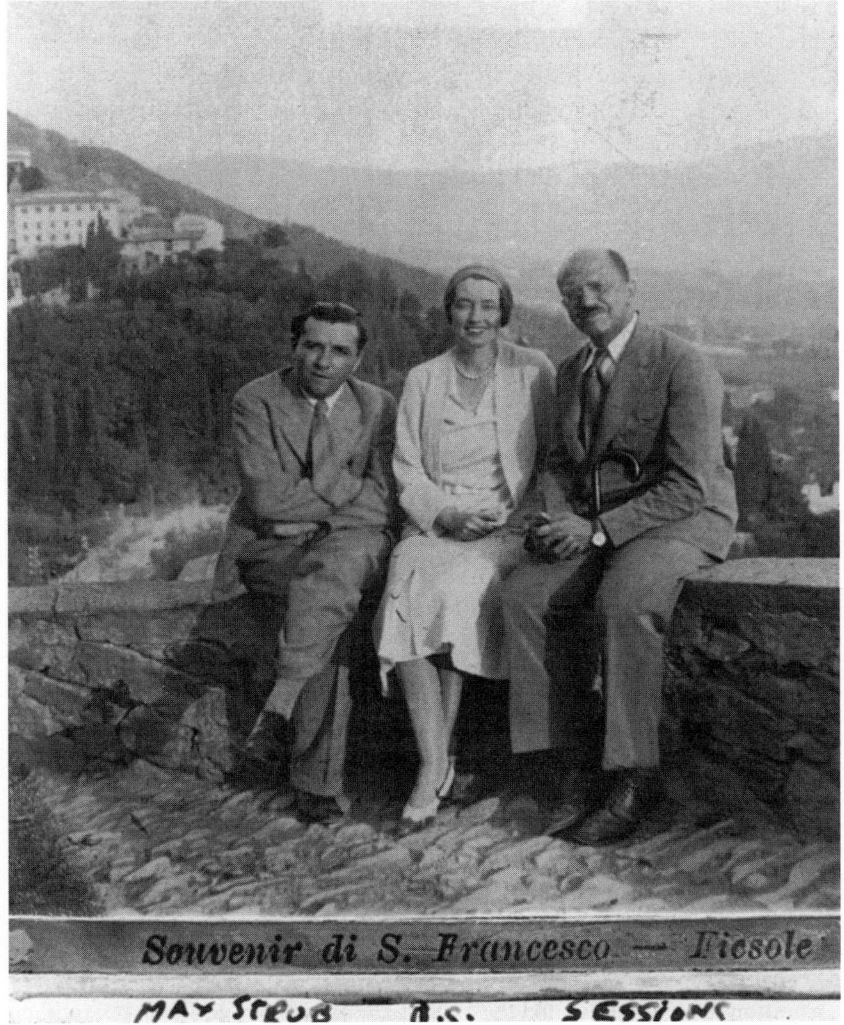

Max Strub (left), concertmaster of the Kroll Opera orchestra, with Barbara and Roger Sessions in the Florentine hills. Sessions lived in Strub's house in Berlin 1931–33.

trip to Europe at I Tatti. Two years later, after the abrupt end of the Bloch regime at the Cleveland Institute, Sessions found his first and certainly the most beautiful haven of his wayfarer years in a Berenson *villino* in Settignano.

Nevertheless, Sessions would always recall 1925–1926 as "the disastrous year." It had begun auspiciously enough with his successful application for a Guggenheim fellowship to finance a year's sojourn in Europe, effective in 1926. On the strength of that, his father agreed to help with funds for an immediate departure and with expenses until the grant money became available. The young couple embarked for Paris in the fall of 1925. But within the year Archibald Sessions would be dead and his son's marriage, never strong, terminally impaired.

Barbara fell in love with Paris and refused to move on. Four years earlier she had followed her husband to Cleveland and endured a cramped existence in a community that had little to offer her. Now she discovered the art capital of Europe, a city whose display of a glorious tradition was matched by a vitality of contemporary painting and sculpture that was about to change the way people would look at the world around them. The Paris of Picasso and Matisse, no less than the Paris of Diaghilev and Cocteau, proved the very place in which to relish the kind of life *she* wished to live, to be who *she* wanted to be. No, she was not about to live in Florence. Italy "did not interest her."[3]

Her husband was impatient to move on. He wanted to write music, and he could hardly wait to be free of the splendid distractions Barbara coveted. Certainly the Paris of 1925 offered riches of musical tradition, creation, and performance to match the comparable splendor of her world; and after years of frustration with Cleveland's meager musical offerings, he might well have welcomed daily opportunities to hear first-rate operatic or symphonic performances. But he did not. Paris, in the year of Satie's death and the birth of Pierre Boulez, impressed Ernest Bloch's former disciple as a confusing and uncertain place in which to find his own way.

Forty years later, recalling his aborted plan to study with Ravel after graduating from Harvard, Sessions would confide in his friend and colleague Edward Cone: "I'm sure it was much better that I didn't [stay in Paris] . . . I don't know at all how being precipitated into French musical life would have affected me."[4] And that reservation on the part of the mature composer seems also to have informed his intuitive urge to leave Paris in 1925.

For all its musical splendor, Paris in the twenties must have been a confusing place for a composer neither ready nor willing to adapt himself to some part of its closely configured musical surface. David Drew, in the first sentence of his trenchant essay on modern French music, goes to the heart of the problem: "For a tradition to have culminated in so commanding a figure as Debussy, and then to have been robbed of him at a time when he was grappling with the problems inherent in his achievement—this was indeed a heavy blow."[5] The foremost figures among composers of the next generation—Schoenberg, Stravinsky, and Bartok—were not French or, in the case of Varese, had left France in disgust. Leading figures in Paris, such as Ravel and Roussel, both in the last decade of their lives, were coping by retrospection.

And then there were Les Six, a group of younger composers of remarkably divergent artistic profile and their "manager": poet and entrepreneur Jean Maurice Cocteau. The collective oeuvre of George Auric, Louis Durey, Arthur Honegger, Darius Milhaud, Francis Poulenc, and Germaine Tailleferre represented neither a school nor a movement; nevertheless, under Cocteau's adroit promotion, Les Six dominated an important slice of indigenous musical life in Paris during the twenties. They met and plotted their lively undertakings at Le

Boeuf sur le Toit, a favorite restaurant named after Darius Milhaud's ballet score and a Brazilian folk song. Many years later, in California, Milhaud was to become one of Sessions' few close composer friends. But in 1925 the aspiring young American showed no interest in the work of his French colleague who, at that time, had already written some of his most important works and occupied an imposing position within the "closed shop" of Les Six.

Last, but by no means least, Paris of the twenties was Nadia Boulanger territory. The famous mentor of American composers, who had received Sessions kindly on his earlier visit, naturally assumed that Bloch's interesting protégé had returned for lessons. Having already spent time and tactful effort trying to distance his work from the surveillance of one master teacher, however, Sessions was not about to subject himself to the authority of another. And somehow, conditioned by a lifetime of peaceable management of a powerful mother figure of his own, he not only succeeded in avoiding an overt confrontation—for the time being—but found friends and future professional allies within the Boulangerie.[6] Nevertheless, the uncomfortable pressure for a full commitment to "that Boulanger crowd" soon outweighed the joys of casual acceptance into a lively group of his peers. He had to move on.

But he moved on alone. In Geneva he visited Jean Binet, his former colleague at Cleveland and, in the fall of 1925, reached Florence. He called on the Berensons, who offered hospitality for an indefinite stay. "People asked, why? Berenson told them 'because I like talking to him.'"[7]

The Berenson establishment, with its heady mixture of splendid art and triumphant commerce, resembled a Renaissance court. I Tatti reflected the Berensons' generous, personally considerate, if socially selective, hospitality. Major figures in the arts and literature mingled with moneyed patrons and their host's clients. Guests were expected to pursue their own work, study, or amusement and were free to use the Berenson establishment as their base as long as they did not get into the master's way. Dinners could become occasions of state, but neither houseguests nor occupants of outlying *villinos* were required to attend. They did have to put up with the noise and activity of ceaseless building and hard-to-please architectural improvement of the estate. The clock tower that now dominates the anterior view of the mansion had been added during the summer before Sessions' arrival, but it was soon deemed too large for the proportions of the facade and reduced during his first year in residence.

Sessions found the place alive with long- and short-term visitors. Recent arrivals included writers Cyril Connolly[8] and Walter Lippmann,[9] dancer Ruth Draper,[10] as well as the twenty-three-year-old Kenneth Clark—future Keeper of the Department of Fine Art at the Ashmolean Museum at Oxford and director of the National Gallery in London—who intended to spend a two-year apprenticeship working on Berenson's great *Catalogue of Renaissance Art*.

Sessions took note of Berenson's arrangement with the young Clark with a comfortable sense of déjà vu: another gifted young man apprenticing himself to a master as he had once done with Ernest Bloch in Cleveland. More than glad to have dodged active involvement with the Boulangerie in Paris, he began to savor his first personal and artistic independence. He thrived at Berenson's "Court" and took some confident steps on the road to discovery of what he would eventually describe as the "musical syntax and grammar of conscious emotion."[11] He found that he could work at his own speed—faster and more effectively, in fact, than he would for many years to come, until he found himself once again in an environment as rich in cultural stimulation and available seclusion as that enjoyed by working members of the I Tatti establishment. His natural habitat as a composer would be that of a privileged member of a major university in his own country. By the time this opportunity would come his way, he would have added, of course, the one additional ingredient essential for such privilege: he would have become a master teacher in his own right.

Meanwhile Sessions set out to test his sense of solid musical structure in a large work. His musical horizon encompassed a growing, no longer "parentally" inhibited enthusiasm for the Stravinskyan alternative to what he came to regard—sometimes—as expressionist morbidity: "I have my influences among modern composers. They are Bloch and Stravinsky. And yet, at times, I know I don't feel the way they feel."[12] His third attempt in nearly ten years to write a First Symphony was a success. For all his false starts on various compositional projects since *The Black Maskers*—always accompanied by euphoric epiphanies about new beginnings—Sessions suddenly knew that he had finally found a way for himself: "Modern music was mostly dissonance. Then, instead of color—movement! I would not have known enough then to define it like that. But people who didn't understand that, thought it was a step back—neo-classic."[13]

His First Symphony careens along with a joyfully jazzy, organized vigor in its fast outer movements. In stark contrast, these are separated by a somberly reflective Largo that yields nothing to overt emotion in its solemn but spare unfolding, later recalled in a hushed close. The glory of the movement, and perhaps of the symphony, is the serenely intimate chamber music at its center. Over a simple accompanying triplet figure, eight solo instruments hold a quiet discourse to which each contributes one or two observations in very free, long, breathtakingly beautiful phrases. Here, as if to preview a much later Sessions, melismatic stretching or shortening of melodic units within austerely self-dependent lines governs an elastic flow—much as the plunging impulse of bunched rhythmic ideas, cross-grained and heavily accented from the start, puffed up or shrank metric values in the fast music on either side of the central Largo. Throughout this work, melodic events control a harmonic fabric that sometimes approaches new tonal regions in such a gradual, almost subliminal way that the result becomes evident to the ear only sometime after the change has already been achieved.

"Instead of color—movement!" he would declare later on: instead of chordal functions, horizontal unfolding of unconstrained yet interdependent lines; instead of expressive dissonance, linear strands thrusting forward—differing from one another in melodic character, as often as not, but clearly separated in orchestral texture. At certain moments of coincidence, the meeting of such strands creates a sense of almost extemporaneous harmonic significance, ultimately revealed as part of a meaningful harmonic movement. Completed in January 1927, Sessions' First Symphony is an impressively self-reliant statement by a young composer in the midst of a turbulent, elated, and tragic period of his life. He dedicated it to his father.

Archibald Sessions died early in 1926. At work on a historical play about the opening of the American West by the building of a railroad across the country in the latter half of the nineteenth century, he shared the concept of the project and his hopes for a successful stage production with his friend, the later legendary David Belasco,[14] who, according to Ruth Sessions' extravagantly bitter account, "stole" her husband's idea in what became a landmark production of his own: "The false friend who stole, and sold, my husband's play and broke his heart; the heart that . . . was not proof against mortal treachery."[15]

Ruth's account omits the specifics of her accusation against Belasco: "Villains are boring to write about."[16] Belasco had indeed written the last of his own plays ten years ago and was devoting most of his time to adapting and producing plays. There is no surviving evidence that one of the productions he mounted on his own might have originated in the mind of his friend and sometime-collaborator Archibald Sessions.

The news of his father's death came as a shocking surprise and a terrible blow to Roger in Italy. He had loved his father deeply and he had no one in Florence with whom to share this sudden loss. Barbara was in Paris. As on quite a few occasions later in life, Sessions would work through great grief with the help of his music. During the spring and again in the fall of 1926, the First Symphony, after years of metamorphosis from string quartet to symphony, came together quickly through the powerful filter of that emotional crisis. The Largo, still center of a very private man's personal grief, owes as much to "conscious emotion" as to the composer's ongoing discovery of a personal syntax and grammar of music.

The summer of 1926 brought work on the symphony to a temporary halt under the evil star of Sessions' unraveling marriage. Barbara was in Paris, Barbara was pregnant, and Barbara wanted an abortion. Barbara had a lover, a fellow foreign student of art history and a brilliant young man, who would eventually head the National Museum of Art in his own country. At the time, of course, he was as poor as they all were. Sessions was told that it was unlikely that he himself was the father of Barbara's child, but the possibility remained. He set off for Paris, but stopped over in Geneva to share his awful dilemma with Jean Binet, who argued strongly against an abortion. In the end it was Barbara's own decision to terminate her pregnancy. When Sessions arrived in Paris the operation had already been done—very badly. Spreading infection required that a hysterectomy be performed. As soon as she was physically able, Barbara left Paris to join her husband at the Villa I Tatti.

Mary Berenson installed the young couple in the "little house" in Settignano just vacated by Kenneth Clark, who, to B.B.'s intense annoyance, had chosen to interrupt his work with the master in order to get married in London. Clark returned with his bride early in 1927, was forgiven and housed in the Cloisters, another recent addition to the Berenson establishment. For Barbara, the arrival of young neighbors with an informed interest in her own field offered some comfort in her personal misery, in her loss of Paris, and in her perceived exile in a lovely place, which soon became a lonely one with her husband frequently abroad in active pursuit of professional betterment. The Sessions marriage would continue for another decade. Roger and Barbara had already achieved a companionable acceptance of each other's inadequacies as partners and a tolerance of their respective extramarital delinquencies. Over time, a mutual understanding of their various incompatibilities would ripen into a diffident kind of detached intimacy.

Meanwhile, the recent family crisis that had first drawn Sessions from his retreat at I Tatti back to Paris soon offered some professional compensations. There was no dearth of young American colleagues in Paris, and, Sessions' earlier misgivings notwithstanding, they were all to be found in the class of Nadia Boulanger. Contact with fellow composers at the Boulangerie played an important part in Sessions' early career, particularly his friendship with Aaron Copland, with whom he was soon to found the Copland/Sessions Concerts of Contemporary Music in New York—Copland to be the U.S. organizer, Sessions the European adviser. Theodore (Teddy) Chanler, his Cleveland colleague, had just joined Mademoiselle's class after two years at Oxford. New acquaintances among the Paris circle included George Antheil, Walter Piston, and Virgil Thomson ("who liked to take me to new restaurants"[17]).

Sessions' new friends took an active part in the Paris musical season, and in the first of a series of articles he wrote for *New Music* magazine in New York Sessions reports on *An American Evening Abroad,* presented by the Societé Musicale Indépendante of Paris. His gift of exploring and clarifying his thinking with words on paper, first exercised under the stern guidance of his mother and later in his editorial activities for the *Harvard Musical Review*, informed long letters to family and friends throughout his life, a large number of published articles on music, and played a constructive role in the unhurried exploration of his developing perspective as a composer. Music performed in the May 1926 concert of the Societé Musicale Indépendante included works by George Antheil, Theodore Chanler, Aaron Copland, Herbert Elwell, Walter Piston, and Virgil Thomson. Sessions writes:

> Among these personalities were three of great promise, and two who, although somewhat less individual, obviously knew what they were about.
>
> Aaron Copland is artistically the most mature of the group . . . a composer of whom one has every reason to expect distinguished things . . . George Antheil was neither so revolutionary nor so original as might have been expected from his enormous publicity . . . With Chanler one has the

> anxious sense of assisting at a precarious dawn . . . Virgil Thomson's *Sonate d'Eglise* is in some ways sympathetic in feeling, especially in the chorale, with certain agreeable instrumental and harmonic sonorities, but on the whole seems decidedly *mal réussi* . . . The work of the two remaining composers, G. Herbert Elwell and Walter Piston, revealed less pronounced individuality, but excellent musicianship . . .
>
> On the basis of this concert one would not be justified in announcing the birth of a new American school . . . rather that an encouraging number of interesting individuals have begun to emerge . . . (who) reflect the diversified character of our national life in a far more healthy manner than would a more unified group based upon elaborate theories before the fact.[18]

The last sentence bears significantly on Sessions' own future. Given his lifelong refusal to recognize or be recognized as a member of a "unified group" of composers, it is hardly surprising that he remained a loner within the musical establishment of his time. Remarkably prescient as his assessment of these composers appears in light of our own knowledge of their works to come, his determination to keep away from groups that established their identity in "elaborate theories before the fact" foretells his future as an outsider among the contentious "schools" of composition that would dominate the musical scene in the United States at midcentury. His abiding concern with the intrinsic *difference* between one composer and another, between one work and the next, rather than with surface similarities, made him a tireless searcher for means appropriate to particular elements in his own work, and his lifelong insistence on finding the particular intuitive requirements inherent in different musical ideas helped him to become a remarkable teacher for several generations of American composers.

For the composer Roger Sessions, his sojourn in Italy could not have been timed more auspiciously if his life had been preordained by a benevolent biographer. He was well prepared for professional as well as personal independence, he had acquired some social ease as Bloch's associate in Cleveland, and he was now able to demonstrate his ability to overcome personal calamity and grief without loss of creative momentum. The one area, however, for which nothing in his previous experience had prepared him was the political one. Five years earlier, the Fascists had assumed control of the government in Rome, and reactions among his new friends and acquaintances in Europe were mixed. Berenson's doubts about the messianic claims for the regime headed by Il Duce were understandable. As a Jew and a foreigner under a regime unfriendly to both, he had every reason to keep a politically low profile. That, however, was not his way. In the year before Sessions' arrival in Florence, Berenson befriended one Gaetano Salvemini, distinguished historian and notorious anti-Fascist. Ernest Samuels, in his Berenson biography, relates the almost incredible story:

> On June 2, 1925 . . . Salvemini was arrested in Rome and incarcerated in the Florence prison. Two thousand Italian scholars and writers published a protest in Turin and letters of protest poured in from abroad . . . Shortly

> after his arrest, Salvemini's wife, Fernande, sent a message to Berenson . . . to ask [him] to lend his passport to Salvemini . . . there was a sort of resemblance between the two men: they had similar beards and similarly shaped heads. But the scheme was not feasible.[19]

Eventually Salvemini was released, but Berenson's status had been so compromised that, at his request, the American vice consul, Henry Coster, would stay at I Tatti to protect the estate while both B.B. and his wife, Mary, were absent during a trip to Sicily in 1927. Furthermore, to ensure long-term security, talks were begun with Paul Sachs of the Fogg Museum in Cambridge, Massachusetts, to prepare a "working understanding" for the eventual donation of the building and its collections to Harvard University.

Already in 1922, shortly after the Fascists' March on Rome, Berenson had written to Judge Learned Hand: "Here we are all pretending like five-year-olds that Santa Claus will bring us all things . . . by believing in Mussolini and the *Stelloni d'Italia.*"[20] But among the social elite in which he worked and moved and into which Sessions was presently introduced, Berenson's disdain was not widely shared. Describing a dinner party given by their Settignano neighbor and friend novelist Edith Wharton, at her Pavillon Colombe in Paris, Mary Berenson reported that "it was only too evident from the two or three remarks on politics . . . that the members of this wealthy and official circle were 'all Fascists,' like members of similar circles in America."[21]

Berenson's English disciple, the aristocratic young Kenneth Clark, also found his host's constant antigovernment diatribes tiresome. Sessions kept his own counsel and soon developed a healthy concern for the possibility of censored mail. The following, to his mother, was written on February 10, 1927, en route from Paris to Florence and mailed from Belgium:

> I said I would write something about Italian politics, and this is difficult, because my own feelings are so complex and so really conflicting that I find it hard to unravel them. It is in no sense an easy situation to judge, especially as it depends as much on the character of one man who is all the time being subjected to tests and temptations of the most difficult kind; and of course the future only can tell how he will ultimately meet them. But what has modified my first unlimited enthusiasm was in the first place, Mussolini's attitude towards France after the attempt on his life in September and the later one in November; an attitude which started a great deal of feeling in Italy and this was met by great *savoir faire* on the part of France; but which even after it was disavowed by Mussolini, had its repercussions in Italian public opinion, or rather public emotion; then, the rather ugly facts that came out in connection with the Ricciotti Garibaldi affair, and were then apparently "hushed up"—I call them "facts" but at best it looked rather suspicious. Then, the agitation for colonial expansion—not for imperialistic war, but for recognition of Italian claims. They apparently expect other nations to give their colonies for an outlet of their surplus population; and at the same time have passed laws taxing bachelors very heavily, and abolishing the spread of birth control information—in other words, forcing

as great an increase of population as possible. Finally—and this goes most against the grain for me—they are trying more and more to control education and thought, in a way that has actually alienated the most intelligent spirits—at least the ones I know—and that will in the end, if it goes much further, make of the Italians a race of parrots.

That of course is one side. The other is Mussolini's personal influence in not only introducing *discipline* but in being a really intelligent factor. The latter he certainly is; and one appreciates the value of these things which are far more important in a *poor* country like Italy than in a rich one like England or Germany or above all the United States. The last thing I balk at, I doubt if it is possible to build a new order without using what was best in the old; and the fact that so many of the highest types of Italian—Benedetto Croce for example—are all but persecuted by the Fascists, makes me pause very long before regarding the good they have done as completely compensatory . . .

Don't in any case answer the part about Italian politics. I don't mean that it would be really dangerous; but it is much wiser for foreigners living in Italy to keep mouths tight shut.

For the young composer, life was very full now. The symphony, completed barely two weeks earlier, was scheduled for performance by the Boston Symphony in April under its new music director, Serge Koussevitzky. Sessions' letter continues:

I wanted to send the music from Paris as that would get it to Boston sooner . . . I finished the copying barely in time—1 ½ hours before my train left. So I was just able to take it to the P.O. and make sure that it would go on the *Mauretania.*

While I was in Paris I played the Symphony to Nadia Boulanger, who was tremendously enthusiastic. She said it was not only a very beautiful but a very important work—the first work showing the Stravinsky influence which is at the same time absolutely personal and individual—and later she told her mother and some guests who were there that it was *"une oeuvre tout á fait remarquable"* . . . I can assure you that it is an infinitely finer, more beautiful and more human work than *Black Maskers* . . . Bloch will like it less well; it is less picturesque and less superficially striking; but it is *solid* both in its structure and in the fresh and perfectly authentic impulses which lie beneath the surface; and while, as I grow older, I shall doubtless write more perfect works—more easy and finished, I shall never write one that is more genuine or more truly spontaneous, in every movement.

I go back tonight, via Strassbourg, Basel, and Lucerne. I shall have wonderful views tomorrow if it is good weather. Barbara has had lots of company and diversion—all the people around the Berenson house have been devoted to her, and even B.B. himself said, before I left, that he was going up to call on her—a very great concession on his part, as he never goes out.

Serge Koussevitzky, who had succeeded Pierre Monteux as conductor of the Boston Symphony in 1924, was a distinguished champion of new music. Like

Leopold Stokowski, his opposite number in Philadelphia, the new master of the Boston Symphony had no need to resort to our latter-day practice of relegating contemporary music to the musical quarantine of an underrehearsed "Discover Series," sparsely attended by the already-converted. The position of these men was very nearly absolute, while their sense of musical responsibility was matched by fine showmanship. After its first performance in Philadelphia, Debussy's *Afternoon of a Faun* drew only tepid applause. Undeterred, Stokowski reproached the audience from the podium for their evident lack of attention—and played the piece again. Whether as a result of improved alertness or for fear of a third reading, the applause was deafening the second time around.

Koussevitzky's sense of mission had not emerged suddenly with his assumption of the Boston Symphony podium. Years before in Paris, as a refugee from the Russian Revolution, he had commissioned Ravel's now-celebrated orchestration of Mussorgsky's piano cycle, *Pictures from an Exhibition*, and Honegger's *Pacific 231*. Koussevitzky had seen at first hand how the musical establishment of European nations favored performances of their own composers, and his long reign in Boston was remarkable for its series of commissions and premieres that read like a *Who's Who* of American composers.

Sessions was fortunate indeed to have such a powerful and dedicated champion for the premiere of his first major work. Like many other composers, however, whose work the maestro chose to perform, he also had to run the gauntlet of Koussevitzky's suggestions for improvement. The maestro was anything but a passive participant in performances over which he presided. He would suggest changes, often drastic, sometimes with comical results—depending on one's point of view. William Schuman used to tell of his amazement when, as a very nervous young composer attending the BSO dress rehearsal of his (now withdrawn) Second Symphony, he heard, instead of the quiet ending he had written, a rising orchestral wave of sound that crested at the top of an enormous crescendo. One can only surmise the stunned composer's reaction when the great conductor turned around, beaming, to shout at him from the podium: "*Stronk, no!?*"

More considerate, if no less drastic, were Koussevitzky's suggested changes in the score of Bloch's *Schelomo* for a New York performance in 1930. In her father's biography, Suzanne Bloch records some ardent pleading via telegram between the maestro in Boston and the composer in San Francisco. Koussevitzky had taken it into his head that the famous solo part for cello, representing the voice of the king, might be stronger and more effective if played by *four* cellos instead. Bloch answered a request forwarded by the symphony manager "to approve or disapprove at once" by pointing out that this would be like having Hamlet's soliloquy recited by four actors. A passionate telegraphic plea from the maestro himself countered that "the greatest cellist could never obtain the same sonority of four cellos [to] give a powerful and imposing impression of King Solomon's voice." Bloch's reply was cool: "If it pleases you, use your own discretion." The concert came and went, followed by a long and generous letter from

Koussevitzky: "Cher ami . . . from the first rehearsal of orchestra I understood at once how right you were!"

Sessions did not escape suggested improvements. But lacking his teacher's gift for leaving ultimate decisions on performance to his adversarial champion, he simply resisted—to the probable surprise and likely displeasure of the maestro. Koussevitzky never played another work of his, but the First Symphony was performed as written. Only after hearing the Boston performance did Sessions himself make revisions in the first movement that are now included in the printed score.

His symphony shared a program that also included fellow New Englander George Whitefield Chadwick's symphonic ballad *Tam O'Shanter*. In his own way, the recently deceased Chadwick, once styled the "dean of American composers," was as much of a risky cause for the new music director of the BSO as the unknown young composer Roger Sessions. Following the Great War and with the emergence of powerful new voices and styles in composition, Chadwick's music had fallen into neglect. Putting his work on a regular subscription program, together with the premiere of a difficult work by a young unknown, argued as much for Koussevitzky's determination as a champion of American music as it did for his aristocratic disregard of popular taste. He did reward his audience and his orchestra, however, by closing with an undoubtedly brilliant reading of Strauss's *Death and Transfiguration*.

By all accounts Sessions' First Symphony received a brilliant performance on Friday, April 22, 1927. Conductor and orchestra had spared no effort in its preparation. Some members of the BSO's notoriously placid Friday afternoon audience—legend has it that Boston ladies never removed their gloves when they applauded—actually shouted, "Bravo," while others hissed; and the music critics of the three major Boston papers wrote lengthy, informative, and generally supportive reviews. H. T. Parker of the *Boston Evening Transcript* actually went to hear the symphony again on Saturday night and wrote a second, even more laudatory account for the Monday paper. Paul Rosenfeld of the *Boston Globe* was "grateful to Mr. Koussevitzky for the opportunity of hearing this American work, which compares very favorably with many of the European novelties we have heard in recent seasons. More of Mr. Sessions' music, and a repetition of this E minor Symphony, would be welcome to those listeners who believe that music is a living art, still near the beginning of its evolution."

In a curiously patronizing and apparently secondhand account of the event in its May 1 edition, the *New York Times* chose to excerpt in full the few reservations expressed by Philip Hale of the *Boston Herald* in his otherwise glowing report but allowed that it was "the doughty [unnamed] reviewer of *The Transcript*, who is nothing if not the penetrating, discerning and final authority on the discovery of new talent, who recorded in his characteristic and inimitable style 'the hearty clapping that saluted Mr. Sessions of the young men uprising.'"[22]

A photograph of Sessions in the *Boston Globe*, April 24, 1927, shows the familiar, intense face in which all features seem round and crowded, as it were, into the very center of his large head. The broad forehead curves from an already distinctly balding skull down to deep-set dark eyes, peering rather fiercely from behind a pair of round "granny glasses." A strong chin supports his generous, handsome mouth below a short, bony nose that seems one size too small in relation to the large ears flanking his wide cheeks. Sessions' carriage is confidently erect. His high, stiff shirt collar, however, and the tie severely knotted over a tight pin seem at odds with the genially rumpled image of the composer in later years.

CHAPTER 7

The Musical Idea I

It must be remembered that for a composer musical ideas have infinitely more substance, more specific meaning, and a more vital connection with experience than any words that could be found to describe them.

—ROGER SESSIONS

The year 1927 had been a vintage one for Sessions. With the first performance of his symphony by a major orchestra it had witnessed the transformation of a very promising student of composition into a young professional and had seen the beginning of a long-term metamorphosis in his life: the gradual discovery of his identity as a composer. This did not come about in a sudden, sweeping revelation of the mystery of musical creation, although it began with a single memorable event that was indeed sudden and remained mysterious. Rather, it brought home to him, for the first time, that a special kind of echoing epiphany was to be the essential precondition for every work he would write—not only at the time of its first conception but also at many stages along the way to a completed score. While the initial vision would come to him unbidden in most cases (not all), subsequent perceptions often required intense and sometimes frustrating effort.

Some twenty years after that discovery, in the summer of 1949, Roger Sessions described the event that became his First Piano Sonata. In the third of a series of afternoon lectures at the Juilliard School of Music, then still in its uptown location at 120 Claremont Avenue in New York, he talked about the musical experience of the composer.[1] The temperature in our little Recital Hall was sweltering. The small audience of faculty and composition students, swelled by young instrumentalists routed from practice rooms to make the numbers look more respectable, was treated to musical examples from Wagner, Brahms, and Beethoven, scores played on the piano with enormous energy and deafeningly loud by our distinguished guest. In fine combative form, Sessions took issue with much of what most of us had been taught in music theory classes:

> We frequently read in a certain type of criticism that in this or that piece of music "the development is superior to the intrinsic worth of the idea," or something of the sort. But what on earth, we may ask, can such a statement mean? Is it not precisely through their development, actual or envisaged, that ideas reveal their worth, whether the ideas are of a musical or of some other type? Or are we perhaps confronted simply with another of those quasi-plausible, important-sounding phrases which cloak more or less effectively either a basic lack of basic understanding or an inability to define exactly what bothers the critic?[2]

While he lectured, Sessions was seated, bolt upright, behind a plain wooden table, the open manuscript of his talk before him. Every time he marched to the piano in order to illustrate a musical point the wooden floor reverberated with his determined tread. At one point, having warmed to his subject, he did not return immediately to his notes but strode to the edge of the small stage and fixed his audience with a silent glare that made at least one member of the audience wonder guiltily, *Who, me?* Then he resumed his seat and, in carefully measured, almost pedantically paced tones, moved to the center of his argument:

> I would say that a musical idea is simply that fragment of music which forms the composer's point of departure, either for a whole composition or for an episode or even a single aspect of a composition. I say "fragment" knowing full well that it can get me into difficulties. For in my experience, in which I include observation and analysis as well as composition, a "musical idea"—the starting point of a vital musical "train of thought"—can be virtually anything which strikes a composer's imagination.
>
> It may certainly be a motif, a small but rhythmically self-sufficient fragment of melody or of harmony; but I am fairly certain that by no means all motifs can be called "musical ideas." On the other hand, I could cite many examples where the most essential musical ideas, the elements that give the music its real character, consist not in motifs at all, but in chords, in sonorities, in rhythmic figures, or even in a single note of a particularly striking context . . . One of the most important musical ideas, in a fundamental and motivating sense, may be not even a thematic fragment at all but some feature of the large design, such as a recurring relationship between two harmonies or keys, or even a linear relationship embodied in different aspects of the music at different moments.[3]

Back at the piano, he struck what sounded like a vehemently arpeggiated dissonant chord and told how, some twenty years before and with that very sound he had encountered such a germinal musical idea: "The first idea that came to me for my first Piano Sonata, begun in 1927, was in the form of a complex

Example 7.1

chord preceded by a sharp but heavy upbeat. This chord rang through my ear almost obsessively one day as I was walking in Pisa, Italy."[4]

As shown in one of the musical examples for the subsequently published lecture, the chord consisted of a minor seventh F#-E in the left hand and an octave G-G surrounding E♭ in the right (Ex. 7.1): "The next day, or, in other words, when I sat down to work on the piece, I wrote the first phrase of the Allegro" (Ex. 7.2).[5] This was immediately hammered out at the piano: an agitated passage that appeared, on first hearing and in this precipitate performance, to have little in common with that complex chord:

> You see, the chord had become simpler—a C minor triad, in fact, and its complex sonority had given way to a motif of very syncopated rhythmic character. Later it became clear to me that the motif must be preceded by an introduction, and the minor melody with which the Sonata begins, immediately suggested itself, quite without conscious thought on my part.[6] [Ex. 7.3]

He played a singing modal phrase, *Andante*, with a left-hand accompaniment figure outlining an octave and its minor, later its major, third:

> A few days later the original complex chord came back into my ear, again almost obsessively; I found myself continuing it in my mind, and only then made the discovery that the two lower notes of the chord, F♯ and E, formed the minor seventh of the dominant of the key of B minor, and that the continuation I had been hearing led me back to B; that the key relationships on which the first two movements of the sonata were based were already im-

Example 7.2

Example 7.3

plicit in the chordal idea with which the musical train of thought—which eventually took shape in the completed sonata—had started.[7]

That shape remained faithful to the musical idea as it was first conceived. The chord with which it all began appears at the close of the first movement, so that the B minor opening of the second (a variant version of the introduction) is preceded by its F♯ dominant as the germinal idea is powerfully reiterated (Ex. 7.4).

What we were hearing—so reasonable and self-evident in the composer's presentation—was not so much Sessions' musical analysis of one of his early works but rather the sum and substance of how a composer, *this* composer, went about creating his works: a process begun with the encountering of an apparently autonomous *musical idea* in which significant elements of a large composition are already prefigured. Sessions did his best to make the point:

> I point out these things in order to throw some light on some of the ways in which a composer's mind, his creative musical mind, that is, works; and more especially to illustrate the nature of the musical idea as I have defined

Example 7.4

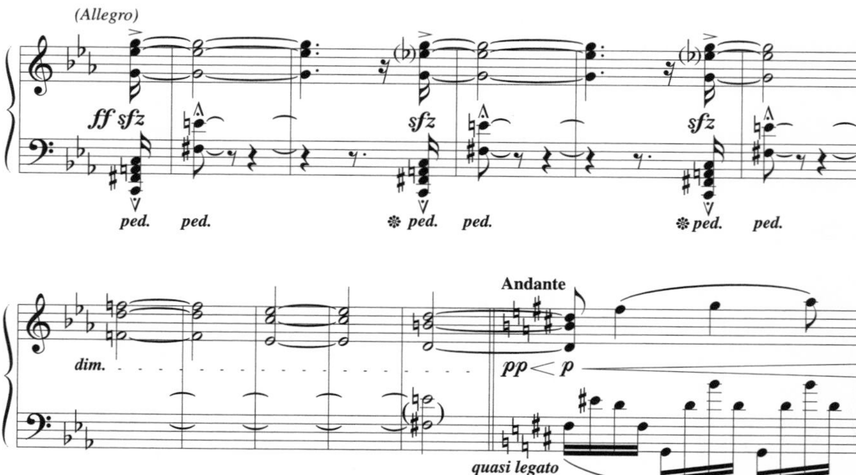

> it . . . The musical idea as I have described it is, then, the element which gives the music its essential character, and I have also referred to it as "the starting point of a vital musical train of thought." The word "vital" is necessary because all composers, and possibly all musicians, have tones moving in their heads all the time, as we all at times follow patterns of association which are not in any sense ideas at all.[8]

What seems remarkable about that moment in Pisa in 1927 is the revelatory disclosure of such a germinal idea as a fully realized musical fact: a chord that provided motivic inspiration, large-scale harmonic rationale, and even its own logical, if unusual, placing in the completed work. Not all the composing of the sonata would continue on that effortlessly subliminal level, of course. In his Norton Lectures at Harvard, forty years after that moment in Pisa, Sessions provided a glimpse of the labor involved in chasing and tying down and managing a controlling vision, as yet imperfectly perceived:

> Many years ago—1930, I think it was[9]—I had come to a point in the piece on which I was working where I needed to introduce a new and contrasting passage. I was working alone in a cottage outside Florence and was experiencing one of those frustrating moments which probably every artist experiences from time to time: moments when one knows exactly what one wants, but has not yet succeeded in finding its definitive shape. I remember wandering over the Tuscan landscape for the greater part of three days, with my sketchbook, making try after try. At some point during the three days, still obsessed by the musical problem, I had occasion to describe in some detail and in quite specific terms what I was looking for . . . The important thing is that I knew—and simply from following the music as I had conceived and written it up to that point—what must come next, and was able to describe it quite accurately in words. I knew it, that is, in terms of everything except the specific musical pattern itself. The latter came to me a day or two later, complete and definitive.[10]

Somehow we find it easier to credit composers of the Classical or Romantic period with such experiences. Mozart's intuitive inspiration has become almost a cliché but surely a believable one: "Then my mind seizes it as a glance of my eye, a beautiful picture or a handsome youth. It does not come to me successively, with its various parts worked out in detail, as they will be later on, but it is in its entirety that my imagination lets me hear it."[11] But when we read that Ravel, "asked about the progress of a work which he was then composing, . . . replied that he had it all finished except the themes" we are tempted to think that he was misquoted or exaggerating. Sessions was "quite sure that it was authentic."[12]

We do have ample documentation of Sessions' approach to composition. In two major lecture series, one at Juilliard in 1949 and the other at Harvard in 1968–1969, he provided articulate and comprehensive accounts of the composer at work; and although the preceding references to his First Piano Sonata are almost the only mention of his own work, he argues persuasively that his approach did not differ from the creative process of older composers. He stipulates an a priori acceptance of the intuitive factor but acknowledges ruefully that, from earliest contacts with the teaching fraternity,[13] he realized the extent to which this basic element in the creative process had become all but unmentionable in professional circles:

> The antithesis between the creative and the analytical attitude toward composition has become a vital issue today, since musical analysis has come to enjoy a vogue of a kind for which I at least know no parallel in the past . . . Musical *analysis* as sometimes practiced today [has] become overspecialized . . . with the implied object of discovering the ultimate criteria of music on a quasi-scientific, supposedly rational basis. Concessions, however, are made, somewhat grudgingly, to what is called "intuition" as a quasi-explanation of what cannot fully be explained in strictly analytical terms.[14]
>
> What is called "intuition"—quite inaccurately, if the word is used with regard to its original meaning—is simply a result of the intensive and pertinent functioning of the *aural imagination.*[15]

In much of his writing and all his teaching, Sessions argued that solid skills of musical analysis constitute an important part of mastering the composer's craft—*after* the fact, when the completed score is available for exploration. He could be ruthless in demanding that a student be able to account, in technically literate terms, for musical events and contingencies at any point in a composition. But he respected, in his own work and in that of young composers, the vital role, *before* the fact, of that personal, powerful impulse that "is certainly one of the forms taken by what is called *inspiration*."[16]

"One of the forms of what is called . . . "—Sessions was a little circumspect, not to say squeamish, about admitting to "inspiration." But how else could he define a musical idea that "rang through my ear almost obsessively one day . . . and a few days later" and, after some preliminary tinkering, "came back into my ear, again almost obsessively [until I discovered] that the key relationship on which the first two movements of the sonata were based were already implicit in the chordal idea with which the musical train of thought—which eventually took shape in the completed sonata—had started?"

At this point of conscious awareness, the composer began to create. With his First Piano Sonata, Sessions' way with musical materials, from the germinal image to the completed work, became his own. And through his writings on the craft of composition we can catch a glimpse of this composer at work: "The composer's point of departure is based on an insight, born of intense and active experience, into the nature of the materials and the creative process of his art."[17]

Sessions' point of departure in composing his First Piano Sonata was "an insight, born of intense and active experience." He never tired of evoking a memory of that experience, his active response to the unbidden emergence of a musical idea, instantly recognized as seminal and fruitful in ways to be discovered.

The problem was always with the latter, of course. Even as a nine-year-old, riding his bicycle, he could realize, suddenly, "that I was whistling tunes of my own concoction."[18] As an undergraduate at Harvard he had written to his mother: "I have already *the germ of the music in mind*" (my emphasis), adding a prescient condition: "If I can carry my ideas out, it will be the best thing, by far, that I have done."[19]

Now he had the technical means to do just that, but he found the going far from easy. Some properties of that musical idea were reflected in his very first sketches (Ex. 13.1): The right-hand G-E♭-G enclosed the downward-tumbling cascades of syncopated C minor triads in the opening Allegro; F♯ and E in the left hand anticipated an implied dominant seventh of B minor, the key in which he had heard an introductory Andante *before* he became aware of the evidence within the musical idea itself. And that evidence, the singularity of this musical idea, wanted to be preserved in "what comes next." Thus began the frustrating search for a continuity that he sensed but could not find: "One knows exactly what one wants, but has not yet succeeded in finding its definitive shape" (p. 95).

To find the pertinent continuity that would inform the entire work with the genetic code within the intuitive given of its musical idea required technical skills beyond those he had acquired in his studies with Bloch. Nevertheless, the solution had to be grounded in the principles of musical unity and logic that his old teacher had first demonstrated to him in his analysis of the opening measures of Beethoven's Sonata op. 2, no. 1.[20] Continuity beyond the unbidden enchantment of the musical idea required intellectual mastery, prescient imagination, and, most of all, a disciplined ear. In an entirely personal way, this unique mix had to be adjusted to the—again partly intuitive—requirements of the original concept, in a technical tour de force that he could only learn to master as the need arose. The process was personal, and Sessions, who could be eloquent and articulate about the craft of musical composition as such, chose to remain stubbornly private when asked about technical aspects of his own work: "The 'technique' of a piece of music is essentially the affair of the composer . . . Do we seriously believe that understanding of Shakespeare, or James Joyce, or William Faulkner has anything to do with the ability to parse the sentences and describe the functions of the various words in *Hamlet* or *Ulysses*?" Nevertheless, he did talk freely and frequently about his work in descriptive terms that were metaphors for his own experience of the elements of music, and he furnished definitions for their use. All of them deal with music as *movement in time*:

> Time [in music] becomes real to us primarily through movement, which I have called its expressive essence.[21]
>
> The elements of [composition]—contrast, association, continuity, articulation, proportion—are not factors of which the composer at his work thinks in the abstract, but rather words that roughly symbolize and classify the immediate demands that his ear makes in concrete musical situations.[22]

For the reader who wishes to have some notion of the verbal descriptions that Sessions used to "roughly symbolize and classify" these elements of composition there follows a brief glossary in his own words. Concepts such as contrast, association, continuity, articulation, and others on the list are not technical terms of musical theory, that is, of the way a composition is *put together*. For Sessions, they are metaphors of those aspects of music that make a composition *what it is* or, during the creative process itself, of "the immediate demands that his ear makes in concrete musical situations" as he follows the bidding of a musical idea. It is doubtful if he could have formulated them at the time of his First Piano Sonata with the precision demonstrated, some twenty years later, in his Juilliard lectures. But by the time of his Harvard lectures, another two decades on, a growing generation of young composers from his classes at Princeton and Berkeley would be familiar with their meaning; and Sessions himself, having clarified his own musical practice in the light of these concepts, would have developed a confident ease in recognizing the technical requirements of a musical idea, an ease that transformed him from a composer with a painfully slow, cautious working disposition into a prolific master.

Careful reading of the short list of the musical concepts he worked out for himself over time should help the reader's understanding of Sessions' struggles as well as his successes with the musical idea as he worked his way to mastery of his materials. Or he may prefer to continue the narrative of Sessions' life in the next chapter, perhaps to return to the list that follows whenever the terms it defines appear in the text later on. For convenient reference, an even more abbreviated précis of these terms is included in this book as appendix 2.

> *Continuity:* is implicit in the very definition of music; after all, continuity might almost be considered synonymous with time itself. As [I] apply the word continuity to music . . . it denotes not only the consistency and logic of movement and its component patterns, but their character as well. Under its heading would come the relation of each tone, sonority, or pattern, each color or nuance, to what precedes or follows it, the nature of the transition between one rhythmic unit and the next, and hence their specific relationship . . . More than any other element, except perhaps individual patterns as such, continuity determines the ultimate character of music: whether its basic movement, in its various aspects, is tense or relaxed, square or asymmetrical, whether the musical gesture is large or small, long or short of breath, and whether the details contribute to the character of the larger line or are simply held together by it.[23]
>
> The composer will certainly find himself deeply involved in questions which may be grouped under the general heading of continuity. Does the movement flow smoothly and consistently in the direction he has conceived, or does it proceed by unmotivated jerks? Does the music, as we may say, breathe properly, or should the phrases be a little more widely spaced here, or tumble on each other a little more closely there? Does a given contrast require an elaborate transition or an abrupt

one? Or, how must the rhythmic pattern established be developed in such a way as to move naturally, under its own momentum, into the next one?[24]

Articulation: Closely involved with the principle of continuity is that of articulation . . . The nature of musical structure [consists] of various levels, groups of smaller units which are so designed that on another level they combine into larger units . . . The smaller gestures of which music consists at the outset group themselves to form larger units of gesture [which] similarly combine into still larger ones, until the overall design is complete. It is on this basis that contrasts and associative elements are organized and that the continuity of a musical work is achieved . . . This is the principle to which I have referred as articulation.[25]

Articulation, in the contemporary idiom, has been achieved . . . to a large extent by means of the organization of small-dimensional contrasts, in greater profusion than was the case in former times. It has been achieved also by various rhythmic means, not in themselves perhaps new but new in the extent and manner of their usage; by means of relevant types of phrase structure, sharply defined; in terms of the rise and fall of the melodic line; and by acute awareness of the element of pacing, by which in this context is meant such things as the distance, if any, in time between the end of one phrase or section and the beginning of the next: timing, so to speak, of the various musical events.[26]

Form: The study of "form" in music is not, in any profound sense, a study of abstract patterns, but of living materials—physiology in as true a sense as any physical organism . . . The student of musical "form" must, then, learn, above all, to hear and to grasp the inner relationships and necessities which form the basis of a living musical organism or train of thought; first of all the musical idea itself, and then the chain of acoustic and psychological necessities to which it gives rise.[27]

Tradition has consecrated the so-called "classic forms"—minuet, rondo, sonata, and variation—and, I fear, raised them a little to the status of superstitions! Actually it is not hard to demonstrate, through reference to fundamental *principles,* that there are very few basic patterns possible, but these are infinitely various in application.[28]

Progression: The *first principle*, perhaps, is the one called progression, or cumulation. Since music is an art of time and not space, its effect must either maintain the level of intensity, or interest, of movement established at the outset, or they must raise it . . . I do not mean here the dynamic curve of a piece of music, the element of climactic tension and relaxation. This is only one phase of the principle. For each facet of the music—meter, pitch, texture, harmonic structure, sonorous quality—has its own principles in this regard.[29]

Association: The *second principle* is association, or, in a much narrower sense, repetition. It serves two distinct purposes. First, through association musical ideas achieve their impact and drive home the precise significance the composer wishes to give them in the mind of the hearer. A musical motif, or even a phrase, means nothing in itself . . . The single impulse is too short, and too isolated; it is a gesture in the void which has not acquired substance. Only through association can it really become effective.[30]

Two kinds of association: The music may be brought into association with words . . . or it must be supplied from within the music itself. The music must, to state it cautiously, supply some element of repetition. The repetition need not be literal or complete, but it must be really associative in effect.[31]

A mere repetition of notes is not sufficient to create association: the internal gesture has to be present in some form. . . . The principle of association thus gives significance to musical ideas and unity to musical forms.[32]

Contrast: A *third principle*, that of contrast.

Articulation, in the contemporary idiom, has been achieved . . . to a large extent by means of the organization of *small-dimensional contrasts* [my emphasis].[33]

The *large contrasts* contained in a work reveal its essential outlines and give it its largest rhythms, through alternation of musical ideas with their contrasting movement, emphasis, and dynamic intensity.[34]

It will be found generally true, and, I believe, almost a psychological law, that the various elements in a work must be so organized that there is only one *major and dominating contrast* in the work when viewed as a whole, and only one at any given moment. That is, on the largest scale only two basic forces can be brought into opposition; and if three or more elements are present, they must be so organized as to present themselves in two main groups.[35]

The principle [of] progression will extend itself to the various elements that are brought into contrast. Just as the level of intensity must be maintained, so the level of *contrast*, which is one of the major aspects of what I have called intensity, must be maintained.[36]

Technique: The composer's technique is, on the lowest level, his mastery of the musical language, the resourcefulness with which he is able to use its various elements to achieve his artistic ends. On a somewhat higher level it becomes something more than this; it becomes identical with his musical thought, and it becomes problematical in terms of substance rather than merely of execution. On this level it is no longer accurate to speak of craftsmanship.[37]

Much of what Sessions described in his lecture series of 1949 and 1968 already informed his First Piano Sonata of 1927, although conceptual formulation of the musical principles had to await his own gradual understanding of the process involved. Beginning with the musical idea that generated the sonata and permeates its melodic, harmonic, and structural outlines,[38] the work—still sufficiently rooted in Classical traditions as to have been identified with so-called neoclassical practice of its time—yields its organic shape far more convincingly along the lines of principles outlined above.

Thematic materials within the outer movements of the sonata certainly support analysis according to traditional principles of evolved and evolving sonata forms, but the often-suppressed contrasts and lines of demarcation between thematic sections argue for an overriding concern with forward thrust, *continuity*, in a linear sense. There are indeed tonal centers, but their shifts seem to endorse rather than to engender the structural joints that they inform. Harmonic movement is apparent mostly in the coincidence of linear events; and, as was the case in the symphony, the composer appears to have been at pains to minimize unmistakable root movement as a potential impediment to forward flow. With the benefit of hindsight, Sessions put it his way:

> The relationships between tones are nothing more or less than the musical intervals, both in an immediate and a far-flung sense . . . Patterns of tones, then, become memorable because we are aware of not merely the tones, but the intervals and the relationships that successions of intervals establish. This is the premise on which the *principle of tonality* was based, and it remains a basic premise today, even though the principle of tonality has been superseded.[39]

Near Munich, in what was once the countryside and is now picturesque suburbia, there stands a Baroque church, Maria in der Wies (St. Mary's in the Meadow). There is nothing remarkable about the exterior of Maria in der Wies. Hundreds of Bavarian churches share its basic shape: a cruciform design with plain white walls, high stained-glass windows, and an onion-domed steeple. The inside tells a different story.

From the main entrance at the foot of the nave to the altar at the top, a gradual crescendo of color and decoration along the walls and the ceiling is supported by sunlight filtered through the right-hand windows as it moves from the back with its dark wooden organ loft, along whitewashed walls, to increasingly dense, bright, and colorful adornment into a riot of blue and gold and red and gold and finally gold upon gold around and above the altar and beyond. There even the flat, ornamented surfaces become three-dimensional, as the chubby legs of exuberant cherubs stick out from the ceiling above the altar, where a cheerful heavenly host blends into a glorious Bavarian summer sky. The eye has been drawn forward and upward by that mounting intensity of articulation along the walls of the nave, and even the light, falling through tall stained-glass windows, participates in a forward thrust of movement as it provides a counterpoint of glowing tints across the increasingly lively colors of the walls toward its intended focus above the chancel of the church.

Sessions' large works, beginning with his First Piano Sonata, share some of that Baroque approach to structure. The articulation of unbroken long lines becomes an integral part of the musical edifice, much as the Bavarian architect's design of a spatial progression of light in his church's interior was essential to the way in which the building "works." There is little of technical novelty for its own sake. Rather, the forward movement of musical continuity ("the essence of the musical experience") is carefully articulated to focus the listener's awareness on the continuum itself: instead of a musical structure predetermined by overall harmonic function of the Classical style; instead of musical flow informed by the richer but shorter-term harmonic dynamism of the nineteenth century; instead of discrete musical events loosely linked (if at all) by a largely illustrative, expressive harmonic gloss of the most recent expressionist past—"instead of color, *movement*!"

CHAPTER 8 Summer of 1929

Kein Pfad mehr! Abgrund rings und Totenstille!—
so wolltest du's! Vom Pfade wich dein Wille!
Nun, Wandrer, gilt's! Nun blicke kalt und klar!
Verloren bist du, glaubst du—an Gefahr.

[No path—silence above and an abyss below!
Your foot disdained the path, you wished it so.
Now, mountaineer, look sharp! Don't count the cost:
If you believe in danger—you are lost.]

—FRIEDRICH NIETZSCHE

The great glacier of Les Diablerets, a few miles east of the far end of Lake Geneva, owes its name to devils and demons who haunt its peak and have, from time immemorial, inflicted serious mischief on villagers in the valley below and on their sheep grazing on its high pastures. According to local lore, these spooks quarrel noisily, chase one another around the peak, and delight in rolling huge boulders against the Quille du Diable, the Devil's Bowling Pin, at the summit. Whenever they miss, those boulders come crashing down into the valley of Derborence on the far slopes of the mountain.

"In reality," reassures the scholarly *Dictionnaire géographique de la Suisse*, "it is just glacier debris falling into the valley on the Derborence side, often with a thunderous noise."[1] The account goes on, however, to confirm the story of a great rock slide in 1714, when, after days of ominous rumbles from the very depths of the mountain, one whole side detached itself and fell on the meadowland at its base, "razing 150 houses and killing hundreds of cows, a considerable number of calves, and 14 people. A shepherd who disappeared and was believed dead, survived on cheese and water while entombed for several months in his hut . . . When the unhappy man reappeared in his native village of Avon, he was assumed to be a ghost, and was accepted back into the community only after exorcism by the priest." F. C. Ramuz, Stravinsky's friend and the librettist of his *l'Histoire du Soldat*, spun a magical tale of that event in his most celebrated novella, *When the Mountain Fell.*

Early in 1929, Jean Binet and his wife, Denise, invited Roger and Barbara Sessions to spend the summer with them in the shadow of the fearsome Les Diablerets. The valley, framed by a spectacular view of the Alpine range and dominated by its own famous glacier, became a popular resort early in the century, offering a variety of easy to moderately difficult walks and climbs in the surrounding hills and mountains in summer and skiing in winter. Would Roger and Barbara like the Binets to find them holiday accommodations near their own summer cottage? Roger and Barbara would indeed.

Drastic changes had marked Sessions' life during the previous year. Roger had returned briefly to America in the spring of 1928, without Barbara. He had planned to be in New York for the premiere performance of his piano sonata in the first of the Copland/Sessions concerts in April but had been unable to finish the work. Instead he retreated to Northampton, working feverishly on the score, which was heard, "in a sort of sketchy first version,"[2] at the second concert. Meanwhile he learned of his award of a two-year fellowship to the American Academy in Rome, effective from the fall of the 1928. On his return to Europe he said farewell to the Berensons and I Tatti and settled in the Italian capital.

Scholars and artists at the academy in Rome were offered living quarters in the institution, but married fellows and their spouses had to make private arrangements in the city. Sessions found comfortable accommodations for Barbara and himself in the Villa Sforza, not far from the academy's Villa Aurelia at the top of the Janiculum, highest of Rome's seven hills. Villa Sforza was home to three families of Russian aristocrats, refugees from their country's revolution of 1917, and offered agreeable living quarters, meals in pension style, informal Russian lessons, and a splendid view over the Eternal City.

Sessions composed slowly in Rome, spending much of his working time with self-imposed exercises to develop the ease of his own musical discourse. But the results pleased him:

> This year has been a good and important one for me. I have written piles of music, with the idea of gaining great facility in technique, and without bothering much about quality. Hence it has most of it gone in the wastebasket. I shall always compose rather slowly; I am that type of worker. But the year has been invaluable to me in giving me more freedom in my work. At the same time I have gotten well started in the Second Symphony[3] and my Violin Concerto—both of them big works . . . As to the Sonata I am letting it come along by itself, as I am convinced that it can only come out that way; I have been too much in a stew about it at various times, and if it is to have any spontaneity it has got to go in just that easy way, now. At the same time, and most important of all, I have done a lot of thinking.[4]

The Piano Sonata, begun in Florence in 1927 and reworked after its tryout in New York, would not be finished until 1930, the Violin Concerto not until

Alpine panorama around Les Diablerets. Writing across the top of the postcard, Sessions informed his mother that "Sex Rouge has nothing to do with the favorite subject of conversation among the younger members of the Smith College faculty."

1935. Two smaller works survive from Sessions' Rome period: the *Pastoral* for Solo Flute, dedicated to Simon Barrère (1929), and a song, "On the Beach at Fontana" (1930), for inclusion in *The Joyce Book*, a dedicatory volume of the 13 *Pomes Penyeach* by James Joyce, set to music by as many composers, and to be published by Oxford University Press in celebration of the poet's fiftieth birthday, in 1932. Arnold Bax, Albert Roussel, John Ireland, and George Antheil were among the other composers who took part in the project, writing music to one poem each. Also completed in that year would be Sessions' orchestration for large symphony orchestra of the *Black Maskers* Suite.

There had also been a splendid break in the quiet routine at the academy in Rome. In April 1929, Sessions attended the European premiere of his symphony, performed as the opening work in that year's Festival of the International Society for Contemporary Music (ISCM)[5] in Geneva by the Orchestre de la Suisse Romande under Ernest Ansermet.

Nevertheless, Sessions did not enjoy Rome. He missed the stimulating company at I Tatti, and an uneasy combination of artistic isolation, political fascination, and a dogged sense of communal constraint added up to a growing disenchantment with life in Mussolini's capital:

> Alas, it has been very nice indeed to see Barjansky, Bloch's friend, a really great 'cellist, and a marvelous person. He is here in Rome just for a few days and has seemed like an old friend—it is wonderful to get out of this stifling, conventional atmosphere up here—where I am absolutely alone, to

be sure, & happy in my solitude, but where my contacts with others are nothing but necessary smiles. Even our Russians, here at the house, are scarcely in the real world—one admires them tremendously, but they do not speak the same language, or really live in the present, keen as is their interest in everything that is going on.[6]

But the real world was moving and stirring quite spectacularly in the Italian capital, and Ruth Sessions' son was not likely to miss a chance to see and hear one of the great movers and shakers of his time:

I must tell you about Mussolini. It was an extraordinary experience; I was so intent while he was there in the hall that I didn't realize till after he had left the hall, what a really strong and deep impression he had made on me. I felt, first of all, enormous power, extraordinarily perfectly directed, and used at each moment with the utmost economy . . . His whole being is of the utmost simplicity; of the fierce expression of certain photographs there isn't a trace, as everyone agrees who has even seen or talked with him. Several times, over his face came the most [illegible] and winning smile that I have ever seen. Not a trace of vanity in his bearing or his face, and at the same time enormous pride and consciousness of power. An impression of inner solitude, of absolute self-reliance—the man who accepts all responsibilities and assumes even greater ones.—I cannot tell you how enormous was my impression.[7]

Ever one to appreciate a fine performer, Sessions could hardly have remained unmoved by a speaker of Benito Mussolini's oratorical gifts, and his spellbinding appeal resonated powerfully with one whose New England grounding approved of individual simplicity and self-reliance. At the same time, a year of firsthand experience at the political and social center of a collectivist Fascist state had made Sessions aware of aspects of life in the new Italy that disturbed him even under the impact of Il Duce's oratory.

Sessions' life in Rome offered more direct contact with Italians in Italy than his experience as a member of Berenson's international colony in Florence , and he did not enjoy his daily encounters with the authorities or the people. Nor were Italian politics in 1929 likely to cheer one accustomed to the free-for-all politics in the United States. As a resident in Rome he witnessed at least one political development of more than symbolic significance to the future of Europe: the Lateran Treaty, negotiated between the Vatican of Pope Pius XI and the Fascist government of Benito Mussolini.

The span of political movements immediately following World War I in Italy had ranged from the ruling Fascists on the right to the currrently underground Communists on the left, with a variety of moderate parties representing the increasingly moot center. Prominent among the latter, somewhat left of center, the Partito Populare (Christian Workers Party) had enjoyed the particular favor of the present pope's predecessor, Benedict XV. "In an age of mass electorates, when even a pope was driven to advise Catholics to accept a republic," writes historian Paul Johnson, "Catholicism had to be identified with popular issues."[8]

Nevertheless, Pius XI, elected in 1922 (the year of Mussolini's March on Rome), demonstrated an overriding concern about danger to his Church from the entire political left, including not only the Communists but moderate socialist movements as well.

Vatican blessing and favor of the socialist Christian Workers Party were now withdrawn, while its leaders were soon to be exiled or jailed by the new Italian government: "The Christian Democrats were broken up. In Germany [also], Pius backed the conservative forces of the right, and gave no countenance to Christian Socialists, whom he refused to distinguish from Marxists."[9] Thus the way was cleared for the signing of a historic covenant between the pope, master of a territiorially independent Vatican in Rome as well as spiritual head of the Catholic Church worldwide, and Il Duce's regime in Italy. Specifically, under the Lateran Treaty of 1929, the pope gave his blessing to Mussolini as ruler of an officially acknowledged *Catholic* Italy and, in his own words, "gave Italy back to God." In return, Mussolini declared the pope "a good Italian."

None of these disquieting events is recorded in Sessions' correspondence from Rome. As he had written two years before, en route from Paris to Florence, "It is much wiser for foreigners living in Italy to keep their mouths tight shut."[10] But for one who would later on describe himself wistfully as a "crypto-Catholic"[11] the political bargain he had witnessed may well have been as good a reason to hyphenate his religious inclination as some of the future positions of the Church of Rome, which the grandson of Central New York's Episcopal bishop found difficult to accept.

Meanwhile, the November elections in the United States had produced Herbert Hoover as a clear winner of the presidency, an event upon which Sessions commented with caustic cheer: "Public affairs [back home] seem to be in a thriving state, just now—I suppose Paul[12] is very happy that Hoover is at last really president; and I can't be seriously depressed, in spite of Berenson's rather apt remark that Hoover's election was essentially "the victory of the 'stick-in-the-muds'!"[13] Berenson's "stick-in-the-muds" included some of his own best clients, of course. The political scene on both sides of the Atlantic saw a shift of power in favor of corporate interests,

> interests of manufacturing industry seen as a sort of cooperative to which, when necessary, the interests of the consumer had to be sacrificed. This was to be the dominant sentiment in Europe between the wars, cutting across ideological and national boundaries . . . The closed system of Stalin's Russia, Mussolini's corporatism and Hitler's autarky with exchange control were all virulent expressions of it.[14]

In hindsight, it does seem remarkable that such an ominous drift to political extremes could so soon polarize a world only recently made "safe for democracy" and that the worldwide shift from free trade to protectionism, from still fairly recent social harbingers as the winning of women's suffrage in the United States (women's voting age in England had just been reduced from thirty to twenty-one) to the triumph of the "stick-in-the-muds," did not raise alarms other than occasional misgivings about dictators who made trains run on time. Sessions continues his letter:

> I read a rather interesting article by Walter Lippman in "Vanity Fair" on the significance of the election in which he propounds the theory that the working people are no longer distrustful of Capital, but they feel that their continued prosperity depends on cooperation rather than insurgency. He doesn't draw any conclusions from this, either of a pessimistic or an optimistic kind; and I must say I feel too little on the spot to do myself, though I can see it might work either or both ways.[15]

It is not known whether Sessions or Lippman would remember to "draw conclusions" about the feelings of newly trusting working people when, only a few months later, on October 28, the world's financial establishments suffered their "Black Friday" with the crash of the New York stock market or when the Great Depression in its train ended continued prosperity until the Second World War would provide a framework for economic revival in a violent new world quite unimaginable in the beautiful Roman spring of 1929.

The Binets' invitation to share a summer in Switzerland arrived that spring of 1929, and in July, August, and September Roger and Barbara Sessions rented rooms in the Chalet Favre-Pernet, Les Vioz, in Vaud, where they could enjoy their very own view of the bedeviled glacier, take long walks, entertain visiting friends, and, not least among summer blessings, were able to write and receive letters without fear of official censorship.

There was a brief reference to life in Fascist Italy in Sessions' first letter to his mother from Switzerland: "About Italian politics . . . now that we are in a free country. A winter in Rome has not been altogether good for pro-Fascist or pro-Mussolini sympathies."[16] Two weeks later, in a closely written seven-page letter, Sessions summarized his bona fide political and personal impressions of people and events in Rome during his first year in the capital:

> I was going to write you a little of this year's impressions of Italian politics, and have in fact been waiting for several months to get to Switzerland where I could write freely without fear of having my letter opened. Don't let me exaggerate; not many letters are opened; but they are occasionally with annoying consequences. In a word, Rome has quite thoroughly changed my impressions of Fascism. The atmosphere there is much *tenser* than in Florence. Although Fl. has always been a rather extreme center of Fascism it is after all a provincial city. Whatever happens there is of local importance, and it is chiefly local issues which are alive there, among the mass of the people. The foreign colony & the intelligentsia are on the other hand of a very fine type in general; I mean that they are civilized & urbane, & among them prevails a very free intellectual atmosphere, in which things can be discussed quite freely provided the mass of the populace doesn't get wind of anything very striking. Of course when I speak of the foreign

colony I refer, rather inaccurately, & I am afraid, to the more serious and intelligent among them, & not to the drinking, bridge & golf-playing, gossiping, & promiscuous love-making ones!

Rome however is quite different & I have to confess that I found that my impressions of the whole thing had been mistaken in certain important respects. It is not that the *theory* on which Fascism is based disturbs me any more than it ever did; I mean that I can accept dictatorship & even admit that it is necessary under certain circumstances. It is rather what Fascism is in the Italian spirit that I find intolerable. Rome, intellectually, I find stuffy, narrow, & provincial to the last degree; one cannot with comfort discuss freely any controversial or even any contemporary subject—in Italian circles, I mean, one is constantly running up against a stupid and rather vulgar Roman & Italian vanity and overbearing arrogance which hinders almost every kind of easy relationship.

And the musical world of Rome is full of men who are using the regime to further their own interests. This I saw at Geneva too, in the spring; the Italians had been rather overbearing in their attitude towards the International Society, and sent in a very poor lot of music, with the result that none of it was chosen. This, of course, made them furious, and those whom I know were not very careful about the way they showed their rage! I don't mean that they are personally disagreeable; but simply that they are obviously not *artists* at all in their attitude; that artistic values are wholly destroyed in a mass of nationalistic propaganda, undiscriminating praise for everything Italian. To Americans they are always agreeable, & personally I have had no unpleasant experiences of any kind. But I often felt oppressed by a sense of quasi-official narrowness, of individual opportunism, and of a vulgarly overbearing attitude which is entirely alien to everything I believe in. And, without exception, all the Italians of the more intelligent and interesting kind that I know are either anti- or perfectly indifferent to Fascism. You see I can admit even nationalism when it means a legitimate pride in the nation's achievements; but when it consists in an extravagant claim for *everything* produced by one's own people, a rather childish vanity about the most everyday things, and in frowning on all criticism, no matter how sincere & well-intentioned, even from one's own fellow countrymen, I find it intolerable & actually destructive of all that makes for real & solid development.

My conclusion is this, for the moment at least; the Italians are by far the oldest people in Europe; civilization has been continuous in Italy since the Roman days. They are a thoroughly disenchanted people, and this is their strength (for they have plenty of vitality) & weakness. They are fundamentally agnostic, indifferent, lazy; in spite of the *tremendous* ability of the individual Italian he is really too indifferent & dispirited & disillusioned to do much about it. Fascism is not, therefore—as the Fascists would like to believe & to have others believe,—a new and [illegible] faith, but purely & simply, in fact, a piece of self deception, more or less conscious, I believe—a piece of able play-acting resulting from boredom & disenchantment; and also in fact a purely self-serving impulse towards power of certain individuals. Naturally I over-simplify; but at all events, after a year in Rome, I am convinced that it is not idealism of any kind that is at its root, and that its benefits to the Italian people are largely material ones. About Mussolini too I have changed. Undoubtedly he is an interesting person, & a powerful one; but "greatness" is a *big* word, and especially after the Concordat with the Vatican I have felt less & less inclined to use it on him. Raffaello prophesied to me in March that the Concordat would give rise to new problems & new controversies; but I think even he was surprised at the promptness with which this happened. Not only did Mussolini make two vulgar, clumsy & irreverent speeches on the occasion of the ratification of the treaties, but he suffered a real diplomatic defeat in so doing. The Holy See, I am afraid, is not so easily outwitted, and one has to be pretty clever in order to escape defeat at its hands, once he begins to raise issues and Gaspari[17] knew how to make the most of Benito's blunders . . .

P.S. Naturally, it would not do if it were too generally known that any American felt this way—also, I still have as little sympathy as ever for the *Lateran!* & still believe the more violent enemies of Fascism are a pretty bad lot.[18]

Clearly Sessions' earlier enthusiasm for Mussolini's magic had not worn well, and the glamour of the Eternal City itself was diminished upon further first-hand experience of its bureaucracy and daily contact with its people. But his observations—judgmental rather than really informative at this first opportunity to share long delayed reactions—also reveal something noteworthy about Roger Sessions. In his unsympathetic portrayal of certain Italian composers' self-image as artistic evangelists for their regime, he forecasts his later misgivings about the role of music as a facile expression of national identity in his own country.

For all of Sessions' reasonable reactions to unreasonable authority, however, there are comments on more trivial matters that seem, at best, unbecoming. His lofty reference to a "civilized and urbane foreign colony and intelligentsia," among whom "things can be discussed quite freely provided the mass of the populace doesn't get wind of anything very striking," patronizes both the civilized and the lower orders, to say nothing of references to "drinking, . . . gossiping, & promiscuous love-making" that seem oddly sanctimonious, coming from a man of his age and personal history—even in a letter to his mother, whose assumed views on social interchange he is at pains to affirm. Roger was not the only Sessions so powerfully affected by the family matriarch. Like his father before him, however, he would finally get away. Others were not so fortunate.

"My mother loved my younger brother most, and ruined his life."[19] But Sessions' frequently expressed regret notwithstanding, elder brother Roger was not much help during that summer of 1929. Important changes had taken place back home in western Massachusetts. After twenty years of service to the community of Smith College, Ruth Sessions retired to the family estate at Hadley, where Roger's brother, John, recently married, had taken on full-time farming of the property. Ruth, with time on her hands, decided to write her memoirs, *Sixty Odd.*

There were adjustments to be made by all members of the family, and new problems that affected their daily lives and relationships had to be resolved. With her young, currently pregnant daughter-in-law as another lady of the manor, Ruth found herself in less than her accustomed charge of day-to-day operations at Forty Acres. More serious difficulties arose when John, in order to improve the financial position of the property, proposed long-range plans, including an eventual sale of the old barn, which held memories of Ruth's girlhood and courtship many years ago. By the end of the summer of 1929 an accommodation was reached among the residents at Hadley. Ruth, however, had written earlier to Barbara in Switzerland about events at home and to inquire about the wishes of her expatriate children with regard to possessions at the farm. Ruth's letter—apparently quite positive about recent progress in family bargaining—is not extant but must have made an unfavorable reference to the role played by John's wife, Dawn,[20] in support of her husband's interests. Roger's reactions ran riot:

Chalet Favre-Pernet
"Les Vioz"
Les Diablerets, Vaud
July 13, 1929

Dearest Mother,—

I was just about to write to you when your long letter to Barbara came; and though I have a thousand things to write you about, I want to answer that first. I can't tell you how happy we were to have it, and to know exactly how the whole thing has gone at the farm this summer. I am so sorry it has been difficult for you, and I can see, I think, pretty clearly what you have been up against . . . I must say that some of the stories you tell do sound, as you say, almost incredible; and at the same time I do believe that the fact that they could happen must be laid to Dawn's condition. At least I hope that is true; otherwise I would be more than seriously concerned not only for the future of the farm, but still more to John's future success and happiness. For, well though I know what discouragement and lack of confidence may mean, I believe that living constantly with a person who not only is incapable of understanding one's background, the deepest part of one, and who at the same time—after the manner of Dawn which I myself have seen—wants to manage everything she lays her hands on. And I have always felt that Dawn had very, very much to learn in that respect, though she is by no means the only one nowadays . . .

I feel at least as strongly as you do that it is quite intolerable that Dawn should consider herself entitled to be a party to any conversation you may have with John, in regard to either the farm, or anything else that concerns the property—or in fact anything you wish to discuss with him! She has every opportunity to influence him, if she likes, in his attitude about such things, while they are alone together; and of course if you want to consult her too, that is your affair. I only mean that it is obviously entirely your affair, and that you will always have my absolute and complete support in insisting on that . . . If it would be of any help to you to quote my opinion in this respect please don't fail to do so, and to lay it on as thickly as you see fit. It is more than an opinion, indeed. If Dawn doesn't know by this time, she must learn how families are run . . .

I am as devoted as I always have been to John, and that is more than any one realizes, I am sure; for I have never been able, in the last years, to quite reach him, much as I have longed to do so. On the other hand I *hope* that all the incidents which led up to your letter to Paul [husband of Roger's sister] are not simply part of a scheme of Dawn's—I mean a frightfully petty and vulgar insistence on her imagined rights and dignity and "position" . . . Please don't think that I am criticizing John . . . but I do find it rather strange that you should be accused of treating him as a "hired man" in view of all the facts of the situation as you write them . . .

I believe that Dawn will learn this in time, but I believe that it should be clearly understood from the first that no one is *obliged* to take her into any consideration whatever, so long as John is there and able to take the responsibility himself.

One need not the apply standards of latter-day feminism to find Roger's reaction outrageous. Denying his sister-in-law's right to participate in family discussions about her husband's property was almost as absurd as to assert, from the not-so-exalted level of his own past performance, that she must "learn how families are run." Clearly some very raw nerve had been touched. The letter closes:

I *must*, I *must* keep in steady touch with you—believe me, I never forget that I am your oldest son, or cease to want to be to you all that that should mean.

Always your devoted
Roger[21]

But there was more. Accompanying this lengthy demonstration of protective filial attachment was an enclosure that sheds a different light on what that outburst may have been about. It was the first page (typed and single-spaced, unlike the bulk of Sessions' handwritten correspondence with his mother) of an unfinished report on the Geneva performance of his symphony three months earlier. The sequence of events was as follows.

On the morning following the concert in April, he had sent an enthusiastic cable:

CABLE VIA COMLGENEVE, SUISSE APRIL 7 1929 745 AM LCD
SESSIONS 121 SEDGWICK STREET SYRACUSE NY
SPLENDID PERFORMANCE LAST EVENING

European reviews do not necessarily appear on the morning after a performance as in the United States or in England. Such may have been the case with the critical "fallout" of the Geneva concert. Some days later, presumably after his return to Rome and obviously smarting by now under a very cold press reception of his work, Sessions typed a draft communiqué for home consumption:

Dearest Mother,—

I have so much to tell you—I hope my cable from Geneva was really not ambiguous. The point is that the symphony was marvelously played, and made a real success with the musicians and everybody that mattered; but I wanted to wire you the first thing, and was not at that moment quite sure whether it had been a success or not. So I said "splendid performance," which was quite true.

The symphony came first on the programme of the whole festival, and was Ansermet's *pièce de resistance*—the largest and most difficult thing which he had to conduct, and also the one which he himself, on his own initiative, had proposed to the jury for the festival. You see, ordinarily the things go through the various national committees; but members of the jury have also the right to propose works on their own account, and this is what Ansermet did, quite without my knowledge.

I heard the rehearsals and realized at once that Ansermet understood the music splendidly. The orchestra is of course second-rate, though not at all bad; and they, under Ansermet's guidance, got hold of the spirit of my music in a way that surprized [*sic*] me from the very beginning. So, when the performance came, I felt that I was hearing the first movement for the very first time—full of life and movement and real incisiveness; and if I didn't feel quite so strongly about the other movements, it is because the Boston Symphony has more and better strings than the Geneva one, and also because Koussevitzky understood those movements better than he did the first.

From the point of view of a popular success it was a great pity that my symphony was the first to be played in the Festival. Ansermet had arranged to have it come at the very end; but at the last moment the German conductor who had been originally engaged to start the whole thing off fell ill, and they had to engage another who could not come till the last concert. So it was undoubtedly a pity that I—an American, quite unknown and in a sense an outsider,—should have had the very opening, when nobody was quite ready to listen with the proper attention. The result was that it was only the musicians who really listened to the symphony, and that the public was quite cold. But it was evident from the start that the musicians *did* like

> it and find it interesting, and as the Festival went on, I had abundant testimony that it aroused interest and enthusiasm of a really strong and intense kind.
>
> As for the critics, I have not read them at all; they are of absolutely no importance or relation to me and my work unless they are people who really know my work and my aims and my personality. I gather that the Geneva critiques were bad—chiefly from the fact that three of the Geneva musicians took special pains to voice their indignation and apologies for their city! But you must remember—in case the thing worries you at all—that this is an international affair, and that there will be critiques of all shades; and above all that I am practically a new name to all of them—and that only extremely rarely does a critic dare to commit himself strongly in favor of some one he has never heard praised by musicians . . . There will be at least two magnificent ones, of which I know—in France and in England; and I dare say there will be others, since I only know of these two by merest chance—someone happened to speak to me about them.

This apparent apology for the enthusiastic cable he had sent before the generally negative reviews of his symphony appeared was not mailed until he had learned, three months later, that a translation of the "magnificent" French review had appeared in the *New York Times*. He explains:

> The echoes which have reached America are for the most part quite unsatisfactory, and do not really give any idea of what the whole thing was; and I suppose I had a certain shyness about writing you about it when some of the things that appeared in print seem rather a contrast with what I myself wrote . . . In translating from the French the article that appeared in the N.Y. Times, the translator changed it in just such a way as to turn it from a really rather good thing, to which I in no way could take exception, into a slightly condescending—and I must add, at the same time rather stupid one.[21]

Taken together, Sessions' letter about his sister-in-law and this three-month-old enclosure reflect on each other. Fervent assurances of filial devotion which introduce his long-delayed rationalization of some bad reviews bring to mind—uncomfortably so—similarly preemptive teenage pleas during his undergraduate years at Harvard. His letter that reported grades of C in History and D in German began: "I think that other fellows would consider themselves extremely fortunate if they had a mother like you. I certainly consider myself the most fortunate fellow in the world in that respect."[22]

He had not been mistaken, of course, about the tiresome level of Geneva reviews for his symphony. The *Journal de Genève* wrote on April 7, 1929:

> The Symphony No. 1 by Mr. Roger Sessions is of such musical poverty that no one could have failed to notice . . . The work is completely lacking in unity, and each of the three movements has its own style, if I may dare to call it that.
>
> A. P.

The *Courier de Genève*, on the same date, begins more kindly:

> The Largo was the best part, truly grand as it expressed, tastefully and calmly, much sadness and suffering . . . The first movement is monotonous in spite of some outbursts in the winds. . . . The last movement opens with a lively and gay theme in the flute. The whole lacks cohesion, and one could wish that its vivacity would stretch from beginning to end without the padding.
>
> G. D.

The most hostile comment came from the *Tribune de Genève* on April 9:

> So, on Saturday evening, in the Grand Théâtre, one heard, first-off, a Symphony No. 1 by Roger Sessions. This composer was born in Brooklyn . . . In 1928 he received the American Rome Prize. One asks oneself for what reasons the jury, consisting of the Messrs. Ansermet (Geneva), Tiessen (Berlin), Ravel (Paris), Sirola (Zagreb), Pijper (Amsterdam) and Dent (Cambridge), one asks oneself, I say, for what reasons did the jury accept this work which does not allow the slightest glimpse of an interesting personality . . . No, truly, this symphony, at least that is what the program calls it, is not a truly contemporary work . . .
>
> Otto Wend

Sessions fared no better at the hands of the European press who attended the Geneva Festival. A notice in the influential German periodical *Die Musik* offered some potted analysis but told nothing in the least recognizable about the work or its performance:

> ISCM Festival, Geneva, Spring 1929. Ansermet conductor.
>
> By artistic intent, an e minor symphony by the American Roger Sessions, resident in Europe, who not only thinks but also writes in linear terms, never doubles or pads, but unhappily is not blessed with a flowering imagination. In the second movement he turns into an all too faithful Bach imitator, with the evident intent to break out of the tedium.[23]

The first American review, however, had been supportive. According to the *Musical Courier* the symphony "aroused more interest than any American work hitherto performed on these occasions" [and] "was warmly welcomed and appreciated."[24]

It is the more curious that the appearance in New York of a translation, even a poor translation, of a French review should goad Sessions into such elaborate efforts of damage control. His public statements on music criticism at the time reflect only lofty indifference. In his review of the Paris premiere of Stravinsky's *Oedipus Rex,* written for *Modern Music* in 1928, he quoted Ernest Ansermet's remark "on the good fortune of Stravinsky in having had his works become known before they were commented on." A few years later, in a solicited reply to an article by *New York Times* music critic Olin Downes, Sessions would write quite categorically that "criticism is in essence none of the composer's business."[25]

But on a private level criticism seems to have been of considerable concern to the son of Ruth Sessions. His idea of himself and of his worth as a composer was stretched uneasily between identification with roots and family on one hand, his sense of belonging to himself alone as the creator of his product on another, and, last, a young composer's alarm at critical judgment taking aim at that product. His creative self, having rejoiced in the leverage and power of a newfound sense of artistic particularity, ached all the more with a need to have its product recognized by those with whom he shared roots, early hopes, and present dreams—who else but his mother?—thus getting hooked on the first corner of the triangle that was his current self-image as a creative artist.

He was already a difficult composer to himself, and he had accepted uncertainty and self-doubt as an appropriate price for the work he assembled in slow labor until it was good. Now he discovered that there was yet another, public price to pay—a price harder to accept, because it involved others' judgment on the final result of his labor. Baffled by his apparent setback in Geneva, he returned to Rome to complete his first year at the American Academy. There he worked, sometimes rejoiced, and often ached but failed to discover that even a bravely sprouting new sense of artistic identity is of little use to one who does not yet fully understand who he is.

In Rome he could now count among his friends and acquaintances a fair number of celebrated performers and prominent composers. He first met conductors Pierre Monteux and Otto Klemperer after their respective concerts with the Santa Cecilia Orchestra in Rome and enjoyed the company of composers Alfredo Casella, "a nice man,"[26] and Gian Francesco Malipiero, "a good composer and a warm hearted human being."[27] But most of the famous musicians who came to town shared little of Sessions' outlook as a composer. Celebrated visitors, of course, had also come and gone at I Tatti; but there, as the American composer in residence, he had held implicit status. In Rome he felt anonymous. He missed the outward recognition that he had expected as a natural consequence of his growing acceptance within the profession at large. Petty, unintentional slights would leave a bruise:

> It has not been wholly pleasant for instance to be called always, in Roman society, a "student" at the Academy, and to be asked if I have a good teacher, etc.—since the general public cannot be expected to know that one can easily be technically a "student" there without being in any sense a pupil; and I don't by any means always have the opportunity to explain that I finished my so-called "studies" eight years ago. One has to achieve some things . . . without allowing oneself to be affected one way or the other by one's fancied "position" or by the props which might come from outside oneself.[28]

To be sure, Sessions showed himself far from unaffected by whatever positive reflections on his "position" came his way. Fancied or otherwise, he gloried in them as he reported to his mother:

> You can take my word absolutely that I have had a splendid start over here . . . and that my future is in my own hands. Jean Binet wrote me, after the Geneva Festival: "I see that you have gained for yourself an important place among European musicians" and that there is no doubt that is really true, though naturally it is only a beginning—inevitably such, and one which has splendid possibilities and let me say inevitabilities of growth.[29]

Friends and colleagues in 1929 would probably have agreed that "splendid possibilities" and "inevitabilities of growth" were fair assessments of Sessions' future as a composer. But it did not seem enough. Jaques Barzun's keen observation about "the need of artists to singularize themselves within the mass of the talented"[30] describes something other than inner maturity. The need of which he speaks is an irrational drive, powered by the very rational recognition of the fact that ultimate judgment of success does indeed rest with others. And who, no matter how involved with an inner quest, would *not* wish to be reassured by outside evidence of his "singularization within the mass of the talented"?—and now!

Sessions' appetite for a public identity contended painfully with an already well established unwillingness to acknowledge the judgment of the marketplace. As a precocious undergraduate at Harvard, much younger than his fellows, as a first-time teacher in a rather alien American Midwest (completely dependent on the care and protection of an even more alien master), and most recently as a resident of I Tatti, where many of his fellow guests were "real" celebrities, the need to see a reflection of his artistic singularity in an outward, public acceptance remained a metaphor of artistic relevance. It was hard to outgrow the incongruity of such a proposition.

Sessions' need to belong drew comfort wherever it was on offer. The fact that his cosmopolitan host in Florence cherished very close ties with his sisters in western Massachusetts reminded and reassured him of his own, much deeper New England roots. He drew needed strength from his membership in a family who still owned land and houses where his forebears had lived for three centuries: "This year has given me a deeper sense of what Hadley and our family mean to me, a realization that all that is strong in me comes from there."[31] In moments of insecurity, artistic or otherwise, he would grasp that sense of belonging with a completely artless resolve. Even some fifty years later, while being bundled into a taxi after an overly celebratory evening in New York, the now-famous composer solemnly reassured the doorman, the cabdriver, his host, and himself, "I am a New England gentleman!"

But meanwhile, at the American Academy in Rome or in the hubbub that attended an international music festival in Geneva in 1929, such considerations were bound to seem ludicrous to his musical friends and entirely irrelevant to the rich and glamorous at I Tatti or in Rome whose recognition he craved. He was an outsider and, for the time being, he was mostly uncomfortable, *mal dans sa peau:*

You see, I was very shy, I had to find myself, to gain confidence.[32]

[A composer's] quest for identity . . . entails the discovery and cultivation of himself, and taking full possession of all he needs. He must discover—and the process is inevitably a gradual one—who he is, in musical terms, what music he wants to write, what forms it must take, and he must work to bring it into being. He must bring it into being, I must emphasize once more, in terms not of his ideas about himself but of the actual music which he finds must come out. The two do not always correspond—as a matter of fact, at least one point in my own development, they did not . . .

In a sense—if his development is a really healthy one—this process will continue throughout his career. He will have found his own way, have achieved his identity . . . and the only inner security—it is, however, very real and very solid—that an artist can have.[33]

In the summer of 1929, in a unique moment of solitary confrontation with himself, under circumstances completely outside his musical pursuits, Sessions had a first, unexpected glimpse of the quality, the need, and the recompense of such self-reliant isolation.

In August, Aaron Copland had announced his arrival for a week's visit to Les Diablerets. Sessions wrote: "I am really touched that he is making this special effort to come and have a week with us. It will be strange to see him in the country."[34] The two young composers got on so well that Sessions agreed to accompany his friend on his return trip as far as Geneva, ticket compliments of Copland as a thank-you present for Sessions' hospitality. They traveled two hours from Les Diablerets to Villeneuve, where they changed trains for a five-hour journey to Geneva on the main line. As they passed along the lake with its magnificent Alpine panorama, future programs for the Sessions/Copland concerts in New York were discussed. Copland tried and failed (not for the first time) to convert his friend to his idea of a distinctively American school of composition.

In town, they called on Jean Binet, who had returned to Geneva a few days earlier, and met Raymond Vernet, Denise Binet's brother-in-law, about to leave for Les Diablerets. Vernet had tried (with no more success than Copland's in converting Sessions to the notion of an "American sound" in music) to persuade Binet to join him in a climb of "their" glacier later in the week; but with the unexpected arrival of Roger Sessions, Vernet had found himself an instant, enthusiastic, if first-time, fellow mountaineer.

The great adventure of the summer of 1929 was planned for Friday, August 16. Sessions left Geneva for Les Diablerets on the Wednesday before. Vernet met him at the station. A guide had been engaged, who told them that in order to reach the *cabane* (hut) at the pass before nightfall they would have to start in the afternoon of the next day. They would stay there overnight and begin their climb to the summit early on the following morning. The weather was not promising, but neither mountaineer was willing to pass up the chance.

Thursday morning was spent in assembling provisions and equipment. Sessions was elated at the prospect of using an ice pick, harness, snowglasses, and other climbing gear. Setting off in a fine rain, they hitched a ride on the mail bus as far as it would take them and walked on to meet their guide. Together they walked up through wooded pastures, and by the time they reached the timberline the rain had stopped. But drifting mist covered the sun and obscured much of their view:

> The mist, that day, added to the impressive sense of dreariness and desolation; & the mechanical, regular action of walking up hill adds to the feeling of immensity & impersonality & loneliness. The gray clouds swept past, sometimes under us, sometimes over us; they seemed to grow thicker & thicker; & as I went up & up I began to realize that one could, if one wanted, let oneself be overcome by a state of terror . . . Finally we came to a very steep staircase of rock; at the end of this the path turned abruptly to the right, & we walked along—always on the side of the mountain—till we came to a place known as *le canapé*—a kind of little grassy platform with a sort of long rocky bench on which one sits, sheltered by the enormous cliff above one's head.
>
> There was still this dark mist . . . to give us only occasional glimpses of the valley beneath, [but] the scene was in itself worth coming for—one felt oneself in safety at the top of the world, & looked down at the tiny valley, three thousand feet below in a straight line. We sat and talked for some time, & then the guide led us over rocks and through rocky passages up to the *cabane,* which is behind the huge ledge, in a sort of hollow, chained to the rock at its four corners—[at] 8000 feet.

Another climbing party had already arrived. During a meal of soup, sausages, bread, and cheese, an easy camaraderie developed "at being in a remote place together," with risks to be shared. The new mountaineer was too excited to get much sleep before the next morning's early departure: "I felt that I could live for weeks in such a place & be perfectly happy to sleep on the floor as one must do, . . . snoring, talking in sleep, whispering, through most of the night . . . I "slept" at a corner of the room; sleep is a rather extreme way of putting it—but one realizes that one sleeps to rest one's mind rather than one's body." Unable to sleep after all, he moved stealthily outside, admiring "a marvelous bright planet just above our dark slope" when someone lit a candle. Suddenly everyone seemed awake, "getting into shoes & sweaters, rescuing glasses and caps & Rucksacks & going in to coffee, bread & cheese." Roger, Raymond, and their guide decided to let the other group leave first.

They watched as the others climbed 400 meters up a very steep slope to the edge of the ice—"a wonderful sight to see in the early morning light, the larger group, roped together, on the side of the glacier." Then it was their turn. They climbed slowly, first the guide, who cut steps into the ice, then Raymond, then Roger. He took pride in his assigned position in the rear, a token of the guide's confidence in him. A mile below they could see the *cabane* and beyond it the green mountains that surrounded their village, way down in the valley. A steep incline of clear ice had still to be crossed; then the slope leveled out. Suddenly the tops of snowcapped mountains began to glow pink in the rising sun:

> The next sensation was almost the most wonderful of all. We were just beginning to arrive at the ridge, in the marvelous, absolutely clear sunlight; and ahead of us, just above, appeared a clear, bluish white, sharp outline,— a little like a wonderful white cloud, but obviously solid and fixed. It was the top of the *Dent d'Herens* (?) just appearing over a slight depression in the ridge. A moment later the *Matterhorn* appeared, then the *Dent Blanche* . . . gradually all the others appeared, *above* the shadow which still covered all the lower slopes. As we crossed the ridge we could see the ice extending for nearly three miles to our left, in a very gradual slope downwards; at one point at its edge a curious steep, absolutely straight tower of rock, called by some people the *Quille du Diable* (Devil's Bowling Pin), by others *Tour de Saint-Martin.*—

They caught up with the other party, shared a snack of chocolate and dried fruit, and finally climbed up a long ridge, with steep drops on each side, until they reached the summit. The sun had fully risen, and the light, glistening on the whiteness of the peaks around them, reached all the way down into the valleys. "Through Dad's marvelous field glasses" Roger could see their chalet 7,000 feet below:

> At 9:20 we started down . . . we lingered a little on the glacier, examining the crevasses, etc. You don't know how hard it was to leave that world—so completely different from the one down here. We reached the *cabane* just before 11:00; we lunched at 12:00, and started down at 1:15.
>
> The only part of the climb that is difficult in the least comes a little after the *cabane* (or rather just a little before, when one goes up)—it is a short stretch where one must watch one's step, & where it would be unpleasant in the extreme to have an attack of vertigo. It is called *La Vire aux Dames* and I think that Raymond and I will always feel a very special affection for each other for having crossed it together . . . When we had gone over it on the way up the precipice was hidden by fog and though we were quite aware of its being there it was not quite the same as really seeing it . . .
>
> I feel that I have had a good & highly successful initiation into the experience of mountain climbing, and that it was, so to speak, something in my life; that I for the first time learned something very important that I had never learned before . . . One faces danger, but danger of a special kind . . . the dangers one faces are dangers within oneself—vertigo, unsteady muscles, or allowing one's nerves to get the better of one.
>
> . . . Even if I should never climb another mountain, I would feel that I had felt for the first time a very rare joy on that occasion, and one which I must find again somewhere—a joy not so far from the joy one has in creating a work of art, where one has constantly come face to face with oneself.[35]

CHAPTER 9

Berlin Interlude

Man's greatest strength lies in his capacity for irrelevance. In the midst of pestilences, wars and famines, he builds cathedrals.

—ALDOUS HUXLEY

There had been a productive pattern to Sessions' years in Rome. During the winter season he worked slowly but steadily on three major works: the Piano Sonata, the Violin Concerto, and another symphony: "These three works are my big job for the winter, & I shan't leave Rome till I have finished them."[1] He did finish the sonata ("I am letting it go along slowly & easily & I think it will come out splendidly"[2]), made solid progress on the concerto, and decided to abandon the symphony.[3] Lesser tasks included the orchestration of his *Black Maskers* Suite and a number of smaller works, most of which he later disowned as exercises: "I have learned to produce much more quickly than I used to or [was] able to, & have turned out innumerable short things in the last year—not, however, most of them good enough to keep, as they were written for practice."[4]

The academy, stuffy and socially sterile though Sessions may have thought it, provided a stable and fruitful environment for work. During the summer months he returned to Les Diablerets, took long walks with Jean Binet, met "his Russians" in Lausanne, where they took the cure, and talked about music. Not for many years would he again enjoy such uninterrupted ease within a self-imposed schedule of work and relaxation. He decided that he could afford time for a brief visit home, paid for by a little teaching at Smith. On his return journey he stopped off in England, where he met Donald Tovey, who played his

Piano Sonata at sight but complained about the seven sharps in the last movement. "Why not five flats instead?" "Because it feels different."[5]

Small wonder then that, with his Rome fellowship nearing its end, Sessions felt less than eager about an exchange of this agreeable and fruitful lifestyle in Europe for that of a job seeker in depression-stricken America. He applied for and received a Carnegie Foundation grant, beginning in the fall of 1931. At the strong urging of Otto Klemperer, he chose to move to Berlin.

Berlin in its last moments before the Nazi regime came to power was a spectacular sunset, a burst of feverish vitality, an ultimate make-believe of glowing health in the terminally ill. Cultural life in the German capital during the final years of the Weimar Republic radiated with such unique abundance and intensity that the darkness to follow seemed ordained by its very excess. Yehudi Menuhin, who at twelve years of age made his Berlin debut in 1929, wrote in his autobiography: "Berlin was then the musical capital of the 'civilized' world, its prestige founded on the music of the past and flourishing still in great orchestras and conductors, not to mention the most informed audience to be found anywhere." As if in support of the latter claim, audience member and sometime violinist Albert Einstein rushed backstage after Menuhin's concert, crying, "Now I know that there is a God in Heaven."[6]

The prodigious cultural wealth of Berlin during the 1920s and early 1930s was nothing like the "old growth" artistic wealth of Paris or Vienna. An interval of only fifteen years stretched between the abdication of Kaiser Wilhelm II, whose ubiquitous civic legacy of architectural monstrosities had culminated in Berlin's Siegesallee (Victory Boulevard), a wide concourse flanked by thirty-two massive white marble statues, promptly dubbed by Berliners the "Avenue of the Dolls," and the advent of Hermann Göring, who would proclaim, "When I hear the word *Kultur* I reach for my revolver."[7] Little enough time in which to explore the riches and luxuriate in the pleasures of the future Reichsminister's *K*-word, but enough to encourage something like a metropolitan orgy. Berlin made the most of it. Following the disorders of military defeat in 1918, the violence of Marxist revolution and right-wing counterrevolution, the economic hardships of reparations, runaway inflation, and rampant unemployment were agonizingly and widely felt. They also helped to put in question the confining restraints of the old order, as the trauma of the war's bloodletting found an almost mystical release in Berlin's irrepressible vitality and its vibrant celebration of life, which thrilled and moved observers:

> This was particularly true [writes Walter Lennig, biographer of the German poet Gottfried Benn], in artistic as well as so-called intellectual circles, but by no means confined there. Not that Berlin of that period was in any way the evil Babylon or the citadel of depravity it was alleged to be in provincial politics. Truth was that Berlin enjoyed a greater openness; hypocrites and moralizers soon risked looking ridiculous.
>
> Completely changed also was the position of women: in Berlin at that

> time; even without special legal sanction, woman's status was one of complete equality. On the whole, this atmosphere was a lot less frivolous than one is inclined to think now. Love and Eros were more highly valued than they are today, and not yet as sexually debased. In addition there was something else which during the "brown" [Nazi] period disappeared completely: an extraordinary politeness in daily conduct—perhaps the only truly democratic achievement of that time. Berlin had the most polite police force and the most polite streetcar conductors, waiters, and shop assistants. All in all, one was proud to be a Berliner; and visitors would make an effort to master the manner, to adjust to the generous lifestyle of the metropolis.[8]

Underlying that remarkable social surface, however, was a postwar political dichotomy that would only be resolved, albeit at catastrophic cost, through the eventual empowerment of the National Socialist (Nazi) Party in 1933. The Marxist uprisings of 1918, which began with sporadic naval mutinies at some of Germany's North Sea ports and culminated in two general strikes in Berlin, the fall of the Kaiser, armistice negotiations, and the humiliating terms of Germany's surrender on the Western Front were powerfully exploited by the extreme left-wing Spartacist movement, whose leaders proclaimed a "Free German Socialist Republic" from the main balcony of Berlin's Imperial Palace, symbolically decked out in a huge red blanket. In response, remnants of the army organized themselves into *Freikorps* (Free Corps), adapted from the name used by independent cavalry units of Prussia's underground resistance during Napoléon's occupation of Europe. When a second general strike was called early in 1919, "to support an armed attack upon the Government and to place Germany in the vanguard of the international proletarian revolution," the Revolutionary Committee distributed arms, stationed riflemen on the Brandenburg Gate, and seized newspaper offices as well as railway stations throughout Berlin. At that point the de facto socialist government, which had filled the leadership vacuum after the monarchy's collapse, turned to the unofficial army units for help: "Delighted to have something on which to cut their teeth, the various bands of *Freikorps* went to work with a will. They gave their adversaries one chance to surrender and then began firing trench mortars and machine guns . . . turning a blind eye to the white flags soon waved by the overpowered Spartacists."[9]

Following this grisly prelude to political accommodation in postwar Germany, national elections were held early in 1919. The mainstream Socialist Party, with 39 percent of the popular vote, succeeded in sending the largest number of deputies to the Reichstag, with the Catholic Center (Zentrum) Party and the "intellectual" Democratic Party helping to provide a moderate balance between the Nationalists on the right and the Independent Socialists on the left. The Communists boycotted the election. A governing coalition under a Social Democrat president and chancellor was formed. It was this coalition that, almost without interruptions, governed Germany until the advent of Hitler's Nazis. In order to lend symbolic weight to its declared independence from an imperial past associated with Berlin, and no doubt persuaded by continuing unrest in the capital, the new National Assembly chose the small town of Weimar, home of Goethe and Schiller, for its deliberations on a new German constitution. In the same theater in which Franz Liszt had once conducted the first performance of Wagner's *Lohengrin*, the Weimar Republic was born.

Historical coincidence aside, the enduring contiguity of exuberant cultural activity and appalling political convulsion in Germany between the wars was at the heart of Roger Sessions' experience of Berlin. Indeed it was the German experience of the time, and it accounted for much that appeared incomprehensible about later events between the end of the First World War and the beginning of the Second. In a country newly riven by a savage pursuit of new wealth at the top and desperate living conditions at the bottom of its social community, culture—to paraphrase a famous maxim—became the opiate of the middle classes. And the middle classes, represented by an almost continuous Social Democratic government, ruled the Weimar Republic from its inception to the coming of Hitler in 1933.

From the beginning, an odd conjunction of art and accepted public peril manifested itself in the daily lives of private citizens. Artur Schnabel was on tour in the Rhineland when revolution broke out in Berlin. He telephoned home to reassure himself about the safety of his family. When he learned that his wife had promised to take their children to the opera that very afternoon to see *Hänsel und Gretel*, he easily persuaded her that it would be too dangerous. "But," he recalled later, "when she saw how unhappy the children were, she did not have the heart to deprive them of the expected pleasure; so they went and saw *Hänsel und Gretel* on the day of the revolution. Many other children were there and they enjoyed it just as much as they could.[10]

The inveterate German diarist of the period Count Kessler wrote:

> France gave open vent for our extermination, expressing it monumentally in her Prime Minister's words: "There are twenty million Germans too many." The continuation of the [Allied naval] blockade was rapidly fulfilling this wish; within six months of the armistice it had achieved a casualty list of 700,000 children, old people and women . . . Berlin had become a nightmare, a carnival of jazz bands and machine guns . . . On the very day [of one battle in the center of the city] the streets were placarded with posters "Who has the prettiest legs in Berlin? Visit the Caviar-Flapper Dance at such and such cabaret at 8:30 P.M."[11]

> In this spring of 1919 [writes Berlin's biographer Otto Friedrich], when the Freikorps forces were battling their way through Berlin and the German government was trying to negotiate for a treaty to end the war, the scientists of the Kaiser Wilhelm Institute in the city's peaceful western suburb of Dahlem were concerned with something more fundamental: an imminent eclipse of the sun. It would provide their first opportunity to obtain scientific proof for the revolutionary theory of the young director of the Astrophysical Institute, Albert Einstein.[12]

A political standoff between extreme factions of left and right continued to trade temporary accommodation for violent confrontation in those early postwar years, while successive administrations wrestled variously, and in hindsight often perversely, with the economy of a country in troubled recovery from its lost war, burdened beyond its capacity by open-ended reparations imposed by the Versailles peace treaty. Inflationary pressures went unchecked. The government in 1922 hired strikebreakers during a printers' strike in order to keep printing money, while the president of the Reichsbank boasted that those presses enabled him to turn out 46 billion marks in new currency every day. Runaway superinflation soon created doubts in powerful circles as to whether the best efforts of a politically moderate but fiscally reckless government could stabilize the economy sufficiently to avoid disaster for a still-compliant middle class and to avert the threat of a final, triumphant Marxist uprising.

Two events in 1923 marked alternative courses for the future of Germany—the appointment as chancellor of Gustav Stresemann, under whom the mark was stabilized; and the federal government of a nation still barely fifty years old's attaining firm control over its restless constituent states. There was one exception: in Bavaria, a failed uprising by the radical right, the so-called Beerhall Putsch by the still-small Nazi Party in Munich, earned Adolf Hitler an insignificant prison sentence as well as very significant national notice. But during the years that followed, the political center seemed to hold. "And so," writes Friedrich, "in the field of international finance, it seemed quite possible for the German government to pay billions of dollars in war reparations to the Western Allies by borrowing even more billions from the same Allies."[13]

Stresemann ultimately succeeded in moving Germany and France to a closer understanding, devoting his last years to successful negotiations on a fixed ceiling for total German war reparations and a three-year moratorium on payments. Nevertheless, soon after he shared the Nobel Peace Prize with French foreign minister Aristide Briand in 1926, Stresemann's policies were fiercely attacked from the political right as selling out to the country's "hereditary enemy in the West," while the left, not to be outdone as keeper of the nation's political conscience, accused him of turning a blind eye to secret rearmament activities by the Reichswehr, Germany's armed forces, in a plot hatched on the large rural estates in the east that were home to generations of Prussian generals.

Stresemann died on October 8, 1929. On Black Friday, October 28 of that year, the New York Stock Exchange collapsed and with it the worldwide paper prosperity of the twenties.

Germany's economy did not respond to the draconian austerity program with which a new government tried to combat the consequences of world depression. The number of unemployed rose from a low of 650, 000 in mid-1929 to nearly 3 million in 1930, 4 million in 1931, and 6 million in 1932. While overall industrial production declined disastrously, the crisis closed banks and forced whole municipalities into bankruptcy. The pain was widely shared. English writer Christopher Isherwood, author of *Berlin Stories*, which was eventually to become the Broadway play *I Am a Camera*, lived in Berlin throughout this time:

> Morning after morning, all over the immense, damp, dreary town and the packing-case colonies of huts in the suburb allotments, young men were waking up to another workless empty day to be spent as best they could contrive; selling bootlaces, begging, playing draughts in the hall of the Labour Exchange, hanging around urinals, opening the doors of cars, helping with crates in the markets, gossiping, lounging, stealing, overhearing racing tips, sharing stumps of cigarette-ends picked up in the gutter, singing folk-songs for groschen in courtyards and between stations in the carriages of the Underground Railway. After the New Year, the snow fell, but it did not lie; there was no money for sweeping it away. The shopkeepers rang all coins on the counter for fear of counterfeiters. My landlady's astrologer foretold the end of the world.

When Sessions arrived in Berlin, in the fall of 1931, the end of the Weimar Republic was not far off. Left-wing press revelations about a secret German air force being trained in the Soviet Union (of all places) brought the army, officially neutral in the struggle between right and left, solidly into the political arena. The powerful Nationalist Party, devoted arbiter of right-wing causes, clamored for a treason trial. The alleged traitor, one Carl von Ossietzky, was editor of *Die Weltbühne* (The world stage), a weekly magazine of the intellectual left. During his trial for espionage and treason, von Ossietzky declared that there was no secret of the German army that he would not hand over readily to a foreign power in order to preserve the peace. Nor did the prosecution attempt to deny that, under the Russian training program, Germany now had three operational bomber squadrons, two fighter squadrons, and eight "observation squadrons"—all expressly forbidden under the Versailles Treaty. The federal judges, for their part, ruled that the army high command was justified in establishing this program "in the interests of national defense," but Ossietzky was sentenced to fifteen months in prison for his indiscreet disclosure. Offered an opportunity to leave the country instead, he refused: "I am remaining here—an inmate of a Prussian prison, a symbol of protest."

Sessions could not have been unaware that the scales of political power were now tipping toward the right. Soon after the Ossietzky trial, industrialist Alfred Hugenberg, having secured the army's support of his own Nationalist Party, undertook major financing for Hitler's 800,000-strong National Socialist (Nazi) Party, which had first flexed its political muscle in the Reichstag elections of 1930. Fellow "Ruhr Barons" Kirdorf, Schröder, and Fritz von Thyssen (who for some years had been paying a private annual stipend to Hermann Göring) followed suit. Competition between the far right and the communist left for the votes of Germany's dispossessed had begun in earnest. Awesome increases in the numbers of unemployed and the perceived threat of a growing Red Menace fueled major industrial investment in right-wing causes, even at a time when the investors themselves were experiencing severe financial reverses—the financial worth of Thyssen's steel empire had just fallen to one-third of its former value. But opportunity beckoned, occasions demanded response, and events took their course with the apparent inevitability of Greek tragedy.

Small wonder that Sessions' stay in Berlin added up to an interlude of inaction as far as composition was concerned. Asked what he was doing in Berlin—as he was obviously not writing—he said with a self-deprecating grin, "I was having a good time."[14] If that sounded uncharacteristically callous, considering the social turmoil and the already-ominous signs of a takeover by either the radical right or the extreme left, it reflects perfectly Berlin's unique match of terminal social convulsions with a brilliant cultural life during these final months of the Weimar Republic.

Evening in Sessions' Berlin must have been beautiful. The falling darkness would transform ponderous buildings of the Kaiser era into a shadowy backdrop for busy streets and squares decked out in bright strips of colorful new neon lights, which decorated as much as they advertised and would turn rainy nights into magical stage sets. Multicolored reflections on wet pavements were cut by the hiss and swish of taxis heading for one of three major opera houses or thirty-two legitimate theaters, like the Theater am Schiffbauerdamm, where Kurt Weill's *Dreigroschenoper* was first performed. After the show, a hundred brightly lit cafés offered a pleasant conclusion to the evening, or one might go on to one of the famous cabarets where world-class entertainers like Josephine Baker performed for lively and cynical Berlin audiences who would themselves become part of a nostalgic memory.

If nightlife in Berlin between the wars compared in variety and vitality with that of any major European city and surpassed most and if the scope of its serious musical offerings and the international cast of composers and performers living and working in Berlin found its equal, if that, only in the respective riches of Paris, the extraordinary range of operatic and orchestral repertory, available in performances by ensembles of the first rank, probably stood alone.

The Berlin Philharmonic Orchestra was the city's premier symphonic ensemble. Wilhelm Furtwängler, who had succeeded Arthur Nikisch as its music director in 1922, reigned supreme in the purely symphonic field: unlike most major European conductors at that time, he did not also head an opera company but, like Nikisch before him, served as chief conductor of the Berlin Philharmonic while occupying a comparable post at the Gewandhaus Orchestra in Leipzig.

The Staatsoper (State Opera) was headed by Erich Kleiber, who became its music director in 1923 and conducted the first performance of Berg's *Wozzeck* in 1925. Two other conductors were part of the Staatsoper's brilliant podium roster: Leo Blech, veteran member of the conducting staff since 1906, when the Staatsoper was still the Kaiser's Hofoper (Court Opera); and a young Hungarian conductor, George Szell, whom Kleiber had engaged in 1924.

Bruno Walter, since 1925 music director of the Städtische Oper (Civic

Opera)—now the Deutsche Oper (German Opera)—combined his operatic activities in Berlin with a regular symphonic series. Two of his associates, Fritz Stiedry and Fritz Busch, took care of contemporary opera: Stiedry, principal conductor since 1923, first performed Schoenberg's *Die Glückliche Hand*; Busch (also music director of the Dresden State Opera) conducted premieres of Busoni's *Dr. Faust* and Hindemith's *Cardillac*, among others. Paul Dessau, who joined the company as resident conductor in 1925, eventually became best known as a composer. Like Sessions, he was to write an opera on Bertold Brecht's *Trial of Lucullus*.

Sessions' sponsor and principal adviser in Berlin, Otto Klemperer, was the charismatic and controversial helmsman of the brief but wonderful musical odyssey that marked his tenure as music director of Berlin's Krolloper (Kroll Opera).[15] Chartered in the early twenties, the youngest of Berlin's major musical institutions opened its doors in 1927 as part of the Volksbühne (People's Stage). With ticket prices "geared to the wages of a 25-year-old manual worker,"[16] and heavily underwritten by the state, the Kroll was fated to become an obvious sacrificial offering to conservative political demands for cutbacks in the government's arts budget during the deepening depression of 1931. Under Klemperer's leadership, meanwhile, the Kroll's meteoric crossing of Berlin's musical firmament was a freewheeling wonder of artistic daring, providing a stalwart home for contemporary opera and a new perspective on operatic staples. The Kroll's 1931 production of Mozart's *Marriage of Figaro* was conducted by Klemperer and directed by Gustav Gründgens—a demonically odd couple of artistic collaborators, considering the contrast of their respective personalities, character, and future careers.[17] The production was both acclaimed and denounced for reflecting present-day social perspectives in its staging of Beaumarchais' lively confrontations and social intrigues at an eighteenth-century court. But with hindsight of history, what could have been more appropriate, in terms of what was to happen either in 1791 or in 1933?

In many ways the Kroll symbolized the summit of Berlin's cultural explosion in the twenties; and its music director—brilliant conductor, fastidious artist, embattled champion of new music, and, not inappropriately, a manic-depressive—represented the best of what Roger Sessions would remember of those unlikely years in Berlin. Ironically, the Kroll had just been forced to close its doors by the time he arrived in the fall of 1931. And yet, as a continuing presence in the minds of detractors and defenders alike, it remained very much part of the musical savor of Berlin, its glory and its controversy a measure of perceived values in an increasingly bitter controversy over elitist culture and the populist politics that marked the end of an era. Sessions' first truly distinctive and personal observations, published soon after his return to America, reflect the profound effect of that experience on his growing convictions about the role of the arts and the artist in our society. It informed his views on music and nationalism that would soon estrange him from much of the musical establishment in his own country.

Not least among Klemperer's accomplishments at the Kroll was the assembling of a skillful, versatile, and mutually supportive conducting staff. The most seasoned of his associates, Alexander von Zemlinsky, had been music director of the German Opera in Prague and was a composer of the first rank. He joined the Kroll when it opened in 1927. Personally close to Klemperer and often consulted by him on touchy artistic decisions, Zemlinsky was "the musical conscience" of the house.[18] But unlike his chief, he lacked even a modicum of essential indifference to fatuous public criticism, let alone Klemperer's taste for the cut and thrust of political infighting. Having watched the bitter end of the Kroll during its last and probably finest season, Zemlinsky chose not to continue a conducting career and devoted himself to composition for the remaining years of his life.

Fritz Zweig, a more traditionally minded though equally effective conductor, was well endowed with political talents that proved invaluable in Klemperer's often-contentious dealings with the Brahmins of Berlin's civil service. Zweig had come over to the new enterprise from Bruno Walter's Städtische Oper. After the Kroll's closing he moved on to Erich Kleiber's Staatsoper.

The number of great chefs in the city's musical kitchen was impressive but not necessarily helpful in creating the best possible menu from the profusion of courses available for the feast that was musical Berlin: so tight was the crush of composers and powerful personages of the podium that even the scheduled performance of a major new work could fall victim to best-forgotten feuds between its irritable author and an annoyed conductor. Otto Klemperer, who had made his Berlin debut with an all-Schoenberg program , asked for rights to the premiere of that composer's one-act opera *Von Heute auf Morgen*, to be scheduled at the Kroll on a double bill with *Erwartung* in 1929. Klemperer was delighted to have the composer's "half-promise"; Erich Kleiber of the Staatsoper, having quarreled with Schoenberg but hoping for the rights to the same work, asked Schoenberg's former student and close friend Alban Berg to approach the composer on his behalf. Berg, in his turn not friendly with Klemperer, announced enthusiastically, if unwisely, that Schoenberg's new work would do better at the Staatsoper than at "Klemperer's Republik-Zirkus."[19] Klemperer withdrew his offer without explanation, and Berlin did not get to hear the opera at all.

All four of Berlin's mighty music directors promoted the music of their time, if not always to the delight of their audiences. Furtwängler's least popular concerts featured works of Schoenberg *et son école;* Walter performed *Bluebeard's Castle* of Bartok and Janacek's *Katya Kabanova* and introduced Shostakovich's First Symphony to Berlin. Kleiber championed Berg and even succeeded, in a final show of artistic defiance before emigration, in forcing the Nazi establishment to let him conduct five scenes from Berg's *Lulu* in a remarkable concert in November 1934.

More than with any of Berlin's other great conductors, Klemperer's well-earned reputation for performing the new and the needful was beyond redemption with conservative listeners, but these were not found in great numbers at the Kroll in any case. Berlin audiences, even allowing for the twelve-year-old Yehudi Menuhin's hyperbolic memory, might well have ranked, if not demonstrably as "the most informed anywhere," then surely among the most opinionated about what they wished to hear. But they did care. Notwithstanding the new repertory that virtually all of the city's major musical ensembles supported vigorously at the time, there were always full houses for important premieres, with a fair share of resident composers in the audience. Klemperer's first performance of Stravinsky's *Oedipus Rex* at the Kroll Opera in 1928 was attended not only by the composer but also by local colleagues Hindemith and Schoenberg. According to Stravinsky, Hindemith was "hingerissen" (bowled over) and Schoenberg hated it.[20]

Hindemith and Schoenberg were the most famous members of Berlin's resident fraternity of composers. Schoenberg, in fact, although the alleged founder of the twentieth century's "Viennese School," had already spent most of his creative life in Berlin before he emigrated to the America in 1933. As a protégé of Strauss, Schoenberg received his first teaching post at Berlin's Stern Conservatory in 1901. Returning to his native city two years later with added professional credentials, he found the musical establishment of Vienna as hostile to his music as it had been to that of Mozart, Beethoven, and Bruckner in their lifetimes. Back in Berlin in 1911, he composed and successfully performed *Pierrot Lunaire*, before the First World War drove him home in 1914. Finally, in 1926, upon the death of Ferruccio Busoni, then one of Berlin's greatest musical icons, he was asked to succeed him as head of the master class in composition at the Prussian Academy of Arts. As we have noted, rights to a Schoenberg premiere were already something worth conspiring about among the resident conductors. Schoenberg, who was writing his Orchestral Variations op. 31 and the opera *Moses und Aaron* at the time, would not again enjoy as prominent a position as he did in the musical life of Berlin.

Hindemith arrived in 1927, leaving his native Frankfurt to become professor of composition at the Hochschule für Musik in Berlin. Only a year older than Sessions, he already had a large number of works to his credit, ranging from the jazzy *Kammermusik* of 1921 to the expressionist song cycle of Rilke's *Marienleben* (1922–1923) and from the Bartókian Third Quartet of the same year to his quasi-Baroque Concerto for Orchestra (1925). During the year of Hindemith's appointment at the *Hochschule*, his opera *Cardillac* was produced in Dresden. As it was for Schoenberg, Hindemith's stay in Berlin was a wonderfully creative period. Among a large number of works written during those years, his *Lehrstück* (lesson play), written in collaboration with Brecht, and the one-acter *Neues vom Tage*, both of 1929, reflect the composer's irreverent vein of social critique and his virtuosity in finding the most fitting musical idiom. In 1930 he began work with the poet Gottfried Benn on his oratorio *Das Unaufhörliche*.[21] Hans Heinz Stuckenschmidt—eminent critic, chronicler, and one of the great movers and shakers on behalf of new music before and after the Second World War—writes:

> It was a stroke of luck for Hindemith to meet this man. Even though the spontaneous welling up of his music and Benn's complex mental stratagems may seem worlds apart, the spark leapt across. For the first time since Rilke's *Marienleben* Hindemith found himself confronted with a text of spiritual grandeur and metaphysical depth. With this oratorio he begins a new creative epoch.[22]

The major work to follow was his opera on the life and the struggle for artistic identity of the sixteenth-century painter Mathias Grünewald, *Mathis der Maler*.

For Sessions' sojourn in Berlin the plot of *Mathis* is pertinent. The painter becomes so involved in the violent political and social upheaval of his time that he forgets to paint. Hindemith, who wrote his own libretto to the opera, presents the artist's dilemma in terms both personal and universal: his need to fulfill a unique obligation to his talent and his urge to share in the common experience of his time. In the climactic scene of *Mathis,* the major characters in the opera appear as symbols of what they represent in the painter's mind: a warlord, an apostle, a merchant, a scholar, a grand seductive lady, and, in a threefold vision, the girl he loves: as a beggar, a whore, and a martyr. He himself is Saint Anthony, helplessly prostrate as he suffers that saint's temptations among the unveiled familiars of his outer world. In the end he is made to understand that, for all his praiseworthy challenge to the inequities of his time, he owes a greater burden of conscience to his talent and must fulfill his own mission by returning to his work.

Sessions, as a man and as an artist, had a chance to test and evaluate his own beliefs while he witnessed the final agony of the Weimar Republic amid a spectacular flowering of all that was best in its musical inheritance. As in Rome, there was political pressure to force the arts into a national mold, but unlike Rome, Berlin still managed to preserve a remarkably diverse musical culture. Nor was Sessions, as an American visitor, in any way neutral—or even sensible—in his daily conduct. Introduced by a British newspaper correspondent to a group of journalists at their *Stammtisch* (regular table) in a Berlin café, he explained his reasons for being in Germany by declaring, "Ich bin Kulturbolschewist!,"[23] cultural Bolshevist, the collective label of right-wing abuse for representatives of so-called degenerate art. Not long after, a German journalist asked Barbara, "Ihr Mann ist Jude, nicht wahr?" (Your husband is a Jew, isn't he?)[24]

As to *Mathis der Maler*'s "greater burden of conscience to his talent," Sessions still had a way to go. Klemperer, who "liked my Piano Sonata and promised to play the Violin Concerto when it was finished,"[25] found a place for him and Barbara at the Lützow Ufer, in the apartment of Max Strub, concertmaster of the Kroll's orchestra: "Not a very central place, side of a hill, in an alley going downhill. Klemperer lived two doors away."[26] The Sessions marriage appears to have been only a matter of form by that time, although they did move around Europe together: "I think Klemperer had an affair with Barbara. I got involved with another woman, we went on a walking tour together, but something happened before we ever went to bed. And I didn't work on the concerto."[27]

No, he was not composing: "I may have made sketches, but mostly I looked around."[28] What he saw was a last look, and he would not see the like again. Two years later, back home, he would disown the response of some American composers to a tidal wave of European artists and intellectuals in flight from Hitler's Germany, a response in which he saw the proclamation of a simplistic right-of-way along the road to American artistic conformity:

> It is a rather striking fact that the highest cultures of the past have been those in which the artist has enjoyed a very large measure of freedom of imagination and expression and the possibility of a rich and varied life, unhampered by the constant pressure of political or other dogma and theory. One thinks readily of the Athenian and Florentine republics, and if the musical florescence of eighteenth century Vienna may seem to be an exception, it is well to remember that music was not in those days regarded as potentially dangerous to any national or political idea.[29]

Individual composers and other eminent musicians in Berlin, of course, were no less partisan in their belief in their own musical bias than their counterparts elsewhere. Sessions recalled: "Schnabel, yes, he was a fine musician but a little dogmatic about it—two thirds music and one third Schnabel. He was 'not in my family': no feeling for French music, Debussy did not exist."[30]

Creative musicians, composers and performers, are naturally territorial in reacting to the work of their colleagues. Hindemith was "bowled over" by Stravinsky's *Oedipus Rex;* Schoenberg hated it, but neither of them, nor any of the leading conductors at the time, would have deferred to the judgment of an officialdom—or an audience—that evaluated the worth of music in terms of national priorities. Even as late as 1934, when Hitler's top tastemakers had been officially in power for more than a year, Furtwängler and Kleiber still managed to perform Hindemith and Berg, whose music had been declared unsuitable for German sensibilities.

But there was also music in search of new audiences. Kurt Weill's *Dreigroschen Oper* was not an isolated musical phenomenon. It articulated something in the economic and social realities of Berlin and elicited a powerful and immediate response far beyond Germany's borders and beyond its time. Weill's aim, before he emigrated to America, was not to make opera economically feasible in hard times but to align it with current popular experience. It related to what went on in the Staatsoper or the Kroll in much the same way as John Gay's *Beggar's Opera* had related to elaborate and expensive eighteenth-century productions in Handel's London. The tough-minded Berlin cabaret that resonated in Weill's *Dreigroschen Oper* and in *Mahagonny* was rooted in its time and place. Not even his felicitous collaboration with dramatist Berthold Brecht could be co-opted by others at another time. Twenty years later, Sessions would write an opera on the text of Brecht's radio play *The Trial of Lucullus.* But it would in no way replicate the powerful sleazy sting or the empathetic sentimentality of Weill's cabaret operas. Weill himself, in the very different cultural environment of New York, would soon lend his talents to the lucrative "musical theater" on Broadway and became rich.

Meanwhile, in a rapidly deteriorating economic situation in Germany, state-supported institutions became terminally vulnerable to political pressure to "downsize" or close. According to Peter Heyworth, "Between 1928 and 1931 theatre subsidies were reduced from 60,000,000M to 35,000,000M and the number of theaters whose season extended around the year with only a brief summer break declined from 106 to 82. Premieres of new operas fell from 60 to 28 . . . A pall of operetta spread over the land."[31]

As Sessions recalled in an article for *New Music*, two years later in New York,

> The movement is to a large extent economic in character, and the necessities to which it responds are outer rather than inner necessities; but in several respects it is symptomatic and must command the attention of everyone who is interested in the way music may go in the future . . .
>
> Composers busied themselves with the formation of a genuinely popular style, with rendering their music more accessible through a simplification of technique, with applying themselves seriously to the new problems offered by the radio, the cinema and mechanical means of reproduction.
>
> New ideals began to appear in opera; younger composers began to produce works designed definitely for momentary consumption, works which were above all striking and "actual," designed to fulfill a momentary purpose and to be scrapped as soon as that purpose was fulfilled . . . The movement deserves close attention, not for its artistic importance, but rather for the questions it raises . . . especially in the field of opera, where it has undoubtedly influenced the character and quality of new productions by enlisting the services of the avant-garde of modern stage production.
>
> Its chief interest, however, lies in the fact that by the very act of facing them, it has drawn attention to certain modern problems and dilemmas which may at any time become acute in other countries than Germany.[32]

The political climate in Germany was now changing at an alarming pace. In the presidential election of April 1932, the eighty-five-year-old Paul von Hindenburg was reelected with 18 million votes to Hitler's 11 million and the Communists' 5 million. The new chancellor, Franz von Papen, dissolved the state legislature of Prussia, and in a stunning election upset, the Nazi Party won 162 seats, while the Socialists, with only 94 seats, lost control of the chamber for the first time since the founding of the Weimar Republic. It only needed an incident to justify seizure of the Prussian executive. When police escorts proved unable to protect demonstrating Nazi storm troopers in a violent brawl with Communists in Hamburg, von Papen mobilized the army. He fired the Prussian government, which in turn set up an exile headquarters across town, while the Supreme Court took the constitutionality of the move under advisement.

Before a ruling on the case could be made, Chancellor von Papen's own federal government was forced to call for new national elections. The results on July 31 showed the strength of the Nazi delegation to the Reichstag at well over one-third of the total membership—almost twice that of the now second-ranking Socialists. Hitler could expect to be offered the chancellorship, with only President von Hindenburg's aristocratic disdain for the "Austrian corporal" standing in his way.

There followed a ludicrous plot of political farce and ineptitude. Papen decided to dissolve the new parliament by decree and actually got Hindenburg to sign the order. But when he arrived at the Reichstag to announce the decision, he discovered that he'd forgotten to bring the document. By the time he returned with the decree, the new Reichstag leader, Hermann Göring, had managed to table a successful vote of no confidence for von Papen's government and declared the decree invalid. Chaos resulted as violence broke out in almost daily confrontations between storm troopers and Communist demonstrators.

Time was running out. The last director of the famous Bauhaus in Dessau, Mies van der Rohe, had been forced by political pressure and radical student unrest to move his school into an abandoned telephone factory in Berlin. A few months later it closed for good. The exodus of writers, artists, actors, scientists, and musicians had begun. "I did not wait for the end," said Arthur Koestler. "I left Germany for Russia in July 1932, a few days after the Social Democratic Government of Prussia was chased out of office by [a handful of] men acting on von Papen's orders."[33] Painter and satirist George Grosz had already received threats to his person, his family, and his paintings. He claimed, however, that it was a dream about the disaster to come that persuaded him to leave. International superstars of science and the entertainment field, already at home on both sides of the Atlantic, simply chose to shift their base. Albert Einstein and Marlene Dietrich, each with a main home in Berlin, were in California at the time of the July elections, one teaching at Cal Tech, the other making a film in Hollywood. Both chose to remain in the United States.

Others waited, but the pace of events did not. In yet another election, in November, Nazi strength in the Reichstag dropped slightly, the number of communist delegates rose, and the level of civil unrest escalated even higher. Von Papen fell and was replaced by the army's strongman, General von Schleicher. His attempt to form a grand coalition that included "moderate" elements of the Nazi Party (according to the Goebbels diaries, the party was virtually bankrupt by then, unable to finance another election campaign), Social Democrats from the political left, and a strong center controlled by the army might have changed history. It very nearly worked.

Christmas passed quietly, but the New Year of 1933 soon proved hopes for the formation of any kind of coalition government illusory. To lure left-wing votes, von Schleicher had proposed to resettle thousands of the unemployed on 750,000 acres of "our thinly populated East." He was promptly attacked by the right as an "agrarian Bolshevist." Hindenburg, a major eastern landowner of ancient Junker stock, was alarmed. Behind the scenes, and leaving Schleicher's army support out of it, Papen went to work again. He privately proposed a joint chancellorship for himself and Hitler. Hitler said no.

Papen's next suggestion had Hitler as chancellor, himself as his vice chancellor, with two of fifteen cabinet posts to be held by Nazis, while all the rest would be given to members of industrialist Hugenberg's Nationalist Party. Hitler said no.

Belatedly Schleicher himself sent one of his army commanders to Hitler, "warning" him of Papen's plot and asking him to join forces with his own government. Hitler said no.

On January 28, Schleicher resigned. On January 30, tired of the game, the old President von Hindenburg appointed his despised "Austrian corporal" chancellor of the Reich.

Ironically, the end of the Weimar Republic took place at Klemperer's Kroll Opera. Following the Reichstag fire in February 1933, meetings of the German parliament took place in the now-vacant opera house. In the republic's final election, called for March 7, Hitler received 44 percent of the vote, his best showing ever, but not enough to control the chamber. He achieved that control by arresting the Communist Party's leadership and banning its delegates. In a personal appearance at the Kroll, he demanded of the remaining members emergency legislation to let him rule by decree. With storm troopers massed outside the building, the assembly gave him what he asked.

That even these developments did not really alarm Klemperer, as a Jew, was astonishing mostly because his aloof reaction matched that of a great many among his non-Jewish colleagues in intellectual and artistic circles. But one cannot admire the marvel that was Berlin's cultural flowering during the violent postwar clashes, years of inflation, brief prosperity, and a disastrous depression without understanding that the same qualities that enabled artists and writers and performers to function in spite of economic chaos and social disorder now shielded many of them from a full realization that this most recent development was of quite a different order. "Hitler cannot last"; "Hitler is not going to be as bad as they think"; "Hitler may provide a period of public order during which more moderate voices can safely be heard." Of such fanatical optimists in denial, none showed a more otherworldly serenity than Otto Klemperer. Sessions recalled that "on the day when all Jewish shops were boycotted, and their owners' names written on their doors, I was with the British correspondents who told me about it. Barbara was not interested and had stayed home. I went back and found Klemperer already there—touched, because the signs on Jews' doors reminded him of Passover."[34] When Sessions explained that this was quite the opposite of the Angel of the Lord identifying Jewish households in Egypt so that their firstborn might be spared, Klemperer was duly horrified but declared loftily, "Mich werden sie aber nicht boykottieren!"[35]

A few days later, he was on a train for Switzerland. With a letter of introduction from Sessions, he next appeared at I Tatti in Florence, still in his buoyant mood of manic confidence. Berenson remembers "a huge, vehement, wild-eyed, loud-voiced, very handsome Jew about forty-five, superb musician, and as jolly and simple as a roistering big boy."[36] But before Klemperer left Florence for Turin he would learn that Bruno Walter had been forced to abandon his concerts in Berlin and had fled to Austria. That finally made it seem real: "I thought that my last hour had also come. I telephoned my cousin Georg Klemperer in Berlin and [told him that] I did not want to return. Now, he told me, particularly now, you must return. Now we Jews must show . . . I still don't know what we were supposed to show."[37]

Sessions met Klemperer again at the Biennale in Venice, where he stopped over on his way home to America. Casella and Malipiero were in Venice, and Sessions was introduced to Alban Berg. By this time he realized that he was not leaving the musical life of Europe behind him: it would accompany his return in a growing exodus of those artists fortunate or rich or famous enough to exchange the troubled old continent for the New World.

CHAPTER 10 Home

Ending the travel was not a return but a kind of departure, which I regretted.

—PAUL THEROUX

You have no idea how lonely one feels in this country, if one's ancestors arrived here in the seventeenth century.

—THEODORE SPENCER

They were a remarkable lot, musicians and artists, whose number almost disappeared in the flood of refugees from Europe seeking shelter and a new start in America. Unlike most earlier immigrants, many of those who arrived in New York had lived prosperous and secure lives in their own country and were driven by a powerful determination to remake their new surroundings in the image of the ones they had left behind. Roger Sessions, returning to the land of his forefathers, was ready to do his bit.

But for our Ulysses, return to New York City of 1933 had to be a shock. He would have been prepared for some obvious differences from his earlier experience of life in America—Boston and Cambridge, Northampton and Cleveland. But the teeming, cosmopolitan cultural life in an urban environment still in deep economic distress had more in common with the Berlin he had just left than the New York of his brief return trips in the twenties, let alone the city that had welcomed visiting celebrities during his father's time or, more recently, offered generous opportunities to the occasional European seeker of musical fortune and permanent residence, such as composers Ernest Bloch and Edgard Varese. Sessions had been a privileged observer of musical life abroad and hardly more than an invited guest at New York's Copland-Sessions concerts. Now he found himself a confused intruder between the European elite of his profession and a resident subculture of native composers busily engaged in fighting one another.

Even with the hindsight of the closing years of our century, initial credit for America's coming of age in the arts is still being ascribed largely to this cultural migration from Europe. "For America, the Hitler years were something like the fall of Constantinople to the Turks in 1453, which sent Greek scholars and artists into exile in Italy and established the Renaissance in Europe. The standards of music education and performance in this country have risen enormously since World War II, largely because of these exiles and their students," wrote Washington *Post* music critic Joseph Mclellan in 1995.[1]

No doubt the influx of the illustrious along with a multitude of once respectably employed European musical performers and composers changed the musical climate in the United States, and it could well be argued that at no time and place since Vienna of the First School did any city hold such an array of distinguished composers as New York during the thirties. But these once and/or future notables included no fewer Americans than European exiles.

The enduring image of a country floating placidly in the wake of European tradition, while awaiting musical instruction and inspiration from the fugitives it welcomed to its shores, omits a remarkable period of indigenous musical life that was eclipsed by the highly visible spectacle of the great migration that followed in the early thirties. Whatever might have been said about musical life in New York as a magnet for performers before, the city's "atmosphere of composition" had long been a lively one as well. It was only its relative remove from the mainstream of musical life at home and abroad that diminished dramatically during the years that followed the arrival of the European exiles.

Unlike Boston of Sessions' Harvard years, New York's active musical establishment could boast a much older history, albeit largely introduced from abroad. The Puritan ethic of New England did not rule the cultural life of Colonial New York. *The Beggar's Opera* was heard at the Nassau Street Theatre in the 1750s, Haydn's music was played together with popular ballads in outdoor concerts at the Ranelagh Gardens from 1765, and John Jacob Astor opened New York's first music shop in 1786. America's principal port of entry, with a population boosted by successive waves of European immigration during the nineteenth century, soon achieved a reputation for its ardent and opulent support of visiting artists from abroad. Jenny Lind, in the first of twenty concerts in the early 1850s, sang for a capacity audience of 7,000 at Castle Garden. In the same decade, pianists Sigismond Thalberg and Louis Moreau Gottschalk (born in New Orleans but educated and firmly established in Europe before his American debut at age thirty-four) gave fifty-six and ninety concerts, respectively.[2] The box office was king, and later in the century New York saw the most renowned artists exchange visits for rich rewards: pianists Anton Rubinstein and Ignaz Paderewski and violinists Vieuxtemps and Wieniawski among many others.

Famous concert halls were built to serve the increasing demand of New

York's audiences: Carnegie Hall, Town Hall, and eventually Philharmonic Hall at Lincoln Center. But opera had an older claim. Invited by Lorenzo da Ponte, Mozart's former librettist, then teaching at Columbia University, the company of Manuel Garcia produced Italian opera at the Park Theatre in 1825/26. This was followed by a season of French opera staged by the Opera Company of New Orleans, America's oldest. New York's first exclusively operatic stage, the Italian Opera House at Church and Leonard Streets, opened in 1833 and burned down in 1839. Palmo's Opera House (named after its builder, an Italian restaurateur) opened in 1844 on Chambers Street. In 1847 opera moved uptown to the Astor Place Opera House, and in 1854 it went downtown again, to the Academy of Music at 14th Street opening with a performance of Bellini's *Norma*. Starring singers such as Henrietta Sontag, Adelina Patti, Lilli Lehmann, and Lillian Nordica among many others, the Academy remained New York's opera house until the opening of the Metropolitan Opera House at Broadway and 39th Street in 1883.

But the senior claim to musical preeminence in the city goes to the New York Philharmonic. Founded in 1842 as the New York Philharmonic Symphony Society of New York, it is the oldest orchestra in continuous existence in the country. And there were other orchestras during that time. Ten years before becoming the Philharmonic's chief conductor, Theodore Thomas had formed his own orchestra in 1867. In 1878, Leopold Damrosch founded the New York Symphony, an ensemble that for many years vied for first place with the Philharmonic. After Leopold Damrosch's death, his son Walter continued as conductor of the New York Symphony, later reconstituted as the New York Symphony Society Orchestra—a tenure which included the opening of Carnegie Hall in 1891. The Boston Symphony offered its own season in the city from 1887 and the Philadelphia Orchestra from 1904. Others, including the Chicago Symphony, now under Theodore Thomas, also visited from time to time. But after its merger in 1928 with Damrosch's New York Symphony Orchestra, the New York Philharmonic prevailed as New York's representative orchestra.

Sessions' decade in Europe had seen a kind of conductors' duel for the podium of the Philharmonic between Wilhelm Furtwängler, who led the orchestra from 1925 to 1927, and Arturo Toscanini, its conductor from 1927 to 1936. To the newly arrived composer, the cultural contest between Furtwängler's German orientation, reaching out from a Romantic base toward expressionist works and scores of the so-called Second Viennese School, and Toscanini's Latin preference for clarity, rhythmic vitality, and Classical simplicity would have seemed very much like the kind of contest he had witnessed within the musical establishment in Berlin. But the discovery that a lively, politically potent confrontation in American composition had yielded influential alliances and mutually hostile camps among American composers was unexpected. It informed an important component of the musical scene in New York of 1933, would eventually claim powerful partisans among the movers and shakers of its musical scene, and would mark Sessions as an outsider for the rest of his life.

The Great Depression had begun to make itself felt in the budgets of American orchestras, drying up much of what enthusiasm there was for presenting new works at the risk of discouraging shrinking audiences. Europe was still the place where living composers were likely to be performed and the ISCM, with its American Section formed in 1923, became a significant venue for Americans hoping to secure a hearing of their work abroad. It did not always happen: "The action of the 'Non-Contemporary Society of Music and Commercial Travelers' is a good one—for our vanity . . . In a new country like ours, children should be obscene and not heard. But the real cause of the situation is the Republican party—they kept us out of the L. of N. [League of Nations] chorus, and we are still out." Thus wrote Charles Ives to Henry Cowell in 1930, after the International Section of the ISCM had rejected his *Three Places in New England* for performance in Europe. Sessions had been on that jury in Geneva, as was Nadia Boulanger, a leading member of the Society, accustomed to being heard with due deference and confident of casting a deciding vote. We do not know how either of them voted on any one of the works under consideration; we do know that the young American, who had once been made welcome at Nadia Boulanger's studio, would not only argue doggedly and at length for or against every work under consideration but also, with a defiant lack of compunction, oppose her own choices whenever it suited him. What suited mademoiselle not at all was that the committee as a whole seemed impressed with Roger Sessions' powers of persuasion and endorsed, by a strong majority, one of his particular choices over her own, strongly voiced, objection. That proved too much for the lady who rose with quiet dignity and left the room. The awkward silence that followed her departure was broken by one Prunier, a Boulanger disciple, who rebuked the astonished Roger Sessions for "this outrageous affront to mademoiselle who, as everyone knows, *invented* American music."[3]

Actually, New York owed much of its awareness and support of new music in the twenties to the energy and political dynamism of a young French composer. Edgard Varese, who despised contemporary French musical life in general and Nadia Boulanger in particular, had come to New York in 1915, founded the International Composers' Guild in 1921, and given concerts of avant-garde music between 1922 and 1927. His forceful and unyielding drive, however, did not easily suffer dissent or criticism, whether from the musical establishment outside or from composers within his own organization. Resenting his authoritarian style, some members broke with the Guild in 1923 to found their own association for new music, the League of Composers. Others organized an American Section of the ISCM in the same year. Notwithstanding their common cause, the overt animosity between these organizations was to enliven but also to divide and sometimes to diminish efforts on behalf of new music in New York for decades to come.

While Varese would refer to colleagues who had broken with his group as "the Ladies of the League" and the League of Composers as "the Vanity Fair of Music," the League proved highly effective in its success in social circles with money to spend on concerts and publicity. Reflecting the musical background of its principal architects, Aaron Copland and Virgil Thomson—both recently returned from Paris and studies with Nadia Boulanger—the league combined a Neoclassicist French orientation with encouraging the ostensible "American" musical style of some of its members. *Modern Music*, the league's influential periodical, nonetheless continued to include articles and reviews from a much wider range of contributors, including those by Copland's friend Roger Sessions. The Copland-Sessions concerts, 1928–1931, were another exception to the doctrinal division of new music activities in New York.

In 1927 Varese dissolved his International Composers' Guild and helped to establish the Pan-American Association of Composers for the promotion of experimental music and its performance in the United States, Latin America, and Europe, and returned to France for five years. Under the continuing leadership of Henry Cowell, with substantial financial support from Charles Ives and the energetic participation of George Antheil, Carlos Chávez, Wallingford Riegger (as treasurer of the association), Nicholas Slonimsky (as conductor of its performances), and Carlos Salzedo, the association pursued its stated mission with some considerable success until the depression brought its efforts to a close in 1934. Not least among the achievements of Cowell's leadership were first publications of a large number of works by promising young composers under the imprint of *New Music*, a quarterly that not only survived the association's eventual demise but eventually sponsored recordings of new works as well. This remarkable undertaking flourished in New York until the death of Charles Ives in 1954. Reminiscing about their brave new world of composition, Wallingford Riegger wrote:

> We had rejected the neo-classicism of a war-weary Paris, and had struck out for ourselves, each in his own way. We formed, of the remains of the International Composers' Guild and the Pro-Musica Society, a new organization, the Pan-American Association of Composers (which included Latin-Americans) and gave numerous concerts here and abroad.
>
> It was undoubtedly the most anomalous chapter in American music, or in music anywhere. Here was a group of serious composers, literally making music history, and yet without the slightest show of interest on the part of those newspaper pundits who are supposed to keep their readers informed. We gave, at no end of effort and sacrifice, concerts of our own and of Latin American works, with a sprinkling of works by younger American composers. In justice I must say that once we did obtain a review. It was of a program given at the New School of Social Research, and appeared in the New York Post, but unfortunately the day before the concert, which had been postponed at the last moment.[4]

It is not hard to see how Roger Sessions, newly arrived after his decade in Europe, found it very difficult to fit into the musical life of New York in 1933. To the main musical establishment of the city he was a footnote, a composer who had received a few performances with major orchestras here and abroad,[5] and had been the nominal codirector of the defunct Copland/Sessions Concerts. The warring factions of the new-music underground welcomed him with provisory open arms. He was soon elected president of the New York Section of the (European-based) ISCM, and he wrote articles for *Modern Music*, the league's increasingly influential periodical, which, according to Virgil Thomson, had become "largely the personal organ of Aaron Copland."[6] But nothing could better illustrate the contrast between Copland's urbane and witty touch and Sessions' not always politic musical rectitude than Thomson's recollection of their respective reactions following the New York premiere of his opera, *Four Saints in Three Acts*, in 1934: "Copland, as always, spoke frankly, in this case glowingly. 'I didn't know one could write an opera,' he said . . . Roger Sessions, on the other hand, told me he thought I had 'not made maximum use of [my] orchestral resources.'"[7]

Nor did Sessions spare the press the benefit of his superior learning. After a performance of Beethoven's Fifth Symphony by the New York Philharmonic under Otto Klemperer, Olin Downes, eminent music critic of the *New York Times,* had taken exception to the conductor's evident neglect of the then-traditional broadening of the symphony's opening bars. Sessions wrote a scornful letter to the paper, assuring its critic that there was no indication in Beethoven's score to justify that tradition or Mr. Downer's objection. Small wonder that, for all his acknowledged deserts, he remained an outsider.

Sessions reserved his most cutting public disapproval for the new "American" style of the dominant League of Composers' musical philosophy. Copland had once praised his First Piano Sonata in terms entirely compatible with that ethos: "Sessions has presented us with a cornerstone on which to base an American music." But years of witnessing simplistic nationalist musical propaganda in Italy, followed by its more ominous display in Germany, had fed Sessions' misgivings about art based on such a program, whether it be government-sponsored or the work of his young colleagues aiming at an "American" style. And he was quick to draw invidious parallels in print: "The *Vaterländerei* [lit.: fatherlandism] of which Nietzsche saw the fatal beginnings in Germany began to reproduce itself elsewhere in a franker and even more accentuated form, in a quantity of national 'schools' of picturesque local significance."[8]

Not that the attempt to achieve "picturesque local significance" in composition was the only item in Sessions' lexicon of musical misdirection. Any contrivance or promotion of music for extramusical reasons was unacceptable, even in the conventional cause of popular appeal: "Many composers . . . were attracted by ideas derived from the quasi-Marxist concept of mass appeal. Their ideas of a cultural democracy drove them toward a type of music which consciously aimed at pleasure for the greatest number. Such ideas suited the aims of the music business."[9]

Sessions' rather original match of Marxist philosophy with American business practice aside, it was the idea of a "national" art, with its implication of some kind of official imprimatur, that really troubled him. Shortly after his arrival in New York, he wrote an article for *Modern Music* on music and nationalism.[10] His point of noxious departure was German Reichsminister Dr. Goebbels' recent answer to an open letter by conductor William Furtwängler, who had written to him in defense of Jewish musicians ousted from their jobs under the new German race laws. Sessions quotes from Goebbels' reply:

> Art must not only be good; it must be conditioned by the needs of the people—or to put it better, only an art which springs from the integral soul of the people can in the end be good and have meaning for the people for whom it was created. Art in an absolute sense, as liberal Democracy knows it, has no right to exist . . .
>
> . . . Artists of real ability, whose extra-artistic influence does not conflict with the fundamental standards of state, politics and society, will, in future as always in the past, receive from us the warmest encouragement and support.

The article goes on to argue the composer's belief in the sovereignty of individual responsibility of the artist over external considerations or programs, no matter how deserving. The only true kinship between art and the community that it serves comes from within the artist himself, not from the externals of his agenda or style. Sessions' response to mandates laid down by the German minister of culture and propaganda tells as much about Sessions in New York as about the new order in Berlin and reflects his views on the musical situation in America as much as it addresses contemporary events in Germany:

> It is difficult not to agree to a large extent with the letter, at least, of much that Dr. Goebbels says of "good art." Such considerations as he implies in his elaboration of the words *volksmässig* and *volksnahe* would seem to be fundamental to any such definition. Who would deny that art must have vitality, as well as perfection, originality, or any other of the current criteria? Indeed the whole essence of artistic form is the intensity of the artist's creative vision, and such a vision cannot grow and develop in isolation, in the dusty atmosphere of esoterism and of theory, either conventional or "radical" . . .
>
> To say this, however, is very different from saying that art must subject itself to the momentary passions or whims of whatever modern demagogues may choose to call the "people." The artist, like any other complete human being, must remain autonomous, at least in relation to his art . . . That art may sometimes be inspired by enthusiasm for a cause may readily be admitted, just as it may be inspired by any really profound feeling whatever. But when it remains on the level of an organ or reflection of popular prejudice, the artist has "made the great refusal" and abrogated his responsibility as a man and therefore as an artist as well . . .
>
> The above considerations do not, of course, apply to Germany alone, nor are the policies which are now being carried out there the exclusive property of the National Socialist party. They constitute, in fact, the basis of

polemics, slogans and theories which are being everywhere increasingly resorted to by advocates of one or anther extremist solution of our contemporary distresses.

Strong language indeed. Nearly two decades later, in the last of his seven Fulbright Lectures at the Cherubini Academy in Florence, Italy, Sessions would paint a more balanced picture of musical life as he found it upon his return to the United States in 1933 and as it had developed during the decade of his absence in Europe. But foremost, still, was his alarm about a conceivable litmus test of national relevance for music by American composers:

> The principal concern of music in the twenties was the ideal of a national or "typically American" school or style and, eventually, a tradition which would draw to a focus the musical energies of our country which, as Rosenfeld[11] once said to Aaron Copland and the author, would "affirm America." . . . Actually the national current in our music dates back to a period considerably earlier than the twenties. Its underlying motives are as curiously varied as are its manifestations . . . In its earliest phases it developed gradually on the basis of a musical culture which came to us from abroad. It consisted, as it were, of a deliberate search for picturesque elements derived for the most part from impressions received from ritual chants of the Indians or from characteristic songs of the colored people in the South; equally, it included efforts, such as MacDowell's, to evoke impressions of the American landscape . . . Next to MacDowell the most significant figure in the American music of that time was undoubtedly Horatio Parker, who, especially in certain religious works, displayed not only a mature technique, but also a musical nature and profile which were well defined, even though they were not wholly original . . .
>
> [Ives] certainly is one of the significant men in American music, and at the same time one of the most complex and problematical. But among the various elements of which his music consists—music which sometimes reaches almost the level of genius, but which, at other times, is banal and amateurish—the folklorist is the most problematic, the least characteristic.
>
> These men, however did not represent a genuininely nationalist trend, but rather idioms which, in much more aggressive and consistent form, contributed to a nationalist current that was to become strong in the twenties . . . More ambitious and possibly more interesting was the effort of Roy Harris to achieve a style that could be called "national" in a less external sense. His point of departure was the evocation of American history or American landscape, but from these beginnings he goes on to technical and aesthetic concepts aimed toward defining the basis of a new American music . . . What is lacking, as in the entire nationalist movement in our music, is awareness of the fact that genuine national character comes from within . . .
>
> One might possibly add one more brand of nationalism . . . the attempt to base a national style on jazz. Such classification is of course artificial and of purely practical value . . . [Jazz] has become an international phenomenon like other mass-produced goods which, originally manufactured in the

> United States, lose their association with it and are assimilated elsewhere . . . One remembers a series of works by Stravinsky, Casella, Milhaud, Weill, and others . . . Aaron Copland in his *Music for the Theatre* and his Piano Concerto (written in 1926) showed his audience novel points of departure such as had been suggested by Europeans . . . The serious composers during the thirties were attracted by the two tendencies which years before had dominated the European musical scene: the *neoclassic* tendency and that which is roughly summarized as *Gebrauchsmusik*, literally utility music. In the United States, explicit "returns" to this or that style or composer were few . . . Widely adopted, however, was a radical *diatonicism*, in the last analysis derived from the *neoclassic* phase of Stravinsky and adapted to utilitarian ends (as in music for film by Aaron Copland or Virgil Thomson), to fantastic and parodistic purposes (as in the opera *Four Saints in Three Acts* of Virgil Thomson and Gertrude Stein).[12]

In later years, Sessions would be careful to separate his reservations about claims of national identity as a basis of judging the worth of music from the particular regard in which he held the work of certain composers on its own merits. For all that he could not share Copland's enthusiasm for the founding of an "American School," he fully appreciated his friend's significant contribution as a composer. In summarizing thirty years of American music for his Italian audience in 1951, he concludes:

> A large share of the various phases through which our music has passed during these decades is summed up in his [Copland's] work. He not only passed through them himself, but guided many young composers as friend and mentor. Notwithstanding his manifold transformations—and it is altogether possible that there are more to come—he has remained a strong and well-defined personality, easily recognizable in the differing profiles his music has assumed.[13]

There can be no doubt that Sessions, after his return from Europe, was a figure of some modest consequence in New York's musical circles, though their politics did not interest him. When, in March 1934, Olin Downes, chief music critic of the *New York Times*, planned to write a Sunday column on the role of American critics in promoting the music of American composers, he invited Virgil Thomson and Roger Sessions to write letters in response. Downes advocated efforts to get American music performed, if not to award it critical preference over the music of other countries. The substance of Sessions' published reply is that "an American music 'nurtured' by special treatment would be only a racket, fundamentally dishonest, dealing in goods confessedly incapable of holding their own in an open market,"[14] was predictable, admirable, and probably resented in some circles. But he was indeed one of the two American composers expressly asked to contribute an opinion. There were others more familiar to readers of the Sunday *Times*'s music page. Sessions was known to an inner circle of the musical establishment as a composer who wrote. Thomson, future chief music critic of the *New York Herald Tribune* and very much a power-to-be in the musical life of the city, was a very different kind of writer. His lively prose could sparkle with a genial wit and a waggish bite that made it refreshing to read, whether or not one agreed with what it said. To some he would become a writer who composed. And he cut with painful precision. In his autobiography, he referred caustically to "sermons by Roger Sessions whose learning was to the cause of modern music as that of Alfred Barr's to that of modern art."[15]

Sessions had indeed begun to speak his mind in a rather Olympian manner and had decided that he was "a kind of celebrity."[16] If the outlines of future distinction may have been evident to some at the time, there was no denying that a mere handful of respected but hardly played works by a now middle-aged composer provided meager support of a claim to any kind of celebrity as a composer. Sessions' return to the land of his fathers was not a happy one, and his feeling of estrangement within the American musical establishment was profound—and justified. Professional alliances with colleagues and active participation in organizations for the performance and promotion of new music were indeed available to him, but his few works had been performed, and he had not written anything new during his turbulent years in Berlin. The Copland/Sessions Concerts were now discontinued, his influence on the current state of music was confined to an occasional essay, and even old friends were not always hankering for Sessions' pronouncements about lessons to be learned from his experiences abroad.

Bloch was in New York. They met, but the easy familiarity and mutual regard of old was missing. Sessions recalled that their meeting, though "pleasant enough, was somewhat casual:

> Bloch was jealous. He was the least civilized of all my friends among musicians. He was up and down and easily thwarted. Very volatile. I was his favorite toy, so to speak, [but]there was more vigor in my music than in some of his. I emphasized lyrical and rhythmic elements instead of colors and "half programs" such as his Jewish references. Bloch's problem was that he came from Switzerland instead of one of the larger countries. He was anxious to assert himself because of that. If he'd been really French, he'd have had a little more confidence.[17]

Whatever Bloch's manner, it might well have reflected the composer's own uneasy sense of the changing musical environment in a very large country in which he himself was a foreigner; more likely, however, it would have been a reaction to the manner of his former pupil and protégé, who had much to say indeed about the state of the arts but who had not yet learned to save his opinions for those who needed to hear them.

The Great Depression was real and New York was a dirty, crowded place in which the famous and the anonymous shoved and schemed for success in the face of daily images of failure. Home was nothing like the image of a sheltered haven that had made Sessions a keen but safely uninvolved observer abroad. He now discovered how much he, too, was a man of his time: as alienated and uprooted as the European refugees with whom he shared an ambiguous sense of cultural identity and belonging. Certainly the New England of his own childhood seemed as far removed from the current reality of his life as the New England of his ancestors. Paradoxically, the urbane Aaron Copland, born rootless, had an easier adjustment to make: with his "invention" of an American school of composition he evoked for himself and for a generation of like composers a bygone America of open spaces, simplicity, and buoyant belief in a future seen through the romantic lens of an imagined past. Sessions' genuine American background did not permit him its posthumous invention, nor would it tempt him to try. The descendant of the Phelps, the Porters, the Huntingtons, and the Sessions of western Massachusetts was a lonely figure in the fast-paced musical binge that was New York in 1933.

He needed a job, and he had already tried to establish a base in Hadley, hoping to commute to the new Malkin Conservatory in Boston, which had offered him "sort of a job": "They engaged Schoenberg at the same time, and I thought there won't be anything for me to do. But there wasn't anything for him either."[18]

So he stayed in New York to teach privately. He rented a room over the Granberry Piano Shop on Third Avenue and 61st Street in New York. And while Third Avenue Elevated trains clattered and rattled past his windows he waited for pupils. Marion Bauer was the first; then came Milton Babbitt. Babbitt recalled his first interview—shades of Ernest Bloch:

> SESSIONS: What do you want to do? To lay a real foundation for your work will take three years. What sort of pieces would you want to be able to write when we're finished?
> BABBITT: The Stravinsky Octet?
> SESSIONS: Hm.
> BABBITT: The Copland Piano Variations.
> SESSIONS: You won't need three years for that.
>
> Babbitt asked about the fee. Sessions, apparently not quite sure what to charge, hesitated. Fearing rejection, Babbitt suggested that his father might offer the whole year's tuition in advance. That paid the rent.[19]

Luck continued to be on his side. On the recommendation of Jean Binet, Paul Boepple, director of the Dalcroze School, not only offered him a teaching post at that New York institution but also, for the year to come, actually allowed it to be renamed New Music School and Dalcroze Institute, with Sessions providing the music component. As de facto codirector of the institute as well as a popular teacher, he now had a very full schedule indeed. The group of students who began their studies with him at the school included some distinguished American composers-to-be: David Diamond, Vivian Fine, Miriam Gideon, and Hugo Weisgall. But by the end of the term Sessions found himself out of a job, "because they felt I was running the place." Ever the optimist, meanwhile, he had bought a car (a Plymouth he called Annabelle) on the strength of his anticipated income and ended up—pace his New England ancestors—in debt. To help make ends meet he gave some lectures at the New School for Social Research in New York and at the New Jersey College for Women in New Brunswick, New Jersey. His was a very precarious existence in that cold depression-era winter of 1934, but in that, of course, he was not alone.

His closest personal friends in New York were not among the musical elite. Struggling musicians mostly, with whom he felt no need to prove his status in the world, they responded to the warm, generous man whose personal charm revealed itself most freely in friendly, familiar surroundings. Even after he moved on to New Jersey in 1935 he would stay in touch and could be certain of a pleased response to his occasional but long and detailed letters.

September 8, 1935

Dear Roger,

Your letter was a great surprise. And we were delighted to hear from you. We are both dying to hear the new viola sonata. Do come to town soon . . . Marcel was here almost the whole [summer]; substituting at NBC for regular house men on vacation. And I kept dashing back and forth between here and Connecticut. I had to go apartment and furniture hunting, both very tedious in the heat.

But we have a place of our own now, and have gone very modern as to furniture. I wonder if you'll like it?

Sept. 15

I stopped, and now a week has gone by. One simply can't write letters from New York. But you'll be here soon. Call us. Sacramento 2-7500

Love from us both
Ann

. . . When can I have the Viola Sonata? I would be too glad to study it as soon as possible. Much love,

Yours,
Marcel[20]

A Sessions viola sonata is not now extant, but he must have been planning to write one, and evidently had it worked out sufficiently to promise it to a violist friend. It would have been entirely in keeping of his way of composing to speak of a new work as "finished," or very nearly so, once he had it clearly in mind, even if little had yet been put on paper. Many a conductor in years to come, the author included, would blithely schedule the perfomance of a commissioned work that, at the time, existed only in Roger Sessions' head.

He wrote nothing at all. It was a confused and confusing time in which to be a composer, worse if one happened to be Roger Sessions. Between the experimental schools of composition that began stridently to promote the superiority of their systems of compositional construction and the politically more powerful adherents of musical *Vaterländerei* it seemed hopeless to carve out one's work according to intuitive benchmarks of a musical idea. At the same time, none of the currently apparent alternatives offered usable common ground to a composer who, at the advanced age of thirty-seven, was just beginning to make out his own way in that confusion of musical tongues.

In an article for *Modern Music*, written in 1934 and titled "New Vistas in Musical Education," Sessions reflects on the "unsureness of instinct" in contemporary composition based, he believes, on "a disharmony in the relation of the composer to his materials—detachment of his musical consciousness from the facts, both 'musical,' in the strictest material sense, and psychological, which form the basis of the musical impulse." He laments:

> The tendency to replace standards based on a sound and self-confident musical instinct, with others culled almost at random from external sources, such as musical history, aesthetic theory, up-to-the-minute fashion, nationalistic, racial or sociological dogma. As far as composers are concerned, even if we leave out of consideration the extremely poor quality of so much contemporary music, we may observe the feverish attempts of certain ones to "explain" their works, the increase of cliques and self-protective, self-adulatory, or self-consoling groups, and the tendency to enroll under banners of various colors—often with the purpose of hiding some half-suspected nakedness. One may even observe a certain tendency, especially in the United States, to formulate principles of criticism in advance of the works to which they are to be applied; one sees composers discussing "style" before any musical ideas have presented themselves, or elaborating external and often complicated formal patterns which have no essential relationship to the specific musical material which is forced into them . . .[21]
>
> Technique, in any really profound sense, is the ability to develop an organic musical train of thought . . . Style, on the other hand, is the individual inflection which an individual, a nation, or an epoch spontaneously and unconsciously gives to music, and has, fundamentally, nothing to do with the conscious and carefully circumscribed choice of materials . . .
>
> Composers cannot, certainly, be taught to keep faith with themselves. The impulse must be there, the courage, and even the intelligence. But they can be helped by teaching to understand their materials and to come to real terms with them. Musical education must make this, above all, its objective, basing itself first on the acoustic fact, of exactly what we hear; secondly on the psychological facts, of how and why we hear as we do, and exactly what effect such and such a musical procedure produces.[22]

One can easily imagine the misery of a composer in the midst of a virtual riot of new music, published, performed, disputed, praised, and damned in a professional environment, all of whose main figures he knows very well—and all of whom seem to be composing all the time. His was the misery of a composer who had known the joy and the urgency of the creative impulse but who could not write unless he was able to meet requirements he has devised for himself and sternly set down in print. If his unrelenting prose sometimes seemed hard for others to take, he was himself the first and foremost victim of its message.

In terms of his immediate future, however, this article was timely and even prescient. Within the year, the teacher Roger Sessions would have a chance to test and develop his "vistas on musical education" in a university classroom. The courage to keep faith with himself, as a composer, would still involve some barren years before he could prove to himself once more how, under the impulse of a musical idea, musical materials that had "nothing to do with . . . conscious and carefully circumscribed choice" would on their own "develop an organic musical train of thought."

CHAPTER 11

Sea Change

The biographer is now faced with a difficulty which it is better perhaps to confess than to gloss over.
—VIRGINIA WOOLF, *Orlando*

In 1935 Sessions joined the faculty of Princeton University, finished his Violin Concerto, and met the woman who was to become his second wife, Lisl, while teaching summer school at Berkeley, California. In 1936 he divorced Barbara—to whom he dedicated his concerto—and married Lisl.

These events, which utterly transformed Sessions' existence in midlife, produced their most immediate effect on his personal way of life. To begin with, and for the first time in a decade, he could now look to the future without the need of either securing yet another grant or earning a living by whatever precarious means were available to an underemployed music teacher in a depressed and highly competitive market. He had played the game of successful grantsmanship with considerable skill—rationalizing a need for continued subsidy, securing prestigious references, patiently awaiting decisions to which there were no agreeable alternatives, and, in due course, facing the whole process again. His reward had been productive, if temporary, leisure and a flexible choice of where to live and work. An appropriate and fruitful way of life as a composer during his early years in Italy, it had no longer served its purpose in Berlin. The last days of the Weimar Republic offered a fascinating opportunity to observe a doomed culture at its superb best, as well as a chance to witness events that changed the course of history, but the end result for Sessions had been creative stagnation as well as a rapidly deteriorating personal life. By the time he reached Berlin he was effectively a cultural tourist, an observer, albeit one who laid up the seeds of his observation for serious future harvest. Considering the very small, if admirable, body of works on which to base a reputable standing among colleagues upon his return to New York, his success in achieving "a kind of celebrity" had certainly been remarkable. But something more was needed.

Roger Sessions' long journey—outward bound from his New England childhood to his student days at Harvard; from his apprenticeship as composer and teacher in Cleveland to his wayfarer years in Florence and Rome; from being a privileged witness of the Weimar Republic's last days in Berlin to his return to New York, just when the implosion of Central European civilization caused his native city to become the cultural center of the Western world in the midst of the Great Depression—this journey, comprising fully half of Roger Sessions' life, had shaped the man but forecast the identity of the composer only in bare outlines. That was about to change. The outlines of the total, complex, creative personality were now to appear in substantial detail, as quickly and fully as a photographic plate suddenly yielding a clear image—albeit a negative—while a picture is being developed.

Nothing had prepared Sessions for his marginal existence in New York, a lifestyle that he mastered and endured during the two years following his return to America. It was difficult to see colleagues getting on with their careers, writing their works, and taking a productive part in the evolving musical life of New York City. He was given initial privileges in that life; his opinions were politely sought and published but not particularly welcome. To musicians, a composer is one who writes music and a performer is one who plays or sings or conducts. There are many who clearly could but don't. Their problem may provoke sympathy, but professionally it is irrelevant. In the musical life of New York in 1933 and 1934, composer Roger Sessions came close.

Nor was there any longer an outward pretense to his marriage. The uncertainty of Sessions' position in New York would have been a strain on a stronger relationship, but he and Barbara had already drifted apart for too many years, making do with respective extramarital liaisons. Neither of them appears to have resented the other's personal lifestyle. When, during the year that followed their arrival from Europe, Sessions got involved, "briefly but intensely," with a student at Smith College, Barbara only commented, "So you're in love again?"[1] They kept in touch but felt uncomfortable in each other's company, living separately on friendly terms but not friends. Two years after his return, it must have seemed to Sessions as if a long and hopeful chapter in his life had ended without any prospect of a meaningful future. But the next page was already being turned for him by hands out of his past.

In 1934 Roy Dickinson Welch was invited to teach two music courses at Princeton University and to design a future plan for musical studies. On the strength of the evident popularity of his classes during that first year, he was in a position, in 1935, to recommend that Roger Sessions, his former colleague

Lisl Sessions

from Smith College, be engaged as a teacher of theory and composition. Although a modest enterprise by any standards, Welch's musical venture within the university soon attracted serious music students in quest of an academic degree as well as Princeton undergraduates interested in a general music course. The conservatories across the river in New York—the newly endowed Juilliard Graduate School and its affiliate, the Institute of Musical Art, as well as the Mannes and Manhattan Schools of Music—trained professional musicians, particularly performers, but offered only a diploma at that time. Edward T. Cone and David Diamond were among Sessions' first composition students at Princeton.

Almost at the same time, a second teaching post opened up for Sessions. At the suggestion of Ernest Bloch, the University of California at Berkeley offered him a job teaching summer school. During his years as director of the San Francisco Conservatory, Bloch had not only proved himself once again to be a highly successful administrator but had also become a highly visible, influential member of the musical community in the lively and cosmopolitan city across the bay from the Berkeley campus. He had relinquished his directorship of the conservatory in 1927 in order to spend part of every year in his native Switzerland, but he continued to be a frequent visitor to the United States and remained a potent force within the musical establishment of the Bay Area. Sessions' invitation to teach in the summer of 1935 began an annual affiliation with Berkeley that endured, with interruptions, until the university offered him a full professorship in 1945. Two women whom Sessions met during that summer in California were to play important roles in his future, one in the immediate future, the other for life.

For her accomplishments as one of America's great patrons of music and as a true believer in the cause of contemporary music, Elizabeth Sprague Coolidge received an LL.D. from the University of California in 1935. There she met Roger Sessions and asked him to write a work for the celebration of Harvard's tercentenary in September 1936. He offered his String Quartet, a work in progress since 1933. Eventually—as so often before and afterward—he missed the deadline, the Harvard performance, and almost his promised fee of $500 (a severe blow to his still-shaky finances). Mrs. Coolidge relented not long after, paying the commission and promoting subsequent performances of the work.

Sara Elizabeth (Lisl) Franck turned up as a student in Sessions' Mus. Lit. class during that first summer in Berkeley. Of Dutch stock, she was a native of Spokane, Washington, where "her father was in charge of big land projects."[2] In the fall she planned to take up a job at the New York Public Library, and she was spending part of her last West Coast summer improving her mind under the tutelage of Roger Sessions: "We liked to talk after class. She also became a private pupil, and we went on boat rides and to San Francisco. Eventually the inevitable happened."[3]

The "inevitable" became a turning point. With the assurance of a stable, if modest, year-round income in a congenial teaching environment, the outward conditions for setting Sessions' life in order had been met. It was his relationship with Lisl, soon to be bound up in a marriage of nearly fifty years, that provided the strong foundation that enabled this composer to function productively in respected, eventually celebrated, professional independence—and isolation.

The extensive body of letters from Sessions to his mother reflects, as we have seen, not only an earnest striver after personal merit and professional achievement but also a man and an artist in need of approval on both counts. Ruth Sessions furnished her son with provisional support throughout the long decline of a bad marriage that, for all her stubborn resolve, she could not save and with a firm focus of emotional identification throughout the travail of a very slowly unfolding professional career. In turn, his need to be valued, indifferently met by the musical establishment at large or by his estranged wife, had offered the family matriarch rather more than a semblance of continuing control.

The events of 1935 and 1936 changed all that. Ruth Sessions turned out to be last among close family members to be told about her son's wedding plans. She probably knew about the impending divorce sooner than her family imagined, but her son's decision to embark on a new marriage was carefully kept from her. Much as she liked Barbara and regretted her daughter-in-law's long-standing estrangement from her son, she had also found comfort in thinking of Roger as relatively unattached and thus the more closely bound to herself. With age the matriarch was beginning to feel vulnerable and needful of others, if often oblivious to their needs. Dealing with her became a shared family problem. A letter from Roger's sister, Hannah (Nan), describes a difficult and unrewarding task:

April 17, 1935

Dearest Roger—

Mother writes that you are at Hadley for ten days' vacation; I am sending off this note hurriedly—which I have been on the point of writing for some time—to see if there isn't some chance of your coming out here either for part of this time or later if you prefer. Part of the motive for asking you is purely selfish—after mother's visit tho' it went off very smoothly, I had a feeling of great loneliness for some of my own people, because I felt such a complete lack of contact with her that her departure left me with no emotion except for a general sense of relief from an exacting & physically exhausting round of regrets. I think she had a good time, but there was less of a sense of pleasure or mental interchange in her presence than I have ever had.[4]

The notion of maintaining, at convenient intervals, the appearance of an otherwise failed marriage should have been a familiar one to Ruth. Long after the separation from her own husband, Archibald Sessions had paid annual summer visits to his family in Hadley that involved, according to Roger, all the franchises of married life.[5] The fiction of her son's marriage had similarly been maintained in his own and Barbara's visits to Hadley during the years following his return from Europe. Even when the plot first started to unravel and the tenuous nature of her son's marriage must have been very clear to Ruth, Roger and Barbara had paid her a joint, if apparently rather stormy, visit. Wrote sister Hannah in the fall of 1934:

Dearest Roger and Barbara,—

I am sending this letter quite trustingly to the school, as I simply don't dare to write either of you at Northampton! . . . I have only the vaguest impression of things at Hadley & Northampton.[6]

Roger and Barbara agreed on a divorce in the summer of 1936. Quick American divorces were granted only in the state of Nevada and even there only on grounds of adultery. Barbara generously offered to be the "guilty party"; Roger's sister, Hannah (whose husband, Paul Shipley Andrews—"stuffed shirt," in Roger's ungrateful description—served as a judge in Syracuse), arranged for legal advice; and Sessions established himself at a place near Reno called the TY Ranch to fulfill his six-week statutory residence requirement in the state. By his own account, he had a "very jolly time" of it all.[7] The late summer and early fall of 1936 were beautiful in Nevada, and he went boating on Pyramid Lake with a lively divorcée-to-be awaiting her own decree.

Lisl, of course, was already very much in the picture, but Ruth would not be told about her until the divorce was final. Roger had laid his plans for that event with consummate care. In long letters from Reno, he first primed his faithful allies at home—Hannah in Syracuse and Boston cousin Catharine (who had already met Lisl and been "enchanted"). They would wait in the wings, ready to move on to the scene as soon as his own letter to his mother had been received in Hadley.

Writes Hannah upon receipt of her brother's news from Nevada:

> Your long letter reached me in West Dennis, day before yesterday . . . Let me say that I am <u>very</u> happy about it. My first impulse was to telegraph the message Paul & I both felt—: "Love to you and Lisl from us both"—then felt uncertain whether to send such a message as publicly as in a telegram might not be indiscreet from your point of view, & we talked it over & considered it would be just as well to write.
>
> I have a vivid impression of Lisl's picture & of a very lovely strong face; & your letter, your whole view point & the profound thought which has led you to this decision make me feel, not only that this is the right thing but also that you have the greatest chance you have ever had of a profoundly satisfying and fruitful life . . . Your relationship with Barbara has had romance & also many of the ingredients of friendship; but that is not enough. It sounds to me as if Lisl had the point of view & the qualities which will give you real marriage. Let me say only this: I consider it merely as a suggestion. Try to free yourself from the pull of your relationship with Barbara & any sense of responsibility for her. I have seen that happen in one or two cases & it made a very happy second marriage not so easy for the new wife. It seems to me that just now you are leaning over backward a bit more than you need.
>
> We saw Barbara in Hadley ten days ago, with Catharine: she (B.) looked remarkably well & seemed thoroughly poised & cheerful & happy about her Washington job. Remember that the break has been absolutely her choice, and that, having made it, she must build up her new life in her own way. You cannot help her & it is really a mistaken kindness to try. You still have a little sense of wanting to shield & spare her. I think you have both made the mistake of trying to compensate for the lack of a complete sense of being mated by demonstration of affection & romantic attachment . . . the moment you have your divorce allow yourself to dwell without restraint or hesitation on the building of your new life with Lisl. I look forward with real happiness to having her as a sister.[8]

Cousin Catharine received her letter about the same time:

> It moved me so much . . . There is so much to say. First of all I went to Hadley with Barbara as you know and it was a very fortunate and strangely simple time—happier than I assume was to be expected—for us all. What was most important in relation to you were several conversations with Aunt Ruth really preparing her for what you naturally dread to tell her. Barbara said to her "I hope and expect Roger to marry again," and Aunt Ruth, evading the significance a little, still took in the idea & accepted it. Hannah—said to me that she certainly hoped that you would marry—& of course Doheny & John seem to really know that you are expecting to. This was startling to Barbara & me—but through some source apart from any of us—and largely from his own impression at the time you & Lisl were in Hadley they had known—saying nothing to others of course. I thought of you in so many vivid flashes when I was in Hadley—so beautiful and mysterious as always.[9]

Clearly Catharine was not immune to the special attraction Cousin Roger always held for women. In any case, she sees his confining dependence on his mother (and his mother's on him) as clearly as his sister saw the negative aspects of his complex relationship with Barbara:

> The center of interest for Aunt Ruth now is so fortunately her book—she seems elated and yet more composed & more realistic possibly. Of course you mean so tremendously much to her—and yet I think that it will be so healthy for you to be re-established on your own base as it were—not that you are not, only that she cannot but think of you as returned to her, and, as you spoke of in your letter to me, begins to wish to guide and feel responsible for you.[10]

Meanwhile, on September 10, Roger's favorite, Aunt Addie, died after a short illness at her home in New Canaan, Connecticut. Family and friends, including many of the dramatis personae of the Sessions divorce, gathered at the graveside: Ruth Sessions, Catharine, Roger's sister, Hannah, with her husband, Paul, and Roger's brother, John, with his wife, Doheny—and Barbara, who happened to be on a visit at Hadley. On September 13, Doheny (who had needed to "learn how families are run"[11]) wrote to her brother-in-law at the TY Ranch in Nevada:

> We have had very nice times with Barbara who was on her way to Washington. And there she was at Aunt Addie's funeral with us. I have never seen B. so well. Catharine—Hannah & Paul & the boys . . . were there too which was nice but very tiring for Granny who of course does not like to admit it. But she has reacted badly in the past few days & says she didn't feel strong enough to write to you herself . . .
>
> Your mother has had a very good summer really but is having a hard time just now with her book & feels the lack of strength to put across what she feels essential—when the editors want to cut.

It does not take a large leap of speculation to imagine why the old lady does not feel up to writing about an intimate family gathering that includes Barbara but not her soon-to-be-divorced-husband, Roger. Is it likely that Ruth had not learned or guessed something of what was being withheld from her—something known to those closest to her in that funeral party: to Barbara herself, to Hannah and her husband, to John and Dawn, and to Catharine? Two more weeks went by before, on his way home from Nevada, her son finally wrote his very long letter to Ruth in Northampton. With the Princeton fall semester upon him, it was too late now for a personal visit to Hadley. Cousin Catharine went instead, to deal with the fallout. Roger's letter, on ISCM, U.S. Section, stationery, with its "President—Mr. Roger Sessions" on the letterhead, follows in full:

Salt Lake City
Wed. Sept. 23

Dearest Mother,—

I am *en route,* as you see, having started from Pyramid Lake this morning. It was a rather wonderful trip, though a long one—wonderful scenery in Nevada, though some dreary desert country too; then over the Utah border the Salt Desert, which is quite extraordinary—the salt looks like snow of course, & the whole effect is of a most wintry expanse in the boiling sunlight.

Yesterday my case was tried, of course; the trial amounted to nothing at all, & though I had dreaded testifying, I did not mind at all in the end. It was merely a matter of testifying in the most cut-&-dried way the facts as alleged in the "complaint"—nothing at all difficult. I felt that the really difficult parts, for both B—and myself, had been fought out by each of us, long ago—& that this was no more than a formality.

I had such a really dear letter from you when I got home.—My quartet was not "turned down" by any Harvard committee—it was in fact to have been played. But the Quartet that was to play it found itself swamped, & did not feel that they could do justice to it. I had a charming letter from Mrs. Coolidge who is having it played in Geneva and in Mexico City this year, by a better organization than the one that played at Harvard. I had quite a scene, for in a previous letter I had a little the impression that she was going back out of paying for it! but apparently I was mistaken—she hasn't paid me yet, but asks me to wait a little while—she will pay me all right, in any case.

I am sorry you had ~~a~~ disappointments about the book, and quite understand how you feel. Only do remember, what I have to remember every time a work of mine is performed, that the public is far less aware of details than the creator is—the main thing is that the substance of the work is there. I sympathize so much with what you say about reviews & advertising & your desire to get away from it all! One simply has to remember that nothing that is said about ones [*sic*] work really has anything to do with it, & to realize that it is perfectly capable of holding its own in the world.

And now I am writing to tell you of a very serious decision which I have made this summer. I must ask you to read everything I say; for I know that when you really understand it & what it has meant, & what it will mean in my life, it is going to make you very happy for me & for all of us. Barbara has known about it for some time; I told her of its possibility back in May—& I have told Catharine about it too. But as long as it was only a possibility I did not want to bother you with it; & later I planned to tell you only on my return, when I could see you, & talk to you about it. For I know that if you did not understand, at first, it might be very hard for you to adjust yourself to it; & I wanted to help you as much as I could. But the other day I wrote Nan as frank & detailed an account of the whole thing as I possibly could. She wrote me a really wonderful letter in reply; but said she thought you were more or less prepared, by things Barbara and Catharine had said to you, for it & that you would rather have the news this way, especially since I can't get to Northampton just yet.

So—I am writing to tell you that in two or three months I expect very quietly to be married again, and to tell you the whole story of my experiences, both inward and outward, that have led to that decision. You will see that it has been very seriously made, & not easily or lightly in any sense of the word—as indeed in view of my whole situation & the way I have felt about it could not possibly be.

The girl I am going to marry is Elizabeth Franck, a girl of 29, with a Dutch father who I believe is the great-nephew of César Franck. She has grown up in the West, however, & her home is in Spokane, Washington. I became first acquainted with her last summer; she was my most intelligent pupil at Berkeley. Quite by chance in a conversation after class one day, we found we had many ideas & points of view in common, & fell into a very pleasant & easy comradeship, with nothing remarkable or emotional about it. We went together to see the lights of San Francisco, & sometimes had dinner together—the first time we dined together I told her a lot about Barbara, & she was so very sweet & understanding that I finally showed her very much of what I was feeling at that time—that the one thing I was really hoping & living for was for Barbara & me to really resume our life together. Lisl (that is a nickname she acquired in Austria in the course of a winter she spent there some years ago) helped me encouraged me more than I can say, at a moment when I need [*sic*] it badly & when she left San Francisco I felt that I had made a real friend, even though we had no particular idea that our paths would ever cross again. We did write each other, however, & after my visit to Brunswick last fall I of course told her how it came out—& she wrote me about it in a way that touched me very deeply.

In the course of the winter she wrote me that she had been offered a temporary job in the N.Y. Public Library, to exchange with a girl from there who planned to go to Spokane. She came to N.Y. at the end of January. She had planned to do some work with me, in addition to the work at the Library; but she found the latter was more strenuous than she had expected, & had to give up that idea. We did see a good deal of each other, though—partly because she knew only a few people in New York & partly because with her directness & simplicity & vitality, she did me so much good. For me, those months of Feb. & Mar. were especially difficult ones. B—& I had already talked of divorce & we had, so to speak, decided—& it was B—who favored it first. But I was having a very hard time indeed being sure what I really wanted, & wondering whether B—was really sure of herself. She was in N.Y. in Feb. & the times we saw each other were infrequent and unsatisfactory & often very painful; we didn't seem to know how to act towards each other, & she was obviously not wanting to come too close to me or to encourage me in any way. Her attitude only served to make me more unsure of myself & though I could not really envisage a return to our life together, I simply didn't feel her as yet to accept the decision we had made. It was a very complicated state of mind & I won't even attempt to explain it to you. After she left I went through a still harder time—& I kept feeling as if it would be in some way failing Barbara if I let myself accept what she so plainly wanted. It was then that I wrote her asking her to talk to me again. She wrote me that she would do so, but that she was sure her decision was final. As a matter of fact what was troubling me at that time was not the real desire to go back to our life together, but a possibly exaggerated & even unhealthy feeling of responsibility towards her. Finally I saw how perfectly sterile this was, & how hard it made things for B—& "snapped out of it."

You will be tempted to think, I know, that I fell in love with Lisl "on the rebound." As a matter of fact it was nothing of the kind. I have many women friends—good ones & attractive ones, & I have been constantly on my guard against that even since B—& I separated. Especially in Lisl's case I have searched my feelings very deeply. You see, in the usual sense of the word I didn't "fall in love" with her at all; there was no sudden feeling of attraction or romance or glamour at all. Just a great simplicity & frankness between us, a capacity for enjoying things & laughing together, & a very beautiful understanding on her part. It has brought me security and peace; & even her Dutch sense of order & management was very soothing & beneficent, when I should have expected it to be irritating. As I found, simply, that I was growing to love her very deeply—

And it took a long time even though I was convinced that Barbara really wanted the divorce, for me really to be sure that I wanted to marry Lisl. When we first seriously discussed it as a possibility, if only in a tentative way—& up to the time just before I went to Nevada we were both agreed that either one of us might perfectly easily decide against it. When I brought her to Hadley, on the only weekend she expected to have free, I was just beginning to recover from the bad time I had in March; I had talked so much about Hadley that I wanted to show it to her, & I also wanted to see her on those surroundings, which were of course quite new and strange to her. She met John and Dawn, of course, but she was rather subdued, & it was so very casual that I doubt whether they got any idea of her at all. Later—& we were much further along then—she had another free week-end, & I took her to Boston to see Catharine. That week-end was a real success. C— will tell you how much she liked Lisl & how much good she felt L— was doing me. Undoubtedly these two visits helped me to decide as I finally did; as did also the beautiful time I had with B— in May; I had told her about Lisl of course before; & in May, after I had absolutely assured myself of what she wanted, I told her of the possibility that I might marry Lisl. She knew then, as she had always known, that she needed only to give me a sign in order to bring us back together—but she had not given me that sign; & when I told her about L— she talked with me about it as if it were the most natural thing in the world, & we even laughed about it together. I realized then, as I had already done before, how absolutely separate are the past & the present; & what a mistake it is to confuse them; & I knew—as Barbara said, very seriously—that for both of our sakes—B –'s and mine—I must absolutely try to look towards the future, & plan my life afresh; and my struggle was then simply to do that—to let the past be what it has been, & keep it & cherish it for what it has been, but to look resolutely towards the future, & determine to make it still better.

I am not going to spend time on many more details—I'm writing now in Cheyenne, & I find that, at the rate at which I am traveling [?] I simply have to conserve my energy & my eyesight—even though I've adored [?] this trip, thus far, far better than any other I've ever made—And I know so well that with your real genius for understanding you will see what an absolutely genuine & [illegible] thing this is. If it were not so I would never have had the courage & strength to make the decision to marry again; it has taken courage, & real thought & effort. For of course I have had to be sure, above all, that I had something genuine to give to Lisl. I can only say that, while it took us both a long time to decide, I have not had a moment's doubt or fear since we did decide.

You see—she had planned, after her work finished in June, to go to San Francisco to spend some time with a married brother. To our embarrassment, David Diamond at the very last minute was offered a commission to go & work in England for the summer—it was a splendid opportunity for him—Lisl & I finally decided that she could go with me alone perfectly well—we made the trip of course in the strictest decorum, which we carried to such lengths that it became a little ridiculous at times! And a transcontinental automobile trip is a strain on the best of tempers or relationships, especially driving through the heat of the Southwest, which is of course something unbelievable. We had the best chance in the world to get thoroughly "fed up" with each other—and yet that trip is a really beautiful memory. We had every chance to talk, and when we arrived we knew each other far better than before we started.—I saw her a good deal in S.F., though of course not every day; & we decided definitely to postpone any decision till just before she had to leave. At that time we had a talk & decided quite simply that we needed each other, & that we wanted to marry as soon as we could make our plans, and as soon as my divorce had been over long enough so that the divorce & the re-marriage would come, so to speak, as separate pieces of news, though we want the latter to be as <u>quiet as possible.</u> She was to go back to Spokane & take up her work again, & as soon as I felt ready financially—with all my debts taken care of so that we can be see our way clear,—I was to let her know. That is the way it stands. Of course, the fact that she is so far away makes things a little complicated as far as the actual date is concerned. We both feel that after all that we have been through, we want to feel, established as soon as possible, & so, as soon as I get back I plan to go over all my affairs & let her know how they stand. She is a splendid manager & is going to help me incalculably much in that way—in fact she has done so already. So I shall probably be married sometime before the end of the year—whether late in November or sometime in December I don't know. She is of course terribly anxious to hear my concerto, & though I don't know whether this will be possible, we both hope it will be.

Of course I will have a very different kind of life than I have had before—built on a different basis, I mean. I know that it is not disloyal to Barbara, & what she & I had together, to recognize that in many ways my life with her was not <u>right.</u> If it had been, perhaps we would not be divorced—when I say not right I mean, of course, not always built on the solidest of bases. What I truly want, now, is to build my future life absolutely solidly; & it is the fact that Lisl can & will help me to do this that has, perhaps almost more than anything else, influenced my decision to marry her. Otherwise you see I would never have let myself feel towards her as I do, under the circumstances. You will see that in spite of being unusually intelligent & warm-hearted she is preeminently a very normal American girl, with, as the saying goes "no nonsense about her"—and that, alone, has done me incalculable good & given me peace & security that I sorely needed.

I'm not going to write more now. Nan wrote me that you said you hoped I would marry again if I found the right person—& I <u>know</u> that when you know Lisl you will feel that I have found her. I know that you will love her & that you will be glad of what she will bring to me. And I know too that what both Nan, who has seen Lisl's picture, & what Catharine, who has seen Lisl herself, & seen her with me, will tell you, will help you to be reassured if you need reassurances. And don't forget, either, that—with all my faults!—I am forty years old, & have seen a good bit of the world, & that the experiences of the past two years, alone, instead of leaving me raw &

exposed as I have often felt, have in reality toughened my fiber & made me much stronger.

So I shall close this letter, which is so important to me, & wish it Godspeed. I know I have your love, & I pray also that I may have your understanding in this—I know I will have it eventually. Dear love to you—and everything good, always.

Your devoted
Roger.

Generations of Puritan ancestors had their say in this remarkable feat of camouflage by disclosure—even though quite a bit of it seems patently untrue. Undoubtedly he did agonize over the decision to marry Lisl. Undoubtedly as well, that decision was made long before he introduced her to Catharine and his brother or wrote to his sister—what indeed would he have written about Lisl but that very news? It is not clear how he had managed a visit to Hadley, with Lisl, without his mother's knowledge.

It is an impressively artful letter, from its chatty beginning to its account of Barbara's determination and to his own faith in Ruth's understanding—"eventually." And it appears to have served its purpose. Far from pleased, Ruth Sessions had to accept an accomplished fact. Hannah, deeply involved by then in her husband's participation in the 1936 campaign for the governorship of the state of New York, writes in haste: "Mother has had your letter—but no comments!" In her rush she signs the letter, "Best love, ~~Hannah S. Andrews~~ Sister (!!)" And it was left to Cousin Catharine to fill Ruth in, tactfully, on Lisl's earlier visit and to write the comforting report from Hadley that Cousin Roger needed:

Dearest Roger

How lovely to hear from you today—and to have you writing as you did—making me feel that I had really mattered in this moment of your life! You have seemed so astonishingly near these last few days and I did really come in fulfillment of your wish to have me on the scene when there might be a chance to voice what possibly no one else could quite voice for you. If that were so I am proud to have played a part. It has all been so much simpler and happier than we've thought in our talks about it—as I remember—but you have been the one to make it so!

Aunt Ruth telephoned to me early on the morning your letter reached her and spoke so buoyantly and freely, insisting upon accepting without hesitation what you had told her of Lisl and your marriage even though she showed that the news was not easy to take. She asked if I felt like coming soon for a visit and I was really very much touched by her wanting me. I also knew that the very thing had occurred to you as possibly a help from your end. Anyhow I am so delighted that I came because it has been very reassuring in every way. We have talked from every angle and I am so im-

> pressed with the grand way Aunt Ruth has taken this very significant change in your relation to her . . .
>
> I was thankful to have had that lovely spring visit [when Catharine met Lisl]—and I hope that I've said everything as you would best like. Of course regarding that visit I said "under my chaperonage" very clearly—you will know why, and whose concern is it—but yours anyhow?[12]

Whose indeed? Nevertheless, Roger's faithful and resourceful advocate underestimated Ruth Sessions. She had indeed realized that, of all aspects of her son's marriage, "this very significant change in your relation to her" would be the part that the old lady would find most difficult to accept. That change had already found painful expression in the discovery that not only her niece in Boston but also her son and daughter-in-law in Hadley had actually met Lisl months before she herself was informed of Roger's marriage plans—by mail. Ruth's friendship with Barbara had seemed to secure for her an intimate place in her son's life and, with the increasing problems in that marriage, potentially a controlling one. Not even Barbara had shared with Ruth what she knew about Roger's plan to marry again. But before Ruth could fully work out her personal disappointment, the cause of true love suddenly won its first matriarchal blessing in a comic reversal. Writes Hannah on October 1: "Mother said of you & Lisl that 'it seems like just the right sort of match.' I think it helps that Aunt Lucy disapproves the divorce, which has made Mother fly strongly in your defense! She even talks of a Hadley wedding."

Surrender was not unconditional, of course. Ruth refrained henceforth from outright opposition, but her misgivings soon found a ready target in her son's still very fragile financial situation. His twin appointments at Princeton and Berkeley offered little more than basic security within very modest limits. Money remained in such short supply that a thirty-dollar loan from Cousin Catharine was repaid in ten-dollar increments—with a very gentle reminder needed some time after the first installment was due.[13] Aunt Addie had lent him $100 earlier in the year.[14] Finding accommodations at Princeton involved some difficult financial planning, particularly since, with summers committed on the West Coast, the need to sublet during those months ruled out a normal one-year-minimum apartment lease in Princeton. Bed-sit digs, adequate for young single faculty, would no longer do. The young couple would need a separate sitting room for Lisl's use while her husband worked in his study.

They were fortunate to find a small house some miles out of town. But getting a whole house instead of renting a small apartment in Princeton resonated as the symbol of a self-sufficient, independent household, a threat to Ruth's role in her son's life—which indeed it was. One more time she asserted her raw capacity for control by questioning the wisdom of committing slender resources merely to assure a young bride's comfort. Roger responded patiently. In a long letter he compared the cost of bachelor digs in New York with the anticipated savings in renting his little house outside Princeton:

> The house sounds more expensive than my N.Y. room—but when everything is added up it turns out to be actually a good deal cheaper, since I had to hire a piano for 12 months at $10.—and board my car at $7.—besides. And in Princeton I found nothing that would have been possible at less than $55.—a month, & no prospect of less than a year's lease, with subletting [for the summer] quite out of the question since nothing is going on here.[15]

The uncomfortable oddity, accepted without demur by a dutiful forty-year-old son, of having to justify the decision of renting a house for himself and his new wife is compounded by what may have been an even odder stipulation with which Sessions began that letter:

> Your letter came yesterday, & I kept my promise & didn't read it, as I promised you not to do. But truly I want you to know that even if I had read it would not have done any harm, in any way. You see I know so well how you will feel about Lisl & even if something I say or leave unsaid makes you temporarily worry for fear I am not doing my part. I know so well that I can reassure you, for I am doing it, dear mother, you see—And you see too, there is no reason at all why you and I shouldn't, really, understand each other better than we have ever done, & I for my part am determined that we shall, & will do everything that I possibly can do in that direction.—

Roger and Lisl were married on Thanksgiving Day, 1936. Ruth accepted what she could not change. She knew, of course, that her own special relationship with Roger, into whose work and success she may have infused some of her own ambitions, had been, for a long time, an illusion. Even if she accepted at face value his reasons for keeping her unaware of his plan to marry Lisl ("as long as it was only a possibility"), from this most intimate decision she, alone among close family and friends, had been excluded. In the life of her son, a sea change had come about, a profound transformation of the way he lived and worked and saw himself as a man and as a composer. In the second half of his story, there would be no matriarch but a fully supportive wife.

CHAPTER 12 Something More

a) Nature holds all of what we find in ourselves
y) and something more.
b) Our Self holds all of what we find in nature
z) and something more.
b) can discover a),
z) can only surmise y).
a) is discernible through direct observation, though
y) is not.
Nevertheless, y) may be made manifest through active involvement.

—GOETHE,
Allgemeines Glaubensbekenntris

In 1815, on the threshold of a century supremely confident in man's ultimate ability to master the world through objective observation and scientific discovery, Goethe proposed the preceding correlation among observable nature, the spirit within, and . . . *something more.* He concluded that "active participation" (*handeln*) would be one way of discovering y), that "something more" *in nature,* but he failed to elaborate on z), the "something more" *within* ourselves that is not necessarily reflected in the outer world.

"Search within, and you shall discover everything; and rejoice that there is an outer reality in nature which says *yea* and *amen* to everything you have found within you," he admonished elsewhere.[1] No mention here either of the elusive *something more* that would include his own most particular sphere of accomplishment, the domain of the creative artist. Writing at the watershed between Europe's classical tradition and the dawn of a new age of empirical observation and discovery, the German poet may have taken it for granted. Twentieth-century composer Sessions had done so as well but had yet not found a way to make it work for him.

He had experienced the essential ingredient of "something more" *within,* z, in Pisa, when the musical idea of his First Piano Sonata came to him, unbidden, in the numinous form of a chord that was to inform the entire composition. Nevertheless, in the years that followed he soon learned that for all his periodic privileged contact with that fertile taproot within, "something more" was needed, the y) outside his own self, which would manifest itself as the result of active involvement. He had been not actively involved in anything much since his teaching days in Cleveland.

New York might have offered that opportunity. He may have been "a kind of celebrity," a status grudgingly acknowledged by some, but he felt no real connection with the musical Babel that was the natural habitat for so many of his colleagues. Local musical turf wars that had developed during the years of his absence in Europe—and would once again dominate music in New York at midcentury—were obscured during the two years of Sessions' residence in the city by the arrival of Europe's most prominent composers. But the New York fraternity of composers had always relished noisy disputes over musical territory.

To his often-expressed bewilderment and chagrin, Sessions belonged to a generation of composers that, more than any other, seemed in constant pursuit of adherence to one *school* of composition or another. Schoenberg, recently arrived and still struggling to find an economic foothold in a newfound land, nevertheless enjoyed the benefit and following of his powerful mystique as founding father of the "Second Viennese School." Young composers like Copland and Thomson—also recently arrived, but from Boulanger's Paris—identified with the so-called neoclassical period of Stravinsky's current writing and proclaimed the establishment of an "American School" of composition. For New York's musical factions, an identifiable "style" of composition determined a composer's relevance to the contemporary musical scene.

It would soon become difficult, even for performers like myself, to maintain friendships with composers on the "other side" of this great divide, and the strictures cut both ways. At ISCM meetings one learned to ignore abusive references to "board members who serve right-wing[2] musical organizations like Juilliard." At the same time, as a composition student of the gently mulish Wallingford Riegger, one could but wonder in respectful silence about remarks concerning Stravinsky's "cheapening of his great gifts by writing derivative rubbish like *The Rake's Progress.*" The language used by Varese about many of his colleagues is hardly printable. But what made all this abuse relevant was the very real harm done, unhesitatingly, by one side to members of the other. Composers and prominent performers in New York had every reason to be on their guard, and mutual hostility, disguised as artistic conviction, was the rallying cry for very effective use and abuse of political power among the warring factions. Arguably in self-defense, members of the musical establishment had much to answer for in the growing alienation of a musical public that remained all but ignored in these internecine quarrels among professionals about compositional theories masquerading as guidelines to the music of the future.

In his brief stay as a resident New York composer, Sessions never experienced the full flowering of infighting that eventually involved major musical institutions and the press. Perhaps the most egregious cabal, twenty years on, would be the deposition of conductor Dimitri Mitropoulos as music director of the New York Philharmonic. His devotion to the cause of contemporary music led him to include many new works in the subscription series of his orchestra and to use unsold services in the players' contract for public readings of new works, a policy that did not win him popularity contests among the public at large or, for that matter, the orchestra itself. But it was his relative neglect of the "right wing" among American composers that resulted in a carefully planned campaign to remove him from his post. In his memoirs, Howard Taubman, chief music critic of the *New York Times*, candidly refers to Dimitri Mitropoulos as "the conductor on my conscience."[3]

Even in its early years, this was not an environment in which the composer Roger Sessions was likely to discover "all of what we find in ourselves" or to achieve Goethe's mysterious y)—the manifestation of "something more"—by active involvement. Toward the end of his life, he would declare, "The way I differed from most American composers: they were writing *kinds* of music; I was writing music without adjectives—including twelve-tone. I am the only American composer without feeling of self-consciousness or inferiority."[4] Hyperbole aside, the inevitable sense of isolation in the face of mutually exclusive, vociferous, and robust coalitions of composers during the midthirties in New York would have made it very difficult for him to maintain the independence he needed to find his own voice. Much as he had already rejected popular roads that were not his own, he had yet to learn lasting reliance on the inward path that had led him to the—painfully slow—completion of his few, carefully crafted works thus far.

> You see, I was very shy, I had to find myself, to gain confidence. And coming back from Europe I found America a very strange place. Some of the musical life had become quite European with the arrival of so many distinguished musicians who had fled the Nazis. At the same time some American composers seemed determined to "invent" American music by external means. I had to discover who I was and what my music was.[5]

For this, he needed "something more."

In his persuasive book, *The Gift*,[6] Lewis Hyde explores the problem of the arts in a commercially oriented society from an anthropologist's point of view. His definition of art as a "gift"—something conceived by its creator as a boon from within and then re-created, *exchanged* as it were, as a gift to others—suggests an interesting relevance to music in our own culture. Hyde illustrates the second half of this process, the essential importance of the gift *exchange*, by a reference to the annual gift-giving rites among Northwest American Indians, the potlatch ceremonies of the Haida, the Kwakiutl, and the Tlingit. These were fishing tribes, depending for their livelihood on the annual upstream migration of salmon along their rivers. The secure, seasonal nature of their work provided for an off-season period of leisure, in which remarkable carvings and other products of highly developed craft *not* connected with provision for food and shelter were created. These objects were the basis for annual ceremonies of a gift exchange, with the essential provision that gifts received at one festival had to be given away again at the following year's event in order to retain the beneficial potency of the ritual.

A comparison to Western musical life of the eighteenth century comes to mind: when composers were also their own performers, the social function of their works, the "giving away" the results, was consummated by themselves, in performance before a socially captive but more or less willing audience. The modern equivalent, in which the composer/performer has been replaced by a performer other than the composer, excludes the active participation of a work's original creator in the actual "gift exchange," the performance. As Sessions himself remarked, a musical work remains incomplete unless it is performed, with the performer "an essential element in the whole musical picture."[7] But as the gradual separation of the respective functions of composer and performer during the nineteenth century became an accomplished fact in the twentieth, there developed an unforeseen consequence: absent regular performance of his music by the composer, what about his *own* need of such a "gift exchange" in order to maintain the relevance of his creative powers by a renewed connection with those who receive his gift?

Those benefits may well have accrued in our time to a new kind of creative musician in his role as composer/*teacher*. Great teachers among the composers of our century have acknowledged the debt owed to their students in the development of their own craft. "This book I have learned from my students," wrote Schoenberg as the opening sentence of his *Harmonielehre* in 1911. Sessions was equally aware of his benefit in exchanging and developing musical ideas with young colleagues during the half-century that saw his own development as a composer while he gave of himself as a master teacher:

> The teaching of composition is essentially personal in character. The composer-teacher will exert a strong influence upon his students, who cannot fail to be to a degree impressed with his point of view. The greater his gifts, and the stronger his personality, the truer this will be . . .
>
> And yet, if the composer is really a teacher he will learn above all to respect the personalities of his pupils, and will seek to develop those personalities and not to mold them. He will take pride not in their likeness to himself but rather in the diversities which result from their maturing development. He will find it not entirely unwelcome when they differ with him . . . He must, naturally, be sufficiently sure of himself to be able to do this, and even be strong enough to let himself be influenced by his students on occasion.[8]

The haven of the university, offering shelter from the confused musical strife of contemporary New York and the assurance of a creative exchange of ideas with mature students, would supply a much-needed "something more" in the ritual of a relationship of learning in which the teacher gained as profoundly as his most gifted pupils:

> We do not in the United States possess a millennial cultural tradition within the framework of which the serious composer, whatever his personal inclinations and tendencies, can place himself. Rather the composer must find his way among a maze of conflicting tendencies, opinions and influences of all kinds, many of which seem more apt to confuse than to help him. He must do this in a society whose public cultural enterprises are supported in very large measure, not by disinterested private patronage nor yet by a governmental department of cultural affairs, but by a competitive commercialism, which, while certainly beneficent in many of its effects, is necessarily compelled by its very nature to be mindful of its own aims, aims which are neither inherently nor inevitably those most calculated to foster healthy creative development . . .
>
> [The composer] . . . needs the experience and knowledge of other standards—not for the purpose of shielding him from contact with competitive standards, but showing him that he is, as a serious artist, subject to far more difficult ones, and must grapple finally with problems for which there are no easy solutions. I believe that in our society, as it is developing in the greatest crisis civilization has yet encountered, the university is the only place where such standards are to a certain extent still upheld; and that its importance and its obligations are growing rather than decreasing as a result of that fact.[9]

Of that quarrelsome lot of American composers in New York, few chose to follow Sessions' example. The great magnet of the country's cultural capital held its own in place and provided them with occasional opportunities for performance, periodic public attention, and, of course, perpetual public controversy. The trek to the university seemed to many an irreversible retreat into academic hinterlands, an unreal landscape dominated by luxuriously secluded ivory towers. Ironically, that very departure was led by the celebrated European émigrés: Schoenberg to the University of California, Hindemith to Yale, Krenek to Vassar, and Milhaud to Mills College, among others. Equally prominent at the time, Weill and Korngold opted for Broadway and Hollywood, respectively, but were negatively absorbed into their new environment.

In addition to offering shelter and support to composers in an increasingly business-oriented musical life, American universities during the second half of our century would become sponsors of musical performance in their own right. Led in this instance by major conservatories, whose gifted young performers provided not only concert series on a high level of proficiency in the orchestral field and the increasingly endangered species of chamber music but also opportunities to perform contemporary music without the commercial restrictions on rehearsal time or the dependence on box office receipts. In the performance of new works, the best of these student ensembles compared favorably with professional forces. Charles Rosen, in *The Musical Languages of Elliott Carter*,[10] writes that Carter's Double Concerto for Piano, Harpsichord, and Two Chamber Orchestras received its best performance from students of the New England Conservatory. As conductor of that performance as well as of performances of this work with first-rate professional forces,[11] I daresay the eventual enthusiasm of young performers (early rehearsals were something else) added a dimension unmatched by even the most successful music making of more experienced professional players.

It must be added, of course, that even a first-rate student orchestra is at a built-in disadvantage compared to a professional ensemble. Because of the transient nature of its membership, even the best conservatory orchestra has no repertoire. Every work performed by the ensemble will be encountered for the first time by most, if not all, of its members, and a performance of Beethoven's *Eroica* will be a premiere. That handicap is partially offset by more generous rehearsal time; and since it is very rare for a new work to be programmed more than once by our major orchestras, the problem disappears altogether in the case of contemporary music. With composers gaining an increasingly effective voice in the administrative councils of conservatories and university music departments; with performance policies of fine student orchestras, choruses, and operatic ensembles being less dependent on the economic bottom line than their commercial counterparts; and with a younger audience than that of regular subscription series, the changing role of institutions of higher education around the country may well have begun to "level the playing field" for living composers to an extent barely conceivable at the time when Sessions first became a "university composer" in 1935.

CHAPTER 13 The Musical Idea II

The painter knows a great deal, but he knows it only afterwards.

—PAUL KLEE

In the spring of 1996, Edward T. Cone, one of Roger Sessions' earliest students and most eloquent disciples, gave a lecture at the Peabody Institute in Baltimore. Titled "The Silent Partner," the lecture was to feature, in the best Sessions tradition, the listener's active role in completing the composer's and performer's work with a truly attentive ear.

The scene was remarkably reminiscent of Sessions' 1949 Juilliard lectures in New York. Peabody's Leakin Hall, small but elegantly refurbished in a recent renovation, was respectably filled with faculty and students, as well as a sprinkling of distinguished-looking visitors. Like his old teacher on the earlier occasion, Cone divided his time between the piano and a lectern onstage, and we were treated to resourceful analyses of examples from the music of Beethoven, Brahms, and Richard Strauss, among others. In the first and most telling illustration, our visitor raised the question of whether the initial four measures of Beethoven's *Moonlight* Sonata should be heard as an introduction or as the first theme. Intuitively, like most of us in the audience, Cone had inclined to the former impression. But it appeared that we were wrong, and there followed an ingenious and absorbing line of reasoning to prove it. As promised, it did indeed make a difference to those of us listeners who took the trouble of forging a silent partnership with Beethoven.

Later we were shown the ending of Strauss's *Zarathustra* with its low pizzicato sounds of C, while a sustained B major chord holds to the end. Again, with persuasive reasoning, we were asked to let our ears reject an intuitive impression of an enveloping B major ruffled by some odd low Cs, pizzicato, in the basses. We were asked to hear Strauss's remarkable ending with a convinced bias for the key of C and told that it behooves the conductor of the work to generate a sense of that tonality at its close. As a listener to Cone's demonstration at the piano I was intrigued and might well have been persuaded, but as a conductor, hearing the *orchestral* sound in my mind, I found myself baffled. The human ear is unlikely to favor those very low, plucked Cs over a sustained B major chord. These pizzicato notes might provide a disquieting reminder of the famous C major sunrise that opens *Zarathustra*, but surely like something no longer relevant or attainable. "The setting sun and music at the close"—nothing short of rewriting Strauss's score could convincingly tilt the tonal balance of this ambiguous ending in favor of C, I felt. But the unsuccessful tug of the ear, away from an already-established final dwelling place, might well be reinforced, as suggested, in performance.

Sessions loved to tell of an argument he had with a distinguished colleague, musicologist Manfred Bukofzer,[1] at Berkeley. Their discussion involved the concept of polyphony. Sessions held that the ear favored the outer voices of a musical work, including a polyphonic one. Replied the scholarly Bukofzer: "The ear has nothing to do with it!"[2]

The glee with which the composer remembered and repeated the famous "-ologist's" unhappy (and surely unintended) dictum never seemed entirely free of personal frustration. For one who spent years of his maturity as a composer in quest of the technical prescription to support particular aural requirements of a musical idea and who trained his own students in painstaking exploration and practice in the use of appropriate techniques to bolster their musical intent, Sessions had a surpassing distrust of the analytical approach, in isolation, as a way to "understand" a work of music. He could indulge in almost morbid resentment of reductive evaluation of his own work in terms of harmonic principles apparent in its construction. On the first page of the foreword to his textbook on harmony he declared: "I have always insisted that it is technical mastery and resourcefulness, and not this or that manner of conceiving so-called 'principles,' which is finally important . . . and that theory in the strict sense of the word is essentially without other than pragmatic value."[3]

Harmonic Practice was written in 1951, based on almost twenty years of experience in teaching a subject that lay at the root of Sessions' musical thinking as a composer. The extent to which the dictates of his inner ear and the respective requirements of musical ideas continued to override assumptions about his own practice remained as much a mystery to himself when, in his late fifties, he realized that he was writing twelve-tone music as it was to the thirty-eight-year-old in 1936, trying to make sense of the unexpected way in which his First String

Quartet made him compose: "With my First Quartet I was really very much surprised and even slightly dismayed to see myself writing the kind of music that I had to write but which was very different from my idea of myself at the time."[4]

He shared the experience of such a mystery with many major composers. Strauss's ending of *Zarathustra* would have shocked Brahms, to say nothing of Beethoven or Haydn. It seems to puzzle us still. Even granting the ubiquitous extramusical dimensions of that score, whether a composition ends in the key of C or in B is no small ambiguity. But in such ambiguity lies an important clue to hearing the music of the twentieth century, the kind Roger Sessions helped to establish—apparently much to his astonishment.

Once again in Sessions' development as a composer, the musical idea had exerted its sovereign dominion over the compositional means required for its realization. With the Violin Concerto, the craft to manage these means had to be acquired in a lengthy process of inner listening and discovering. The First Quartet, sketches for which were begun in 1933, found Sessions in enhanced command of grammar and syntax implicit in its musical idea, but its final realization did not come as quickly as he hoped. Quite aside from the obvious personal distractions of a divorce and an anticipated new marriage, it was a musical language that surprised and bewildered the composer as it came forth.

Coming so soon after the completed Violin Concerto, the String Quartet might have had some benefit from Sessions' renewed self-assurance as a composer, but the nature of its discourse, as it emerged in his work, posed new problems and suggested unexpected answers. As always, the composition of the quartet demanded its own treatment of the materials that informed its fabric. But the composer had to accommodate these demands to a point where he began to wonder at his image of himself. He had no choice, of course. The time when the structure of music was a function of the tonalities involved was long past. And while Sessions did not hanker after that function in shaping his music any more than most of his contemporaries, his own sense of tonal centers as arbiters of musical structures was so much part of his musical thinking that he accepted it as part of himself as a composer. And it remained so, in a sense, even in his later so-called twelve-tone works. Meanwhile, however, in 1935 harmonic function—no matter how subtle the means by which its direction might be masked by contrary articulation of the musical line or how ingeniously a musical line be lengthened by delaying its ultimate harmonic revelation—was still part of Sessions' musical language and distinguished it, in the composer's own eyes, from other contemporary trends in composition. But it had already come a long way, longer than he realized at the time.

Charles Rosen, in his book *The Classical Style*, demonstrated how, in the early music of the Classical age, tonality *was* the form. Classical usage expects a dominant seventh chord to be resolved into its tonic, thus producing a sense of release in the attentive ear. Failing that, there is a sense of musical frustration, setting up the listener for eventual fulfillment or even further new expectations.

Ultimately, the articulation of musical continuity[5] with additional tonal references and associative or contrasting elements provided the possibility to expand the scope and the structural complexity of a musical work, while still maintaining organic cohesion through the functional integrity of its overall harmonic framework. The nineteenth century saw a flourishing exploration of these possibilities. In the Introduction of his A-Major Symphony Beethoven introduced the keys of C major and F, far-off tonalities, which nevertheless, in all four movements, were to play a consistent and powerful role in determining, extending and ultimately confirming A major as the principal tonality while the work unfolds.[6]

Increasingly sophisticated means within the harmonic syntax soon complicated matters. The functional ambiguity of diminished and augmented chords, growing components of late-nineteenth-century musical discourse, required increasingly elaborate harmonic strategies to maintain overall tonal perspective and structural coherence. Some composers went to great lengths to fulfill that requirement, while others chose to elevate unrelieved uncertainty to the level of musical experience itself. Our best textbooks on harmony, including Sessions' own, deal with that reality.

As listeners, however, we cannot avoid the fact that a huge repertory of widely performed music—mostly of less recent vintage—conditioned our ears and our musical response long before some of us sat in a harmony class. In this we are no different from the young Sessions, to whom Bloch opened a world of inherited musical perception, or the now forty-year-old composer of his First Quartet, who found himself "surprised and a little dismayed" at the music he "had to write." As a musical craftsman he thought of his work in terms of warranted convictions about the music he had come to know—evidence that, surprisingly and even painfully, failed to accommodate some of his current musical choices as a composer.

A dilemma of musical orientation was built into Sessions' self-image as a composer from the start, and future directions reflected an evolving musical perspective over time. While at Harvard, he was powerfully moved by the music of Wagner and found himself intrigued by works of Debussy on one hand and of Schoenberg on the other. Later, under Bloch's guidance, he received solid grounding in the German tradition. Later still, however, in Cleveland, he discovered the works of Stravinsky and, to the sometime chagrin of his teacher, was profoundly impressed. The so-called neoclassic turn of Sessions' opus during the ensuing years coincided with the coming to prominence of a new generation of French composers, who willingly adopted the label and its implied aesthetic in a kind of backlash against the mighty German musical hegemony. Most of the young Americans during their European sojourn in the twenties were drawn into the French fashion. Sessions empathized, although he had avoided active membership in the Boulangerie in Paris and soon experienced a very different musical environment in Berlin.

We have already seen how, following the flash flood of European refugees that swamped New York in the midthirties, both native and immigrant composers allied themselves with one of two hostile musical camps, identifying either with Stravinsky and the new French "neoclassicists" or with Schoenberg and the so-called Second Viennese School. Most of the musical establishment in New York, including the press, favored the former. In this climate of confrontation, Sessions, who according to Milton Babbitt was very much "down on Schoenberg at the time,"[7] wrote a long and revealing article, "Music in Crisis," in which he reserves his highest praise for

> a new manner of expression, a new sobriety and at its best, as in the finest pages of Stravinsky, a new inwardness. The grandiloquent and neurotic self-importance which characterized so much of the music of the years preceding the war has, in fact, practically disappeared and is only to be found in a few provincial survivals . . .
>
> All that is ambiguous and profoundly problematical in the music of Schoenberg is to be traced to its definitely esoteric character . . . its tortured and feverish moods, its overwhelming emphasis on detail, its lack of genuine movement, all signs of a decaying musical culture, without fresh human impulses to keep it alive . . . Such esoteric and discarded devices as the *cancrizans* variation of a theme, a technical curiosity which is admittedly inaccessible to the most attentive ear and which was used with utmost rarity by the classic composers, becomes a regular and essential technical procedure . . .
>
> Such reflections, however, are necessarily but approximate and by no means dispose of this music and the problems which it raises. A work of art is a positive reality and must be considered, quite apart from the principles which are found to be within it. Thus one may reject many of Schoenberg's ideas and modes of procedure while acknowledging not only his historical position as the initiator of even more in contemporary music than is usually accredited to him, but also his work, and that of some of his followers, as in itself an important and fundamentally unassailable element in the music of this time.[8]

On the side of his currently acknowledged angels, "neoclassicists" all, Sessions' survey straddles a number of approved virtues, none of which relates to his own music except possibly in intent:

> It is idle to inquire when and by whom the somewhat sweeping and inexact term "neo-classicism" was first applied to certain contemporary tendencies. It has been applied rather disconcertingly to such essentially different composers as Stravinsky, Hindemith and Casella—composers of whom a certain more or less conscious traditionalism (not a new thing in art) is apparent, but who differ widely both in the traditions which they represent, and in the roles which tradition plays in the composition of their styles . . .[9]
>
> This traditionalism, however, can in no real sense be called a "return to the past." Rather it should be considered in the light of a *reprise de contact;* and, in spite of its prophets, essentially nothing more than a point of depar-

> ture. It was significant chiefly in that it marked the beginning of an instinctive effort to rediscover certain essential qualities of the older music with a view to applying them to the purposes of the new, an experiencing anew of certain laws which are inherent in the nature of music itself, but which had been lost from view in an increasing subjectivism and tendency to lean, even in "pure" music, more and more on association, sensation, and *Stimmung*.
>
> This traditionalism, then, was essentially a part of a new attitude toward music—new at least for its time. Music began above all to be conceived in a more direct, more impersonal, and more positive fashion; there was a new emphasis on the dynamic, constructive, monumental elements of music.[10]

In the end, he does get around to one attribute of central importance in his own work:

> Whereas the earlier tendency was to be more and more conscious in regard to a "meaning behind the notes" and to construct the music according to principles derived from this indirect and not strictly musical source, the composers of the newer music proceeded directly from their musical impulses, seeking to embody these impulses in musical ideas which should have an independent existence of their own, and to develop these ideas according to the impetus inherent in them as musical entities. In other words, with the latter the *musical idea* [his emphasis] is the point of departure, whereas with the former extra-musical considerations consciously determine the choice of the idea.[11]

With the advantage of hindsight and foreknowledge of the composer's future, one might suspect a covert subtext of the article to be "Sessions in Crisis." That a musical thinker of his background and sophistication failed to recognize the direction and development of his own work in terms of the current musical environment is perhaps remarkable but not unique—Brahms thought of himself as the Cherubini of his time. That Sessions' creative instinct proved stronger than his intellectual and even his aesthetic bias, to the point of his evident surprise and dismay at the kind of music he "had to write" in 1936—is a matter of record; but how such a contradiction underlies Sessions' lifework as a whole and how it determined the relation of his opus to the music of his contemporaries is something we shall examine briefly before we continue with the narrative of his life.

The Violin Concerto had seen Sessions at work in Rome, in Berlin, in New York, in Princeton, and, during summers, in California. The work represented, in his own view, an important turning point in his life as a composer. It was certainly the current culmination of a search for his own musical language, sufficient unto itself and capable of serving the full-blown aural image of a musical idea conceived without attendant literary or psychological association. At the same time, it also represented a first closure, a near restoration of the dark, passionate musical ambience of his incidental music to Andreyev's *Black*

Maskers twelve years before, albeit without the illustrative element of that music:

> Earlier reflections [on *The Black Maskers,*] as I look back on them, seem quite unfair to that piece now. But one is always looking at it from a personal point of view. I was a little disturbed that part of its interest seemed to be in the fact that it portrayed interesting states of mind, and I wanted to cultivate more solid virtues in my music. I suppose that was the way the whole neoclassic movement of music at the time presented itself to me, though I never thought of myself as being a devotee of neoclassicism, as such.[12]

Be that as it may, his First Symphony had certainly been a corrective move in the direction of neoclassic virtues, with the Piano Sonata, albeit a much more complex work, still able to bear the same label. The first movement of the Violin Concerto, composed in Rome, offers a similar point of departure before its author embarked on a creative journey that spans eight years of musical experience, finally distilled into four remarkable movements. The solo violin—literally solo, for the string section of the otherwise large orchestra consists only of violas, cellos, and basses—wings its way across the space of the first three movements in a long soaring flight, high above the rich diversity of the changing orchestral ground below, until it descends to lead all the forces in a relentlessly driven final dance that certainly seems much closer to the haunted atmosphere of Andreyev's play of yore than to the playful musical manipulations of the concerto's beginning. And yet what was achieved in this new work was *progression* or *cumulation*[13] over a long line of musical thought that not only maintains "the level of intensity, or interest, of movement established at the outset" but also raises it.[14] Notwithstanding the long gestation period of the concerto and even the somewhat different stylistic treatments of its movements, persuasive musical unity derives from a masterful application and elaboration of its musical idea over its entire range.

The opening measures of the Violin Concerto include all the material not only for an ever-changing pattern of thematic development but also for seemingly equivocal, if nonetheless organic, longer range connections between musical gestures, across whole sections of the work and among its four movements. Edward Cone said it eloquently, in recognizing the various levels at which such music may function, "as when a tone resolves once in the immediate context but turns out to have a different goal in the long run."[15] The three sections of the first phrase of the concerto consist of a trombone motif in stepwise upward motion (a), a jagged trumpet figure (b), and a an oddly equivocal little cadence (c), prolonged and made even more equivocal by its extension in the flutes: altogether a more complex musical idea than that of the First Piano Sonata.

The complexity of its organic implications for a large-scale work goes a long way toward explaining the eight-year span of its creation. Sessions was fond of applying to himself Picasso's famous quote: "I never experimented, I discovered."[16] He had his work cut out for him merely to discover the possibilities and

Example 13.1 Opening of Violin Concerto

requirements of that initial musical gesture above. In a wonderfully searching and imaginative analytical essay, "Roger Sessions, in Honor of his Sixty-fifth Birthday," his former student and later colleague composer Andrew Imbrie,[17] dissects that musical idea and traces some of its implications for its immediate musical environment. The reader with requisite theoretical knowledge and a desire to gain some insight into the formidable compositional complexity of this work is urged to examine that remarkable birthday gift. In the course of it, Imbrie refers to Elliott Carter's more general but, in its implications, even more thought-provoking review of the concerto. Carter recognizes the unique feature of its "over-all unification of themes"—Sessions' ubiquitous musical idea—but also points to a result that, might well have surprised and perhaps dismayed that composer as he watched the work emerge under his hands:

> There are obviously many degrees of similarity possible between phrases controlled by the same directional motif, and when directionality is used with other kinds of remote relationships such as imitation of outline, ornamentation, and simplification, directional inversions, etc. the play of these could be likened to the use of metaphor and simile that results in the fascinating effects described in Empson's *Seven Types of Ambiguity*.[18]

Ambiguity of musical building blocks with which tonality is established and recognized by the ear was already an element of Wagner's late harmonic language. But much as Sessions understood and valued what was happening in that music, he did not consider himself a compositional heir in that mold. His admiration for Stravinsky, whose early ballet scores, so fascinating when he discovered them in Cleveland, certainly did not suggest any post-Romantic yearnings for long-delayed harmonic resolutions, and Stravinsky's identification with the neoclassical movement continued to intrigue him. The Viennese School still remained suspect, not necessarily because of its way with musical materials but because of its perceived inclusion of extramusical elements as part of the message. The Violin Concerto as a whole was as far removed from Schoenberg or Berg as from the Stravinsky's current neoclassical aesthetic.

But ambiguity? The concept might seem to hark back to musical practice of the late nineteenth century, but at its most successful, ambiguity then was a means to attenuate and stretch the harmonic parameters of a work within an organic framework that was anything but ambiguous. The intellectual avant-garde of the early twentieth century concerned itself with ambiguity as uncertainty. That was what Carter had in mind and what caused Sessions to be "surprised and a little dismayed at the music [he] had to write."

Composers were not alone. Carter had alluded to Empson's field of literary criticism, but contemporary science moved in similar paths. In 1935, the year in which Sessions completed the Violin Concerto and began his Second Quartet, physicist Erwin Schrödinger published his article about a cat with which his name will probably be associated for all time.[19] Schrödinger's cat was an imaginary one. Placed in a soundproof box in which a radioactive source could randomly activate a poison gas device, the cat faced instant death *if*, during the brief moment the apparatus was switched on, the built-in poison device was triggered by the decay of one atom. Since the sequence of radioactive decay occurs entirely by chance, it can be predicted only statistically. The device in Schrödinger's box was timed so that there would be a fifty-fifty chance of decay—instantly killing the cat; alternatively, the event might (randomly) *not* take place—allowing the cat to live. Unless he were to open the box, an outside observer would have no way of knowing whether the poison gun had fired and whether the cat was alive or dead. The result is ambiguous; the cat is half-dead, half-alive. Nevertheless, as physicist Bruce Rosenblum commented, "This does not mean that the cat is sick."[20]

Would that musical analysis were always conducted so vividly and with so much fun! Physicist Schrödinger had a problem—who but other professionals in his field would care to consider the arcane mathematics involved? But, like a composer, he wanted the widest possible audience. "If you cannot, in the long run, tell everyone what you have been doing, your doing has been worthless," he wrote.[21] The great scientists of the period were good at that. Einstein himself used plain metaphor to make the principles of his theories understandable to a general readership. "Most of the fundamental ideas of science are essentially simple, and may, as a rule, be expressed in a language comprehensible to everyone."[22] In 1938, he also used the analogue of a sealed box to illustrate the perplexing uncertainty of physical reality:

> In our endeavour to understand reality we are somewhat like a man trying to understand the mechanism of a closed watch. He sees the face and the moving hands, even hears it ticking, but has no way of opening the case. If he is ingenious he may form some picture of a mechanism which could be responsible for all the things he observes, but he may never be quite sure his picture is the only one which could explain his observations. He will never be able to compare his picture with the real mechanism and he cannot even imagine the possibility of the meaning of such a comparison.[23]

It is likely that Sessions was unaware of the conundrum of Schrödinger's cat or Einstein's sealed box and even more likely that he would have denied the relevance of theoretical physics to his work as a composer. This is not to say, however, that the theoretical physicist and the working composer have nothing in common. Both work in a world of inner reality whose eventual application in the "real" world may be immediate or delayed by decades of confirmation and proof. Some of Einstein's theories awaited physical vindication years after his death, and J. S. Bach's legacy, soon overlaid by popular musical fashions in his day, is being reexamined and argued to this day. But both Einstein and Bach knew the inner reality of their own minds, the pure world of an inner vision. And in the first half of the twentieth century, the inner vision of theoretical physicists and some composers began to project an unexpected, autonomous, and, in Sessions' case, quite unwelcome image of ambiguity on the screen of their imagination.

Who can look into the mind and penetrate the creative inspiration of a composer? We examine his text and listen to the ticking clock that is his work, and we "may form some picture of a mechanism which could be responsible for all the things [we] observe." The terminology of musical analysis may seem as arcane as the mathematical language of the new physics and often appears self-limited indeed to a demonstration of technical devices used in constructing a musical work. Public lectures and discussions among professionals may seem to take place in such a profound aura of learned mystery that even the most ardent music lover may feel that he is watching a debate among medieval scholastics. Schrödinger was right all the same: we must be able to "tell everyone what you have been doing." And while the success of analyzing a piece of music depends on who wants to know, how much, and for what purpose, the attentive listener to Sessions' First Quartet will have to trust the composer for a musical continuity within the richly articulated continuum of harmonic—ambiguity. He is not meant to open the clock:

> For it should be properly a truism that analysis, however brilliant and even imaginative, can never penetrate below the surface of a work of art. It is possible approximately—though only approximately—and valid pragmatically, to demonstrate some of the connections and syntheses that go into a work of genius, The work, however—and this is true of the humblest as well of the greatest—remains still inaccessible and mysterious, and above all unique—a deed of which the attempted reconstruction is, and must perforce always be, a mere reflection, without content or value of any genuine kind.[24]

But what about the reader? Neither a technical analysis of musical grammar and syntax nor a mere general description of a musical surface would seem very useful, unless the reader had actually heard that particular work and retained some aural impression. Sessions himself doubted the usefulness of the exercise, even with familiar works: "I can imagine no duller, and certainly more laborious, reading than someone else's technical analysis of a piece of music."[25] To the extent, however, to which a composer's works represent major experiences in the course of his *life,* we need to account for them, and our story of Roger Sessions' life shall continue to trace his development as a composer, as a musical thinker, and as a teacher in the reflection of his work.

For Sessions, there was nothing ambiguous, of course, about the way in which the later movements of the Violin Concerto, and then the String Quartet, took shape under his hand according to the dictates of their enlarging musical ideas: "It must not be forgotten that a living seed contains not only the possibility, but the determining elements of organic development along a certain predestined line; it is these determining elements, and not the inert ingredients of which they are composed, which indeed make a living organism possible."[26] Written two years after the completion of the First Quartet, these words reflect a newfound, hard-won confidence in subordinating freshly acquired realization of how music works to the dictates of his imagination. There was still a difficult and sometimes uncertain way to go, but Sessions was no longer limited to what he had long considered fundamental to organically conceived music: the overriding harmonic function in a cadentially buttressed musical fabric. There were passages in the second movement of his quartet, for instance, that defied useful rationalization in terms of established tonality. And yet he insisted that he had heard and felt his emerging music in terms of the full gravitational force of tonal centers. Ambiguity—even though it had involved him in puzzling and even dismaying choices—became established musical reality *after the fact*.

Marveling at ingenious analyses such as Imbrie's of the opening of Sessions' Violin Concerto or Carter's discoveries of connective tendrils of shapes and outlines across the divide of its movements, one can hardly help wondering if the composer was consciously aware of the intimate profusion of such connections and the "simultaneous" relationships of widely separated harmonic entities, all of them traceable to an initial musical idea. One is reminded of the alleged and largely demonstrable construction of Bartok's mature works according to the Fibonacci series.[27] Can a composer's mind encompass such an apparently confining series of extramusical considerations and yet write music that is so vibrantly alive? As to the first, we really don't know; as to the second, Bartok's did.

It was during the period of his early teaching at Princeton and Berkeley that Sessions began to develop analytical terminology to suit his conceptual requirements. We have already referred to some of the terms he found useful in exploring music with his students and summarized them in chapter 7: "The Musical Idea I." A glossary for quick referral appears as appendix 2. These terms grew out of his own work in progress, of course, and proved increasingly helpful in organizing his own thinking about composition: *continuity, long line, articulation, association,* and *contrast*, among others. None of these was a new concept as such, and every one could easily be applied to any music. But to the extent that Sessions' inner musical vision had gone beyond the exclusive utility of harmonic functions as they were commonly understood, these terms were capable of reflecting more meaningfully his musical thinking as a composer and the growing insights of his teaching.

A quarter-century after Sessions' completion of the Violin Concerto, some of these concepts became part of a general technical vocabulary concerning the craft of composition: "inner relationships and necessities forming the basis of a living organism or train of thought; first of all the musical idea itself, and then the chain of acoustic and psychological necessities to which it gives rise."[28] As his musical ideas required fresh perspectives on the organizing of materials, and as accustomed references to musical form appeared more and more corrupted into formulas, the idea of the long line of musical *continuity* itself, as a formative, quickening element of a composition, was bound to emerge as the principal challenge and liberating concept. Elliott Carter observed at the time that

> Roger Sessions's music has increasingly come to grips with the most serious and important task of finding new forms for the new material. Many composers have been aware of the need to find a continuity that would allow them to translate into the most typical of musical dimensions, subjective time, the implications of the new 20th-century world of rhythms, linear and textural shapes, harmonic fields, and all manner of physical sound . . . It is not an easy thing to develop a new and meaningful type of musical continuity. It must be undertaken by slow, rather intuitive steps, since the condition of "meaningfulness" presupposes a cooperative development in the composer and some qualified listeners of a grasp of musical relationships not previously clearly recognized, coupled with the ability to test them against some standard of interest and meaningfulness . . .
>
> The significant continuity techniques, one of the explicable things that give his music its interest and importance, seem to have become mush more focused and intentional in the Violin Concerto (1931–35) than in the previous Piano Sonata (1930) and the First Symphony (1927), a fact that does not detract from these latter works of art.[29]

As a composer and fellow craftsman, Carter illustrates with persuasive examples how the shape of the opening measures of the Violin Concerto, the threefold musical idea, is organically reflected, developed, and deepened across the wide reach of Sessions' four-movement work. As a listener, he remembers "a work whose main feature is a wealth of long, beautifully shaped singing or rhythmic lines and figurations that move in very broad sweeps."

Harmonic ambiguity in much of Sessions' First Quartet is offset by carefully plotted constructive contrast: "The *large contrasts* contained in a work reveal its essential outlines and give it its largest rhythms."[30] Surely, for performers seeking to penetrate beneath the musical surface of this work, an analytical exploration of its "largest rhythms" should be more helpful than laborious classification of harmonic events so complex as to defy long-range function regardless of their constructive significance. Scholarly deconstruction will inevitably, and rightly, register ambiguity. This puzzled the composer, who eventually dealt with it as a given. Performers will have to look for the organic shapes, the creative rhythm of contrasts, and the "rhythmic downbeats" that the composer furnished and the listener is to hear.

CHAPTER 14 Teacher

Education is, in any real sense, nothing more nor less than experience, and teaching, purely and simply the directing of experience with the object of saving the student from as many wasted motions and as many blind alleys as possible.

—ROGER SESSIONS

Sessions joined the Princeton faculty in 1935, accepted the offer of a full professorship at the University of California at Berkeley in 1945, and returned to Princeton as William Shubael Professor of Music in 1953. Following his retirement from the university in 1965, he taught young composers in Buenos Aires and returned for a year to Berkeley as Ernest Bloch Visiting Professor in 1966. From 1967 until the end of his life in 1985, he taught composition at Juilliard in New York.

His beginnings at Princeton were bound to be difficult and his feelings about the new environment uncertain. He had committed himself to a taxing schedule—eighteen hours of teaching theory classes in addition to his time with composition students—but prospects of a steady, if modest, income should have tilted any comparison with his hand-to-mouth existence in New York strongly in favor of the new appointment. Of course, he also paid a price for that security. His earlier, freewheeling decade as an honored visitor among the artistic elite in Paris, Florence, Rome, and Berlin could not help but make his modest role in the fledgling music teaching enterprise at Princeton seem disappointing. Even in New York, without employment commensurate to his professional stature, he had moved in professional circles as "a kind of celebrity"; now, without any actual break, formerly close connections with colleagues on the other side of the Hudson River unraveled in a way they never had even while he lived on the other side of the Atlantic Ocean: "I saw hardly anyone in New York after I started teaching at Princeton. My father had died and I had a home of my own. I went to see my aunts occasionally."[1]

Princeton itself fell short of his expectations at first. For all of his own undergraduate frustrations with a Harvard curriculum that seemed to him a mere musical supplement "to the education of young gentlemen" and the sadly remembered words of Harvard's Edward Burlingham Hill: "We are not in a position here to give you what you need"[2] or even his uneasy memory of the disappointed Horatio Parker at Yale, such teaching of music as Princeton provided, when Sessions first joined its faculty, could not compare with the offerings of those established university music departments he had once found wanting.

To begin with, there *was* no music department at Princeton. Sessions' former colleague from Smith College, Roy Dickinson Welch, had only been invited to teach two undergraduate courses on the appreciation of music and to draw up plans for the eventual development of a music curriculum. On the strength of the remarkable popularity of these classes, Welch was offered a full-time post at the end of that academic year, and able to persuade the deanery to fund modest steps toward an expansion of his pioneer enterprise. Musical instruction remained under the respectable aegis of the department of arts and archaeology until 1949.

In his Italian Fulbright Lectures in 1950, Sessions recalled the genesis of the Princeton music department as a late example of how music found its way into an American university curriculum:

> The appreciation course usually consisted of propaganda for "serious" music, and it can be stated frankly that its true aim was often to attract as many students as possible to the music department in order to win the graces of the university administration, which in the old days frequently retained a degree of skepticism regarding the legitimate place of music in the university.[3]

Welch proved to be an effective spokesman for his group and, in his appointments, a fine judge of the mix of personalities and professional expertise that would help in making a fully recognized music department within the university a reality. Following his early death in 1951, only five years after he had finally realized that goal, he was mourned as "father of the Princeton music department."[4]

Alexander Leitch's *Princeton Companion* sketches a vivid retrospective of those earliest years that Sessions shared:

> By 1937 [Welch's] two experimental courses had increased to seven and the original thirty-five students had grown so that one-tenth of the student body was taking at least one music course sometime in their college career. The enlarged curriculum allowed undergraduates to begin concentrating in

> the theory and history of music. Welch made several distinguished appointments for the future—Roger Sessions in Theory and Composition, Oliver Strunk in History and Literature, and in 1940 a one-year M.F.A. program was begun . . .
>
> The phenomenal progress of the early years occurred despite the fact that there was very little money and no building. Instruction was given in the basement of Alexander Hall, the Peking Room of Murray Dodge (shared with Theatre Intime), and the crypt of the Chapel. Books and scores were stored in McCormick Hall, and practice facilities were virtually nonexistent.

When Sessions was engaged to teach Theory and Composition in 1935, the excitement and the frustrations of being part of the founding team might have rekindled fond memories of his exciting years at the budding Cleveland Institute under Ernest Bloch; but he felt himself no longer the beginner he had been then, and—on a personal level—Roy Dickinson Welch was not the charismatic Bloch who had inspired a young faculty with participatory zeal. For all his qualities as a skillful planner and politically astute spokesman in dealing with the academic power structure, Welch lacked the professional esteem Bloch had commanded among his young faculty, as well as the ability to show his own unstinting support and respect for members of his own team. Milton Babbitt, who followed Sessions to Princeton for continued composition studies, claims that Welch—"who illustrated his lectures at the piano, with the same wrong notes every year"—let it be known that he thought Sessions "a crude composer,"[5] notwithstanding his evident effectiveness in the classroom.

There is no evidence that Sessions knew of this, but he may well have sensed that empathy with the most cherished part of his work was not to be expected. Much as his teaching duties now allowed him time and opportunity to write, Sessions hungered for primary status as a *composer.* Confusion between status and function was hardly a novel problem for composers, but this one came with a twentieth-century twist. Composers were not part of the academic elite on an American university campus in the 1930s. Unlike their most distinguished colleagues in the humanities, members of the music faculty depended more on their efficacy as teachers for recognition within the academic community than on the distinction of their creative work. Sessions himself would be among those who changed that assumption in academia, but first he had to understand his role as a teacher. As he had, ten years ago in Rome ("It has not been wholly pleasant for instance to be called always, in Roman society, a 'student' at the Academy, and to be asked if I have a good teacher, etc."[6]), he now chafed under real or unintended slights in an environment that saw no reason to value his presence beyond his evident effectiveness in the classroom. He clung to his status as composer as if too great an identification with his function as teacher might impair his creative integrity.

It seemed difficult for him to see that in order to gain the full benefit of the great "sea change" in his outward condition, no inward change was required, no

Roger Sessions sketches in preparation for Tristan analysis in class. Courtesy of the Library of Congress.

change of artistic identity—ever the perceived threat to the creative ego. As a result he hesitated, even resisted in some ways, to commit himself fully to a professional lifestyle that suited him perfectly and warranted the means for full employment of his creative gifts. Such rewards were not subject to approval by the professional establishment, offered abundant opportunities to use, share and exploit the great intellectual and musical booty of his wayfarer years, and only needed to be accepted by himself as a base from which to explore *something more within*. But the potential of a numinous gift exchange, "something conceived by its creator as a boon from within, and then re-created, exchanged as it were, as a gift to others,"[7] was inherent in his future as a master teacher of composers.

Other problems intruded upon his early tenure at Princeton that were hard for him to live with but needed to be solved by the institution and the society in which it functioned. Milton Babbitt's recollections of humiliating beginnings in his own teaching career at the university touch upon darker aspects of that period in America. He first applied for a teaching position in 1937 but was turned down "because I was Jewish."[8] He tried again in 1938. This time Welch asked Babbitt, "Are you native-born?" Being able to answer in the affirmative, he believes, made the difference and allowed him to begin his own long and distinguished teaching career at Princeton.

Paradoxically in a land of immigrants and in a culture that, until very recently, had identified itself with European models to a point of near self-abasement in the arts, resentment of the foreign-*born* was nothing new. When Cubism and Fauvism first arrived in America in 1913, conservative critics railed against "Ellis Island art."[9] During the very founding days of the Republic, Benjamin Franklin deplored a new German settlement in Pennsylvania. Chinese, whose cheap labor helped to lay the rails that opened up the American West, were targeted by the Exclusion Act of 1882. Refugees from the Irish potato famine who settled in Sessions' own Boston and Italian immigrants in New York and Chicago experienced public prejudice and discrimination until they were assimilated into the mainstream of American life. Newcomers worked hard for less and often appeared as an economic threat to earlier arrivals. The late 1930s, with aftershocks of the Great Depression still strongly felt, were years of some resentment about employment opportunities offered to newly arrived refugees from Europe, most of whom happened to be Jewish this time. Universities were large employers, offering highly prized jobs. There is no evidence that anti-Semitism as such informed Princeton's hiring practice, although such charges against other major universities were not uncommon. Babbitt's appointment on his second try and indeed Welch's own question argue less for racial or religious prejudice as such than for an effort, at a time of widespread economic hardship, to save valuable employment for native-born Americans.

Nevertheless, to one who had felt at home abroad, from Berenson's cosmopolitan I Tatti to the musical Götterdämmerung of pre-Nazi Berlin and who, for all his straitened financial circumstances in New York, had known himself to be among the best and the brightest young composers in a de facto international musical environment, a minor teaching position within great Princeton University's WASPish social environment seemed very confining—especially if one was a WASP: "How lonely one feels in this country, if one's ancestors arrived here in the seventeenth century."[10] Sessions was fond of quoting his lifelong friend Antonio Borgese, refugee Italian writer and author-to-be of the libretto for his opera *Montezuma:* "An American is one who was dissatisfied at home." Ernest Bloch, Swiss Jew, had been such a one. Sessions' most cherished composer friends in the future would be the Italian Luigi Dallapiccola—who had to spend months underground during the German occupation of his country because his wife was Jewish—and the Jewish Frenchman Darius Milhaud. Sessions' distaste for personal or social prejudice in any form resonated also in solid convictions based on the history of Western culture in general and its musical heritage in particular:

> It is to a large extent precisely the best of Europe which has come to us.[11]
> The great musical tradition of the Renaissance . . . was founded very largely by Netherlanders—Josquin de Prés, Verdelot, Arcadlet, Willaert, Cyprien deRore, Orlando di Lasso—of whom no one asked whether they were native Italians. The great Germans of the eighteenth century—Bach, Handel, Mozart—were never tired of studying Italian models, and they and their successors were in fact the inheritors of the Italian musical tradition, which was, in fact, European music. Vienna itself was the crossroads of European culture where currents from South and East and West met and mingled in the greatest musical culture the world has known. And French musical culture was largely, through two centuries, the creation of foreigners—Lully and Cherubini the two Florentines, Gluck the South German, and Chopin the Pole, in whose style are mingled influences from his native Poland, from Italy, and even from the Irish composer John Field.[12]

Needless to say, there were indeed other members of Princeton's first music faculty who shared Sessions' views on race and foreigners. Oliver Strunk, appointed in 1937 to teach Music History and Literature, became deeply and actively involved in organized efforts to welcome and help newly arrived colleagues from abroad. Strunk came with impressive career credentials: in order to teach at Princeton he had resigned as head of the music division at the Library of Congress and as a faculty member of Catholic University in Washington, D.C. Being a considerable "catch" for Welch, Strunk was given an office of his own—a mark of rare distinction at a venture notoriously short of space. Sessions took it as a personal affront. Babbitt recalls how, ten years later, when "Roger came racing through the corridors to tell us about his offer of a full professorship at Berkeley," he ended by saying, "And they gave Oliver Strunk an office of his own and none to me!"[13]

Contrary to the impression of Olympian self-possession he liked to demonstrate long before he eventually achieved it, Sessions, perhaps more than most composers, remained oddly reliant on his environment. For a long time his pent-up appetite for outward recognition remained in conflict with a need for its very opposite—peace of mind to undertake the labor of an undisturbed *search within.* A respected place within a musical environment that he could respect in turn would provide the remedy for his sense of professional isolation that had encumbered him since his return from Europe. The Princeton offer seemed to promise such a remedy, but playing an as yet peripheral role in a distinguished academic environment made for an unpromising start. It could hardly have been otherwise, as the changed outward circumstances were, in fact, experienced by a man as yet unchanged. His personal bearing still bore the stamp of one who had learned, during his freelancing past, to manage and manipulate outward appearance of situations to suit a desired image. He had cheerfully lost his job at the Dalcroze School in New York because "they felt I was running the place," i.e. there was merit in being fired. In his new position, with academic territory the more strongly defended for the very novelty of his professional stake in it, he devoted much of his energy to matters that concerned the outward conditions of his professional environment, rather than the inner search he had sought as a composer, the means for which should now have been at his disposal.

In an article published in 1945, Mark Schubart, an early student of composition who became dean of Juilliard in the year his former teacher left for Berkeley, remembers how Sessions,

> during his recent tenure as a professor of music at Princeton University, followed closely the issues of the day, addressed numerous meetings, served on committees . . . There were many times when music was forgotten or laid aside to make way for the larger issues which Sessions knew had to be met before any of the arts could flourish.
>
> At this point of his career, Sessions may seem a somewhat aloof figure to those who do not know him, and there are those among his admirers who wish that he would do more towards fighting the good fight for progress in music. But Sessions is a man who has fought the good fight, and is now at a crucial point in his life where he must produce without distraction. For he feels that in this production lies the proof of his validity of his endeavors.[14]

At the time this was written, Sessions had already begun to withdraw from the "good fight" in order to search within. And he had begun to write the works of his maturity. But the university, which had offered him privileged shelter from economic insecurities, could not assure his immunity from current social and political affairs. Throughout his later years as a teacher, while faculties and students throughout the United States would debate issues of the day and were able to assume radical positions the more readily since their place within the institution was not at risk, Sessions staked out his claim for the inner sanctuary he needed in order to discover that *something more* he required as a composer. His students loved him. Miriam Gideon remembers how "one day I arrived for my lesson to find the door open, no one there, and a large note on the piano which read: 'From today on, I want all my students to call me 'Roger.'"[15] The Olympian Roger Sessions had given way to the sharer of the Gift.

His manner of presentation was much the same as that of his everyday conversation: informed but informal, drawing on all aspects of his professional and personal experience, mixing organized thought and momentary diversion in quest of conclusions that could confound their apparent connection until he actually got to the point—often by a train of thought rather like free association in search of an objective, predetermined but yet to be discovered. Andrew Imbrie recalls:

> Roger's teaching was maddeningly discursive: one thing would remind him of another, this would trigger an anecdote, and so on for perhaps ten minutes. Then he would pause, place the palm of his right hand behind his left ear, and say, "BUT . . . " and would return to his original topic. The curious thing was that this topic now had acquired a new depth of focus brought about by the apparent digression.[16]

During the early Princeton years, Sessions dealt mainly with craft that *informs* composition rather than with composing as such. But even in practicing elementary harmony exercises students had to recognize and respect the inner logic of musical discourse, while their teacher went to endless trouble to ensure that the rationale not of a merely possible solution but one that suited and enhanced its particular musical environment was found. Schoenberg in his *Harmonielehre* of 1911 had demonstrated how, under certain circumstances, a longer working out might establish a sense of arrival at a new tonal center more convincingly than an equally "correct," shorter modulation. From the start, Sessions insisted on harmonic movement as a *rhythmic* event, with "upbeats" to be fulfilled in eventual harmonic "downbeats" in order to articulate phrases and establish musical continuity according to musical logic. To the extent that such logic was subject to individual insight, the training of an attentive inner ear to monitor and guide the movement of harmonic rhythm was as much part of his teaching as the appropriate manipulation of texture, voice leading, or instrumentation involved in the event.

Primacy of inherent musical logic remained the determining principle in Sessions' teaching, even in basic harmony exercises for beginners—not "right" or "wrong" according to certain rules but effective or less effective in terms of a heard harmonic rhythm. It becomes quite clear how, seen from this perspective, Sessions' way of teaching differed from approaches to musical theory most common in his time—and ours. Even in front of a class of undergraduates taking a general music course he remained a composer, teaching music from within its audible core rather its visible surface. When former members of his classes at Princeton or at Berkeley—most of whom never intended to write a note of music after they left his class, boasted that they had studied composition with Roger Sessions, they were quite truthful in a way. Their experience with Sessions may have dealt only with music chosen to illustrate his course, but their learning revealed the fundamental stuff of which that music was made and the way in which it came to be the way it was:

> A Fugue or a Sonata is not an abstraction but a living organism, and must be studied as such, in relation to the *musical content* [his emphasis] which it embodies and not to any abstract scheme. It will be found that the Fugues of Bach, all quite different in form, are dependent for their form on the nature of their themes, as are the Sonatas, Quartets, and Symphonies of Beethoven.[17]

Sessions was always the composer, and his students learned to deal with principles of composition, with musical realities relating to the work at hand, just like their teacher. The sum and substance of that approach, first published in the year before he came to Princeton in his article on new vistas on musical education, grew out of his own work with Bloch, were tested in his European years of apprenticeship with himself, and would develop but not change in fifty years of teaching to come. Beginners gained insight into the creative aspect of music, and young composers had to *earn* the liberty they enjoyed ("in whatever style") by meticulous attention to the craft and to requisite requirements that would inform their work: "The artist is free in proportion to his mastery of his materials." Sessions brought to his classes the conviction and the urgency of one who, in the midst of finding his own way, shares what he discovered with young companions who are walking the same road:

> Education is, in any real sense, nothing more nor less than experience, and teaching, purely and simply the directing of experience with the object of saving the student from as many waste motions and as many blind alleys as possible. The teacher of music, therefore, has the unique function, not of retailing abstractions, but of *bringing the student into contact with facts* [his emphasis]—facts of a demonstrable and fundamentally inexorable nature. First of all, the elemental sonorous and rhythmic facts on which music is based, and to which it is subject.[18]
>
> Such elementary facts as these are the subject-matter at the basis of harmony and counterpoint, the "rules" of which are purely devices for limiting the student, for pedagogical purposes, to the simplest modes of procedure and teaching him to make sharp distinctions of a type which would become necessarily modified by the use of more complex material . . .[19]
>
> The study of "form" in music is not, in any profound sense, a study of abstract patterns, but of living materials—of psychological entities which have their anatomy and physiology in as true a sense as any physical organism. The Fugue, the Sonata, the Variation forms arose because the ideas of composers inevitably took certain shapes, and not because of any abstract or conventional pattern which the composer concocted independently of his musical ideas . . .[20]
>
> The student of musical "form" must, then, learn above all, to hear and to grasp the inner relationships and necessities which form the basis of a living musical organism or train of thought; first of all the musical idea itself, and then the chain of acoustic and psychological necessities to which it gives rise . . .[21]
>
> For technique, in any really profound sense, is the ability to sustain and develop an organic musical train of thought.[22] . . . In other words, the primary task of the teacher is to help his pupil to *hear* straight, and then, as a consequence, to *think* straight and *feel* straight in musical terms.[23]

In order to achieve that ability, the development of the student's inner ear, to monitor and guide his realization of a musical image, became a matter of prime importance. Like a virtuoso pianist's fingers, the composer's ear required not only natural aptitude but also disciplined, practiced, and specifically directed proficiency.

> A "good ear," in terms of musicianship, is not simply the ability to identify sounds, rhythms and musical patterns accurately. It is not simply the ability to read music and inwardly hear it. It includes also the ability to coordinate sounds and patterns of sound, even on a very far-flung scale; and of course, for the composer, to conceive and construct them, with precision and clarity.[24]

Naturally, given the categorical role of the composer's inner ear, the student's aural image had to be accepted as its own point of departure. Among his young composers Sessions was the most undogmatic of teachers. He respected their ideas, insisted that they did likewise, and provided them with the necessary craft to apprehend, refine, and ultimately realize their inner vision:

> No one can possibly be a good teacher of composition if he attempts or wishes to mold the style of his pupils in any way further than that of helping them to envisage and become aware of the problems in their own work, and if necessary suggesting lines along which the solution might possibly be found. In such cases it is indispensable that the ultimate solution be at least as satisfactory to the pupil as to the teacher. Otherwise, the problem has not been really solved, nor has the pupil really learned anything.[25]

Sessions had serious problems only with theoretical preconceptions in default of the formative power of underlying musical ideas:

> Many times I have been asked by young and inexperienced composers whether a given formal scheme. thought out and planned in advance of its eventual musical content, will "work." But such a question can only be answered by the composer himself, in terms of specific musical material and the way he treats it—it makes no sense whatever in any other terms at all. If it is really a musical idea—one which has its origin in tones and rhythms concretely imagined and "heard"—it may be of some value to him, and in that case it is up to him to realize it in such a manner that it does "work."[26]

How does one "realize" a musical idea "in such a manner that it does work"?[27] "You have to work something out in your mind, compare it with the idea of it, put something on paper, compare that with what you had in mind."[28]

After careful examination of a student composition, and allowing for unconstrained participation of the young composer ("the composer decides!"), Sessions' advice centered on specific areas in the work in relation to their larger environment: "Perhaps it needs more contrast here, or it needs emphasis—the question is always, what comes next? Go a little further then, look a little further ahead: Thin out the texture here? Fatten it up there? Should this melody have a little more variety or movement?"[29] Arbitrary as such directions may appear at first sight (they are direct quotes in answer to specific questions by the writer, as suggested earlier), they go to the heart not only of Sessions' teaching but also to his way of being a composer. "The composer decides." Once one had disposed of the cookbook variety of formal construction, how else could decisions be made? Arbitrary they may seem; subjective they are indeed, as they shift the final responsibility to the composer. After all, if not on the basis of personal responsibility, under what guidelines should the composer decide "what comes next"?

We have already touched upon an aspect of Sessions' own "style" that has become entirely idiosyncratic to any of his former students who wrote or talked about their teacher's work: *the long line*. And yet, as one of the most distinguished of that group concedes, "We all knew what he meant, or thought we did. But I have heard no one attempt to describe it precisely."[30] Perhaps a great novelist's flexible command of his story line, to be culled from continuing interaction of various characters while it is woven into the fabric of an unfolding narrative, comes close. The novelist has no abstract "form" to dictate "what comes next." As with composers, there are many reports of novelists who are themselves surprised at the way in which their protagonists affected unexpected twists and changes in the story as it unfolded. A story, like the continuity of a musical composition, involves an evolving projection in time of ideas in the mind of its author. It makes for long lines:

> This concern for projection through time led Roger to the penetrating analysis of rhythmic, and especially metric, organization. His incisive and intuitive grasp of the essential role of accent in penetrating such organization was seminal. He would have us "periodize" the Beethoven and Mozart work we were studying—that is, measure the distances between important downbeats to discover the larger structure of measure groups. What with the introduction of such startling ideas in both the linear-harmonic and the metric-rhythmic realms, and in view of his informal manner of presentation, rich with allusion, anecdote, humor, and tolerant debate, it is no wonder that (during my senior year at Princeton) we spent an entire year on Beethoven's [string quartet] op. 132 without getting to the last movement.[31]

Sessions also encouraged active exploration of works by the great masters as a starting point of an exercise in composition. Babbitt recalls a typical assignment: "Take a movement from a Mozart string quartet. Find what makes it work, and incorporate that into a movement of your own—in whatever style."[32] But the central core of Sessions' teaching—as in his own work as a composer—rested firmly on a combination of essentials: active imagination and an attentive inner ear. "You work with your mind and your imagination, when you compose, but your imagination starts with your ear and is checked by your ear while you think about what comes next."[33]

One of the problems Sessions encountered during his first tenure at Princeton was the limitation of his program to undergraduates. Not only were "serious" students of music necessarily in the minority among members of his classes at that time, but even they often lacked the breadth of a general musical background he required as constant reference in his teaching. The young not-yet-department of music was making every effort to move from its origins in "music appreciation" toward a program devoted to the training and nurturing of musically gifted minds. But the numbers of students required to justify the university's overall investment in music during the early years necessarily tilted the balance of instruction toward the needs of those who chose merely to extend their four-year exploration of their cultural heritage into the field of music.

Unobjectionable as such aims are in the context of an undergraduate curriculum, the consequences for those with already well defined interests and skills in music—as well as for their teacher—were confining. Eventually, the degree of Master of Fine Arts was added to the university's offerings in music, even before a music department as such was approved:

> The study and teaching of composition is essentially graduate work of the most advanced type. Its nature, however, makes exceptional cases inevitable—students of a generally undergraduate status who through private study have achieved adequate preparation and for whom special provision must be made if the student is not to be forced into a wasteful repetition of ground already covered . . .
>
> It seems to me wholly sound both to require of the student of composition a degree of knowledge of musical history and especially of musical literature, and at the same time to allow his achievement of a certain grade of technical mastery in composition to count in an essential way toward his Magisterium.[34]

Sessions' early years at Princeton were among the least productive of his life. To blame that comparative dearth of creative results on problems in his still-unaccustomed role as a university teacher would be quite wrong. He taught brilliantly and happily from the start, he enjoyed a settled and satisfying family life, and he found ample opportunity to take stock of himself. But then there was the war, and the need to confront unresolved issues.

As with the First World War, Europe had been fighting for two years before America's active entry on the side of its allies. Sessions, who, in 1916, had been chary of his country's imminent involvement, had himself lived in Europe meanwhile, had witnessed the Nazi takeover firsthand in Berlin, and was deeply conscious of his own place in the Western cultural tradition that appeared threatened by the near victorious forces of Fascism in December 1941. As before America's entry into the First World War, there were plenty of voices warning the country not to get involved in "England's war," but Sessions was not one of them this time.

He wrote two articles for *Modern Music* that suggest a very different attitude from that of the graduate student at Yale who had alluded to Mathew Arnold's "armies on a darkling plain" in a letter to his mother.[35] The first of these articles, "No More Business As Usual," is a straightforward affirmation of his personal convictions about the composer's role in America and his particular responsibilities in the current national crisis. Beginning with "a recognition of concrete and urgent perils and tasks, and a gradually focusing determination to clear the way for the larger task of complete and effective victory," he goes on to the question of "what such considerations have to do specifically with music. Why, in fact, does one discuss music at all, at such a moment?" Making short shrift of the notion of "serious musicians having any very important connection with 'morale,'" he declares that

> it is also in his opinion childish, if not worse, to speak of 'keeping alive the flame of culture' or any similarly disguised plea for artistic 'business-as-usual.' Culture, in so far as such an abstraction exists at all, is not 'kept alive'; it either lives or dies.
>
> Fascism itself is only the logical conclusion, as it is certainly the result, of what one might all too easily regard as the dominating tendencies of our time. Its ultimate horror is not the fact that it is cruel beyond all conception but the fact that from the beginning to end it is *phony*. It is an almost inevitable product of a culture which contains so much that is phony as does that of pre-war Europe and America. This fact—the core of the present situation—is the primary key to the understanding of the war; it is the key also to the contradictions and the embarrassments of American and of so much of Allied policy, which have led us directly to our present painful situation . . .[36]
>
> For this reason it is urgently necessary that everyone—the artist no more and no less than everyone else—examine candidly the shortcomings of the present state of society, as a preliminary step toward the achievement of a more honest and more human future . . . What does this mean in terms applicable to musical life?[37]

In some lapidary paragraphs to follow, he then summarizes an indictment of what he sees as the primary failings in American musical life:

> American musical life is convention-ridden as has been that of no other modern nation . . .[38]
>
> Musical life today is theory-ridden and musicology-ridden . . .[39]
>
> Our musical life is propaganda-ridden . . .[40]
>
> We are in fact prone, in our musical life, to a kind of fetish-worship which is at best a provincial mannerism and at worst a provider of alibis. We are a "young country," so we say, without any place in European tradition—therefore our most "vital" composers are expected to write music which, artistically, or otherwise, is something less than mature. (They do not, of course, always oblige.) Or we dig into the unpretentious music of the American past, recent or otherwise, hailing all crudities and gaucheries as signs of originality and of the emergence of an "authentic" American style . . .[41]
>
> Our composers will, of course, be serving the country in ways immediately relevant to the conduct of the war. The situation is too immediate and too urgent for any thought of "business-as-usual" even for the most gifted,

> for the American composer any more than, for instance, Shostakovich in the siege of Leningrad. But in doing their share for the common cause they will not cease to produce . . .
>
> And the artist does not so much reflect the spiritual climate of his age as help to create it, in proportion to the validity and the inwardness of his product. Even the size of the public is irrelevant; the greatest art has, in fact, always been, and perhaps always will be, accessible to the comparative few.[42]
>
> The task of the American musician is, then, now as always, to *create*; to help build a really new and better inner world.[43]

A heavy burden for a composer, but a still heavier one for a man not yet entirely at ease with himself as a composer. We have already referred to "Artists and This War,"[44] Sessions' "Letter to an Imaginary Colleague," apparently caught between conflicting responsibilities of creative and patriotic priorities. Written later in 1942, it records Sessions' own change of heart following America's entry into World War I, from active pacifism to highly determined efforts to enlist during the following year. Addressing an "imaginary colleague," evidently in a comparable current dilemma, Sessions justifies mention of his own past experience

> to remind you that although, as you have hinted, we are not in identical situations today, we in 1918 had been shown during three and one-half years what war was like . . . You are now far more than the aspiring but thoroughly untried sub-beginner that I was in 1918. You have already large works to your credit, and have earned a following, both professional and lay. Above all, you have learned to know, basically at least, what you want, both as a musician and as a human being.[45]

In the body of his "letter," except for its ending, he develops ideas already contained in the earlier article:

> First of all, I am afraid that I do not feel that any of us are very good guardians of culture. For, after all, culture is not an object d'art, or a set of books, or a manufactured product made to order by specialists; rather it is the total spiritual product of any given time and place . . . Secondly, I am not referring, by any means, to only the slowest witted among us when I say that nearly all of us are still hugging some cherished status quo . . . never have we artists had so clear a vocation. For if our successors are to find a world tolerable to live in, it is a new world we have to create—there is unlimited space to be filled . . . Meanwhile we have an immediate and immensely threatening crisis to meet. In view of this, can any of us . . . do less than try to fulfill with credit and without complaint? . . . The survival of culture seems to me to depend to a far greater extent upon the ability of artists to do this than on their physical survival as individuals.[46]

By any measure, this is a strange document. There is the passionate final plea to ensure "the survival of culture [by] whatever task is assigned to us." Sessions' earlier article had argued with equal passion to renounce all cant of "keeping alive the flame of culture" or similarly disguised pleas for artistic "business-as-usual." And then there is the device of an "imaginary colleague," embellished with some very specific references: "You have already large works to your credit, and have earned a following." As the subtitle suggests, the addressee is no longer a student but has a following for his works. He is also a confidant: "[You have] hinted that we are not in identical situations today." Do "imaginary" colleagues hint? However, what "real-life" colleague would know about Sessions' conversion from pacifism to seeking active participation, even in the forces of an allied country, during the final months of the First World War? To publish an open letter on such a sensitive issue, even under the fiction of an "imaginary" addressee, about the soul-searching of an *actual* colleague (in a periodical read by a small group of mostly well acquainted colleagues) would have been extraordinarily indiscreet. It is difficult not to conclude that Sessions was his own imaginary colleague, asserting his belief in the current cause (again), while reciting the resolution of his own quandary twenty-five years ago, "because I would have been unable to live at peace with the self that had willingly allowed others to leave me behind in offering their lives in a cause in which I was vitally interested." In what follows in this open letter, such a cause is eloquently argued in terms of the Second World War—even its title specifies "This War"—but nothing we know of Sessions' thoughts at the time of the First World War supports either his vital interest in its "cause" or a belief that armed conflict offered a desirable solution.

Thus in 1942, when university populations, faculty and students, shared in the national outrage that followed Pearl Harbor, he may well have felt uncomfortable with his former notions on armed conflict. Confession was in order, confession that was also denial and might serve as a guide to an "imaginary colleague." From Sessions' youthful defense of poor grades at Harvard to his mother to announcing and rationalizing to her his forthcoming marriage to Lisl in a very belated letter, we have seen quite a few "confessions" to someone in whose eyes he could not afford to have done wrong—not only his mother's but his own.

Interestingly, the crowning achievement of his *music* would be that very presentation of coexisting contradictions, without any attempt to account for their concurrent appearance by conventional interaction or development. As a composer who lived his entire life in active discourse with musical ideas "within," Sessions was not given to psychological introspection for its own sake. He was eminently qualified, however, to recognize and re-create a Blakean "fearful symmetry" of complementary opposites when they surfaced in his special domain as a musical idea. But that was still in the far future.

The war years found the Princeton campus bereft of most of its undergraduates and many members of the faculty either in the services or undertaking emergency assignments in addition to their normal teaching duties. Sessions, by now an associate professor, resumed charge of elementary classes, "the emergency having claimed both the younger instructors and the older students."[47] He also taught classes in American history. Welch worked part-time at the Treasury Department in Washington, and Babbitt did advanced mathematical research for the Department of Defense. Personal and artistic priorities had to be adjusted to meet the demands of the national crisis. Nobody minded. But for Sessions, such treasure laid up in heaven failed to yield its expected earthly rewards soon enough after the conclusion of hostilities in 1945. Princeton, with a host of urgent financial needs and priorities, simply had no funds available just then for promoting an undoubtedly deserving and greatly respected professor in the music section of the department of arts and archaeology to a tenured position. Thus when the University of California offered him a full professorship beginning with the academic year 1945–46, Sessions left for Berkeley, "where, as a result of that institution's enlightened policy, he found ample time to compose."[48]

A number of distinguished future American composers and musical thinkers had by now learned their craft from Roger Sessions. In private lessons in New York he had taught Milton Babbitt, David Diamond, Vivian Fine, Ross Lee Finney, Miriam Gideon, Leon Kirchner, and Hugo Weisgall. Babbitt went with him to Princeton, where he received his M.F.A. in 1942. Edward T. Cone joined his class in 1936, received his B.A. in 1940 and his M.F.A. in 1942. Babbitt and Cone remained at Princeton as members of the new music department's faculty. Andrew Imbrie enrolled in 1938 and graduated in 1942. After service in the U.S. Army, both Imbrie and Kirchner joined Sessions at Berkeley in 1946.

CHAPTER 15

Family, Friends, and *Montezuma*

Jack shall have Jill;
Nought shall go ill;
The man shall have his mare again,
And nought shall go ill.

—SHAKESPEARE,
A Midsummer Night's Dream

Mar. 18, 1937

Dearest Lisl,—

This is a long-intended letter; I have thought of you a great deal, these gray winter days, & hoped that your household was running smoothly & the house not too lonely. Mother gave a very happy account of you . . .

. . . I felt rather worried while she was here, about times when she seems confused & forgetful—in fact, it would seem as if at times, for a short period, her mind was almost a blank, & then if some one from outside came in, she would "click" at once, & be her keenest self. I wonder if you noticed it. Even so, however, I feel she is so much happier living as she does, that it would be unkind to make her feel she ought to have an attendant.

Also, of course, Roger will have heard from John this last few days about his problems. We have written that we will plan to give a definite amount yearly toward keeping the place for Mother, & beyond that I think we should have a family discussion as to the matter of trying to retain all the land permanently. I wish Roger, if he can, would find time to write me what he feels on the whole subject . . .

With love always to you both,
Nan

The old order was passing, and the health and fitness of the aging matriarch in Hadley became a matter of concern for a family once accustomed to deferring to her authority. The letter from Sessions' sister, Hannah (Nan), addresses intimate concerns: their mother's uncertain health, her future financial maintenance, the eventual disposition of family property. The newcomer to whom it was addressed and with whom these concerns were shared had been a Sessions for barely five months but had already gained the family's confidence, affection, and respect. This marked the second part of the sea change that transformed Sessions' life in ways that proved to be as fundamental as his professional move to the university. An important departure for the entire clan, it would be hard to overstate its importance in the life of either the composer or the man Roger Sessions. Its name was Lisl.

During Sessions' early years of learning to be a full-time husband and family man, throughout the difficult adjustment to being a composer within an academically oriented establishment, and in a lifetime of being an artist in an increasingly indifferent world culture, Lisl's support of her husband remained total and unconditional—even when he allowed himself to be drawn into situations about which she might have felt some initial doubts. Her son was to write much later:

> When you speak of her "marvelous protectiveness" of my father I can only suggest that you have no idea of how far it went, or at what cost to her. Her ironclad precept—that with regard to my father's psychological well-being anything that wasn't part of the solution was part of the problem (a precept that if I may say so went so far as to include both her children) took over her life completely.[1]

This was new. Barbara had pursued her own career ever since she had first decided, more than ten years before, that for an ambitious young art historian the cultural riches of Paris justified a separation from her husband, whose work required the relative seclusion of I Tatti in Florence. Sessions' mother had slighted his personal sensibilities and preferences from earliest childhood, whenever she believed that it would serve his future prominence and professional success in a field that had been denied her. Ruth had succeeded remarkably well in this, but at the price of her own eventual exclusion from the most important personal aspects of her son's life. The outward display of an affectionate relationship was maintained, of course; she rejoiced in the birth of two grandchildren and lived to take pride in her son's prestigious appointment as a full professor at Berkeley a few months before her death in December 1946. But she had long ceased to be a principal partaker in his life.

New marriages that follow a failed match carry an extra burden, no matter how friendly and reasonable the separation of the previous union. Herself the daughter of a second marriage, Lisl empathized with her husband's need for sporadic absolution from uneasy feelings of guilt. She even encouraged Barbara's continued inclusion (some thought intrusion) in family gatherings and put a brave face on painful early snubs by some of her husband's old friends and colleagues. Sessions never forgot: "Nasty friends—Theodore Chanler et al—snubbed us both when I first took Lisl to the Library of Congress."[2] Teddy Chanler was now on the staff of that institution, and the snub was no small matter when her husband's First String Quartet, commissioned by Elizabeth Sprague Coolidge for the Library, came up for performance there.

But with the birth of a son, John Phelps Sessions, in May 1937, Lisl joined the ranks of the matrons, and the sense of family in that small household in Pennington, New Jersey, acquired a new meaning. Writes the proud father, a fortnight later:

> The nurse left us yesterday, & Lisl has been doing wonders in taking care of him for nearly 24 hours now. We kept Mrs. Schroeder on for some extra days, because I wanted Lisl to be able to profit by her mother's visit & to get a good rest, besides, before tackling John herself!—It did her a great deal of good, I think, because she was able to get a lot of extra practice in taking care of him—so that now she bathes him & feeds him & changes his diapers like a veteran. I am now the understudy & in another week I dare say I will be relieving her at regular intervals on the night feedings. He weighs now 8 lbs. and 10½ ounces, and it is truly amazing to see how he has developed in the 12 days since he came home. He is as active and strong a little fellow as one could hope for, with the arms & legs & back of a little athlete. Two or three times a day he cries lustily, but on the whole he is very quiet. He is beginning to push himself around in his bassinet or his baby carriage—he spends long hours—the whole day, in fact, except when he is being fed—in the latter out on the porch. Popo [the dog] is quite used to him, & we feel sure is going to be very good to him.

The arrival of daughter Elizabeth Phelps Sessions (Betsy) in September 1940 completed the new Sessions family.

Like Ruth, Lisl had grown up in an environment that neither expected nor easily allowed a woman to develop talents that were considered a man's province in a man's world. Her daughter, also Elizabeth and a prodigiously gifted woman, would be more fortunate in her own upbringing. She remembered her mother's regrets:

> My mother would obviously have been a lot happier if she could have developed her intellectual talents more—she constantly lamented the fact that in her day the only careers open to a woman in Washington state were that of teacher or librarian. She spent much of her time seeking perfection in cooking, sewing, and keeping a household—in latter years, as you may know—she did the most difficult crossword puzzles from the London Times and the Observer.[3]

But Lisl also had her own special advocate, her mother and lifelong best friend. Grandmother Franck, wife and by this time widow of a successful, if personally rather difficult, banker of Dutch extraction, was a great family favorite. Writes granddaughter Betsy:

> Urry,[4] as we nicknamed her (she had a marvelous sense of fun) influenced me tremendously—and obviously was a greet influence on my mother. She had a mixed heritage—apparently a mixture of Maine and Louisiana (?); she told me about how at age 15 she traveled miles through the snow to reach school in a small town in Nebraska. She had a marvelous common sense ("good common horse sense") and a sense of common decency. Both these characteristics rubbed off on mother, and on John and me as well. We used to look forward to her visits; as a child in California I rather frequently went to Palo Alto to visit her for a couple of days. My mother frequently commented on how nice it was that Dad was so nice to his mother-in-law and welcomed her visits. This rather surprised me—after all, who wouldn't be happy to have Urry around?[5]

Grandson John recalls the powerful bond shared by his mother, Lisl, and her beloved Urry in even stronger terms:

> I feel very strongly that anyone who didn't know . . . [my mother] before the death of *her* mother in late summer of 1962 really had very little sense of what she was like. The two were extraordinarily close (my mother was even born on my grandmother's birthday), really in many ways like sisters. Certainly I feel I was "brought up," essentially, by the two of them. When my grandmother died, a crucial part of my mother's identity and, rather soon, her vitality and ability to cope with a good many things, went with her.[6]

The young mother of that new Princeton family was a player who determined her own role, and that role revolved first around her husband's needs. She was no less resolute in pursuit of a related objective—to keep husband and household solvent and working smoothly. Lisl soon found herself the sole manager and treasurer of the Sessions ménage. Daughter Betsy wrote: "Everybody knew that my father would have been in the slammer if my mother had not been around to do things like pay bills, organize finances, keep track of dates, and so forth."[7]

Nor was the extent of Lisl's administrative oversight confined to the Sessions finances or the composer's professional obligations. Organizational skills and a firm hand were required when the whole family accompanied their famous father on major trips abroad, as during Sessions' Fulbright year in Florence, 1951–52. According to daughter Betsy, "she could be rather forbidding at times." And she had plenty of practice as the family tour guide, for there were regular shared summer holidays, reflecting Lisl's Western background and lifelong regional preference in America.

> A feature of the family's life during those years was a kind of mobility: there were always summer vacations—hiking at Yosemite and later Yellowstone National Park, stays at Lake Tahoe (in a rented cabin) and lakes in Washington state and Oregon, and so forth. I think I am correct in my calculation that by the time I was 14 or so I (we) had crossed the country by

automobile five times—never driving more than 330 miles (I think that was the record) per day. Always between Princeton and Berkeley, of course.[8]

Mobility had been a well-established aspect of Sessions' life before his marriage to Lisl, but now, for the first time since his memorable summer of 1929, professional considerations or past personal obligations did not necessarily determine where he might spend his free time. As the children grew older, especially after the move to Berkeley, there was time for shared family activities in which their father appears to have been an enthusiastic participant—and occasional victim, as John reports: "Every evening he would play catch with me in the backyard—a ritual which was terminated when I was in about the fifth grade and managed to knock out some rather expensive bridgework with a high fastball."[9]

Closer to Sessions' more normal pursuits, his son took cello lessons and eventually became a distinguished performer and teacher.

Daughter Betsy would take ballet lessons until her twenty-first year and wanted to be an opera singer. She loved horses and (with some help from the regular coachman) got to drive a horse-drawn carriage on the Champs Élysées during the family's first visit to Paris, in 1951. Later, according to her proud father, she "collected languages including Hungarian, Estonian and Sanskrit, in addition to the usual ones."[10]

To Sessions, the change in his lifestyle may have seemed one of degree at first. But when small new players appeared on the home stage, little Sessionses who required feeding, changing, and absolute respect for schedules that owed nothing to their father's professional priorities, the condition of fatherhood began to seem as fundamental as that of a university instructor who also happens to be a composer. For the first time in his life, others looked to him for their needs. He, who had been given much and had been expected to prove his worth by being a dutiful son, a stimulating companion, and a perceptive disciple of his role models in the field of composition, now found himself the designated giver in his personal life as a father and in his professional life as a teacher. These responsibilities, however, needed to accommodate a point of convergence in his work as a composer. He had expected it to be hard. Instead, far from feeling constrained by his new personal and professional surroundings, he learned to accept them as the ultimate benefit of the great sea change that had transformed his life.

How does such acceptance begin? Very slowly, like every other personal and professional discovery in Sessions' life. With Lisl's help he adjusted eagerly to his new role of paterfamilias, but he grew only gradually, cautiously, and on occasion resentfully into his new professional environment. He enjoyed the teaching, but absent an academic equivalent of Lisl in the workplace, it would take him most of the next decade to see the university as an institution that could serve his own needs while he served those of his students.

Thus the first benefits of the sea change appeared in his home life. Like most successful artists, Sessions had always given more thought to professional decisions than to personal commitments. The composer's concerns came first, and the rest would have to look after itself. Family and friends, including his amicably estranged first wife, used to provide a natural audience to admire, support, and empathize as his musical fortunes warranted and his artistic ego required. Until now, his mother had occupied the royal box in the theater of a performance that played to family, friends, and the world at large as a select audience, out there beyond the proscenium lights, but not as fellow actors on his stage. He had achieved some notable results in spite of having played, far longer than most, the role of a dutiful son, a perpetual student, and a performer of his self-absorbing life. Now, as husband, father, and teacher, he found himself in the role of provider, nurturer, and exemplar—full-time.

The new household, self-contained though it proved to be in its wide range of demands and rewards, was never a lonely one. Sessions had a talent for friendship. Shy and often self-conscious at large gatherings, he relished the intimacy of close communication, and he maintained valued relationships for life. Having chosen with care, he suffered "nasty friends" the more keenly, but most of his friendships—even the temporarily strained ones—were for life: Roy Dickinson Welch, his sometimes-difficult boss during the early Princeton years; Jean Binet, fellow student of Bloch, with whom he had shared summers in Switzerland as well as intimate personal problems such as Barbara's pregnancy; Bloch himself, of course, a lifetime champion and supporter, if an occasionally uneasy colleague; Berenson in Florence; Casella in Rome; and Klemperer, who had brought him to Berlin. Of the young Americans he had met in Europe, Copland remained close, while the Hudson River and Sessions' new life at Princeton proved to be a big divide from many of his colleagues in New York.

There is a relatively narrow window in the life of most creative artists, which presents unique opportunities for friendships among mature equals. Young adulthood was a time of learning and of receiving the benefits of experience from older masters who might eventually choose to befriend the former pupil. In later life, such roles are reversed: the mature artist, now himself the giver, may befriend younger colleagues and former students, even though the underlying pattern of giver and receiver is likely to endure in the background. Young midlife—a time that came late for Sessions—is for reaching out to one's chosen equals among contemporaries in the field.

Ernst Krenek came into Sessions' life because he wrote a book on contemporary music, and he became a close friend mostly through historical happenstance. Krenek's music, like that of other major composers of his generation—like that of Sessions himself—has almost disappeared from our concert halls and opera houses since. And yet, at the time he and Sessions met, Krenek enjoyed a substantial reputation as one of the most important living composers, particularly of opera. From the early international success (*sensation* might be a better word) of his jazz opera *Johnny spielt auf* (Johnny strikes up the fiddle) to the vast, forbidding twelve-tone opus of *Karl V*, Krenek remained a commanding figure at opera houses around the world, from the Staatsoper in Vienna to the Metropolitan Opera in New York. Not unlike the music of Stravinsky, however, Krenek's work defied facile academic and journalistic characterization. No sooner had he been classified as representative of one "style" than he disappointed friend and foe alike by adopting another—just as persuasively. By his own admission, he was often torn between an urge to write only according to the dictates of his present musical image of himself or a sudden, quite contrary notion of a musical idea (he did use that term) that seemed to prefigure the kind of music it wanted him to compose next.

In 1938 Sessions reviewed Krenek's book, *Über neue Musik* (About new music),[11] for *Modern Music*.[12] There was a great deal in this book with which he could empathize completely, and Sessions' article left no doubt of his strong regard for its author: "Krenek's book is not only the product of one of the most subtle and profound minds which concern themselves with contemporary music; it is a confession of faith, and has all the compelling force of such."[13]

Indeed, much of Krenek's critical writing on music was bound to have amazed and delighted Sessions in its likeness to his own musical perspective:

> On a superior level of musical thought, we find a still broader concept which I shall call the musical *idea* (Krenek emphasis). One might think of it as an analog of the overall concept of a work, incorporating aspects of form as well as of content . . . This is so to speak the highest level of the process of musical creation, bordering on the outer world of extramusical contents, and attaining hence a variety of impulses which, thoroughly transformed and assimilated according to the composer's inclination, find their way into his musical world within. [my translation][14]

It is fair to say that Krenek's concept of the musical idea was less narrowly defined than Sessions' own. According to Krenek, it may indeed inform an entire work and, in the creative imagination, anticipate it, but it may also encompass extramusical impulses, images, and ideas—something to which Sessions would hardly admit at the time. Nevertheless, there was a large and fully acknowledged part of the book that Sessions might well have written himself. "Krenek proceeds in the second chapter to a clear and highly interesting discussion of musical elements; he adduces illuminating and original conceptions of the nature of the musical 'idea,' 'language,' 'articulation,' 'binding elements,' and 'form.'" Much of this seems to anticipate concepts that Sessions himself articulated, ten years later, in his Juilliard lectures.[15] His current reservations about Krenek's musical philosophy, however, centered on the book's polemic on behalf of the twelve-tone system:

> In a remarkable passage Krenek demands not a "natural" (*Naturgegebenen*) but an intellectually determined basis (*Geistesbestimmten Voraussetzungen*) for music. This writer's antipathy for the twelve-tone system is expressed precisely in these terms, provided that by "nature" is understood not only

> physics but the response of the human ear and spirit to the simplest acoustic facts, He is profoundly out of sympathy, therefore, with the conception which Krenek boldly avows, of music as an abstract system like geometry. On the contrary it seems to him that its human meaning—and this has nothing to do with "success," "conformity," or any of the current and more pretentious synonyms—lies ultimately in the fact that elementary musical phenomena as the fifth, and the measurably qualitative distinction between consonance and dissonance, are psychological as well as physical facts, out of which a whole language has grown, and which even in music based on the twelve-tone system seem often more powerful binding forces (*Relations-momente*) than those inherent in the system itself.[16]

But for all his declared reservations about Krenek's twelve-tone argument, Sessions sensed a kindred spirit. The chance to discuss with a distinguished colleague such concepts as the autonomous role of the musical idea as a central matrix of a new work promised a welcome diversion from the internal politics of a Princeton music-department-to-be under the aegis of arts and archaeology. And he saw to it that such a chance should come his way.

In 1937 Krenek first visited the United States with the Salzburg Opera Guild, for whom he had adapted Monteverdi's *L'incoronazione di Poppea* (The coronation of Poppea). In the following year, the year of the Sessions review of his book, he came back to perform some of his own work and, as a last stop before returning to his native Vienna, accepted Sessions' invitation to visit Princeton and to play his Piano Variations for colleagues and students at the house on Carter Road. One must assume that the visit was a success, for the two composers parted on very cordial terms, with promises to stay in touch. Then history took a hand. On his way back to Austria, Krenek stopped over in Amsterdam, where he learned that the Anschluss, merging Austria into the German Reich, had just taken place. Clearly Vienna was not a good place now for returning Jewish citizens in general and for the twelve-tone "cultural Bolshevist" composer of the politically unacceptable new opera *Karl V* in particular. Krenek decided to come to America. His urgent appeals for help in securing employment in the States—one of the conditions upon which immigration visas were granted at the time—included letters to his new friend at Princeton University. Sessions wrote letters on Krenek's behalf and helped him to secure a teaching appointment at Vassar College. With none his own students quite ready for friendship on equal terms and with mature colleagues such as Darius Milhaud and Luigi Dallapiccola still in his future, Sessions soon felt closer to Krenek than to any other composer at the time. Upon his own acceptance of a professorship at Berkeley, he tried—unsuccessfully—to secure the Princeton post for him. Two years later, Krenek moved to California himself.

Another friendship, which dated back to the first weeks following Sessions' return from Europe, profoundly affected his own work for many years to come. Antonio Guiseppe Borgese, as future librettist of Sessions' opera *Montezuma*, became his partner—and sometime sparring partner—in the planning and de-

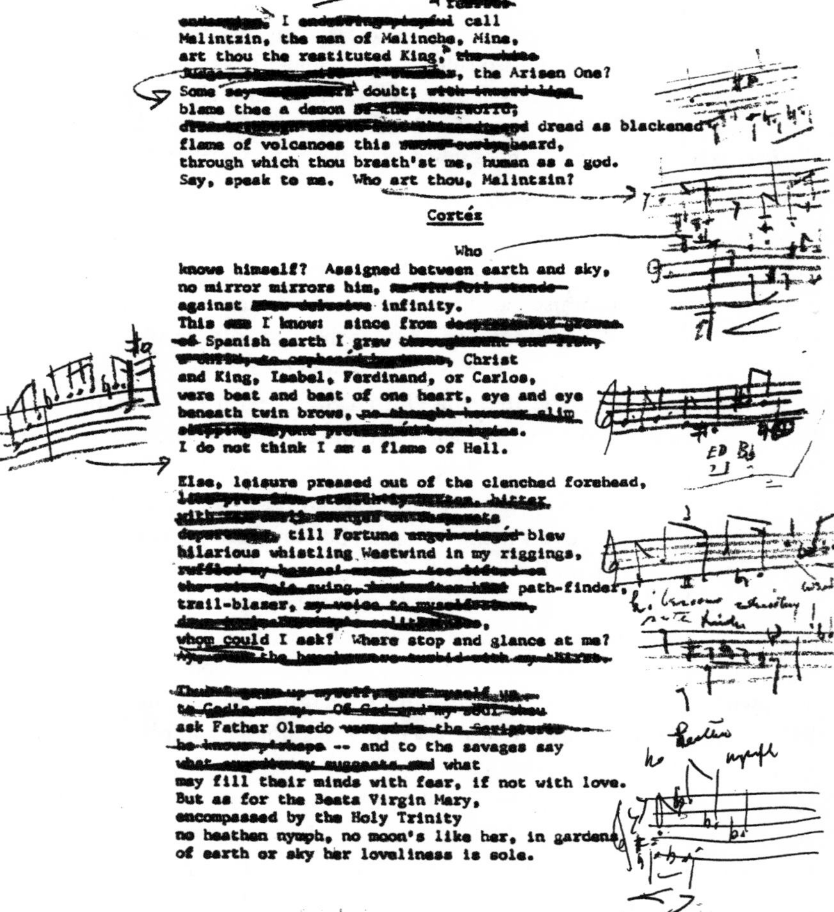

-24-

Art thou Quetzalcoatl? Whom

(Only occasionally a belated Indian or a group of three scuttle mutely along the darkening soon to slip, mouse-like, in the maze of the piteous city.)

I call
Malintzin, the man of Malinche, Mine,
art thou the restituted King,
, the Arisen One?
Some doubt;
blame thee a demon
dread as blackened
flame of volcanoes this beard,
through which thou breath'st me, human as a god.
Say, speak to me. Who art thou, Malintzin?

Cortéz

Who
know himself? Assigned between earth and sky,
no mirror mirrors him,
against infinity.
This I know: since from
Spanish earth I grew
, Christ
and King, Isabel, Ferdinand, or Carlos,
were beat and beat of one heart, eye and eye
beneath twin brows,
I do not think I am a flame of Hell.

Else, leisure pressed out of the clenched forehead,
till Fortune blew
hilarious whistling Westwind in my riggings,
path-finder,
trail-blazer,
whom could I ask? Where stop and glance at me?

ask Father Olmedo -- and to the savages say
what
may fill their minds with fear, if not with love.
But as for the Beata Virgin Mary,
encompassed by the Holy Trinity
no heathen nymph, no moon's like her, in gardens
of earth or sky her loveliness is sole.

Provisional cuts and musical sketches on copy of a draft libretto of *Montezuma*, 1941

velopment of his most ambitious project. Sicilian by birth, anti-Fascist by conviction, and a resourceful writer by the grace of God, Borgese had earned Il Duce's acute displeasure with some sharply critical articles in Milan's *Corriere della Sera* and was forced to flee to America. There he happened to find asylum as William Allan Nelson Professor at Smith College, across the river from the Sessions ancestral home in Hadley, Massachusetts. For Sessions, barely returned to America, and still suffering personal withdrawal symptoms after eight years abroad, the discovery of a distinguished European exile as his mother's near neighbor was reason enough to organize an early meeting. A weekend visit to Forty Acres was arranged. Talk ranged from the political clouds over contemporary Europe to past European aggression in the New World, and without either man realizing it at the time, the most formidable undertaking in their creative lives was already "in the air." The actual genesis of *Montezuma* as an operatic project came gradually into focus over the next two years, but would take thirty years to complete.

The idea for a dramatic epic on the tale of Montezuma, penultimate emperor of the Aztec nation in sixteenth-century Mexico, was Borgese's. The European was fascinated by the story of confrontation between two civilizations, represented on one side by the forces of Catholic Spain under Hernán Cortéz with his small band of conquistadors, his priests, his cannons, and his frightening horses, and on the other by a powerful native empire with warrior traditions, mutinous subject nations, annual human sacrifices, and a visionary king ultimately abandoned and stoned to death by his own people. A mysterious link between the two was the slave woman Malinche, Cortez's future lover, who joined the Spanish march into the heart of Montezuma's empire because, by law, only the emperor could set her free. In the end, the great emperor, abandoned by all, would die in Malinche's arms.

The story appealed to the American composer, whose ancestors had come to the New World barely a century after these events. Here was material for an opera, his opera, and he set to work on his notes at once, sorting out his ideas:

> The cataclysm—End of a civilization—the death of the old gods—universal destruction by greed and ambition.
> Also—a new "sun"—beginning of a *new unity* . . . a new land, a new epoch. looking at two pasts and one future.
> This is, of course, *America* in its purest essence, its only possible destiny . . . containing the seeds of legitimate hope and possible fulfillment.
> The drama is therefore the *mystery* of America—the cataclysm which gave birth to this continent as it is for us.[17]

In a later talk at Kenyon College, "Europe Comes to America,"[18] Sessions would introduce such thoughts within the context of a latter-day American perspective:

> America is in its truest sense of the word un-American. Let us once more face this great fact—which is the ultimate source of all that has made our country great, either in material or moral power: America is, and always has been, not primarily a land but an idea. Its very name is the name of one of a series of European dreamers who dreamed of a greater Europe extending beyond the seas. Cortez himself destroyed an American empire based on mystical, conceptions of "blood and soil"[19]—especially, and in the most drastic sense, blood. He brought to take its place a spiritual framework which aspired, as it still aspires, to include all mankind.

I am well aware that Cortez and his warriors were human beings, and that their motives were as mixed as was their Christianity. Something quite similar is true of the founders of our nation. What I want to point out is that when Europe first came to America, she was in fact even consciously serving the ends of a vast historic process—that of creating something which is greater than either Europe or America; and it could, I think, be shown that each successive decisive movement in our history has continued to serve that end, often in spite of ourselves.[20]

The notion of the Mexican conquest "creating something greater than either Europe or America" was not original with Sessions or Borgese, of course. Writers in other fields saw it in much the same way at the time. In 1962, the year in which the score of *Montezuma* was completed, George Kubler published a study, *The Shape of Time: Remarks on the History of Things*, that also focused on the underlying, once-and-future significance of the Mexican conquest by Spain. Kubler's point of departure involved concepts of varieties of historical simultaneity from the viewpoint of the visual arts, architecture, and language. He speaks of "a Mexican paradigm":

No historical crisis shared by so many millions of people has ever displayed its structure more simply or plainly. A great cultural distance separated native behavior and Spanish behavior in the 1520's. This distance is like that which separates Old Kingdom Egypt or Sumerian Mesopotamia from the Europe of Charles the Fifth. [In] such dizzying confrontations of altogether different stages of cultural development upon a continental scale . . . new behavior is learned from the victors, but during the learning period, the new behavior is itself changing.[21]

A shared vision of "such dizzying confrontations of altogether different stages of cultural development upon a continental scale" informed Sessions' and Borgese's collaboration on *Montezuma*, and their friendship grew over time. With Sessions' move to Princeton, meetings were no longer dependent on other people's hospitality. Among the many strengths Lisl brought to her marriage was her gift as a hostess. Borgese became a frequent visitor at the composer's home. It was here that he met fellow exile writer Thomas Mann's daughter Elizabeth and married her on his hosts' own third wedding anniversary, in their new house on Carter Road, Princeton, on Thanksgiving Day of 1939.

It is precisely because Montezuma had become so real for both Borgese and myself, that we found ourselves so gripped by it. I do not remember ever speaking with him directly in those terms, but they were implicit in everything we said to each other about it, and became more and more so as time went on, and the essential nature of our thoughts became more and more explicit and concrete. We spoke more and more, that is, about the characters and their motivations, in terms not only of history as such, but in terms of human beings and the forces—historical and political and religious—which moved them.[22]

The collaboration lasted until Borgese's death in 1952.

In 1941 Sessions received the first draft of the *Montezuma* libretto, a huge manuscript almost three times the length of the final version: "I read the text over and over; each time I read it, portions of the text—speeches and episodes—would take definite melodic shape—always in the context of the character and the situation in question, and I would note this down."[23]

The genesis of *Montezuma* reflects what has already been said about Sessions' very gradual discovery of his own way of composing and about his unwillingness to settle for results that would not meet the test of that discovery on every level:

> The composer's technique is, on the lowest level, his mastery of the musical language, the resourcefulness with which he is able to use its various elements to achieve his artistic ends. On a somewhat higher level . . . it becomes identical with his musical thought . . . The large contrasts contained in a work reveal its essential outlines and give it its largest rhythms, through alternation of musical ideas with their contrasting movement, emphasis, and dynamic intensity. On this level it is no longer accurate to speak of craftsmanship.[24]

From the time of his receipt of the first draft of Borgese's libretto in 1941 it took nearly twenty years before Sessions wrote in his work diary: "Work on *Montezuma* begun" (i.e., the actual musical composition) and another three years to complete the task. These twenty years saw the composition of three symphonies, the Piano Concerto, a number of chamber and solo works, the one-act opera *Lucullus,* and, in 1953, another "preparatory" work, the beautiful *Idyll of Theocritus* for soprano and orchestra. Meanwhile, he tried (ever since the completion of *Lucullus* in 1947) to make and develop some musical sketches for the opera. Under pressure of a deadline agreed upon between the collaborators, Sessions thought that the end of his labor was in sight in the summer of 1952.[25] He was mistaken, and the work on *Montezuma* was suspended. Borgese died, and with him an immediate prod to finish had gone. Eventually Sessions wrote in his notebook: "First of all, opera is drama; it is also music. It is not *drama with* music, but *drama in* music."[26]

His efforts had not succeeded as long as they merely reflected—no matter how appropriately—characters and situations in Borgese's text (*drama with* music). Before he felt confident enough to compose the epic drama of *Montezuma*, he had to take yet another step in learning to liberate "the musical syntax and grammar of conscious emotion" from limitations not yet completely understood—*drama in* music.

The sure-footed instinct that was evident in all his work and was the ever-present condition of its ultimate acceptance by himself is nowhere more remarkably demonstrated than in the fact that sketches as far back in time as the late 1930s would be incorporated in the final composition completed in 1962. By that time Sessions had realized that musical ideas conceived years before, in what he still considered a tonally based harmonic framework, were in fact easily adaptable and more easily managed in a twelve-tone environment: "I set to work on the score in the fall of 1959—and *with the help of very many sketches I had made over a period of eighteen years* [my emphasis], finished in two and a half years the complete particell—the condensed score—of the work, the final page of which bears the date July 1, 1962."[27]

Sessions' notes on *Montezuma,* exploring aspects of dramatic characterization and their possible musical representation, are now part of the collection of Sessions manuscripts in the Music Division of the Library of Congress. Much of his initial labor involved editing the libretto itself, cutting it down to manageable size:

> My first efforts in cutting consisted in slowly eliminating lines and even words which I thought could be dispensed with . . . However the moment soon arrived when I found myself obliged to eliminate whole scenes—some of which I had already sketched musically in some detail . . .
>
> Each excision was made with some reluctance, as it involved not only some small scenes of great beauty, which added life and depth to the characterization, but even whole episodes which seemed . . . important links in the chain of events. It was necessary to find more concentrated equivalents for some portions which were omitted. The final consideration was always that of setting the essential elements of the drama into sharpest possible relief. When the definitive text was finished, I felt unexpectedly happy with the result.[28]

An odd reaction: "happy"—of course—but why "unexpectedly" so? Perhaps because the whole process of editing the libretto had been so much like his approach to fine-tuning a musical composition. He discovered that editing a large dramatic text posed a comparable challenge. Finding himself capable of meeting that challenge made him happy, unexpectedly so, because he was not yet confident whether, in music, he would be able to match that effort on such a scale. The time would come when his music on the grand scale of *Montezuma* would match the imposing structure of its text; and the very existence of a "definitive text" seemed a big step toward a musical realization of the work that set "the essential elements of the drama into sharpest possible relief." The immediate years to follow saw a determined attempt—near to completion, according to the composer—but the time was not yet. We shall observe how it was begun afresh and how it succeeded.

"E nato difficile," Casella had consoled Sessions about his intractably hard Violin Concerto, "It was born difficult," and the time of its composition proved a long, slow, and difficult birthing period. With Lisl's help, with the new stability of his growing family, and with his friend Borgese's evolving drafts for *Montezuma* providing long-range focus throughout the restrictive day-to-day existence in a nation at war, the years that led up to Sessions' move to Berkeley in 1945 proved to have been more fruitful than they seemed to the composer at the time. His entire creative output during that period consisted of Chorale for Organ, *Pieces from a Diary*, the Duo for Violin and Piano, and a choral work for

Princeton, *Return O Libertad.* These were not "major works." But that in itself was a sign of settling down as well as of maturing in a composer's oeuvre in which—in his own mind—all previous work had been either singular and "major" or expendable as an exercise. These new, smaller works were real enough in a growing opus—by no means insignificant, though never intended to prove their creator's professional sense of self-worth at the time. If ever in Sessions' life an outward sign of his growing reputation in the field was perfectly timed to contribute to his effectiveness as a composer, while providing the full benefit of "something more," it would have been the call from the University of California at Berkeley to become its composer in residence and master teacher of composition.

CHAPTER 16

Berkeley

"What did Sessions do for you?"
"He made me feel important."

—EARL KIM

In the fall of 1945, Sessions moved to California to take up his new post at Berkeley. Ten years earlier, teaching summer school on the magnificent campus that overlooked San Francisco Bay, he had met his future wife, Lisl Franck, then a student in one of his classes. Now he would settle into this fondly remembered place as a full professor and honored resident composer:

> What was it like? Shortly after I got there I saw Bloch, who was visiting at the time. "How do you like it here?" he asked. I said, "I think it's the most marvelous place I've ever been." He thought for a moment before he answered and said, "Yes, but after a while you'll see: *Ach wie flüchtig, ach wie nichtig.*" It was a little better than that, and I think I helped it become so.[1]

It is doubtful that the older man's rueful forebodings cast a shadow on Sessions' immediate pleasure in his new surroundings, and Berkeley turned out to be very much more than "a little better than that." For his prospective students, the arrival of their teacher was an event anticipated with extravagant expectations. This is how, for Gordon C. Cyr, "half a month after the end of World War II," the fall semester began at the University of California in Berkeley:

> A handful of students who considered themselves composers—myself, an entering freshman, included—were all aglow over the impending arrival of

> Roger Sessions at our campus. He was to be, for most of us, our first contact with an American composer of national stature, even if at that time he was barely more than a reputation . . . Those few of us devoted passionately to "new music" also noted with pleasure that the composer was a perceptive commentator, and that for many of the newer works we ourselves held dear, he had expressed a kindred enthusiasm and understanding.[2]

For the "American composer of national stature," the prospect of teaching would-be-composers "all aglow" over his impending arrival could not but compare favorably to the music component of the arts and archaeology department at Princeton, where "one-tenth of the student body was taking at least one music course sometime in their college career."[3] To be working with a leavening of students whose hopes for their own future as composers were buoyed by the very prospect of study with him must have brought fresh comfort to an ever precarious professional ego. Berkeley's "enlightened policy" with regard to his teaching schedule, to quote Mark Schubart's essay,[4] made it reassuringly clear that Sessions' presence as a composer was prized as highly as his skill in the classroom. Performances of his works at Berkeley and in San Francisco soon provided tangible evidence of his welcome in the Bay Area. In this supportive environment, the artistic ego was less likely than before to expend valuable energy in searching for reasons to assume defensive positions. Sessions' tenure at Berkeley marked a noticeable change in how he felt about his place of employment. He knew himself to be the dominant figure in music on campus. By his own admission he had rarely set foot outside Princeton, even to see former New York friends just across the Hudson River. Now he established companionable relationships with fellow composers and other colleagues throughout California. Such was the paradoxical result of his *inward* turn as a result of the sea change in his life during the decade before that now, with increased *outward* recognition, he began to compose with growing ease and confidence.

For Lisl, a West Coast woman who had never felt entirely at home in her husband's working environment in the East, their arrival in Berkeley was a near homecoming, albeit in a milder climate than that of her more boldly colored, seasonally defined native state of Washington to the north. Moving into their commodious hillside home in the Berkeley hills seemed happiness enough for the whole family. John Sessions, eight years old at the time, remembers his childhood home:

> The house on 107 Tamalpais Rd. was rather large, with wooden shingles, stained dark brown (I think)—built into the hillside so that the front entrance was on the second (and main) floor: living room, dining room, kitchen, hallway, etc. The bedrooms were upstairs, and on the bottom floor was a living space—an apartment, really, inhabited over the years by various students—and my father's study. This floor opened up onto the rather large back yard. The "neighborhood" was typically Californian, architecturally speaking: no two houses alike—across the street, for example (but not facing: built much higher on the hillside) an outlandish white stucco

pseudo-Spanish castle, turrets and all, several houses down the street, a house that was completely Japanese, inside and out (except for the occupants). A very nice street, very much the Berkeley hills in atmosphere.[5]

At home, both parents enjoyed joint sessions of reading orchestral scores in four-hand piano arrangements. Judging by their repertoire, Lisl must have been quite a skilled pianist in her own right:

> In those days there was a piano in the living room and I vividly remember hearing my parents play—especially Mahler symphonies, which I got to know quite well long before hearing them in orchestral performances. When I began being taken to concerts in San Francisco (orchestral or the opera) I was often "prepared" by hearing the music—either in four hands or occasionally simply being walked through the score by my father—most memorably, perhaps, in the case of *Tristan*. . . . I have many memories of the Berkeley years and what was, I think, an exceptionally happy childhood

To my question of what one could see from the windows of the new Sessions home, he replied,

> Certainly, the living room had a view, but for the life of me I can't recall how far it extended. I don't recall being able to see the Golden Gate, certainly—but the bay, I think, was occasionally visible—bay area fog & haze permitting only rarely. I have vague memories of being able to make out the outline of Alcatraz island, but that may be the power of suggestion: the famous jailbreak attempt and subsequent siege took place during that time and for a while that was all one heard or talked about.[6]

One's mental image of the University of California's Berkeley campus, at the time of this writing, is inevitably colored by the lingering memory of events that caught nationwide attention some time after Sessions left the university to return to Princeton in 1953: riots in the 1960s, protests of the Vietnam War, and a smoldering political milieu that seemed instantly combustible over left-wing causes. In fact, this was far from the social climate at Berkeley when the Sessions family arrived in 1945. With the end of the war, the University of California's student population had literally doubled in size to more than 25,000. The most immediate problem was teaching space, and returning veterans were more interested in making up lost study time than in raising America's political consciousness. The most highly visible event at Berkeley in 1945 involved neither faculty nor students but the birthing of the United Nations in San Francisco. Campus conference facilities served the manifold needs of ongoing international negotiations, which resulted in the founding charter of the organization—a document that was "translated, designed, and printed in four days at Berkeley, in time [to be] signed by delegates to the historic session."[7]

All five regional divisions of the University of California were then administered by a central authority under socially conservative president Robert Gordon Sproul. The war years had provided $57 million for government-sponsored research at Berkeley. In partnership with the federal government, the university at large administered the research laboratories at Los Alamos, New Mexico, where Berkeley faculty, among others, had helped to develop the atomic bomb under the leadership of Berkeley professor J. Robert Oppenheimer. With industry funding adding to its government-sponsored programs, "Cal" was well on its way to becoming one of the most important American research universities.

Sproul oversaw the university's march to greatness with autocratic independence, but diminishing faculty support for unilateral control of the university's enormous enlargement forced him to grant the five regional UC campuses a measure of independence. Each division would be administered by its own chancellor, and in 1952—Sessions' last year as a tenured member of its faculty—Berkeley was able to welcome its industrial relations professor Clark Kerr as new administrative head. When, five years later, Kerr followed Sproul as university president, a new era of participatory academic rule had already begun.

Not least among the unaccustomed attractions of Sessions' new post was the vibrant musical life in the Bay Area, with Berkeley as a willing and productive contributor. Pierre Monteux was music director of the San Francisco Symphony Orchestra when Sessions arrived. Appointed two years earlier, Monteux's tenure spanned roughly the same period as that of the composer across the bay. Under his guidance the symphony soon achieved parity with other major American orchestras as a virtuosic and sensitive instrument. In terms of forward-looking and courageous programming it would put some of its illustrious sister organizations across the country to shame. The brilliant premiere performance of Sessions' Second Symphony under Monteux's baton proved to be one of the highlights of the composer's California years. And in Alfred Frankenstein, music critic of the San Francisco *Chronicle,* the area had the benefit of a distinguished and stalwart musical mind in the press.

There was no shortage of prominent composers in California. Arnold Schoenberg had held a professorship at UCLA since 1936. In 1940, after the fall of France, Darius Milhaud found American refuge at Mills College in Oakland, just to the south of the Berkeley campus. Bloch returned to the United States in 1941, settled to the north, in Agate Beach, Oregon, and taught summer school at Berkeley. Stravinsky, who had moved permanently to the United States in 1939 and received citizenship in 1945, lived in Hollywood. Unlike his three major colleagues in California, he did not teach;[8] nor did Krenek, who had also become a citizen in 1945 and moved to Los Angeles in 1947.

Schoenberg and Sessions were the powerful magnets who drew gifted young composers to their respective studios on campuses of the University of California. Schoenberg however, now in his seventies, found himself ensnared just then in one of the bureaucratic traps of academic employment in mid-twentieth-century America: mandatory age limits. Seventy in 1944, his retirement had been postponed before and now became unavoidable. His pension, based on only eight years of employment at UCLA, was small. Recently married and a father to two young sons, even his great musical eminence could not support his young family. His 1947 prize from the American Academy of Arts and Letters for outstanding achievement was accompanied by a check in the amount of $1,000—and unlike other European composers newly arrived in Southern California, he had not been very successful in efforts to improve his financial situation with lucrative work in neighboring Hollywood. Thus the period that followed his retirement was devoted to an energetic buildup of a private teaching schedule at his beautiful home in Brentwood Park, Los Angeles. He wrote little during that time of transition, but then, undeterred by a brief though almost fatal illness in 1949, the teacher Arnold Schoenberg flourished alongside the composer of the great works of his old age: the String Trio, *Survivor from Warsaw*, the Fantasy for Violin and Piano, as well as work on the unfinished opera *Moses and Aaron* and the tantalizing beginnings of his *Modern Psalms*.

Two among Sessions' most outstanding students at Berkeley had worked with Schoenberg before they came to him. Leon Kirchner received his B.A. under the European master at UCLA in 1940, started graduate studies at Berkeley, won one of the music department's prizes, and was able to work with the just-returned Bloch in his second year. Kirchner went to New York to study privately with Sessions in 1942 and, after active service in World War II, followed him to Berkeley in 1946. Earl Kim had begun his studies with Schoenberg at UCLA in 1939, moved to Berkeley when Bloch appeared back on the scene, served in the war, and returned to Berkeley to study with Sessions. Andrew Imbrie, however, was entirely Sessions-taught as a composer. He received his B.A. from Princeton in 1942 and, after service in the U.S. Army, followed his teacher to Berkeley. All three eventually held chairs in composition at the respective universities most closely associated with Sessions' life: Harvard, Princeton, and Berkeley. In their turn they taught some of the most distinguished composers of the next generation, some whom, like Imbrie's Del Tredici at Harvard, soon continued a living and sustaining legacy of Sessions' teaching into the third generation. Kirchner, Kim, and Imbrie had been general music students at university before they began private composition lessons with the master. In theory classes at conservatories and university music departments, young composers learn the basics of musical structure in classes alongside instrumentalists, singers, and conductors. Schoenberg, Sessions, and Bloch all taught general music classes in California for a large population of musical performers as well as future composers.

Sessions' young composers were required to take part in general class work according to their needs. There they learned how musical building blocks relate to the materials from which a work is constructed and vice versa. As always with Sessions, that process began with the work itself, the hearing of the work, and a gradual, cumulative familiarity with what was heard. In such classes he could not take for granted either the trained, attentive ear he would later demand of his composition students or the general musical background that warranted familiarity with a wide range of musical literature:

> Once, with a class of fifty students, all relatively unprepared and some quite innocent of contact with contemporary music, I tried the experiment of familiarizing them, at the beginning of the course, with Schoenberg's Fourth Quartet, one of the composer's most "difficult" works. My whole effort was to bring them into contact with music, and I deferred speaking of the problem of tonality, or the twelve-tone system, until the students knew the music thoroughly. By that time—believe it or not—one could hear the opening theme of the quartet, or other passages, being whistled by students on the campus. At the end of several weeks I spoke only briefly about technical questions involved and they fell, it seemed to me, in their proper place. My students learned to know—some to love—the music their ears had conquered.[9]

In his teaching, Sessions trusted his own intuitive awareness and growing experience as a composer in order to find appropriate, if sometimes surprising, solutions. In writing his First Quartet he had imposed the same trust on his instinctive grasp of what was needed, even though he found himself "surprised and even slightly dismayed to see myself writing the kind of music that I had to write."[10] Now there were days when he surprised himself by the way he had to teach his classes and his private students.

The epigraph to this chapter, Earl Kim's response to my question during an interview for this book, provides a striking clue to that part of a great teacher's way with gifted students, a way that transcends honing of compositional craft—"he made me feel important." In light of Sessions' own acknowledged uncertainties in the past—"you see, I was very shy, I had to find myself, to gain confidence"[11]—and how for years, and in the face of ample evidence of ability and success, a lack of self-confidence choked the productive flow of his creative energy, Kim's response reflects a need that was met by one who knew.

Oddly enough, the effective potential of having composers teaching the basics of how music is made was not widely appreciated. When William Schuman became president of Juilliard in 1945, he insisted that only composers be permitted to teach classes in the literature and materials of music that were to take the place of a traditional theory curriculum. Understandable protests of a faculty long established in teaching harmony and counterpoint classes were overridden in the firm conviction that it took a composer to make music students—performers and composers alike—comprehend how a piece of music was made and what it was; how, in light of examples from a large amount of musical literature, the materials that inform a work govern the procedures and techniques according to which it is constructed. For students with an urge to write, only a teacher who, through personal experience, knows about the brittle and vulnerable nature of developing a composer's relationship to his ideas enjoys the special credibility and trust needed to address that most vexing aspect in the development of creative talent.

Sessions commanded such immense respect among his students that the mere fact of his taking their work seriously was reassuring. Gordon Cyr, in his retrospective essay, paints a persuasive picture of just how seriously Sessions took the results of his students' efforts:

> The usual procedure was for Sessions to read the score silently. Occasionally he would put questions to the composer concerning some ambiguity, whether of tempo, dynamics, phrasing, or other musical intention imprecisely stated. Once in a while, Sessions would play a few notes, a single chord, or an isolated melodic fragment, after which another long period of silent reading would ensue.
>
> The process would continue for several minutes . . . Only after this perusal I have described—and after all of the instructor's questions had been answered to his satisfaction—did Sessions then speak about the student's work. The suggestions he offered extended from purely practical considerations of instrumental and vocal choices and limitations to the thornier, more controversial areas of development, balance and contrast . . . Never did Sessions impose his own style or methodology, but made every effort to deal with the student's work in terms of that student's own compositional manner.[12]

Student participation in the preparation of their teacher's new works for performance was as much part of being a member of "the class" as helping to celebrate their completion. Sessions had begun the composition of his Second Symphony during his last year at Princeton and finished it at Berkeley in 1946. The premiere with the San Francisco Symphony under Pierre Monteux was scheduled for 1947. Andrew Imbrie gives a vivid account of the class at work before the first rehearsal:

> At the time I was a graduate student at Berkeley, and along with my colleagues was willingly conscripted for the correction of the instrumental parts before the rehearsals began. These parts had been copied by well-meaning amateurs, and were full of errors. We stayed up late at Roger's house the night before the first rehearsal, Roger himself doing the string parts. At about four in the morning he discovered an omission of perhaps ten measures of music for the first violins, which of course had to be corrected in each individual part. There ensued a string of Anglo-Saxon monosyllables, punctuated by "Excuse me, gentlemen." Meanwhile the tantalizing glimpses of the music that we saw as we corrected merely whetted our appetite for the events of the next day.[13]

That this feverish activity took place only during the night before the first rehearsal was fairly standard Sessions routine. The problem was not necessarily limited to poorly copied parts. Sessions never understood why his own work on a new composition should be considered done until no further last-minute improvements would occur to him. Even with copying errors—the bane of all first orchestra rehearsals—he might find on discovery that the whole passage might be improved—involving changes in *all* the parts.

Imbrie's account of the Second Symphony's first rehearsals caps the joint experience of the class, as it witnessed the final stage of a process in which new works must eventually prove stronger than the human and musical problems that obstructed their preparation:

> At first what we heard was chaos. With infinite patience, however, Monteux rehearsed each passage—sometimes only two or three measures at a time—with Roger at his elbow and the concert-master, hating every note, pulling out his pencil at each pause and marking his part. As the rehearsals progressed, the sense of the music miraculously began to take shape, like an unfinished Michelangelo. The sculptural simile is intentional: I do not recall ever hearing music that had such tactile quality: the ideas and their transformations unfolded for me with breathtaking palpability; yet of course they were constantly in motion. They rocketed around me, echoing through the vacant auditorium of the San Francisco Opera House like guided missiles. The eloquence, the excitement, and the luminous triumph at the end left me in a daze. I haven't recovered yet.[14]

In addition to the premiere performance of the Second Symphony, San Francisco had already heard Sessions' Second Piano Sonata (1946), played by Bernard Abranowitsch at the Composers Forum Workshop. Berkeley itself went all out in fielding the fruits of their resident composer's newly revitalized creative productivity. Works of his last two Princeton years, the Duo for Violin and Piano (1943), with violinist Barbara Rahm and Sessions at the piano, as well as his choral setting of Walt Whitman's "Return O Libertad," were performed on campus. But the big event at Berkeley proved to be the preparation and performance of his new opera, *The Trial of Lucullus, Drama in Music* (1947).

Sessions later described *Lucullus* as a preparatory exercise he needed to write before he could undertake the huge project of the opera *Montezuma*. It turned out to be a good deal more than that. Michael Steinberg in the *Boston Globe* called *Lucullus* "a masterpiece, nothing less." David Drew, writing for London's *Observer,* suggested that Sessions, "the first American composer to have achieved mastery in Schoenberg's sense, has written an opera that towers over the American operas favored by the Met." In all, the opera has had only three performances in fifty years, none of them with fully professional forces, all of them highly acclaimed. Here is yet another aspect of the problem of "difficult composers" such as Roger Sessions.

Berthold Brecht wrote the radio play *Lucullus* in the 1930s. It was first performed in 1941 in Lausanne, Switzerland. In late 1946 or early in 1947, in California, he offered the text to Sessions (having already given the rights to Paul Dessau, some years before, in New York[15]).

The Trial of Lucullus pictures an afterlife experience of the great Roman general, conqueror, and colonizer, recently deceased. At stake is his eligibility for an honorable afterlife or his sentence to damnation. All but two former-life witnesses, including his most powerful political contemporaries and defeated adversaries in war, testify against him. Only a cook and a gardener speak in his defense. The curtain closes as the judges withdraw to weigh the evidence, leaving the verdict to the audience. I, for one, think he's going to walk (that cherry tree music).

Sessions' score reflects the availability of instrumentalists on campus at the time: 2 Flutes, 1 Oboe (also English Horn), 1 Clarinet, 1 Bass Clarinet, 1 Bassoon (also Contrabassoon); 2 French Horns, 2 Trumpets, 2 Trombones; Piano; Tambourine, Military Drum, Tam-Tam, Bass Drum Cymbals (two percussion players total); Violins (only one section—there are no second violins), Violas, Cellos, Double Basses. The vocal cast is very large, but singers can be double-cast in some roles.

If the preparation of orchestral materials for Sessions' Second Symphony was a major participatory exercise for the composition class, the Berkeley premiere of *Lucullus* involved the entire music department. A large cast of singers, instrumental performers, and production staff had to be found, rehearsed, and coordinated. Sessions conducted. Imbrie, Kirchner, and Kim coached the singers —all but one of whom were students—and helped some of the players with their difficult parts. It would be hard to imagine a more telling illustration of that remarkable happening than the sketch (Ex. 16.1) by former student and (according to his own graphic evidence) hapless horn player for the event S. Earl Saxton, being forcibly restrained by assistant conductor Leon Kirchner. Sessions himself, still composing while he conducted the rehearsal, was

> unbelievably plain and humble, unpretentious, soft-spoken and kind, any of us would readily given anything for this opportunity to work with him.
>
> There were so many moments of fun, even hilarity, sprinkled throughout the rehearsals, I couldn't resist the temptation to do some sketching of the personalities involved, and eventually to put them all into a cartoon. The idea of making a cartoon came so late in the production schedule that no attempt was made to include every one of the 144-member company.[16]

Sessions composed *Lucullus* in six weeks. Whether or not the one-acter was in fact meant to be a preparatory exercise before the composition of his magnum opus, *Montezuma*, its success encouraged him to take on the much larger task of organizing and realizing his musical ideas for that complex drama. In his work diary, a small notebook measuring about two by three inches, into which he entered dates of beginning and completing works in progress, there is a 1947 notation: "*Montezuma* begun." Obviously this refers to work on the music, not the dramatic revision and editing that had gone on since he first received Borgese's manuscript in 1941. Sessions made enough progress to feel, some five years later, that he was only months away from completing the score. That goal, as we have seen, was not reached for a further decade and after a completely fresh start, but *Montezuma* remained in the foreground of his creative efforts during his remaining years at Berkeley.

Dramatic musical representation of the earliest confrontation between Native American and European cultures may well have been part of the common interests that drew Sessions to his colleague Darius Milhaud at Mills College.

Example 16.1 Cartoon by S. Earl Saxton of a *Lucullus* rehearsal at Berkeley under the baton of Roger Sessions

Their initial association, of course, was a natural result of their teaching at neighboring schools. They shared, among other respective chores, the duties of visiting arbiters at the San Francisco Composers Forum Workshop, where contemporary works, including their own and those of their students, were performed and discussed. Soon, however, Milhaud and Sessions would have discovered another topic of shared interest, *Christophe Colomb,* Milhaud's own opera on a fifteenth-century conquistador. Written in 1928 on a text by Paul Claudel, Milhaud's *Columbus* shares some striking similarities of concept and language with Borgese/Sessions' *Montezuma*. In Borgese's libretto for *Montezuma*, the Aztec slave Malinche, aka La Marina, "Lady of the Sea," sees in her lover Cortez the human form of the legendary god Quetzaquatl, "snake that pluméd night uncoils." "L'esprit de Dieu descend sur les Eaux sous la forme d'une colombe [The spirit of God descends upon the waters in the form of a dove]," writes Claudel in a mystical association of the name of the conqueror from across the sea with the dove (*colombe*) that represents the Divine Spirit.

Ernst Krenek, in 1930, had commented on Milhaud's *Colomb* in words that anticipate Sessions' own view of the significance of the cultural confrontation inherent in the drama of *Montezuma:*

> The deed for which Columbus may yet go to heaven, his numerous human failings notwithstanding, is a spiritual deed. America represents an expansion of man's horizon, compared to which questions about an increase of happiness on earth, or even misgivings about the suffering for most of those who had to live through the experience, assume secondary importance.[17]

The French composer newly become American and the New England heir of some three hundred years of American tradition, each in his own way, lived the effects of a more recent cultural collision. In biannual visits to France after the war, Milhaud maintained his bond with the country of his birth, which, as a Jew, he had fled during the Vichy regime; while Sessions, unlike some of his more radical colleagues, came closer to La Malinche's welcoming view of the European ascendancy within America's cultural citadel. Both of them looked to—and embodied in their work—a future based on cultural fusion, in which the resulting whole would be greater than the sum of its parts.

That fusion and its consummation among major creative figures of the time represented an important, if in retrospect curiously ignored, aspect of the period. The process of accommodation was no longer centered in the musical turf wars of the polarized, competitive New York scene, as it had been during the first wave of immigration before the war. Many of the major protagonists in the arts and in literature now taught at colleges and universities throughout the United States, where their influence and interaction with American colleagues took place in an atmosphere of shared economic security and where the cultural "gift exchange" among the highly gifted produced that "something more" for all and helped to turn the postwar decades in this country into one of the most fertile periods in American arts and letters.

Much of this activity took place on the West Coast, and as often before in his life, Sessions found himself to be in just the right place at the right time. Contact with Schoenberg in Los Angeles took longer to establish. Letters went unanswered for some time. In his second year at Berkeley, Leon Kirchner, who had joined the class after his release from the army, took some of Sessions' music to play for his former teacher in Los Angeles. That evoked a letter:

Dear Mr. Sessions:

I feel I am indebted to you for the good letters I received from you. Were it not that my eyes are an obstacle to my writing and thanking you, I would have written you, after Mr. Kirchner played your music for me. I was very pleased that I could follow your thoughts almost throughout the whole piece and it is that, why I said: "This is a language." I mean, it conveys a message and in this respect it seems to me one of the greatest achievements a composer could arrive at.

Thank you again for your kind words. I am very pleased to be in contact with you not only by the music we both love, but also through pupils, who love what we love.

Cordially yours,
Arnold Schoenberg

July 17, 1948
Too bad that your son has to leave today; my son Ronny would have liked to have a playmate like him for both cello and tennis.[18]

Contact between the families was eventually established on an informal, friendly basis, affording many opportunities for serious discussions between the two composers. Sessions was particularly fond of recalling an occasion when he told Schoenberg that even in his twelve-tone works he could always hear tonal centers: "I said, 'Fred [*sic*], you know that I think the 12-tone method has been distorted'. Schoenberg looked glum. Then he said, 'Yes, you're right, and I must admit it's partly my fault. But it's mostly the fault of my students!'"[19] At the time of this conversation Sessions had not yet incorporated elements of the "12-tone method" into his own musical language and resisted its appeal in an ultimately unfounded fear that, as a "system," it might require a fundamental change in his approach to composition. His obvious pleasure in relating Schoenberg's disavowal of his students' twelve-tone procedures was usually followed by some declaration of his abiding distrust of the Webern "School"—"they want rules!"[20]—and his disdain of "their avant-garde music festivals in Darmstadt," always happily referred to as "Bowelville": "Remember one thing: Schoenberg was a giant . . . Webern, to my mind a much lesser figure, is for that reason much easier to handle. I think that is why he is in higher favor among certain circles now."[21]

The first five years of Sessions' tenure at Berkeley mark his long-overdue transformation from diffident discoverer of ways in which his musical imagination might trim creative response to assured acceptance of his role as learner and sharer of what composing his works had taught him. Since his first encounter with the generative force of a musical idea, a chord destined to become his First Piano Sonata, he had tested, tried, and enhanced creative assumptions that informed his work not only as a composer but also as a teacher. The first generation of young composers with a name to come—Babbitt, Cone, Diamond, Imbrie, Kirchner and Kim—had shared the exploration and the discoveries of that inner territory and had been rewarded with their own musical evolving. Schoenberg, himself a constant explorer and discoverer of his own way with music, had recognized in his younger colleague's music something that must have meant more to Sessions than any other praise he might have been given: *this is a language!* And having just written a small masterpiece, *Lucullus*, with the apparent ease and confident dispatch of an eighteenth-century composer, Sessions had finally achieved what Ernest Bloch, thirty years earlier, had promised as the result of two years' hard work: "you'll be able to do what you want."

At this stage, Sessions himself felt sufficiently assured of the results of his search for something more *within* to sum up his discoveries in the already-mentioned 1949 lectures at Juilliard. In the following year they were reprinted in paperback, by arrangement with Princeton University Press, under the title *The Musical Experience of Composer, Performer, Listener.* To anyone identifying with at least one of these ways of musical experience, this little book makes important and often provocative reading. In addition to summing up his own encounter with music as a composer and providing illustrative musical terms that go beyond traditional theoretical terminology, he raises the special problem that distinguishes music from her sister arts: music needs to be *performed*, and the composer's text requires decoding before performance can take place and before listeners can hear the work performed. His conclusions are refreshingly apt:

> What then is the task of the performer? Is it simply fidelity to the composer's text, or of the performer himself a creative artist for whom the music is simply a vehicle for the expression of his personality?
>
> Stated thus, the most obvious comment is that it is not "simply" either one or the other of these things, or, in fact, simply anything at all.[22]

Musical notation in the score, that is, the "code" in which the composer writes his instructions for performance, is far from a precise blueprint of its execution. While some of its indications are unconditional, for example, pitch and instrumentation (with some latter-day disagreement even in these areas), other composer's instructions are clearly relative as to what is heard before or after ("how loud is loud?") or call for largely subjective decisions on the part of the performer: determining the shape of a phrase, although far from arbitrary, depends on a number of considerations that, albeit based on textual evidence in the score, may be weighed differently by different performers and result, cumulatively, in quite different yet entirely justifiable performances of the same work: "We experience music as movement and gesture, and that movement and gesture [must] be constantly reinvested with fresh energy . . . A sense of energy . . . comes from the fact that the energy is really and unavoidably fresh, from beginning to end. . . . Every moment conditions the one that follows, and the whole is conditioned and sustained kinetic impulse."[23]

Because strict observance of the composer's printed instructions still requires many subjective decisions on the part of the performer and because the effect of such decisions will be cumulative over the continuity of the music played, the result has to be a performance unique in itself, every time the work is played: "There is no such thing as a 'definitive performance' of any work whatsoever. This is true even of performances by the composer himself."[24] With this self-evident truth Sessions allied himself to convictions expressed by many of his predecessors. Gustav Mahler, composer *and* performer, went even further, writing wistfully that "the most important things in music cannot be noted in the score."[25]

Sessions adds the variable of the listener to these relative elements of the musical experience of the composer's score. Over three centuries of Western music, and specifically in Sessions' own time, the listener's role in the experience of music changed as profoundly as that of composer and performer. The nineteenth century had seen the professional separation of the latter roles and the rise of the specialized only-performer, the virtuoso whose celebrity no longer depended on any kind of reputation as a composer. No less significant was the advent of the twentieth-century listener who, unlike the typical member of earlier audiences, no longer played a musical instrument. Nineteenth-century music lovers shared their musical experience in playing quartets, trios, and solo works at home, a musical experience limited by individual adequacy as instrumentalists but enhanced by personal effort and practice. With the growing availability of virtually the entire musical repertory on recordings by superior professional forces, music became something like a spectator sport, geared to perfection and prestige, removed from personal experience, and ultimately reduced to popular entertainment.

Sessions' view of the problem—and as such he does introduce the subject—was largely sociological: art music, after three centuries of general acceptance as a privileged pursuit, was now competing for support in a business economy. The problem was one that Sessions solved for himself, as a composer, by his move to the university. His 1948 article on the subject, "The Composer in a Business Economy," would be the focus of his 1950 Fulbright Lectures in Italy. But he also adds another consideration to our *relative* experience of music—he compares it to audience experience in the theater:

> [A member of the audience] has talked in prose all his life. His feeling for the values of both visual and literary art consists therefore in a degree of refinement, and an extension, of experiences which are thoroughly familiar to him, through analogies constantly furnished by his ordinary life.
>
> In the case of music there are no such clear analogies. The technical facts which are commonplace to the composer, and even many of those proper to the performer, have no clear analogies in the ordinary experience of the non-musician . . . And if the latter finds it difficult to conceive of the mere fact of inner hearing and auditory imagination, how much more difficult will he find such a conception as, for instance, tonality or the musical facts on which the principles of what we call "musical form" are based . . .
>
> The "technique" of a piece is essentially the affair of the composer; it is largely even subconscious, and composers frequently are confronted by perfectly real technical facts, present in their music, of which they had no conscious inkling. And do we seriously believe that understanding of Shakespeare, or James Joyce, or William Faulkner has anything to do with the ability to parse the sentences and describe the functions of the various words in *Hamlet* or *Ulysses*?
>
> Of course not . . . In the primary sense, the listener's real and ultimate response to music consists not merely in hearing it, but in inwardly reproducing it, and his understanding of music in the ability to do this in his imagination . . . The really "understanding" listener takes the music into his consciousness and remakes it actually or in his imagination, for his own uses.[26]

Sessions was not a performer, but he was well aware of the performer's vexing problem with the musical expectation of listeners' ears, conditioned by centuries of evolving changes in the musical language itself:

> I once read a bit of criticism which struck me as one of the best I had ever seen, in spite of the fact that I had not heard the performance reviewed and therefore had no means of judging whether or not the critic was right. The critic spoke of a performance of Mozart's G Minor Symphony in which the conductor, he said, had performed certain sharply dissonant intervals in the last movement "as if he were not aware that they were there."[27]

As a composer, of course, Sessions enjoyed the advantage of raising the problem without having to provide suggestions for its solution. What was shocking for eighteenth-century ears may indeed pass unnoticed in its musical discourse before an audience today, and allowing this to happen, no matter how carefully the textual evidence of his score was observed, would certainly be contrary to Mozart's intent. What was the hapless unnamed conductor to have done? Surely something. But whatever slight liberty might have helped to suggest Mozart's intent to shock might also have roused the ire of ever-present guardians of textual purity. Every conductor knows that the Introduction of Beethoven's First Symphony begins with the "wrong" dominant leading into a "wrong" tonic. The "right" dominant, immediately following, then escapes into yet another "wrong" tonic. Only on his third try does Beethoven finally field the dominant of the "right" dominant (G major), resolving it properly and triumphantly as the symphony's tonal root of C major.

Contemporary ears in Beethoven's day did not take kindly to such harmonic circumlocution at the very outset of a work. Listeners today don't even notice. Beethoven obviously meant—what? An arduous establishment of the key of C? A joke? Evidence in the score, particularly its orchestration, could support either, and it behooves the conductor to make his own choice on the basis of Beethoven's text. But how is the result of one or the other—surely very different—interpretation to be gotten across to the audience? The one thing that can *not* be reproduced in any performance today is the shock of harmonic bafflement that, to Beethoven's certain knowledge, his opening of the symphony was bound to produce in listeners of his time. Sessions' comparison with the listener's experience of the spoken drama, where language provides "analogies constantly furnished by his ordinary life," illustrates a significant difference in the performance of music. Our experience of music, the very art that Sessions defined as "controlled movement of sound in time,"[28] is remarkably unforgiving of the passage of historical time.

A significant aspect of how the composer furnishes and explicates passage of time in his music is treated in Sessions' *Harmonic Practice*,[29] a textbook that, like Schoenberg's *Harmonielehre* of 1911, represents a major composer's practical experience in the organic management of harmonic events. Like its predecessor, it is carefully organized by a great teacher as a compendium of the cumulative process of study, exercise, and learning. At this time of his own suddenly revitalized creative energy, Sessions was tempted at first to resist the suggestion that he publish the mass of materials he had used in his teaching:

> I found the field already crowded with textbooks on harmony, ranging all the way from theoretical treatises of the first order to less ambitious but quite practical works expressly designed for classroom use. I have, furthermore, always insisted that it is technical mastery and resourcefulness, and not this or that manner of conceiving the so-called "principles," which is finally important . . . and that theory in the strict sense of the word is essentially without other than pragmatic value.
>
> It was, however, just this consideration which finally convinced me that the project was worth undertaking.[30]

Begun as a purely practical set of mimeographed notes to aid him in teaching his elementary courses at Princeton, the copious exercises with which the book was ultimately furnished serve one primary purpose: "The goal of harmonic study must be precisely that of liberating the ear through mastery of resource. The aim is that of enabling the ear to become constantly more aware of, and more sensitive to, the relationship between tones and between aggregates of tones, and constantly more resourceful in making coherent use of these relationships."[31] Emphasis on the primacy of the ear, in this context as in any other aspect of musical thinking, will not seem very extraordinary to the reader who has followed our development of Sessions' ideas as a composer and as a teacher. But the ear as something to be liberated, that is, made independent, through mastery of harmonic resource, shifts ultimate emphasis from the tested practices of a great musical heritage to the pragmatic birthright of the living composer in enabling so subjective an organ. It had certainly struck as preposterous Berkeley's distinguished musicologist and Sessions' sometime sparring partner in discussion Martin Bukofzer. His irate "the ear has nothing to do with it!" we have already reported.

Sessions' final literary labor before leaving Berkeley on sabbatical in 1950 was a brief article for the *New York Times*, "How a 'Difficult' Composer Gets That Way," from which we have already quoted and whose title, changed to the past tense, became the subtitle to this study of his life. Sessions was well aware of his "difficult" reputation, even in those professional circles in which he enjoyed unvarying respect. He accepted that conclusion philosophically, taking comfort in another favorite anecdote: "I remember a remark of Albert Einstein, which certainly applies to music. He said, in effect, that everything should be as simple as it can be, but not simpler . . . I try only to put into each work as much of myself as possible."[32]

On August 1, 1946, the U.S. Congress passed what became known as the Fulbright Act, named after its sponsor, then freshman senator J. William Fulbright.[33] Funded by the sale of war surplus properties and by exchanging nonconvertible currencies of countries with scarce dollars, the act was "to amend the Surplus Property Act of 1944 to designate the Department of State as the disposal agency for surplus property outside the United States, its Territories and possessions, and for other purposes." One of the "other purposes" developed into the now famous international exchange program of students and scholars. Following this authorization to pay American recipients of Fulbright grants out of foreign debts owed the United States—in currencies of their host countries—American universities were asked to fund temporarily the equivalent stateside costs for fellowships, assistantships, and visiting lectureships of foreign applicants. The Carnegie Corporation and the Rockefeller Foundation helped to defray these costs until, in 1948, the U.S. Information and Educational Exchange Act of Congress extended the U.S. government's own authority to the appropriation of funds for educational exchanges worldwide.

An old hand at grantsmanship, Roger Sessions, with a sabbatical leave of absence in the offing, applied for and was awarded a Fulbright scholarship to Italy for the academic year 1950–51. He chose his ever-favorite Florence as his base abroad, and the Florentine Academia Luigi Cherubini obliged by issuing the official invitation for his lectures. As the months before his departure from Berkeley turned into weeks, the pressures of winding up his teaching duties, getting his harmony textbook ready for publication, and attending to the glut of routine chores involved in moving a family with two young children to Europe were compounded by an intense campus controversy.

At the conclusion of the decade that had seen the end of World War II, and only a few years since the Soviet Union had been a wartime ally of the United States, the so-called Cold War was in full fury, and its effects were beginning to reach into the private lives of Americans. Fear of communist subversion became endemic in conservative political circles, while early excesses in containing the perceived threat enraged the liberal wing. Universities were among the first to be drawn into the debate. Political power in California stretched over a wide range of opposing views at the time. Earl Warren, its governor and a political moderate, was soon to become the fourteenth chief justice of the U.S. Supreme Court and would preside over the court's landmark equal rights decision in *Brown vs. Board of Education of Topeka, Kansas*, a trial that ended legal segregation in American public schools. Future Republican president of the United States film and television actor Ronald Reagan, then still a member of the Democratic Party and for many years a champion of Franklin Roosevelt's New Deal, was just beginning to speak out against "big government" as well as communism. Robert Gordon Sproul, however, powerful president of the University of California and "violently anti-Communist,"[34] decided to make an example of his convictions. Even before U.S. senator Joseph E. McCarthy made his famous speech about "card-carrying members of the Communist party in the State Department," in February 1950, faculty in the five divisions of the University of California were asked by their administration to sign a "loyalty oath," a sworn statement affirming that the signer was not, nor ever had been, a Communist.

In a national climate of growing tension over the perceived threat to employment and livelihood for anyone tainted with former communist associations, the fact that university administrators (among other employers) across the country were beginning to demand a sworn statement concerning past political association raised the signing of a loyalty oath to a controversy in political and personal morality on both the left and the right wing of the political spectrum. In California, where major careers in the film industry, among others, were to be ruined in a wave of national hysteria ("better dead than red"!), the university faculty was in an uproar. Sessions did not take an active part in prolonged faculty deliberations on whether to sign or refuse in a body. At the end of the 1949–50 academic year he left Berkeley for his European sabbatical without having signed the document or recorded his intent to abstain.

The subsequent misunderstanding pained him for the rest of his life. Some thirty years later, on my very first visit to his Princeton home in quest of information for this book, both he and Lisl insisted on giving me an account of the event—"to set the record straight." At the time, I had not even heard of the event that troubled them both so much, but I shall relate their story as it was told, Roger sitting in his big chair in the living room of their small house in Stanworth Lane, with Lisl coaching from the kitchen:

ROGER: All the faculty of California State institutions were asked to sign a loyalty oath. Nobody took it seriously. I certainly didn't. We were just leaving for Princeton, at the beginning of the summer—1950, I think it was—on our way to Italy.

LISL: In Princeton we got word that Roger had better sign.

ROGER: Well, in order to get it over with before our departure for Europe, I did. At the Public Notary on Witherspoon Street. And we sent it off. Later came word that everybody else had refused.

LISL: Berkeley apparently decided to accept the faculty refusal.

ROGER: Then Lisl and I decided now we have to leave Berkeley.

Lisl, now seventy-four, is not well. In addition to coronary fillibrations, she has balance problems and cannot manage the stairs without Roger's help. She says it's "circulatory" and believes the eastern climate makes it worse.

LISL: I loved California. I hated to leave it. Roger was quite ready to come back east.

ROGER: But you couldn't live there now?

LISL: Of course not, I'd hate it.[35]

It must not be imagined that the decision to give up his teaching post at Berkeley was forced on Sessions because of his hasty signing of the university's loyalty oath. At worst his carelessness would be a social embarrassment for him when he returned after his sabbatical in Italy. He did return, of course, for another year—a major figure on campus and very active in musical affairs at Berkeley and in San Francisco.

But his self-conscious defense, some thirty years after the event, is oddly reminiscent of his elaborate justification of an earlier social disposition of which he no longer approved. Such a need to make amends for something long forgotten by anyone but himself had informed his 1942 "Letter to an Imaginary Colleague,"[36] providing a belated public disavowal of his pacifist views when America went to war in 1917. The hardheaded, personally unforgiving nature of his mind worked slowly on such matters but ground almost as exceedingly fine in pronouncing eventual judgment on himself as the proverbial justice of his New England God.

CHAPTER 17

Dallapiccola

Tout sur terre appartient aux princes, hors le vent.
[Everything on earth belongs to its princes, except the wind.]

—VICTOR HUGO

The Europe to which Sessions returned in 1951 was altogether different, of course, from the continent in crisis that he had left nearly two decades before. In the two countries he had known best, Italy and Germany, physical signs of appalling destruction still marked ruined cities and the paths of contending armies could be gauged in the grim remnants of what was left by the side of the road. It was the more astonishing, therefore, that cultural life not only flourished everywhere but also functioned in a much healthier way than the feverish fervor of denial with which a grand cultural tradition in a dying age had embraced its doom in the Berlin of 1933. For six years the war had been an impartial broker of mutual destruction among the nations of Europe, but the will to rebuild had succeeded so remarkably that a visitor ignorant of the war's outcome might have found it hard, on first arrival, to determine who had won and who had lost. Thanks largely to the enormous help which the U.S. Marshall Plan had granted to the losers in the Western orbit of occupation and to the energetic rebuilding of their national economies, outward appearances might well have made it seem that victorious England, under its self-imposed austerity program, had been defeated by an apparently more prosperous Germany and a far more cheerful Italy. But there was unmistakable evidence that newly formed governments, in virtually all the major European countries, supported a robust revival of cultural life as a national priority. A society still in deep distress had found its first healing in those areas of civilized existence that had not been tarnished in the catastrophe.

Arguably, the herald of Europe's cultural renaissance after the Second World War was the British Broadcasting Corporation. "Auntie," as the network became known affectionately or was called in moments of exasperation, depended for financial support on license fees on all privately owned radio (and later television) sets; administrative oversight rested with an appointed board of governors, while artistic policy was the responsibility of controllers of respective departments. Taking office in 1945, a new Labour government introduced significant changes of emphasis in programming for its broadcasting franchise. A new BBC Third Programme (No.'s 1 and 2 having been the Home Service and the Light Programme, respectively) aimed proudly at providing for "minority tastes": tastes of an educated listenership, too small to be commercially viable. Inevitably these goals were labeled elitist, but as in the rest of Europe, national pride in a great cultural legacy overrode stubborn objections to a government-sponsored monopoly that served the greatest good for a comparatively small number of listeners. The looked-for result was that this number would grow. And so it did.

Musical resources were so remarkable as to be unique. The BBC employed its own symphony orchestra in London—one of the best in Europe—as well as fine regional orchestras in Manchester, Scotland, and Wales. For many years it also engaged the services of London's four other major orchestras, the Royal Philharmonic, the London Symphony Orchestra, the London Philharmonic Orchestra, and the Philharmonia Orchestra (later the New Philharmonia orchestra), to sustain a vast program of live as well as prerecorded performances.

The so-called Proms, century-old promenade concerts that dated from a debut in August 1895, with "full orchestra" under Henry Wood in Queens Hall, had by now moved to the Royal Albert Hall, filled 6,000 seats for eight weeks in the summers of postwar London, and offered symphonic programs that employed not only England's own ensembles but also many of the world's finest orchestras under some thirty conductors. Many programs were so long and so diverse that they required one conductor for the first half and another for the second half of the performance. The cost for the series was underwritten by Auntie, with the BBC Orchestra under Sir Adrian Boult, its chief conductor since 1942, contributing the major share of concerts. Inclusion of contemporary works became a principal concern in programming. Sir Adrian was a master at lightening the orchestra's often tedious task of preparing an unfamiliar score for performance. Leslie Ayre, for many years music critic of the London *Evening News*, recalls how "on one occasion he [Boult] spotted a decidedly odd passage in the score and, turning to the orchestra, asked, 'Is the composer here?' On being told that the composer was not present, Sir Adrian gave a sigh of resignation and said, 'Ah, well, I shall just have to play it as he wrote it.'"[1]

With the appointment of William Glock as Controller of Music, Auntie moved firmly into the international music scene. A fine pianist, pupil of Schnabel,

Luigi Dallapiccola

Glock had himself appeared at the Proms before the war. True to the BBC's established dedication to cultural minority interests, the world's finest soloists and conductors were now actively encouraged by its new Controller of Music to learn and perform major contemporary works, many of them commissioned by the BBC itself. Not until 1980 did the market-driven reforms of Margaret Thatcher's Conservative government succeed in bringing about changes that marked the end of this grand, freewheeling musical enterprise. With television rapidly emerging as the dominant arm of broadcasting, these unhappy reforms were patterned on the developing American model, in which privately owned channels would soon be run for advertising profit by "business school graduates . . . who regard their new acquisitions as cash cows to be milked for a creamier bottom line."[2]

In the years after the war, however, the BBC model of government-sponsored broadcasting became the pattern of national radio all across continental Europe. For the great European radio networks, programming in support of "minority culture" became the accepted norm *because* it would have been a losing proposition in commercial terms. An era of unprecedented creative vitality and general acceptance of musical innovation followed. American composer William Schuman may have had something similar in mind when, in what was perhaps his finest hour as president of Lincoln Center in New York, he answered his board's reprimand about an alleged lack of interest in fund-raising and a lack of attention to the realities of the marketplace with the statement: "At Lincoln

Center, it is your job to find the money, and mine to tell you what to lose it on." What he lost, of course, was his job.

Ironically, in postwar Europe government support for the arts *bolstered* comparable enterprise in the private sector and established fruitful cooperation between individual initiative and public assistance. The Musica Viva (Live music) in Munich was an outstanding example. Founded by composer Karl Amadeus Hartmann in 1945 and actively supported by the publicly funded Bayrische Rundfunk (Bavarian Radio), this remarkable enterprise offered concert programs that combined the music of established twentieth-century classics (e.g. Debussy, Ravel, Schoenberg, Stravinsky, Bartok, and Varese) with works of younger and as yet unknown composers. As in other cultural centers throughout formerly Nazi-occupied Europe, a significant stimulus was the urge to *nachholen* (catching up) for years of artistic denial, years during which contemporary works already in the acknowledged mainstream of Western music had been proscribed as *Entartete Musik* (degenerate music). K. H. Ruppel, leading music critic in Munich, wrote in 1958: "It was in the air at that time to revive the foundered, barren German musical life through the performance of modern works, not least because one of the most repellent cultural lies of National Socialism had been that modern art was rotten, decadent and devoid of creative force."[3]

Quite aside from being one of Germany's most important composers, Karl Amadeus Hartmann was a unique human being. During the ascendancy of the Nazi regime and the war that followed, he had so internalized his distress over the malignancy of the Nazi regime that he not only withdrew completely from active musical life for the duration but also was unable to compose. Even after the war, when the Munich opera house was being rebuilt, he would thunder whenever he passed the site, "They should leave it in ruins to remind them forever of what they've done!" He could not have looked less one's image of a lean, hungry resistance hero. Chubby, gregarious, with a loud voice and extravagant gestures, he ruled much of Munich's musical domain from his large high-ceilinged apartment, furnished in extravagant late-nineteenth-century taste. He owned a car that only his wife, Louise, could drive and harbored an extravagant affection for Bavaria's Mad King Ludwig (Ludwig II), Wagner's patron, who had very nearly ruined his country's economy by building too many exquisite palaces and proto-Disney Richard Wagner theme parks for the king's personal use. He eventually drowned himself in one of Bavaria's most beautiful lakes, but he lived on in the heart of Karl Amadeus Hartmann.

In its role as presenter of a vast amount of new music that had been banned in Nazi-occupied Europe, Hartmann's Musica Viva was soon joined by Pierre Boulez's Domaines Musicales in Paris and by Luigi Nono's Incontri in Milan. The ISCM also availed itself of resources offered by the new government radio networks and their superb orchestras. Under such auspices, new music was not only performed but performed by artists of the first rank. For all the material and psychological ravages in the wake of the war, an exciting sense of cultural renaissance was unmistakable in that potent mix of efforts at reconstruction.

This writer well remembers his astonishment and pleasure when a representative of Schott Music Publishers arrived at his office at Juilliard in New York with a bulging briefcase full of new scores, not merely for perusal but as a gift. Most impressively, moreover, someone had done real homework on assembling this collection: there was not a single score that did not match my particular interests at that time, and, needless to say, I performed most of them in the years to follow. Nor was there a mystery about the identity of the man who had done his homework: Howard Hartog, an Englishman whose active service in the war was followed by his appointment as Controller of Music in the newly formed North German Broadcasting Service in Hamburg and his service, until 1949, as director of Austrian Radio, both in the British zone of occupation. After leaving the service, he was handpicked by Schott in London to promote new music around the world. Nowhere in postwar Europe were the winds of change felt more powerfully than in the arts and their allied fields.

The Sessions family left Berkeley immediately after the end of the academic year 1950–51. This was to be their first major journey as a family, and relocation for an entire year strained even Lisl's organizing skills to their limits. Nonetheless, the logistics of the Sessions exodus were firmly under control, as far as the home front was concerned, but departure from the university, in the midst of the annual flurry of final examinations and graduation, was less carefully planned. We have already mentioned the still-pending matter of the university's loyalty oath.[4] Ever the faithful partner, Lisl blamed *herself* later on for letting her husband sign the official declaration on the mere rumor that "everybody else is doing it." As he had signed it, however, apparently in a minority of one, Sessions' subsequent stop-over in Princeton became more than a casual visit among old friends. But as Lisl put it: "Roger was quite ready to come back east."[5]

For Fulbright Lecturer Roger Sessions, arriving in Italy in 1951 on a cultural exchange program sponsored by his own government, presenting a fair picture of the composer's situation in the United States was a challenge. For all of America's generous support of economic reconstruction in Europe, the idea of public patronage of the arts at home inevitably aroused bitter political opposition in Congress, while a business-oriented society expected cultural goods and services to be paid for by those who wanted them.[6] In his seven lectures at the Cherubini Academy in Florence, Sessions succeeded remarkably well. He provided a balanced picture of musical life in the United States without inviting invidious comparisons with the current condition of composers in the musical life of the old continent.

Establishing the unique historical background of music in a young country as a point of departure, Sessions neither glossed over problems he had identified in an earlier article, "The Composer in a Business Economy,"[7] nor dwelled on personal frustrations he had endured while trying to find his way through the cultural maze of the musical scene at home after his return in 1933. He emphasized the growing strength of musical instruction in American higher education and traced the increasing role of the university in providing independent alternatives to the highly polished, expensive, and necessarily business-oriented musical enterprise of major musical organizations in the private sector of the economy:

> In our universities the most independent forces of American culture seem to gather—influences free from political or commercial pressures; the universities, more than any other institutions, sustain their role as strongholds of independent and liberal thought, and, with a few regrettable exceptions, they are jealously committed to the conservation of that independence. They shelter the cultural activities which have difficulty acclimatizing themselves to the excesses of commercialism, and they provide means for the independent existence of worthy activities within their own walls.
>
> . . . Some universities such as Michigan, Wisconsin, and Illinois possess Schools of Music which are genuine professional schools similar to our medical and law schools. Others such as California, Columbia, Harvard, and Princeton have music departments which, though integrated in the Colleges of Liberal Arts, include in their curricula not only composition courses frankly professional in standard and aim, but also generally high-quality courses in the performance of choral, orchestral, and chamber music and, frequently, in opera. Some universities support "Quartets in Residence," generally established ensembles which are under contract to contribute their services during a certain portion of the year for campus concerts and instruction as well. The Pro Arte Quartet at Wisconsin, the Griller Quartet at the University of California at Berkeley, and the Walden Quartet at the University of Illinois are examples.
>
> In some respects, this program constitutes a radical departure from the traditional role of the university as established in Europe. It is the result of a long and frequently complex evolution.[8]

In providing perspective on the historical background of musical life in America and tracing its expansion into the American university, these lectures elaborated themes already developed in Sessions' earlier writings. In the final lecture, however, he touched upon a new topic: European influences on American music, resulting from the settlement of Europe's foremost composers in the United States during the recent world crisis:

> The influence of European musicians who found refuge here during the thirties and the early years of World War II, the most distinguished as well as the most modest, can scarcely be overestimated. It is unnecessary to speak of the important role they have played, since that is well known; looking back at the situation as it presented itself at the time, one can be impressed both by the cordiality with which they were nearly always received and the spirit in which, with few exceptions, they embraced the entirely new conditions history had thrust upon them . . .
>
> We are dealing, in other words, with a concept of American music differing sharply from that heretofore discussed: one which views the United States basically as a new embodiment of the occidental spirit, finding in

> that spirit not only the premises but the basic directives which have given our national development its authentic character. Such a view assumes the cultural independence of the United States both as a fact and as a natural goal . . . The same view also recognizes that real independence is an intimate and inherent quality which is acquired through maturity, and not a device with which one can emblazon one's self by adopting slogans or programs of action . . . Only when the ideas are no longer preconceived, when, in other words, a large body of music of all kinds will have brought a secure tradition into being, then the American musical profile will emerge and the question of American style or character assume meaning . . .
>
> The "great line of Western tradition" provides the most fertile source of nourishment also for American music . . . In the absence of an indigenous tradition expressing itself in our criticism, our music education, and our practice of music, there is no group of composers which would or could identify itself with a conservative traditionalism, nor is there a means of opposition to new music on that level . . . The word "tradition" here assumes the most dynamic of its senses: that which implies *continuity* rather than that which fosters domination by the past.

The great American "melting pot" had indeed begun to include a diverse and distinguished group of European composers, who chose to stay on after the end of the catastrophic upheavals that had driven them abroad: Schoenberg, Stravinsky, Hindemith, Bartok, Varese, and Milhaud, to name only a few whose work may fairly be said to have created "a large body of music of all kinds [that] will have brought a secure tradition into being."

American composers meanwhile continued to identify defiantly with one or another of these luminaries and engaged in an ongoing polemic that rested heavily on disparaging the followers of another superstar composer. At the same time, a full range of *new* composers had begun to dominate the musical life of postwar Europe, and here it was Fulbright Lecturer Sessions' turn to sort himself out against a largely unfamiliar professional environment.

Most immediately striking would have been a discovery that powerful sponsoring institutions supported new music with feverish enthusiasm. At home it was up to composers and their occasional sympathizers to interest the establishment as best they could. In the new Europe, composers actually controlled much of the musical life. From the remove of half a century it is hard to do justice to the excitement and enthusiasm that informed that vibrant musical scene. Composers seemed less concerned with their associative affinity or the putative importance of "schools" than with a mutual effort, on a very wide front, to apply Wagner's famous exhortation to "make it new!" They could afford it. Like painters of the Italian Renaissance, they could compete successfully for commissions and support in the here and now, rather than to write in pseudoseclusion and worry about posthumous musical museum space. For some three decades to come, that competitive, thriving, and healthily self-serving way of musical life resembled nothing more than the confident cut-and-thrust of an artistic scene dominated by the *condottieri* and merchant princes four hundred years ago. Government and publicly funded institutions took the lead in supporting the commission and performance of new music much as secular and religious rulers of the Italian Renaissance had once vied for the prestige of securing the services of the best artists and craftsmen of their day.

A new generation of composers had transformed the European musical landscape. Hans Werner Henze, born in 1926, Karlheinz Stockhausen, born in 1928, and Bernd Alois Zimmermann, born in 1918, in Germany; Pierre Boulez, born in 1925 in France; Gottfried von Einem, born in 1918 in Austria; Janis Xenakis, born in 1921 in Greece; Luciano Berio, born in 1925, Luigi Nono, born in 1926, and Riccardo Malipiero (nephew of Gian Francesco), born in 1917, in Italy, would soon dominate the New Music festivals at Darmstadt and Donaueschingen. At the same time, a group of older composers—too young to have participated prominently in prewar musical life in their own countries or too independent, musically or politically, to have pleased the cultural chiefs of totalitarian regimes—had grown influential after the war. Karl Amadeus Hartmann in Germany was such a one, as was Olivier Messiaen in France, while the most prominent new Italians were Goffredo Petrassi and Luigi Dallapiccola. In Florence in 1951, Dallapiccola became Roger Sessions' friend:

> Among all my contemporaries Luigi was the one composer with whom I always felt I could speak freely and without reserve; he was the one whose music and whose thoughts I valued above all others, and the one living composer who represented for me my awareness that the continuity of music at its highest point is still unbroken and that truly great achievement still existed and may still be possible. Perhaps above all a human being to whom I was devoted, whose friendship I treasured very deeply, and for whom my admiration was completely unsullied.[9]

Casella had first mentioned Dallapiccola to Sessions just before he left Rome for Berlin in 1932. Not long after, as a member of the ISCM jury that selected works for performance at the 1934 festival in Amsterdam, Sessions had cast his vote for Dallapiccola's Partita for Orchestra, the first performance the young Italian composer would have in an international setting. But only now, eighteen years later, did the two composers meet.

> The evening of our arrival [in Florence] my wife and I met our friend Leonardo Olschki, who knew I hoped to meet Dallapiccola; he immediately proposed to call him by telephone, in order to arrange a meeting between us.
>
> The result was an invitation to spend an evening which I shall always remember . . . I felt an instant and lively sympathy which, as the autumn, winter and spring passed, developed into a deep affection, and an ever-growing admiration for a personality that was vivid, profoundly cultivated, and gifted, all in the highest degree . . . In the years that followed our first meeting my affection and my admiration have grown steadily, and although geography, and the involvements of our respective lives, made our meetings ever less frequent, I remained constantly aware of him, of his music, and of its high significance for myself personally.[10]

What exactly was the high significance of Dallapiccola's music for that of Roger Sessions? Most certainly it involved the sung word. Dallapiccola was primarily a vocal composer. Poetry, excerpts from sacred literature, and even philosophical works could suddenly prod his musical imagination into providing a musical complement. His autobiographical sketch is filled with references to literary sources of his musical inspiration:

> I had just read the biography of Mary Stuart by Stefan Zweig (1935), and I am indebted to this book for the knowledge of a brief prayer which the Queen of the Scots wrote during the last years of her imprisonment . . . All of a sudden the music began to impel me, so forcefully that I had to interrupt work on [the opera] *Volo di Notte.*[11]
>
> In two phrases from *De Consolatione Philosophiae* by Severinus Boethius, I found the text I needed for the second movement of *Canti di Prigionia.*[12]
>
> Only by memorizing a poem can I truly appreciate it—by turning it over and over in my mind as I walk the streets, savoring every word and every syllable. Without such a process of gradual absorption, I don't believe I could possibly find a musical equivalent for the poem.[13]

On the face of it, nothing could be more unlike the autonomous musical idea that informed Sessions' approach to composition. The intuitive, unbidden musical image that aroused his imagination had no a priori literary reference, on which he let his musical imagination dwell and elaborate until it eventually emerged as an *extramusical* image, enlivened by the words of a chosen text. It might well have given Sessions pause had he not been trying to write his operatic magnum opus at that very time. *Montezuma* happened to be the only work with which Sessions occupied himself during his trip to Italy in 1951–1952, and an opera libretto does suggest a "musical equivalent" of the dramatic gestures of a prior text. But even here the difference between the approaches of the two composers remains unmistakable. As we have seen, Sessions believed that "opera is not drama *with* music, but drama *in* music." *Drama in Music* first appeared as the subtitle of his earlier opera, *The Trial of Lucullus*. It would be some years before he realized that a musical idea sketched ten years before and destined to appear in the very first measures of *Montezuma* would continue to inform the entire work until its final version, whose very beginning still lay years in the future.[14]

In spite of these differences, a ripening friendship encouraged mutual exploration of respective musical strengths, Dallapiccola's approach to composition, stimulated largely by lyrical poetry, soon found an unexpected echo in the work of his American colleague. The last of the three quotations cited earlier comes from the composer's notes about *Cinque canti* (Five songs) for baritone and eight instruments, dedicated to Roger Sessions. In turn, after his return to America, Sessions tried his hand at a comparable work, *The Idyll of Theocritus* for soprano and orchestra, dedicated to his Italian friend who had suggested the text. *Theocritus* was unlike anything Sessions had composed before; with its mesmerizing refrains, perceptible musical equivalents of the poem's "O magic wheel, draw hither to my house the man I love" or "Bethink thee of my love and whence it came, O holy Moon," it stands as a harbinger of Sessions' greatest lyrical work, twenty years hence: his cantata on Walt Whitman's "When Lilacs Last in the Dooryard Bloomed."

For all that, it might have seemed an unlikely friendship, had Sessions and Dallapiccola not shared, each in his own way, a private point of creative orientation and the assumption of an inward source that empowered and gave direction to their work. Given the mutual discovery of that kinship, their primary differences in musical approach yielded a challenge of opposites, complementing and eventually enriching the creative dispositions of both composers.

There was yet another, equally basic contrast between the two men, and here again Sessions was the primary beneficiary of their friendship. In paying tribute to his friend as a "composer who represented for me my awareness that the continuity of music at its highest point is still unbroken," Sessions expressed more than admiration for Dallapiccola's work: he voiced an American composer's very real concern about the future of an art that, in his own country, seemed increasingly relegated to academic sanctuary within the university, while, in the "real world" commercial control of the most powerful and expensive musical outlets threatened to shrink a narrowing public base. For all of Sessions' more recent disclaimers, the early memory of Mrs. Wilmerding's reservations about American composers still resonated. Dallapiccola, on the other hand, never harbored the slightest doubts about his inborn legitimacy as an Italian composer. If Sessions' development reflected his conservative New England background in an America—a national background that had not yet fully engaged on the cutting edge of Western musical heritage, Dallapiccola, six years younger and from an equally provincial, if almost archetypally ambiguous, European setting, never doubted his place as the proud heir of a grand tradition. Born in an ethnically mixed Austrian border region that was only ceded to Italy after World War I, he felt himself as Florentine as Dante, when he made his home in that ancient city. He identified with his Renaissance hero even to his lifelong dislike of Rome. Pride in a great cultural heritage and in a magnificent, frequently cruel but quintessentially European past had inspired and empowered his work even in the quite recently brutal present. In Dallapiccola's Florence, and in the wake of the Inferno of the Second World War, the Italian composer quite naturally played the role of Virgil to Sessions' Dante as they explored the Purgatory of Western music in midcentury Europe. Completing this extravagant metaphor, Lisl would guide her husband's eventual journey through the Paradiso of his musical harvest to come.

The two composers occupied comparable positions within the profession. Dallapiccola, like Sessions, enjoyed considerable international acclaim in his lifetime but earned only the grudging respect of colleagues who did not care for his music. Both composers were difficult and expensive to perform, and their works would be more widely praised than played. Sponsorship of live performances via the newly potent national radio networks in Europe and enterprising music schools in the United States provided a tenuous but effective lifeline between composer and listener in midcentury and enabled them to develop a rich store of new works in active engagement with real audiences. But once bereft of the institutional support for music that appealed to "minority tastes"—a support on which Western music had depended for three hundred years—the works of Dallapiccola and Sessions, among many others, would fall victim to the popular marketplace on both sides of the Atlantic, an event at which corporate sponsors and a sizable segment of the profession itself heaved an almost audible sigh of relief. The latter discovered the virtues of a *new romanticism* for mass appeal and *minimalism* for a new elite, much as fifty years earlier their predecessors had acclaimed the *new classicism* and dismissed an entire generation of "difficult composers" as if they were motorcars recalled for faulty design. Eminent writer on music, Michael Steinberg, said it best in his introduction to a review of Karl Amadeus Hartmann's Second Symphony: "Hartmann is one of those composers—Roger Sessions and Luigi Dallapiccola are others who come to mind—with whom the distance between achievement and reputation is absurd."[15]

Who was Luigi Dallapiccola?

> The background is the family of a teacher of classical languages at the only Italian secondary school permitted by the Austro-Hungarian government in the middle of that tiny peninsula called Istria . . . The little Istrian peninsula where I was born lies at the crossing of three borders. When the train stopped at the station of my hometown, the conductor called out: "Mitterburg, Pisino, Pazin" . . . I was ten years old and just beginning high school when, in 1914, the first phase of World War I convulsed Europe . . . Our home life continued to be calm and uneventful. Sometimes I would hear about the Irredentist movements of Italian-speaking subjects of the Austro-Hungarian Empire, I was also aware of the rivalry between Italians and Slavs. But in a region like mine, one of mixed population, all this seemed quite unexceptional. And so my childhood passed calmly . . .
>
> Only today, many years later, can I express the swiftness of the change when I recall meeting a friend of my own age in 1916, on the morning the newspapers reported that the Austrian prime minister Count Karl von Stürgkh had been assassinated by the socialist Friedrich Adler. Winking at me, my friend whispered: "Another one gone." Thus even twelve-year-olds had been infected by the new mentality: Human life had lost much of its value . . . [The Irredentists]were to be expelled from the border zones and sent to the interior of Austria. The school my father had directed with such love, where he had taught for so many years, was closed overnight on the grounds that it was a "protest school" *(ein Trotz-Gymnasium)*, in the jargon of the authorities. And so my family, escorted by a policeman, was obliged to arrive in Graz on 27 March 1917 . . .
>
> We were never treated harshly. My father was under no particular obligation, except to report periodically to the police. However, the sudden

> change from the tranquil rhythm of the first ten years of my life to what later happened was a little too abrupt. I had the impression that an injustice had been done and felt deeply humiliated.
>
> The food situation, already very serious when we arrived at Graz, deteriorated from one day to the next . . . Eighty cents wasn't enough to purchase black-market bread, but it could be used to buy a ticket for the gallery at the opera. Unable to give me bread, my mother sent me to the theatre.[16]

A musical future was already on his mind, but there was neither an equivalent to Harvard with the Boston Symphony just across the Charles River nor an Ernest Bloch to guide him through the uncertain early stages of becoming Luigi Dallapiccola, composer. Every step in his gradual advance toward his own "grammar and syntax of musical emotion" was immediately questioned by himself, carefully developed, and then most often rejected. His fierce integrity would not let him accept solutions to problems that he felt were not his own:

> Put yourself in the place of a boy who, at the age of fifteen, goes to Bologna for Easter—his first trip to Italy after the War. This was in 1919. I was in the company of my old uncle, who was very fond of me. We of course stopped, enchanted, in front of the window of the music store of Pizzi. I saw: Claude Debussy, *Pelléas et Mélisande*. And I asked my uncle, who was an ardent music lover: "Do you know this work, *Pelléas et Mélisande*?" "It's Debussy's masterpiece," he replied. I was ashamed that he, though not a musician, knew the name of a composer I had never heard of before. After I returned home, I resumed my piano lessons. And then by way of *La Cathédrale Engloutie* I began to discover what there was in Debussy . . . It had such an effect on me that for three years I did not write another note because I understood that I would have merely imitated Debussy.[17]

Twenty-five years passed and another war. Following the defeat of Mussolini's armies, large-scale deportation of Jews began in the German-occupied areas of Italy. Dallapiccola's wife, Laura, was Jewish:

> Nazi troops occupied Florence on 11 September 1943 . . . A friend generously offered us asylum in his villa at Borgunto, north of Fiesole. Here I finished *Sex Carmina Alcaei* and then fell silent . . .[18]
>
> At the beginning of February, the villa in Borgunto was requisitioned by a German command. We had no choice but to return to our apartment in the Viale Margherita and remain there until we received the next warning. Then some fraternal friends would cordially welcome us to wait long days and interminable evenings with them for the hour of liberation . . .
>
> What totally unnerved me were the insidious persecution and the constant threat of anonymous denunciations—always carried out, in fact—the vulgar journalistic prose and the petty Fascist functionaries sporting the Roman eagle on their caps, who stared meaningfully when they met you in the street.[19]

As long ago as 1929, Sessions had also expressed his distaste for Fascism:

> . . . what Fascism is in the Italian spirit that I find intolerable. Rome, intellectually, I find stuffy, narrow, & provincial to the last degree; one cannot with comfort discuss freely any controversial or even any contemporary subject—in Italian circles, I mean, one is constantly running up against a stupid and rather vulgar Roman & Italian vanity and overbearing arrogance which hinders almost every kind of easy relationship.[20]

But what had seemed merely "stuffy, narrow, & provincial" to the young American visitor a quarter-century ago became life-threatening for his European colleague, an omnipresent darkness that foreshadowed much of his creative work to come. Dallapiccola's opera, *Il Prigionero* (The prisoner), begun during the war and first performed in broadcast version by the Italian Radio in Turin in December 1949, reflects an existential, old-world acceptance of the reality of evil, much as Sessions' *Montezuma* expresses its composer's optimistic American faith in an eventual advent of great good to overcome an apparent triumph of evil. Both operas are set in the occupied dominions of Philip II of Spain, *The Prisoner* in the Netherlands, *Montezuma* in Mexico. Both are about hope, and the protagonists of both are doomed. But the hero of Dallapiccola's opera based on Villiers de l'Isle-Adam's story, *La Torture par l'espérance* (Torture by hope), suffers an illusion of hope that becomes the Grand Inquisitor's most refined instrument of torture; while the tragic death of Borgese/Sessions' Montezuma holds out acute faith in the historic fulfillment of an eventual union of his people with the race of the invaders, conqueror and conquered, Old World and New.

Popular reaction to the broadcast premiere of *The Prisoner* in 1949 protested furiously against the evident winds of change that would soon, albeit briefly, compensate artists in the Old World for the cultural ravages of two world wars: "Letters to the government, one of which said: 'It is a disgrace that an opera which casts a dim light on the Holy Spanish Inquisition should be performed in Italy during the Holy Year' . . . Of all the insults hurled at me during the first half of 1950, this was the only one that deeply wounded me."[21]

For all his passionate belief in democracy and freedom, Dallapiccola was also heir to a musical way of life that had once depended on the protection of aristocratic patrons—some more perceptive than others but all of them convinced that their support of intellectual and artistic "minority culture" was part of noblesse oblige: "A unique instance of 'aristocratic' minority is that of Queen Marie Antoinette who, with her authority and diplomacy, saved one of the *Iphigenie* operas by her old teacher Cristoph Gluck. I believe that the minority was on the right side . . . and is it necessary to recount the vicissitudes of *Lohengrin* and *Tristan* and Ludwig II of Bavaria?"[22]

"Aristocratic minority" may be an appropriate way to describe the impression Dallapiccola's own personality made in most gatherings of more than two people, but the customary solemnity of his bearing—which might have seemed comical in a lesser man—could vanish instantly in the warmth of his huge smile. Slow, expressive gestures enhanced and sometimes belied the soft-spoken intensity of his speech, a mode of communication that knew little of small talk but made equally persuasive points in lively reasoning or by eloquent indirection. The most remarkable aspect of his appearance was his carriage: scrupulously erect, as if to make sure that his head—very large for a man of his small stature—would not overbalance. It all added up to a sense of authority, not by force of any kind but by the power of a presence.

> Perhaps my most treasured memory of Dallapiccola, man and artist, is of the final, few precious moments of a rather tense recording session in London. I was ready to try for the last "take" of a very difficult section in one of his works. The red recording light came on, and went off again as the small figure with the majestic head emerged from the control booth—to my frank despair. There was so little time! Oblivious and unhurried he walked to the podium, took my score, examined it in the deafening silence of our arrested final plunge and pointed across the most complex page with that curious circular motion of his extended thumb and hand. Then he looked up and smiled: "*Leggierissimo*," he said.[23]

As Sessions' Fulbright year in Florence came to an end, Dallapiccola left for his second visit to the United States, as a member of the faculty at the Berkshire Music Festival at Tanglewood. The Sessions family prepared to return home via a leisurely detour through Austria, beautiful Sils Maria (of Nietzsche and Rilke) in the Engadine, and Geneva. In late summer, before embarking on the American Export SS *Excambion* at Marseille, Sessions wrote a farewell letter[24] to his new friend. In Vienna he had met Lukas Foss, composer, conductor and longtime adviser to the Boston Symphony's (and Tanglewood's) maestro Serge Koussevitzky, and had heard about Dallapiccola's success at Tanglewood firsthand. Dallapiccola, meanwhile, had chosen to take an even longer detour after his summer school in the Berkshires, visiting Juilliard in New York and taking a holiday—in Mexico. Sessions expresses his hope that Dallapiccola enjoyed that visit to Montezuma country and ends on an extraordinarily optimistic note: "My *Montezuma* has grown wonderfully during the summer in Austria; I have reached a point at which I am working very fast and with great confidence. Right now I am impatient to get back to my own desk and my own study, because I expect to have it all finished within three or four months, and then on to the orchestration!"[25] No doubt—as always—he had a nearly complete image of the work in his head, although the evidence of sketches from this period does not include anything like a nearly finished particell score of *Montezuma.* But pressures other than creative ardor were indeed calling for the completion of his long labor on the opera. A year before, Borgese had reminded him that after their previously agreed deadline of September 1952 for the finished score the libretto could be given to another composer—and Borgese made no bones about his determination to do just that, adding his intention to offer his dramatic text to film and television producers.

Sessions replied with sanguine progress reports to one and all, including Borgese. In response to such a report in January 1952, his long-suffering librettist is "thrilled," while asking politely for an opportunity to approve Sessions' "final version" of his *text*. That version, including substantial cuts that Borgese had never seen, was now being composed: "The poet is, how should I say?, 'blank' about what the composer-surgeon has done to his child." Nor had the poet been apprised of the fact that Sessions was living in Florence while he himself had been in Milan. Borgese died soon after in 1952.

Upon return to Berkeley, Sessions found himself in a changed atmosphere, differing not only from the freewheeling musical life in Europe but also from the situation he had left at the university the year before. On the one hand, following the death of Schoenberg in July of 1951 Sessions was now the "big man" among teachers of composition on the West Coast and some of Schoenberg's students, Dika Newlin among them, came to study with him: "Roger Sessions proved to be a fine teacher; his criticisms seemed gentle after Schoenberg's, but were always to the point and insightful. (He could be sarcastic too; when I brought him a grandiloquent operatic hymn of which I was rather proud, his only comment was, 'Humph! Sounds like Grand Central Station!')"[26] His newly empowered European connections, moreover, made it possible for him to refer young composers who wished to continue studies abroad to famous colleagues abroad (he sent two to Dallapiccola). On the other hand, his hasty signature of the university's loyalty oath, just before last year's departure for Italy, estranged him from some of his colleagues, at a time when his rapid rise to international prominence also caused some grudging resentment. Whatever the reason, he soon abandoned his immediate hopes for completing the large-scale *Montezuma* in order to begin more concentrated work on his Second String Quartet.

Meanwhile he threw himself into active musical politics on behalf of Dallapiccola. On Sessions' initiative, a concert had been arranged for him in San Francisco, immediately following his return from Mexico, as well as a lecture and symposium event to discuss his works at Berkeley. Dallapiccola, whose English was not up to his own standards of acceptable public presentation, insisted on giving his lecture in French, punctuated at prearranged points by encapsulated English summaries by Sessions. On short notice, the fee offered by the university for his appearance at the event appears to have been much smaller than he had hoped. Sessions was outraged, ready to assign the worst motives for the music faculty's hesitation to fully endorse and for the university authorities to adequately fund this multilingual venture: "I need not tell you—they [the music department] know nothing, and unhappily, because the bureaucracy is so powerful in the university, there is little I can do . . . I am sorry—."[27] Somehow his sorrow reached a sympathetic ear, either of the gods whose profitable timing throughout Sessions' life appears to have been flawless or of the powers at the now fully established new music department of Princeton University, where it was decided that the time had come for the prodigal son's return. Beginning with the academic year 1953–54, Sessions would move east again to become William Shubael Professor of Music at Princeton.

CHAPTER 18

The Musical Idea III

I wot myself best how I stand.

—CHAUCER

The only genuine security an artist can find is the knowledge of what he wants, in terms of his art, and in getting it, by whatever means he has at his disposal.

—ROGER SESSIONS

Most composers in mid–twentieth century were "difficult" or suspected of doing their best to become so. Schoenberg and his twelve-tone disciples had appeared hopeless from the start—*nato difficile*—while Stravinsky, after an early scandalous success with such works as *The Rite of Spring*, seemed to have opted for near respectability as the symbolic leader of the so-called neoclassicist movement—until, to the disgust of his true believers, he chose to adopt twelve-tone procedures from 1953. As it happened, Sessions wrote his first twelve-tone work, the Sonata for Solo Violin, in the same year. To the uninitiated, neither composer sounded very different in 1954.

The commercial musical establishment accommodated itself to what it could not alter. Music heard in public venues fell into in three categories: "old" music (Bach, Vivaldi, and before) for the cognoscenti and for musical background in bookstores; Mozart, Haydn, and most of the nineteenth-century classics for the whole family to enjoy; and "modern" music, in small doses, because it was there. One did not have to see the point of it, let alone enjoy it, but it was to be endured as a civic duty and was assigned, in the name of cultural enrichment, to long-suffering audiences. Predictably, the generation to follow would largely dispense with such elitist shuffling.

Sessions' son, John, recalls

> one little anecdote which might amuse you. When my father's 5th Symphony was given its first performance in Philadelphia (Feb. 1964) I was told by my parents to go as a sort of emissary—they were both in Berlin—and that Mr. Ormandy was expecting me to show up backstage after the concert.
>
> Inside the program booklet was an extra sheet informing the audience, more or less, that they were in for a rough ride, because Mr. Sessions wrote very complex and difficult music—signed: Eugene Ormandy and, beneath the signature, printed: General Music Director, the Philadelphia Orchestra.
>
> After the concert I was taken back and introduced to the Maestro, who was very cordial and nice—until he suddenly became somewhat agitated and said: "I'm really very angry about that extra sheet they put into the program . . . "
>
> Me (trying to be polite) "Oh, er . . . I think it was a little unnecessary . . . "
>
> Mo. O (by now pink with rage, brandishing the offending sheet and stabbing at the bottom of it with his forefinger) "UNNECESSARY? I mean . . . look at this thing—you see this? 'General Music Director, the Philadelphia Orchestra' . . . I mean, my God!, as if there was anybody around here who doesn't know who I am!"[1]

An amusing story, instructive but not very funny. After first blushing for Mr. Ormandy, one remembers that ever since Bach's congregation complained about his "distortions" of the Sunday hymns in church and Mozart was called a hunter of dissonances, there has been a fairly widespread assumption that perfectly respectable composers make their works difficult on purpose. The truth is that even very respectable composers found it hard to "hear" the new music of their time, let alone relate it to their own very different (and in the ear of the contemporary listener perhaps also difficult) realization of their musical ideas.

In Franz Werfel's novel *Verdi*,[2] the aging composer confronts the appearance in Italy of his powerful, controversial German colleague Richard Wagner, idol of young enthusiasts and instant ogre of the old operatic elite. Less dogmatic than Wagner's conservative detractors but increasingly doubtful about his own work after a decade of near impotence as a composer, professionally curious but personally vulnerable, Verdi manages to ignore for a long time a piano-vocal score of *Tristan,* which a young Wagner fan has smuggled into a drawer in his hotel room in Venice. But when, in a moment of unattended crisis, he opens the score, he is disappointed! Whatever he might have expected—some utterly new and strange musical language—he found only harmonic devices he himself had used in his later work. Werfel explains that his Verdi is a "poor reader," meaning presumably that he has problems in translating the visual image of a score into an immediate aural experience within. Whatever the historical evidence for such an assertion, the author makes expert use of it in what his Verdi encounters next. The composer is struck by apparent harmonic ambiguities, which Wagner seemed to encourage by his lavish use of diminished and augmented chords. It seems to him that this affected the clear contour of phrases, requiring definition by means other than the distinct closure of harmonic cadences such as the ones that articulate his own work. Thus the essence of musical continuity in *Tristan* was different; time passed differently in Wagner's music. That he found intriguing. His own *Otello* and *Falstaff* were not far off, and the real as well as the fictional Verdi was about to take another step.

"*Continuity* . . . might almost be considered synonymous with time itself."[3] Sessions spent the first half of his professional life mastering this self-evident proposition before he discovered how the passage of time in his music was controlled by the pursuit of aural requirements laid down by a priori musical ideas. He certainly was an excellent reader-translator of inner images offered by his own musical imagination, and it would be very hard to imagine that this experienced teacher of composers had problems "hearing" the work of others. It would also be hard to believe that of the real Verdi, but the reaction of Werfel's fictional composer on first perusing the *Tristan* score is nonetheless very much in keeping with the self-limiting approach of an expert musician who applies his accustomed craft to the examination of a score without also willing himself to experience it with his inner ear: he recognizes what is different in the grammar and syntax of its construction and may well be intrigued by the way the composer manages the result in terms of musical continuity, but failing to *experience* the music in the audible silence of his own mind, he cannot respond to it.

In our earliest training in musical analysis, most of us were conditioned to think about a composition as a frozen kind of visual reflection of the notation on the printed page. We learned to speak about it in borrowed spatial terms—*shape, structure, image*—without any sense of what the ear may experience in the quickening effect of time. In this, even after his excellent instruction by Ernest Bloch, the young Roger Sessions was no exception until, during his Berkeley years, he finally became fully conscious of the primacy of time and continuity in music: "Music is controlled movement of sound in time."[4] On those terms his remaining problems of compositional craft resolved themselves. Full realization of the ultimate authority of his inner ear finally allowed him—a composer in his fifties—to compose fluently and trustingly at last, without being "dismayed to see myself writing the kind of music that I had to write but which was very different from my idea of myself at the time."[5]

Some of the greatest creative artists appear to themselves as a constantly endangered species. The more powerful and intriguing another's work may appear to a composer on the cutting edge of mastery, the more threatening it becomes to the integrity of his own creative identity. In hindsight, Verdi's paralyzing notion of Wagner's music as a menace to his identity might seem absurd, but it seemed real enough to the composer at the time. In my own experience, the gentle Dallapiccola calling Stravinsky's *Agon dirrty* music, or William Schuman, brilliant head of America's best music school, going out of his way to discourage press coverage of a Schoenberg premiere at Juilliard seemed shockingly and gratuitously churlish. But in an equally incomprehensible posture of needless self-defense, Sessions—who had once asserted that rather than avoid the influences of Bloch and Stravinsky he would try to absorb them in his music[6]—assured his friends, his pupils, and of course himself that the twelve-tone "system," intriguing and even admirable though he found it in the best work of Schoenberg, Berg, Krenek, and Dallapiccola, would never be for him. No wonder he was dismayed when he discovered that his ever autonomous musical ideas nonetheless had led him firmly toward that environment.

Sessions' early steps in that direction were small enough to be almost unnoticed, even by the composer himself. But having allowed himself to make ever more puzzling concessions in order "to write the music he had to write," he eventually found himself in musical territory in which neither the principles of functional harmony nor yet the new concepts of serial composition (with important contributions from his student Milton Babbitt to come) had primary relevance along the way from musical idea to completed work. The attentive inner ear, a valued companion during the years of his cautious advance over the years, now became his indispensable guide.

Long before, Schoenberg had attempted comparable departures from the vestigial remains of harmonic function in some of his pre-twelve-tone atonal works (e.g., *Erwartung*) and had to pursue his musical imagination and his creative intelligence wherever it would lead. Sessions now found himself—surprised and dismayed, by his own admission—in a similar quandary. The tonal center would not hold. In his program notes for the first performance of his Second Symphony in San Francisco, he wrote: "The subject of tonality is complex and even problematical these days, and if I use terms which I myself find inadequate to the facts of contemporary music, it is because they possess certain essentials more satisfactorily than any others I know."[7]

He did know. During the following summer, in his Juilliard lectures on the musical experience, he articulated a number of basic structural terms that, used as organic reference in the process of composition, proved entirely adequate to the facts of his work: "The elements of . . . [composition]—contrast, association, continuity, articulation, proportion—are not factors of which the composer at his work thinks in the abstract, but rather words that roughly symbolize and classify the immediate demands that his ear makes in concrete musical situations."[8]

"Words that roughly symbolize and classify the immediate demands that his ear makes." They are not necessarily an improvement over standard analytical terms *unless* the ear and aural imagination have played their part. *Then* they allow for and indeed facilitate the involvement of aural imagination, are descriptive of the work and of the process in which the work takes shape, avoid any suggestion of formula, and, most important, will clarify continuity, the dimension of time.

Being Roger Sessions, it took him some years more to concede that here, in fact, were concepts that would form a coherent matrix for further creative development. Schoenberg was quicker to realize the import of that accomplishment. After Leon Kirchner had played the Second Piano Sonata for him in 1946, he wrote to Sessions: "Here is a language! By which I mean the greatest achievement a composer could arrive at."[9]

The musical language of a great composer is the unique vehicle that conveys his message. It is not the message. Again Sessions would come to quote Schoenberg: "A Chinese philosopher speaks Chinese, of course, but the important thing is what he has to say." Twentieth-century musical debate involved so much theory and terminology disguised as language that what composers were actually trying to "say" often seemed lost in scholastic contention within the profession. Small wonder it sounded Chinese to most listeners. The ear had little to do with it, and given the formidable cast of battling schools and systems, it would almost seem as if individual composers had not much to do with it, either.

Poor Sessions. Ever since he was a boy on a bicycle, delighting in the discovery that the tunes he whistled were of his own making, he was aware of the ear as somehow connected with a musical idea. Twenty years later, with the benefit of Bloch's training in compositional craft, he found that one musical idea could generate an entire musical organism. "[Then] I had to discover who I was and what my music was."[10] That was hard when "the kind of music that I had to write . . . was very different from my idea of myself at the time."[11] Another twenty years were to pass before his inner ear and his critical imagination were finally in exclusive control of the organic evolution of large and complex works. As a composer, he was at peace with himself at last, but "all I wrote about music was in self-defense. I felt very much alone."[12]

In order to show how little any of this had to do with contemporary jargon of "schools" and "systems" of composition, we shall look briefly at the creative path suggested by three major compositions on which Sessions worked at the time: the Second Symphony, the Second Piano Sonata, and *Montezuma*. In the first two, a musical idea was powerfully at work from the start. The third, enthusiastically undertaken and carried forward, failed for the time being. Eventually *Montezuma* would be a twelve-tone work; the others were not. Sessions had yet to discover his own kind of twelve-tone process, and although the development of his musical thought from the Second Symphony and the Second Piano Sonata to that discovery seems clear in hindsight, the composer had to experience it first and gain confidence in its bearing on his musical thinking at the time.

The Second Piano Sonata (1946) was written in a feverish encounter with its musical idea, which, as usual, knew better what it wanted to become when it grew up than its composer had reckoned with. Intended as a "short piece" for pianist Andor Foldes, in five weeks it grew into a sonatina and finally revealed itself as a full-fledged sonata. Its musical idea is introduced (Ex. 18.1) as a steep melodic reach, a poised balance at its peak, and a stepwise downward release

Example 18.1

of the resultant tension. Michael Campbell, in his comprehensive analyses of Sessions' three piano sonatas, writes:

> It is impossible to overestimate the generative role of the opening gesture, the nuclear idea of the [second] sonata. It shapes the sonata in all important aspects, influencing its development through a complex network of associations based on the character of the gesture, as from the melodic and/or rhythmic shape, in conjunction with the intervallic relations within or between melody and accompaniment. The associations are remarkable for their comprehensiveness; they determine relationships in all dimensions . . .
>
> One of the most characteristic features of the sonata highlights the emphasis on long-range continuity: Sessions anticipates each major articulation with climaxes which suggest tension in stasis, The music builds to, briefly remains at, and then recedes from a peak with little release of tension, harmonic or otherwise, either during the detensification or at the articulation which follows. Both the quality and the location of these climactic moments help maintain tensions through and beyond articulation, yet they are forceful enough to define clearly the formal design . . .
>
> The tonal plan of the sonata is the ultimate expansion of the harmonization of the appoggiatura-like release motive: it outlines a descent from D to C.[13]

It is easy to identify the long-range reflections of the *musical idea* in the musical shape of its first appearance in Example 18.1. It flares up, sustains itself at the top, and sinks back by a whole step, briefly, on its last eighth note. The idea of a pervasive, characteristic musical shape informing a large work was not new, nor did Sessions invent it. I have written elsewhere, in some detail, about such an omnipresent shape in the Third Symphony of Brahms, among others.[14] What is particular to Sessions' work, however, and relevant to his development as a composer is that a single generative musical idea anticipates that shape and determines structural, harmonic, and gestural aspects of the work in an organic fashion.

Recognition of such a generative musical germ presents an essential clue—for the performer as well as for the listener. Sessions, in his writing and in his teaching has given us abundant evidence of its importance to him as a composer. The genetic code, as it were, of a new work began for him with an idea, a musical idea, which continued to develop itself in his mind—and sometimes quite independently—as he developed it on paper. That this genetic code is not nec-

Example 18.2

essarily a theme as such—there are always other themes and shapes and gestures related to it—has been evident since the First Piano Sonata. But with the Second Symphony (1944–1946) that relationship itself had become looser and freer, so that stimulated remembrance of musical events—*association*—became his aim rather than literal repetition and recall. Thus he was free to modify and develop even the musical matrix itself and to establish differences of kind and degree in consequent relationships.

For the listener, recognition of what is being modified requires whatever help the composer may be able to give. This may have moved Sessions to restate the consequential chord (Ex. 18.2) that opens the Second Symphony at each of the connecting points between the five parts of the first movement—three *molto agitato* sections enclosing two *tranquillo* ones. To describe that chord as D minor (second inversion) with additional notes B and G (twice) hardly does justice to its overall function in a work that, its ending in unmistakable D major notwithstanding, often defies unambiguous tonal definition. More immediately memorable to the ear is the fact that it consists of three two-note tone clusters of a major second, as an instant jog to memory and association even when only two of these clusters appear later on. It is designed to be heard and remembered by attentive, if not necessarily experienced, listeners.

In a 1972 essay, Andrew Imbrie emphasized the significance of the way in which Sessions uses this chord as the musical continuity evolves:

> The use of this chord clearly demonstrates a fact that is crucial to the understanding of Sessions's music, namely that function does not follow formula. The identity of the chord is not literal but approximate. The deviations from literal identity are small enough to permit the listener confidently to form the necessary association. Yet these same deviations are large enough to give variation of light and shade, allowing the chord to take on a coloration appropriate to its immediate context. Sessions's music is always apt to make one consider what are the necessary and sufficient conditions for establishing a musical idea; but the question remains theoretical because in Sessions's practice it is so successfully and resourcefully answered.[15]

"Function does not follow formula." It would be hard to find a more apt characterization of Sessions' approach to music at any time, but in this period of ultimate recognition of his identity as a composer it has particular relevance. The simplest function, even repetition, as long as it is recognizable as such, may be varied and thus may render additional interpretive clarification of the musical narrative by taking on "a coloration appropriate to its immediate context."

During Sessions' last years before he moved to California and throughout his entire tenure at Berkeley, his general way with music—his "style," one might say, if he had not disliked and mistrusted that word so much—was in a final state of transformation. The musical idea and its manifestation in the inner ear remained unchanged, of course, but its appearance and its role *within the continuity* of the work it had generated began to change very gradually: the musical idea became a musical *environment.*

Musical environment and its active relationship to overall structure of a composition were concepts that resonated—very differently—in two areas of contemporary musical thinking: Schenkerian analysis and Schoenberg's twelve-tone system. Ever skeptical of "systems," Sessions disapproved of them both as long as he could. But he could not ignore them.

When Heinrich Schenker died in January of 1935, Sessions undertook to write an appreciation of his achievement for *Modern Music.*[16] Inevitably the article reveals as much about Sessions' own work and musical outlook at the time as it did about the body of theoretical critique it examines. Central to Sessions' reservations about Schenker had to be the latter's well-publicized animosity to contemporary music—and for practical purposes that included almost any music after Brahms. While some of Schenker's disciples extended the range of composers to whom his analytical verification might apply into the twentieth century, the very idea that the validity of a piece of music needed to pass the test of theoretical verification under any system of analysis could not but raise Sessions' doubts. Nevertheless, in his earlier writings Schenker established ideas on musical analysis that were indeed apposite to contemporary music and writings on music at that time. Sessions' examination of these perspectives allowed him to express his contempt about some of what was still being taught by way of so-called theory instruction, as well as to confront, in terms of Schenkerian analysis, some questions about his own work:

> At the basis of Schenker's teaching lies the most important possible goal —that of effecting some kind of *rapprochement* between musical theory and the actual musical thought of the composer . . . The older theory of harmony, virtually a compilation and standardization of the purely practical teachings of earlier days, consisted of little more than a systematic catalog of "chords"—and what was a chord but the simultaneous sounding of any two or more notes, regardless of their syntactical significance? That the harmony books catalogued only the simplest of such phenomena does not in the slightest alter the fact that fundamentally the conception went no farther . . . There even exist textbooks which dogmatically assert the inferiority of certain cadence formulas, on the ground that the

masters used them *less frequently* than others of a different structure! [RS emphasis]

Schenker's concept of harmony was hierarchical, suggesting a grand structure in which no single chord needed to be a harmonic event and in which a harmonic event did not even have to be a chord as such but might be a purely melodic reference. A series of *Stufen* (literally steps, meaning sections of which harmonic events are comprised) governed the harmonic sequence of events as perceived by the ear. To this Schenker added the concept of *Tonikalisierung*—as ugly a word in German as its English equivalent, *tonicization*, but a very useful concept readily adopted by Sessions in his own teaching. By surrounding any note in a scale with the equivalent of its own emphasis as a quasi tonic (e.g., approaching it with its own dominant seventh chord) it is treated as the main chord of a new tonality without having earned that status by way of an actual modulation—the cadential establishment of a new tonality, with all the confirming harmonic implications pertaining thereunto. This sophisticated and potentially complex harmonic structure became a hierarchical one by the assumption of a detailed and colorful "foreground" of events, supported by a far more basic harmonic "background," which only demonstrated the most fundamental overall relationships. It is easy to see how such a concept provided the possibility of visualizing the harmonic image of any piece of music in a single moment of contemplation, no mean advantage to any performer or student of the work and one that certainly commended itself to Sessions in its affinity to some aspects of his own concept of the musical idea:

> Every composer is aware through his own experience of the reality of "background" in his musical construction that goes beyond individual traits of melody which constitute the most immediately perceptible features of his work. He is conscious, that is to say, of a type of movement which takes place gradually and over large stretches, and which embodies itself in the need which he feels, say, at a given moment, for such and such a high note, or for this or that particular harmonic or melodic intensification. This is in a very real sense one of the most essential features of the composer's impulse and is far more than a part of an impulse towards "design" in the usual sense of the word.

Schenker might well have made objection to some of these assertions. Sessions, in fact, continues by *emphasizing* the very difference in viewpoint.

> Musical line is, in its full significance, an extremely complicated affair . . . a single note may be fraught with a hundred implications and embody a hundred relationships within a given work . . . This holds true, ultimately, of Schenker's work just as fatally as of the older systems which formed the basis of the training of the composers themselves and which governed a large part of their speech about music.

Three concepts informed Schenker's later work: *Auskomponieren* (literally composing out), the *Urlinie* (prime line), and *Ursatz* (prime setting) as evident in a musical composition. Schenker's notion of *Auskomponieren* is concerned with linear and contrapuntal aspects of music, concepts of line that arrive ultimately at the stipulation of a very plain *Urlinie* and an *Ursatz* behind and beyond the busy foreground of any work. Sessions could hardly help but object to this theoretical condensation of a composition to prime elements in a behind-the-scenes setting that the composer might or might not have correctly attended:

> There are two fundamental objections, therefore, to such a conception as Schenker's *Urlinie* and *Ursatz*. The first is that it is far too primitive a description of the actual events which constitute a musical work, or the sensations and apprehensions that constitute the ultimate comprehension of that work. With an arrogance that is all too characteristic he makes the claim, on the title page of his treatise on the Eroica Symphony, that the latter is "Zum erstenmal in ihrem wahren Inhalt dargestellt [for the first time presented in its true content]!" The reader may follow him through pages of analysis, some of it brilliant, some of it overingenious, and if he is thoroughly familiar with the text of the symphony he will find it comparatively simple to "hear" it in the manner laid out by Schenker . . . [But] there is no possible substitute for a highly evolved musical ear and a robust musical instinct, and if he is possessed of these he will certainly find Schenker's description all too insufficient.

Schenker's dogmatic insistence, moreover, on "right" settings and inferior ones, according to the reckoning of his theoretical analysis, did not stop at the work of Beethoven. Sessions cites the Bach harmonization of a chorale that, according to Schenker, should have been better executed—and was—in a "corrected" version by Schenker:

> [According to Schenker] Bach's settings of *Gelobet seist Du, Jesus Christ* prove, in spite of certain admirable features, how the instincts of even a great master may be sidetracked at moments by false teachings. It is easy enough to follow the logic of Schenker's argument. But unfortunately he asks us to choose between theories which, for all the clarity, sincerity, and verve with which they are advanced, remain speculative and, on the other hand, the actual deeds of the greatest masters . . . Schenker's harmonization of the chorale in question, which he offers as the correct one, is precisely that which any reasonably competent musician would make. Only Bach's versions, as a comparison shows with devastating clarity, happen to be actual deeds of a man of supreme genius, and as such carry us to a realm of far more profound musical reality. And the history of music, like history of other kinds, consists of deeds and not of theories.

Schenker's rejection, moreover, of even the possibility of valid contemporary additions to the history of music, absent the analytical principles he proclaimed, becomes a final and unacceptable provocation. At this point Sessions, even in the context of a posthumous appreciation, could not refrain from entering the domain of sweeping polemic and firing back without further pretense of dispassionate academic esteem:

> A culture which no longer can grow through its own vitality will end up gnawing the bones of its past; for the past can be kept alive only through

> vital growth into a present, in which the creative impulse is still alive and the ultimate criterion no artificially cultivated set of judgments based on analysis or research, but the living response of sensitive and exacting minds. It is precisely when Schenker's teachings leave the domain of exact description and enter that of dogmatic and speculative analysis that they become essentially sterile . . .
>
> It is hardly conceivable that Schenker's proud boast should be fulfilled and a revival of the older tradition take place in Vienna, under the standard of the *Urlinie* and *Ursatz* . . . A far more exacting discipline—that of the directly perceiving and spontaneously co-ordinating musical ear—is demanded of the musicians today and tomorrow, if they are to be equal to the task before them. And they will derive much profit and help from the clear and profound conceptions in Schenker's earlier works, just as they will turn away from the Talmudic subtleties and the febrile dogmatism of his later ones.[17]

"Every composer is aware through his own experience of the reality of 'background' in his musical construction that goes beyond individual traits of melody which constitute the most immediately perceptible features of his work." If not "every composer," then certainly Sessions, for one, was aware of a musical "background" that dominated the overall structure of a work and into which the events of the immediate "foreground" had to be fitted. It will be as useful for us to mark the point at which Sessions' work departed from what he considered Schenker's "clear and profound conceptions" as it was for Sessions himself. Again he provided it clearly enough. "Musical line is, in its full significance, an extremely complicated affair . . . a single note may be fraught with a hundred implications and embody a hundred relationships within a given work." The long musical line that was to become a hallmark of Sessions' work is nowhere more clearly defined in its complexity and its structural portent within a large composition than in that apparently casual commentary.

Schenkerian analysis applied its particular focus on existing works after the fact; twelve-tone composition offered the composer a way of managing the musical materials of a work in progress. With Schoenberg's arrival in the United States, twelve-tone composition had already become a movement in the minds of supporters and detractors alike, a cause in which to counter the allied forces of neoclassicists bound to Stravinsky and the "American school" identified with Copland. There certainly was a xenophobic aspect to the notion that the twelve-tone system was something imported by European refugees and thus somehow "un-American." Sessions' own reservations, however, concerned the rigidly dogmatic methods promoted by some twelve-tone composers but were tempered by his genuine admiration for the work of Schoenberg and Berg.

Sessions' eventual adoption of twelve-tone principles in his work is the more difficult to trace as in all his writings on music he rarely discussed his own—and not without apparent contradictions when he did so. But in 1944, roughly a decade before he was to write his first twelve-tone work, Sessions published an article titled "Schoenberg in the United States"[18] in the English magazine *Tempo*. Inevitably the article reflected his attitude toward the "system" at a time when he still considered it unlikely that he should ever use it in his own music. By happy coincidence perhaps, or rather by inspired design on the part of David Drew, editor of *Tempo* in 1972, a reprint of Sessions' 1944 article includes a number of substantial notes by the author, citing changes in his compositional outlook and practice over the period of nearly thirty years since the article had first appeared in print. Thus, with the hindsight of 1972, we are offered a rare perspective of the final stages in the development of Sessions' musical language before his advent as a "twelve-tone composer." In 1944 he wrote:

> I believe that in [his] works written since 1936 Schoenberg has achieved a freedom and resourcefulness which carries them in this respect far beyond his earlier works, especially those in the twelve-tone technique. Regarding that technique itself much misleading nonsense has been written. I am in no sense a spokesman for it; I have never been attracted to it as a principle of composition.* But one must distinguish carefully between technical principles in the abstract and the works in which they are embodied; even a great work does not validate a dubious principle, nor does a valid principle produce in itself good or even technically convincing work.[19]

A footnote, appended in 1972 at the point of the asterisk in the preceding extract, suggests how in the course of time the "dubious principle" found itself into his own work after all:

> * I used the twelve-tone principle for the first time in 1953, in my Sonata for Violin Solo, and have used it to various degrees and in various ways ever since—always, of course, in my own terms. My first use of it was, at the beginning, quite involuntary. I had at various times, for my own self-enlightenment, carried out quite small-scale exercises with the technique, but I still envisaged it as not applicable to my own musical ideas. It was therefore a surprise to me when I found the composition of the Sonata flowing easily and without constraint in its terms. I used it consistently in several well-defined sections of the piece; but on several grounds I decided not to mention this to anyone. However, a colleague to whom I showed the piece immediately recognized the twelve-tone procedures, and afterwards observed, with some surprise, "But it's still your music."[20]

Sessions' amusing hesitation about mentioning his apparent lapse to anyone was not all that was undone when his colleague—Andrew Imbrie—spotted it. His evident fears that the use of a "system" might affect the identity of his music were absolved in the same sentence as well. It was still his music.

That Sessions' eventual use of a twelve-tone process in his work was in no way an epiphany on the road to Vienna becomes quite clear from his 1972 account, and was affirmed by the composer in several recorded conversations since then. Nor did it affect, in any outwardly obvious way, how his music sounded—any more than Schoenberg's own pre-twelve-tone compositions had sounded less "like Schoenberg" than the ones immediately following his adoption of twelve-tone procedures. But 1953, the date of the Solo Sonata and some preliminary twelve-tone exercises, suggests that Sessions' open-minded discussions with his new friend and seasoned twelve-toner Luigi Dallapiccola may have helped to ease his suspicions about the system in principle and encouraged him to explore the usefulness of its techniques in his own work

In Florence, Sessions and Dallapiccola had spent a happy fall, winter, and spring of 1951–1952 talking. The Italian, whose small talk was of poets, painters, and composers, and the American, who had found "the one composer with whom I always felt I could speak freely and without reserve,"[21] found that they already shared a great deal and were able to give each other even more. Laura Dallapiccola, accustomed to her husband's intense opinions on anything from world politics to music, marveled: "I'd like to find something you two disagree about."[22]

For Sessions, who probably knew Schoenberg's oeuvre better than most of his colleagues on either side of the Viennese divide Dallapiccola's mature works would have been instructive, if nothing else, in their fundamental difference from works of the so-called Second Viennese School. Among the three chief representatives of the latter—Schoenberg, Berg and Webern—Berg's work, with its relatively flexible application of the row, appeared most sympathetic to Sessions, Webern's the least. But Sessions never knew (until I told him) that Dallapiccola had in fact studied with Webern. Indeed, there were aspects of Dallapiccola's approach to twelve-tone composition that recalled Webern's practice and which Sessions could only reject for himself. In particular, Dallapiccola's construction of the row for a new work "in the abstract," the arrangement of a dominant intervallic sequence before he began actual composition, would have seemed at odds with Sessions' belief in the primacy of a musical idea. Similarly, the use of carefully constructed subrows, entirely inaccessible as such to the ear but intellectually perceptible for purely illustrative purposes, might carry any notion of intuitive guidance by the composer's inner hearing almost beyond credibility.

During Sessions' 1951–1952 visit in Florence, Dallapiccola was composing an operatic work, *Job*, his one-act "Sacred Representation" based on the biblical text and set, with a timely eye toward American performance, both in Italian and in English.[23] Central to the work's story is the appearance of Job's friends during his testing. Hans Nathan, in a 1958 article for the *Musical Quarterly,* quotes a letter he received from Dallapiccola, in which the composer describes his musical treatment of that scene:

> That there is a single row cannot be doubted: D, E♭, G, A, B♭, E, C, F♯, C♯, B, F. In the scene of the three friends, however, there is a transformation, as you correctly noted. This transformation has been obtained (following the example given by Berg in *Lulu*) by applying one of his three methods—in the present case, by selecting tones that are seven tones apart while the row is seen as a circle, i.e., tones 1, 8, 15, etc. Thus one obtains: D, C, A♭ [G♯], B♭, F, E, E♭, F♯, A, B, C♯ [D♭]. It is up to you to decide whether, critically, one can still speak of the singularity of the row.[24]

At other times a certain playfulness of allusive correlations moved Dallapiccola to fashion visually illustrative ideograms in his scores. He was particularly proud of the aspect of a page in his *Cinque canti,* on which the graphic image of the music revealed itself as a cross, reflecting the pain suggested by the text of that passage. None of that could have drawn a very empathetic response from Sessions, to whom the work was dedicated. At the same time, the extraordinary freedom that Dallapiccola achieved within the row and its permutations, including suggestions of tonality, the appearance of plain triads and of harmonically propelling chromaticism, was bound to have intrigued the American composer, whose acquaintance with "permissible" usage in twelve-tone music had largely been limited to that of its Viennese apostles.

We have already remarked on Dallapiccola's keen interest in poetry, literature, and the visual arts. Unlike Sessions, who insisted that his creative imagination was entirely aural, his new friend confided freely that some of his critical discoveries in fields *other* than music translated naturally into creative ideas in his work as a composer. He greatly admired and avidly studied the work of Proust, and although he remained uneasy about actually speaking or writing in English (he wrote to me in French, and I would answer in German), he claimed to have learned a great deal about composition from the work of James Joyce. "I found in the works of [this writer] confirmation of what I had dimly felt after hearing the works of Schoenberg and Webern," he writes in *On the Twelve-Note Road.*[25] Hans Nathan, in the previously cited article for the *Musical Quarterly*, elaborates:

> In Joyce [Dallapiccola] observed a method of imparting a totally new meaning to a word through a change in the order of its letters, through omission, addition, or replacement of a letter by another, even through a reading from right to left (i.e., retrograde), "From this I believed I understood up to what point in music an identical succession of notes could take on a different meaning by being *arranged* in a different way." On the other hand, he was fascinated by Proust's manner of building up a character by dropping hints, so to speak, before it entered the story. This procedure Dallapiccola related to the row in these words (though he himself applied its lessons infrequently): "Before reaching . . . [the] rhythmic and melodic definition of the series, we may find it compressed into a single chord of twelve notes, two chords of six notes, three of four notes, or even six two-note chords . . . to speak only of the most elementary possibilities."[26]

As for "aspirating" the genetic chord of a work long before it would actually appear in the music, Sessions, in his First Piano Sonata, had already demonstrated how a musical idea may inform a work "by dropping hints, so to speak, before it entered the story." Contrary to the dogmatic restrictions that had largely comprised Sessions' American acquaintance with the twelve-tone usage thus far, Dallapiccola's wide-ranging cross-references and comparisons and his almost prankish departures from an established code were bound to have engaged Sessions' interest in exploring the creative *opportunities* offered by the process. Dallapiccola's simple statement that "twelve tones would enable me to articulate a melody better than seven—to write a richer and (as far as my capacities would allow) more expressive melody" might not only have brought to mind Sessions' own declaration: "Musical line is, in its full significance, an extremely complicated affair . . . a single note may be fraught with a hundred implications and embody a hundred relationships within a given work, but also have furnished an enticing prospect of additional choices in selecting that note." By intended association and reference, his own use of the musical line, in all its expressive sovereignty, was already more closely woven into the overall fabric of a work than Dallapiccola's melodies in their sometimes frankly decorative and frequently descriptive way. For all of Sessions' insistence on linear supremacy in the way his music was composed and to be heard, he could hardly have helped being intrigued by the freedom with which his Italian colleague's compositional practice suggested triadic and chromatic events that would not have been "allowed" by the twelve-toners he knew and on the basis of whose tenets he had doubted the usefulness of the system for his own work.

In the first scene of Dallapiccola's opera *Il Prigionero*, the protagonist, a prisoner of the Spanish Inquisition, is visited by his mother. As evidence of new hope—the ultimate thwarting of which will be his most refined torture—he tells her how the jailer addressed him as "my brother," *fratello*, a word that dominates the opera from its very opening in a descending three-syllabic motif. Its cruelly deceitful explication, *dolcissima parola*, is composed on six tones of one row, while the remaining six provide a harmony of two plain minor triads, B minor and C minor. A highly chromatic vocal line, in which the prisoner expresses his fragile hope, elaborates a second tone row. The concluding arioso of the scene, "Signore, aiutami a camminare" (Lord, help me to go on), returns to the original row.

Certainly minor triads and expressive chromaticism had been part of Sessions's own technical vocabulary and usage from the start. But in extending that technical usage with melodic lines using twelve notes instead of seven—without the penalty of an abstract and overriding code of musical conduct—promised very attractive new possibilities. Intrigued, and "for [his] own self-enlightenment, [he] carried out quite small-scale exercises with the technique," even though he "still envisaged it as not applicable to [his] own musical ideas." Be that as it may, a year later Sessions was surprised "when I found the composition of the Sonata flowing easily and without constraint in its terms."[27] He discovered that the so-called system could provide a pervasive aural environment, distinct for its discrete set of pitch classes, involving, by definition (if not necessarily in practice), the twelve different tones available within the octave in certain intervallic relationships, while also allowing for their interchange according to possible symmetries within the original set and its transpositions. Thus a work could be endowed with *a constant and recognizable environment of sound.*

There was really no need for Sessions to adjust his musical thoughts and his particular approach to composition to include this new environment of sound.

Milton Babbitt had told him for some time that his work was increasingly bordering on twelve-tone territory. Perhaps the most striking illustration is provided by the history of his work on the opera *Montezuma*. Sessions brought his sketches, begun in the late 1930s, to Florence in 1951 and was busily working on the opera during his year in Italy. As we have seen, the work was interrupted soon after his return to Berkeley and not resumed until 1959. In its final version, *Montezuma* revealed itself as a twelve-tone work. But materials that were sketched years before Sessions' conscious acceptance of a twelve-tone environment were indeed used in the final composition of *Montezuma*. The musical idea itself did not need to be adjusted to the system; the system allowed for its incorporation as the generative root of the work.

In Edward T. Cone's unique compendium of the composer's life, work, and thought, published as *Conversations with Roger Sessions*,[28] the following exchange is recorded:

> RS An original musical idea was the basis of the row in *Montezuma*. It is, in the very first measure of the piece, divided into trichords. Now, you can pair these trichords. There are three possible combinations: you can group I and II together, or I and III together, or I and IV together. If you take I and III together, or I and IV together, you can generate a complete symmetrical row. If you do I and II together the row isn't symmetrical. This gives a good deal of leeway. However, a good deal of that I discovered in the course of the work. I forgot just at what point I became aware of what I was doing.
>
> ETC But your sketches go back many years before you were working twelve-tone at all.
>
> RS Exactly.

"Exactly." Upon first reading Cone's record of this conversation, I found that hard to believe. It would have been one thing to accept the notion of musical ideas now emerging spontaneously within the composer's newfound twelve-tone frame of reference but quite another to assume that ideas conceived long ago, within a tonal environment, were presently capable of being "translated" into a musical syntax within the framework of a twelve-tone matrix. And yet the extant record of sketched materials that eventually became the opera *Montezuma* provides exactly that evidence.

We have already quoted Sessions' claim that "I set to work on the score in the fall of 1959—and *with the help of very many sketches I had made over a period of eighteen years* [my emphasis], finished in two and a half years the complete particell—the condensed score—of the work, the final page of which bears the date July 1, 1962."[29] The Sessions archive in the Library of Congress provides the record of that work. *Montezuma,* from its earliest sketches to the final score, arches over a period in the composer's creative life that includes the greater number of Sessions' mature compositions. His own notes on *Montezuma* as a work in progress suggest a stretch of years from 1947 to 1962,[30] but his musical sketchbooks now in the Library of Congress include dated musical sketches *with key signatures* from the late 1930s. Even the earliest ones already show unmistakable melodic and rhythmic outlines of themes as they would eventually appear in the final twelve-tone score more than a quarter-century later.

Clearly the generic musical idea in Example 18.3 and its counterpart, Example 18.4, in the final version of *Montezuma* owed nothing to any compositional system in terms of their melodic shape, rhythmic identity, or even a possible emotional message. In essence, they are the same. As always in Sessions' music, the role of an a priori musical idea remains unchanged even in its eventual translation into a twelve-tone environment. In this his work differed from that of the Viennese masters and their disciples, including Luigi Dallapiccola, whose musical ideas were drawn from the row itself.

It was in the working out of the musical idea that Sessions found that the twelve-tone system made a difference. This is how he described uses of the row in *Montezuma*:

> An original musical idea was the basis of the row in *Montezuma*. It is, in the very first measure of the piece, divided into trichords. Now, you can pair these trichords. There are three possible combinations: you can group I and II together, or I and III together, or I and IV together. If you take I and III together, or I and IV together, you can generate a complete symmetrical row. If you do I and II together the row isn't symmetrical. This gives a good deal of leeway. However, a good deal of that I discovered in the course of the work. I forgot just at what point I became aware of what I was doing.[31]

We have already noted a comparable quote from Luigi Dallapiccola's writings: "Before reaching . . . [the] rhythmic and melodic definition of the series, we may find it compressed into a single chord of twelve notes, two chords of six notes, three of four notes, or even six two-note chords . . . to speak only of the most elementary possibilities."[32]

Where Dallapiccola had looked to the row for formative potential, Sessions statement about the way *Montezuma* worked out for him begins with the musical idea. He, too, examined the way that idea blended into the twelve-tone environment of the first measure, and he came up with possible groupings and subgroupings every bit as forbidding as Dallapiccola's diagnosis of his row. Any craftsman examines his medium, be it wood or marble or a set of notes, before he sets to work. Sessions arrived at an awareness of "what he was doing" in the course of the work on *Montezuma*. And perhaps the most telling sentence in his statement that describes the potential of the opening measure of *Montezuma* reads: "If you do I and II together the row isn't symmetrical. This gives a good deal of leeway." The freedom of leeway was crucial.

Long ago, in working on his First String Quartet, Sessions discovered the creative uses of apparent harmonic ambiguity, a way of leaving something in the "understanding" of what was happening in the music, not to the theoretical analyst within him but to the attentive listener, the willing ear. He learned to raise

Example 18.3 Opening measures of *Montezuma* in a late 1930s sketch

questions within the musical continuity that were not necessarily rooted in what had gone before but would receive satisfying, even remarkable, answers somewhere down the road where the music led.

In order to entrust his working out of musical ideas to a so-called system still widely associated with a notion of inevitable rigidity in the uses of composition with twelve tones Sessions needed practical evidence of its capacity to include and evolve the musical reality of such ideas. What Sessions had learned from his Italian friend was the way in which a twelve-tone melody might be combined with elements of apparently tonal reference, as in the case of the

Example 18.4 Opening measures of *Montezuma* in a final particell version, 1962

minor triads that underlie a deceptive message of hope at the beginning of Dallapiccola's opera *The Prisoner*.[33] Conversely, a tonal idea could become an integral part of a twelve-tone environment, as Sessions found when he really set to work on *Montezuma* in 1959.

Traceable tonal references were anathema, of course, to the accepted founding father of the twelve-tone system, Arnold Schoenberg. This entirely personal preference of a great composer caused a great deal of misunderstanding among future followers in his footsteps and among many who had hesitated. Composers of very different musical dispositions began to explore the musical potential of composing with twelve tones about the same time as Sessions, Stravinsky, Copland, and Benjamin Britten among them. Perhaps the most damaging effect of a misunderstanding among composers was its lasting impact on musical audiences.

We have already noted Sessions' own recollection of a talk with Schoenberg on the subject: Schoenberg looked glum. Then he said, 'Yes, you're right, and I must admit it's partly my fault. But it's mostly the fault of my students!' "[34] "It is one thing to define a twelve-note set and quite another to define twelve-note composition," declares the *New Grove Dictionary of Music and Musicians*.[35] From the beginning, there were so many ways of using sets of twelve tones that some of the early pronouncements by dodecaphony's founding fathers were soon recanted: Webern held to the injunction that a twelve-tone work should not be made of more than the permutations of a single row; most others did not. Even within that limitation, segments of the series might be found to duplicate a succession of pitches in other parts of the row, in one of its four permutations (Prime, Inversion, Retrograde, and Retrograde Inversion) or in the forty-eight possible transpositions of these. Such correspondences allowed new combinations and relationships, not unlike the enharmonic respelling of chords and their consequent new meaning in the erstwhile context of functional harmony. Berg was particularly fond of exploiting such possibilities. Choice soon became the hallmark of twelve-tone composition. As *set theory* developed, along with new works created over the years, it was Milton Babbitt who mapped the limits of its musical territory and defined its almost endless possibilities within a theoretical framework he called combinatorialty. But strong personal differences in their approach to twelve-tone composition were already reflected in the works of Berg, Webern, and Schoenberg, challenging the notion of theoretical rigidity, which was promoted by some of some early advocates and gleefully cited by their opponents. Schoenberg himself allowed that much in the conversation with Sessions we have quoted.

Sessions had to work out his own inferences, as always, in terms of the work at hand. For him, twelve-tone came to be a musical environment produced by the same intuitive process that had generated his musical idea earlier on. That environment was capable of incorporating, presenting, and developing musical ideas along the entire range of twelve available tones instead of the seven notes of major and minor scales. The difference, after all, between the "Pisan chord," which informed his First Piano Sonata, and the two hexachords on which his Third Symphony was built lies in the fact that the latter chords add up to twelve tones, as do the trichords of *Montezuma*. The musical shapes and melodic entities in works to come need not feature a set of twelve tones as such but exist in a twelve-tone environment, infinitely variable as it takes its actual character and recognizable identity from the primary musical idea.

Within this musical environment, thematic materials could evolve as of old, while at the same time providing a discrete experience of sound regardless of thematic, rhythmic, or textural events. Such an environment is "home" within the Sessions work it informs, and the attentive ear becomes aware of it without any prior need for theoretical analysis.

Given Sessions' complete reliance on the inner ear while he composed, it seems only reasonable that, for a while, he should have continued his intellectual reservations about the dodecaphonic approach to composition, even while young colleagues like Imbrie and Babbitt found near twelve-tone environments in his works. Sessions' diffident acceptance of a potentially useful enlargement of his musical vocabulary into a new musical syntax, persuaded him eventually to attempt "quite small-scale exercises with the technique." And rather than having to chart a new course, he discovered that the composition of his twelve-tone Violin Sonata was "flowing easily and without constraint in its terms." Campbell describes the effect of Sessions' own way with twelve-tone composition in his analysis of the Third Piano Sonata:

> The nuclear idea of the sonata exerts a generative influence that is more obvious in the largest dimensions, yet ultimately not as direct as that found in the earlier sonatas. The nuclear idea provides a background in a Schenkerian as well as an acoustical sense: the chromatic inflection of a minor third that governs so many important relationships seems once removed from its first expression, the halting phrase that opens the sonata. This phrase serves, directly or indirectly, as the source of important thematic material, but does not control less obvious pitch relationships in the manner typical of the first two sonatas. Sessions' adaptation here of twelve-tone procedures enables him to maintain considerable consistency of pitch choice without predicating pitch succession.

With the adoption of a twelve-tone musical environment, not only the uses of thematic material but also the rhythmic articulation of musical continuity, the outlining of phrases, and the establishment of cadences became matters of choice to be resolved according to the composer's ear. In his *Conversations with Roger Sessions*, Cone asks:

> EC: What takes the place of the harmonic definition of a classical cadence?
>
> RS: I think a lot of things. The movement of the outer voices, certainly. The rhythmic flow, sometimes the curve of the line, sometimes something in the instrumental scheme or the sonority. A composer today must be aware, and then cause the listener to be aware, of a close of some kind, a rhythmic articulation at this point. There are innumerable ways of doing that, of course. After all, in classical music, you can have IV, V, I in the middle of a phrase and yet you know that it's the middle of the phrase.
>
> EC: In other words, the rhythmic aspects are probably more important in defining a cadence than the harmonic.
>
> RS: I would say all the aspects together. But one can never tell in advance what will work in a specific place. One can only tell what *has* worked.[37]

The composer's only arbiter of what has "worked" was his inner ear. With the realization that the twelve-tone approach offered optimal choices for his aural imagination, Sessions finally arrived once more at a point in his work that Bloch had promised to him in 1919—"you'll be able to do what you want."[38] Fifty years later, as a composer who was able to reap a rich harvest of works freely and easily at last, Sessions wrote:

> The tone row is an organic pattern of sounds and intervals, created by the composer's imagination in terms of sound and of the relationships between sounds; it is a framework of reference the composer establishes for specific purposes—just as the composer of a larger work decides in advance the instrumental or vocal combination for which he is writing. It is in other words the composer's ear, not arithmetic and not dogma or theory, necessarily of an arbitrary nature, that is involved here.[39]

Over and over again, as a teacher and in his writings as a composer, Sessions stressed the primacy of the ear as chief guide in the process of realizing a composition from its musical idea.

I must confess that I sometimes wondered how far and in what detail this admirable reliance on the inner ear could be relied upon when it came to the minutiae of his complex scores. It was during my own preparation of Sessions' Eighth Symphony in 1968, then fresh from his pen, that he provided an impressive answer. I had written to him about a few apparent inconsistencies in the published text. One of them involved a D♮ that later reappeared as a D♭, the only changed note in an otherwise identical corresponding passage.

He replied promptly and at length (the emphases are mine):

> . . . The question of the D♭ (m. 126 as against m. 17) has intrigued me very much. The D♭ *is* correct (in m. 126, not m. 17); but it took me some effort to be sure of this fact, and even more to discover the reason for it. I looked at the blueprint of the Ms. & there it was, D[♮] in m. 17, D♭ in m. 126. Then, as I read the passages through, *my ear confirmed it*—I still wanted it that way, but couldn't discover the reason why. I started a letter to you last night in that vein. This morning I looked at it again, just to make sure I was not deceiving myself; and the reason jumped out at me. Excuse me if I go into some detail, but is rather interesting to me, as I hope it may be to you.
>
> First of all, the two passages differ in that the first one goes on for 3 more measures—the phrase ends at m. 20. The next one breaks off abruptly in the next measure (127) & is interrupted by a very sharp contrast. Now—since the 3rd horn, which takes the lowest voice at this point, establishes F—D as a bass over five beats, *my ear undoubtedly shied away from the D♮* following the F in the previous measure. I admit that it is a minute point, and in a way has more to do the way my mind works (or rather my ear, since *it was probably unconscious & and simply the result of my "hearing ahead"* to the next measure—one never "thinks" such things "out" & I don't see how one could do so)—than with anything at all noticeable in performance. But the D♭ is correct here, as the D♮ is in the earlier passage.[40]

Schoenberg said it all when he closed his harmony textbook of 1911 with the memorable words: "Who would dare to demand theory here!"[41]

CHAPTER 19

Harvest

He who marries the spirit of the age will quickly find himself a widower.

—W. R. INGE

The best was now to come. The creative flowering that had begun in Sessions' Berkeley years ripened into a truly astonishing harvest during and after his second tenure at Princeton. The composer who had labored almost half his musical life to write one symphony, one piano sonata, a violin concerto, and a string quartet produced, in roughly the same number of years, seven more symphonies, the Rhapsody for Orchestra, two operas, a piano concerto, a double concerto for violin and cello, two more piano sonatas, a second quartet and a string quintet among other chamber works, the solo violin sonata, choruses, and three extraordinary cantatas: *The Idyll of Theocritus*, *Psalm 140*, and the work he loved best: *When Lilacs Last in the Dooryard Bloomed.* From 1973 to 1976 there followed a creative pause until his Ninth Symphony was begun and completed during the next three years. His work was concluded in 1981 with the Concerto for Orchestra for the Boston Symphony Orchestra, which had given the first performance of his First Symphony more than a half-century before. Lisl died in 1982, and the creative impulse ceased.

What was it like, this life of a newly prolific composer and acclaimed master teacher? No longer on the musical margin of a great university, on his return in 1953 Sessions found himself the acknowledged star of Princeton's newly created music department. No longer confined with his family to the modest home of a faculty member without tenure, he now resided in spacious university property on Alexander Street. Among teaching colleagues, Milton Babbitt, Edward Cone, and Earl Kim were former students. Among students, now there were musical grandsons like John Harbison, distinguished composer-to-be, who studied not only with Sessions but also with Kim. And in his very first year he completed two important works, the Sonata for Solo Violin and *The Idyll of Theocritus* for soprano and orchestra, dedicated to Luigi Dallapiccola in exchange for his friend's dedication of *Cinque canti.*

Nothing could now describe Sessions' life less accurately than the notion of a cloistered university professor. His restless urge to seek new worlds to conquer was not to be worn away by the physical comfort and professional security of his home base in academia. His talent for lasting friendship, which had marked his way of life ever since Smith College, Cleveland, and his early wayfarer years in Europe, found ample recompense during the two decades to come, while his abiding pleasure in travel now helped to shape a career in which personal associations within the profession were stimulated and fortified by an abiding delight in "being there." His Fulbright trip to Italy, resulting in his close friendship with Luigi Dallapiccola, had only been the first of many excursions during those harvest years, some so extensive that one might wonder how Sessions managed to compose at all, let alone with his now-prolific creative output, and some so brief, rapid, and extravagant in style as to raise questions about how he could afford them. To be sure, Lisl shared his *Reiselust,* and she contributed gladly from her own inherited financial resources, while nevertheless maintaining firm and sensible control of the Sessions budget. As once she had planned family trips to Yosemite, Yellowstone National Park, and Lake Tahoe from Berkeley, she now organized and often shared excursions to London, Berlin, Zurich, and Florence, where her husband renewed old friendships and formed new alliances. And as is often the case with such a lifestyle, professional connections and friendships-to-be not only accrued in those faraway places but sometimes led to other, even more distant travel destinations. Argentinean composer Alberto Ginastera, whom Sessions had met during a summer in Tanglewood, invited him to teach young composers in Buenos Aires, a project that resulted in a long South American sojourn in 1965, including stops in Rio, Santiago de Chile, Lima, and Mexico City. In later years such travels would grow once more into actual vacation trips to Scandinavia, leisurely stays in Liechtenstein or, closer to home, quiet summers in Franconia, New Hampshire ("I don't remember the name of the place, but there was a great restaurant!").[1] There were times, however, during those glory days of the fifties and sixties, when being there would grow into such a crammed schedule of just getting there that composer Sessions had to assert himself:

> Lisl & I have decided that we are sick of driving around in that car, and are anxious to settle down for the last weeks in England before sailing from Southampton on Aug. 23 [1956] instead of touring Scotland as we had thought of doing. I have very urgently to finish the score of my [Third]

Sessions and the author during a rehearsal of Symphony No. 4 in Boston 1962.

Symphony at that time, and cannot work properly under these peripatetic conditions.

Just how peripatetic his life had become during the final weeks of work on the Third Symphony is illustrated, in the same letter, by a list of poste restante addresses in France and England for the end of the trip:

July 21–22	Amboise
July 23	Louviers
July 24	Boulogne
July 25	Canterbury
July 26	Lavenham
July 27–28	c/o John Sessions, Deanscroft, Oakham

That letter was addressed to Sessions' newest friend and future champion, William Glock,[2] founder and editor of the prestigious English musical periodical the *Score.* Glock was to become the BBC's powerful Controller of Music during its truly golden years in the sixties and early seventies. As a student of Arthur Schnabel Glock lived in Berlin when Sessions stayed there during the early thirties, but the two did not meet at the time. Back in England, Glock worked as music critic for the London *Telegraph* and the *Observer* before he began his remarkable career as a musical administrator, which eventually made him one of the most influential men in the musical life of England and earned him a knighthood. A discerning and energetic champion in the cause of contemporary music, Sir William became one of Sessions' most effective advocates among the power brokers of Europe's musical establishment.

At the time of Sessions' plea for summer asylum for himself and his travel-weary family, Glock had several jobs in addition to being a music critic. He ran a club for musicians in London (which lost the financial support of its chief patron when Glock's management made it self-supporting) and administered a summer school at Dartington Hall in Devon where, thanks to the philanthropic generosity of the American Elmhurst family and Glock's enterprise as founding father, gifted music students from British conservatories studied with a select group of international performers and composers, enjoyed the amenities of a reconstituted twelfth-century castle and one another's company while a receptive musical audience, in turn, had the advantage of nightly performances, lectures, and panel discussions by international luminaries of the musical world. The Sessions family was given shelter at Dartington, and arrangements were made immediately to have the new Sonata for Solo Violin played. A later performance was planned for his own favorite at the time, *The Idyll of Theocritus*, with the great English singer Claire Watson as soloist.

Sessions' proven gifts as a writer had long since made him a frequent contributor to American musical journals, and as editor of the *Score* Glock engaged him in that capacity as well. "Song and Pattern in Music Today," the first of Sessions' articles published in the English periodical, was originally presented as an informal lecture at Dartington Hall in that summer of 1956. From personal experience I know that Glock would sometimes prevail on one of his guests to give such lectures on only a few days' notice. Addressed to an audience that consisted largely of serious music lovers, with a small leavening of composers and performers, Sessions' talk, as later revised for publication in the *Score*, allowed some revealing insights on his outlook on music as a composer and a teacher of composers. To accommodate his mixed audience at Dartington Hall, he had to keep his remarks as free as possible of professional jargon, and he managed to provide a plain summary of his views as a composer and a teacher for listeners unfamiliar with more specialized terminology:

> We teach and study harmony, counterpoint and instrumentation; and in speaking of music we isolate as it were a number of other elements: melody, rhythm, line, metre, tempo, dynamics, texture, articulation and possibly

Roger Sessions and Elliott Carter

> other matters. We frequently speak of these things as if each of them were a separate and independent element, and as if a total musical impulse or impression could in actual fact be adequately analyzed as the sum and interplay of these elements, each proceeding according to its own laws. But surely it is our thinking that is in all its essentials highly artificial. These elements are not even *ingredients*, but rather dimensions, facets, or aspects of an integral *musical* experience, and are inaccurately conceived in any other terms . . . Each one of these various aspects derives its function from the total and indivisible musical flow.[3]

Another article, "Thoughts on Stravinsky," was published in the *Score* in 1957. In the following year, Sessions neatly sidestepped Glock's suggestion of an article about the ISCM, offering instead a long and complete statement of his views on the training of composers. Its strangely neutral title, "To the Editor," may have been the result of a tardy manuscript delivery and a publication deadline too urgent to permit further clarification. It still appeared under this title in *Perspectives of New Music*,[4] and in Perspectives on American Composers,[5] but acquired the more helpful title of "What Can Be Taught?" in Edward T. Cone's anthology, *Roger Sessions on Music*.[6]

> May 24, 1958
>
> *Dear William,—*
>
> I have no idea what this might be called—I thought of it more as a "Letter to the Editor" than anything else. I'm sorry that it is so long; but there was that much, at least, that I felt needed to be said. I would rather

that you made no cuts if you can possibly help it, as it is all of one piece; but if you can't avoid it I will understand . . .

This is written in a rush; the month of May is a kind of stretto in a quintuple or sextuple fugue here.

Love to all, from all
Roger[7]

Stretto in a multiple fugue was an apt metaphor. Quite aside from the normal end-of-academic-year rush at Princeton, 1958 was the year in which Sessions, together with three other American composers, had been asked to take part in a State Department–sponsored trip to the Soviet Union. In the wake of the *Sputnik* launching by the Soviets a few months before, official American sensibilities, barely assuaged by young pianist Van Cliburn's spectacular first-prize win in the Tchaikovsky Competition in Moscow, were ready for any prestigious U.S. showing abroad, preferably on Soviet soil—even if only in the field of classical music, as Michael Steinberg notes wryly in Cliburn's *New Grove* biography. Courtesy of the State Department, the Philadelphia Orchestra and the Juilliard Orchestra were sent to the Brussels Worlds Fair, and composers Roy Harris, Ulysses Kay, Peter Mennin, and Roger Sessions would pay an official visit to Moscow, Leningrad, Tiflis, and Kiev.

All in all, Sessions' recollections of that trip were those of a sightseer rather than those of a cultural ambassador. He thoroughly enjoyed everything, Leningrad in particular. As to his companions, their mutual unease as composers of rather disparate musical persuasions soon gave way to an easy camaraderie among fellow tourists. Even Roy Harris, whom Sessions found a little overbearing at times, became a boon companion for the duration: "In Tiflis, Harris and I drank to our friendship, etc. out of ceremonial horns—cows' horns with metal bottoms. Harris wanted them to give the horns to us. They didn't."[8]

For Sessions and Mennin, who met on this trip for the first time, it was the beginning of a long professional relationship. Mennin had just given up his teaching job at Juilliard to accept the presidency of the Peabody Conservatory in Baltimore. Four years later, he would return to New York as president of Juilliard, by then in its new midtown location as one of the member institutions of the Lincoln Center. Sessions would be taking a long look toward Princeton's faculty retirement policy at age seventy, and he would think back to their joint Russian trip: "So I just asked Mennin for a job. He thought for a minute or two and said, yes."[9]

This was before the era of mandated search committees and federal employment guidelines, of course, and faculty appointments were made largely at the discretion of the director. Mennin himself used to refer to his role as head of Juilliard as that of "benevolent dictator." As a composer Mennin was no more comfortable with Sessions' music than his predecessor, William Schuman, had been, but as Juilliard's CEO he recognized a valuable musical acquisition for his school, and he bought it. To his great credit, he would continue to separate his

Curtain call after *Montezuma* in New York, 1982

own musical preferences from what he saw as his artistic responsibility to Juilliard and to the community it served. In the preparation of major performances of new music the school in his day spared neither effort nor expense, and the choice of contemporary repertoire ranged over the entire spectrum of current musical composition. When, in planning for Sessions' eightieth birthday, he asked the composer which of his works he would most like to have performed, the unhesitating reply was, "*Montezuma*." According to reports, Mennin never blinked before agreeing to mount the most costly production in Juilliard's history.

The year of the Russian trip was also the year of the Fourth Symphony, a strangely conceived three-movement work in which—as in Mahler's Fourth—the slow movement, an Elegy on the recent death of Sessions' brother, John, serves as gravitational center and expressive focus of the musical narrative. It is as difficult to forgo its direct and moving appeal to the "willing ear"[10] as was that of the sorrowful Largo in his First Symphony, dedicated to his deceased father, or the musical eulogy for President Franklin Roosevelt in his Second Symphony (originally inscribed to Ruth Sessions), or the grand vista of mourning in what was to become Sessions' own favorite, the Cantata for Robert F. Kennedy and

Martin Luther King, set to the words of Walt Whitman's poem commemorating the slain Abraham Lincoln, "When Lilacs Last in the Dooryard Bloomed": "The way I differ from most American composers: they were all writing 'kinds' of music. I was writing music, without adjectives—including twelve–tone. I wrote some works (I've forgotten which they were) that were strictly in twelve-tone. Then I forgot about it. It wasn't necessary."[11] In a contemporary musical culture polarized between the claims of rival "schools" Sessions had found the ease of knowing that musical language in itself was only a way in which to develop generative musical ideas, and those musical ideas remained his own. Long ago, in a program note for the premiere of his First Symphony in Boston, he had written: "I have tried to absorb rather than to escape [influences], since I have no sympathy with consciously sought originality. I am not trying to write 'modern,' 'American' or 'Neoclassic' music. I am seeking always and only the coherent and living expression of my musical ideas."[12] Much of the struggle of his early years as a composer had been about "coherent and living expression of my musical ideas." By the time of his Second Piano Sonata he realized that he had achieved his aim. Now it was a matter of following the most appropriate way in which a musical idea had to evolve, whatever the needed revision of choice among the available range of technical means.[13] In a 1957 letter to William Glock, he wrote of his work on the Third Symphony:

> It is—as I did not fully understand before—one of those works, at which one arrives periodically, which are a kind of new inner departure, & in which nothing one has done before seems to be any real help—one's "style" has, from one's own inner point of view, become a cliché & of no further use to one. It is an experience that I have had several times before & it is at least a satisfaction to find oneself having it again at the age of sixty.[14]

His increased productivity owed everything to this newfound confidence in the very fact of not being beholden to any method, no matter how well it might have served him in the past. His recent adoption of twelve-tone procedures in composition had discarded previously assumed limitations on its practice and had widened the usable scope of language within his own work: "My String Quintet, written in 1958,[15] was a departure too. I used the twelve-tone system in a much more thoroughgoing way than I'd used it before . . . I think I became more aware of the full resources of the twelve-tone system from then on."[16]

This was hardly an advance in technical expertise as such but rather the happy result of discovering fresh opportunities for the elaboration of musical ideas.

> People don't realize that composers have ears. They have ears and they have feelings. And they have a direct relationship with their music.
>
> It's hard to find the right words. I suppose it's a conception, but it's more than that. I am absorbed with music, and I can tell where certain ideas belong. or I make them belong. But that sounds more cut and dried than it really is.[17]

The newfound confidence of a composer who enjoyed a direct working relationship with his music did not necessarily extend to the finished work. Earl Kim told a story of *The Idyll of Theocritus*. In honor of the completion of that score there had been a celebration at Sessions' Princeton home. The composer really enjoyed himself, playing and singing from the new work, with colleagues and students sharing in his pleasure. On the next morning it was pouring rain, and sodden walkways that crossed the university campus were deserted except for solitary figures hurrying to reach their destination. Kim was one of those hurrying figures until, peering out from under his umbrella, he saw his former teacher standing quite still, soaked and dripping, in the streaming downpour. Startled and worried, he asked him if he felt ill, whether he needed help. Sessions turned to him slowly, his face filled with pain, and asked softly, "But suppose it's *shit?*"[18]

The musical establishment at large could no longer deny its recognition to a composer of Sessions' growing reputation, although it managed to enfold him in the kind of embrace that keeps a man at arm's length. He had achieved the public stature that would be his for the rest of his life: an imposing position in professional circles and name recognition among the musical public that greatly exceeded familiarity with his work. Most of his major compositions would now be on commission by enterprising major orchestras and important musical institutions. In performance, they were assured of a well-publicized premiere and a respectful reception. Critical acclaim would most often be restricted to praise for his compositional craft, a pat on the back for the performing organization, and a metaphoric shrug of reviewers' shoulders in reaffirming Sessions' reputation as a "difficult" composer. To the current crop of mighty maestros of American symphony orchestras—the generation that followed the truly trailblazing Koussevitzkys and Stokowskis—occasional condescension to the cause of complex contemporary music was a meritorious duty but one to be undertaken with care.

We have already quoted John Sessions' letter about a backstage exchange that followed the premiere of his father's Sixth Symphony by the Philadelphia Orchestra under Eugene Ormandy.[19] Mr. Ormandy's priorities of status were a far cry indeed from Leopold Stokowski's insouciant repeat of Debussy's *Afternoon of a Faun*, when he decided the merely polite patter of applause after its first performance in Philadelphia warranted more than a polite bow from the podium. Conductorial conviction in taking on the performance of new and "difficult" works was becoming rare, while unhelpful and often whimsical apologies for the benefit of the orchestra's precious subscription audience tried to assuage the expected pain. Even the intrepid Leonard Bernstein relegated the New York Philharmonic's first performance of two movements of Stefan Wolpe's three-movement symphony—arguably the most difficult orchestral work in the literature, and not performed complete until its subsequent premiere by the New England Conservatory Orchestra—to his assistant. By way of introducing the new work to the Philharmonic audience, Bernstein explained that the young conductor to whom he had entrusted its premiere was a particularly apt choice because he had been a mathematics major in college.

Among the unsung heroes in this struggle were members of the much maligned press, music critics who had convictions, took the trouble to become familiar with new scores *before* their performance, attended rehearsals, and wrote relevant and persuasive reports on what they had heard in concert. The contradictory flowering of contemporary composition in midcentury in the face of popular indifference owes a great debt to a small number of serious and knowledgeable music critics, among whom Andrew Porter and Michael Steinberg in the United States, David Drew, William Glock, and Peter Heyworth in England, and Hans Heinz Stuckenschmidt in Germany were only a few of the most distinguished and effective. Sessions was well aware of these champions and maintained cordial, if properly reserved, relations with most of them. He was less astute in the face of adverse criticism. From the early days of his homecoming to New York in the 1930s, when he fired off a disdainful letter to the *New York Times*'s all-powerful Olin Downes, in defense of Otto Klemperer, to his furious protest in 1961 when Ross Parmenter, also of the *Times,* quoted overheard negative comments made by Lisl Sessions on the performance of her husband's music at Northwestern University,[20] he left an uncalled-for trail of avoidable resentment where he could ill afford it.

Hubris, perhaps—Sessions was "riding high." At the time of the latter incident, in the spring of 1961, he had been granted a semester's leave of absence from Princeton in order to attend rehearsals and the premiere performances of *Montezuma* in Berlin. That project had to be postponed when it became clear that his work on the opera would not be completed in time. Nevertheless, the excitement that attended the endgame of a thirty-year project must have been huge. Life was very full. In January he attended John F. Kennedy's inauguration in Washington as an invited guest. From there he proceeded to conduct his Third Symphony at Oberlin and *The Black Maskers* in Evanston, Illinois, where *Lucullus*, his mass, and the Fourth Symphony were performed by other conductors and Lisl's displeasure with one of these performances was quoted in the press. Symptomatic of her husband's ambivalent standing in the music world, he received an invitation to spend an all-expense-paid week at a music festival in Japan, at which none of his music was to be played. He declined. Instead, he took advantage of his already-scheduled university leave ("to remain in Princeton while on leave is like not being on leave at all"[21]) by taking a long trip with Lisl to visit his colleague Boris Blacher in Berlin,[22] and his friend Luigi Dallapiccola in Florence, to travel in Scotland and France, and finally to see Athens and the Greek islands, including Cos of *Theocritus*. He returned via Switzerland in time for the fall semester. In February of 1962 he was off again to Boston, where I had invited him to conduct his Fourth Symphony at the New England Conservatory of Music.

His first appearance before our orchestra was memorable. The work had been rehearsed, of course, before his arrival, and the young players had begun to look forward to a performance of a new work, whose technical problems had been resolved, under the baton of its eminent composer. Having been introduced to polite applause, Sessions, a stocky figure in rumpled trousers, shirtsleeves, and a sleeveless sweater, mounted the podium and made his first error of judgment: before he had heard a note of his symphony, he provided the orchestra with a list of *likely* mistakes that had not yet happened. Then, on hearing a reading that apparently exceeded his expectations, he seemed to react with some errors of concentration of his own. There were enough nervous mistakes for the orchestra to declare they "could not watch him." After being informed—by me—that they were free to close their eyes but that they would have to play in any case, they settled down. Eventually they gave a fine performance, and the maestro, having meanwhile requested and received some conducting pointers on coping with frequently changing meters in the score, did them proud.

Sessions' charisma was of a curious mixture of the humble, the magisterial, the irrepressibly elated, and the unconsciously superior. He was alone in Boston during his week of rehearsals. Lisl would join him for the concert, and meanwhile he came to dinner most evenings. He had no small talk, but he was a marvelous guest. Even our dog was devoted to him—which may have been the result of a special Sessions way to make his hosts feel at ease. He told us that "on our trip to Normandy,[23] we couldn't find a place to spend the night. A nice lady found us a place with a peasant family. We were looked at askance at first, because they were not used to having strangers. But we were nice to the dog, so they took us in."[24]

He also confided to us that he did not own a dress suit. His Princeton neighbor, a choral conductor who usually lent him his tailcoat, had a concert himself during that week. We looked up a rental establishment for him, and the next evening he appeared with a large carton under his arm. He had not bothered to rent a suit: "They let me bu*y* it for *eighteen dollars!*" he told us triumphantly. The modeling session that followed left us speechless. But such was the spirit and zest of his conducting at the concert two days later, that his unusual appearance, with brown shoes and coattails that nearly reached his ankles, went quite unnoticed. In fact, in his performance of the wonderful slow movement of his symphony, the Elegy for his brother, John, he more than justified the concert program's inadvertently jumbled statement: "Symphony No. 4 by Roger Sessions, the conductor composing." A week later, I received a letter from him, headed: "Dear Teacher."

The score of *Montezuma* was completed in 1963 and its premiere rescheduled in Berlin for April 1964. In June of 1963 he had also finished work on a commission from the Princeton Theological Seminary, the piano/vocal setting for soprano and chorus of *Psalm 140*, first performed by Janice Harsany in 1966.[25] Early in 1964 he completed Symphony No. 5. But all hopes and expectations now centered on the magnum opus, which had occupied Sessions for nearly thirty years. On a Ford Foundation grant he settled with Lisl in Berlin, two months before the premiere.

Berlin in 1964 was a depressing place. Even his brief earlier visit there to Boris Blacher had not really prepared Sessions for the profound transformation of a city he had known well, more than thirty years ago, during the final years of the Weimar Republic. Its physical devastation was only the most obvious reminder of a lost war. The pretentious monuments of the Kaiser's Siegesallee as well as the extravagant architectural projects of the Third Reich lay in ruins, but in a transformation that seemed even more poignant to the composer, the former German capital's feverishly driven cultural life had yielded to an almost provincial mix of prosaic public entertainment in a city isolated and divided among mutually estranged occupying forces, a city held hostage not only to a reflection of the contending worldviews of its foreign occupiers but also to daily confrontations of insular local interests and concerns among its German inhabitants. As a launching site for *Montezuma*, an American opera rife with potential historical analogies, it proved to be a very bad choice.

Public reaction to the premiere on April 22, 1964, was mixed at best. There had been bravos as well as catcalls from the audience, but the press, with notable exceptions such as Stuckenschmidt's review, was almost unanimously hostile. The work was attacked largely on political grounds, with some reviews going as far as to suggest an investigation of why public funds had been spent to produce it. Sessions himself was disappointed in the staging and the stage direction.[26] The musical performance under conductor Heinrich Hollreiser,[27] with a fine cast, suffered mostly from inadequate rehearsal. First-night nerves aside—a serious "train wreck" caused by a momentary lapse of concentration on the part of Montezuma himself was narrowly saved by the astute Hollreiser—the score appears to have been given a far better hearing than might have been expected, considering its enormous demands on all performers and the apparently very niggardly provision of preparation time.

"Per Montezuma, che cosa dire?"[28] wrote Sessions to Dallapiccola on the day after its first performance:

> The situation in Berlin worries a lot of fair-minded people. There is concern about an increasingly reactionary (and xenophobic) trend especially among young people, of a complacent apathy now that Berlin is no longer felt to be at the flashpoint of an international crisis (at least since the Cuban crisis of 1962), and also because young West German men can find shelter here to avoid the draft. My sources for these observations are responsible and well-informed, but I accept the information with some caution nevertheless, because I cannot vouch for it myself. I do know, however, that the 1961 project to attract foreign artists and intellectuals to Berlin has not worked out very well, at least for the time being. Many of them (I should say of us) are more or less uncomfortable and unhappy here. One hears *very* little—actually almost no—contemporary music other than Henze,[29] who is the hero of the hour, and whom I find a friendly and

> agreeable young man but in no sense a great figure, at least so far. Except for *Montezuma,* which is in no way connected with this project [sponsored by] the Berlin Senate as well as the Ford Foundation, there does not appear to be any reason why Elliott Carter, Xenakis,[30] Gilbert Amy,[31] to name some of the composers involved in the program [and] whom I see from time to time, should live here—no performances, little communication, as well some resentment of the program itself by people concerned with their own *way of life*, who take umbrage (quite openly) at what they call an American effort to "bring culture to Berlin." Needless to say this notion is based on a complete, if more or less personal, misunderstanding of the idea. But contemporary music aside, this concern I have mentioned may not be an entirely bad thing from a world-wide perspective, even though it is a little sad for Berlin.[32]

According to her son, John, Lisl never quite recovered from the public rejection of her husband's opera, a work that had occupied his mind and imagination during all the years of her marriage. Sessions thought it best to treat her to a vacation in Sicily in May. But if he had hoped that Lisl's depression would soon lift in a place filled with all the sunshine, color, and physical beauty they had both come to love about Italy, he was mistaken. She lacked her husband's hard-earned inner defenses of creative confidence and professional resilience. Sessions had come a long way. It is well to remember how, nearly fifty years ago, hostile reviews of his first European reviews in Geneva had to be hidden from his mother, Ruth, the long-ago woman in his life. When he wrote to her that "criticism is in essence none of the composer's business,"[33] he may well have believed it to be true—in theory. By now, however, his abundant and still-burgeoning harvest of works had provided him with a very simple kind of personal security—he was no longer "a kind of celebrity"; he was Roger Sessions.

Nevertheless, Berlin had been a great disappointment. The *Montezuma* premiere was to have capped Sessions' growing prestige within the profession by turning his already-commanding position as an American composer into prominence as a composer without an implied need for the national qualifier. That never happened.

Following their holiday in Sicily, Roger set to work on the orchestration of *Psalm 140*, but now there was another change to be faced: his retirement from Princeton in 1965. This time it was Lisl's turn to take charge. She arranged for a sensible move to more modest quarters in town. He put a cheerful face on it, saying that he much preferred the new little house in Stanworth Lane and joking about his small study, where whatever he wanted was within arm's reach. Judging by the condition of that study in later years, it must have been hard even to get in the door. Not that he spent a great deal of time in his new home. His South American odyssey was begun in the summer that followed his retirement (i.e., the winter season south of the equator). During the next academic year, 1966–67, he served as Ernest Bloch Visiting Professor at Berkeley. In 1967 he joined the Juilliard faculty, and he lectured as Charles Elliott Norton Professor at Harvard during the academic year 1968/69.

A daunting schedule for a septuagenarian, even aside from the remarkable creative flow of major musical works that continued to accompany it. Piano Sonata No. 3 and Symphony No. 6, as well as Two Pieces for Solo Cello for his son, John, were completed in 1966; the dark Symphony No. 7 followed in 1967 and the densely charged Symphony No. 8, for his daughter, Elizabeth, in 1968. That was also the year of another summer holiday in Sicily: "Two important things happened in Syracuse: I was cheated for the first time in Italy, and I received a letter from the U. of Cal with a commission for their 100th anniversary."[34]

That commission engendered his cantata on Walt Whitman's "When Lilacs Last in the Dooryard Bloomed," Sessions' largest work other than *Montezuma* and the one he loved best. In his half-humorous, self-deprecating way he would happily recall his old friend and colleague Darius Milhaud's reaction after its 1970 premiere at Berkeley: "About my music, Milhaud always said I *almost* made it. But after *Lilacs* he said I made it."[35]

Whenever it was performed, *Lilacs* enjoyed striking public acceptance. Compared to Sessions' symphonies, which, after their premiere by whatever orchestra had owned rights of first performance, were more likely to be repeated in Europe than at home, *Lilacs* enjoyed a somewhat better record of second performances in the United States. Five years after its premiere in California, *Lilacs* came to Harvard in a performance sponsored by the Fromm Foundation. A year later, George Solti conducted it as part of the Chicago Symphony's bicentennial celebration.

Introducing the Harvard performance, Michael Steinberg wrote about the work in a long preconcert feature article in the *Boston Globe*:

> Sessions is in the anomalous position of being a great eminence on the musical scene—not least as a teacher whose students have included composers as distinguished as Milton Babbitt, John Harbison, Andrew Imbrie, Earl Kim, Leon Kirchner and Fred Lerdahl—whose own music remains relatively little known. That music is immensely difficult to perform. There is so much going on in it, with no idling, no coasting and with accompaniments apt to assume so "specific a character as to become independent lines. "Lilacs" at 40-some minutes is hardly less concentrated than the intense and witty Symphony No. 8 at 15. But the music immensely rewards superb performance, not only careful performance, which is of course essential, but performance with flair, with a sense of "the large gesture," for the rhetorical and—let us not shirk it—the ethical assumptions of the Beethoven-Brahms-Schoenberg tradition which Sessions uniquely represents today . . .
>
> When you listen, attend to the poem: it is the way into the music, as the music is the way—a way—into it. Some details I love especially: the plaintive conversation of flute and clarinet with which the work opens; the whippoorwill phrases for off-stage flute and piccolo (sometimes with xylo-

> phone); the undulating, swaying violins for the "sea-winds blown from east and west," the vaulted melody with which the violins follow the phrase "Night and day journeys a coffin," the wonderful mixture, part doublings, part variations, near the end, at "Yet each to keep and all, retrievements out of the night," the last phrase for bass clarinet, alto flute, trombone, clarinet, which does not stop so much as move across the last double-bar out of earshot.[36]

Sessions and his Boston audiences for that performance on March 24, 1975, were fortunate again in having a music critic in the grand tradition of their city's Philip Hale (*Boston Herald*), H. T. Parker (*Boston Evening Transcript*), and Paul Rosenfeld (*Boston Globe*),[37] who had written generously as well as knowledgeably about the premiere of his First Symphony, half a century before. A sense of the reviewer's having actually been there and having cared—a sense of immediacy more often found on the sports pages of our newspapers than in musical reviews—emanates from words that share experience and invite discovery. Nevertheless, on the matter of Michael Steinberg's mention in the *Boston Globe* of Sessions' acknowledged standing as a master teacher the composer had become quite touchy:

> I had a strange experience at Ann Arbor [in 1967]. I had a pupil there, and I had written the 7th Symphony for their 150th anniversary. They wanted me to conduct, but I said no, I won't write it unless you engage the Chicago Symphony. Luigi Dallapiccola also had something for them. The way the symphony was put on made such a difference between the way it was introduced: Luigi was a great *composer*. I was a great *teacher*.[38]

Surely it would have been nothing if not churlish had the University of Michigan, on whose music faculty at Ann Arbor Sessions' former pupil Ross Lee Finney held a prominent position, refrained from grateful public acknowledgment of the connection. Certainly Luigi Dallapiccola enjoyed no wider recognition, even in smart musical circles at the time, than his American colleague. But for Sessions the apparent distinction rankled enough to be recalled twenty-five years later in more than one interview for this book.[39]

Ironically, at least part of the problem was, in the true meaning of the word, *academic*. The profound change in the American way of life in the 1960s, with civil rights marches that protested racial and gender inequities as well as a widespread reevaluation of civic liberties, had deep roots within the American university. Concurrent with a new affirmation of social values both within and outside the campus, however, populist sentiments flooded the national debate. A peaceful but nonetheless powerful cultural revolution rejected much of what had suddenly become an elitist heritage, with some significant commercial support. The country at large had very little time for the emperor Montezuma.

It seems doubtful that Sessions fully appreciated the extent to which, at that time, his academic prominence, his books, his lectures, and his fame as a teacher supplied an essential underpinning to his stature and identity as a composer. To be sure, major American orchestras *did* commission Sessions symphonies for the rights of first performance. At fund-raising time and in aid of foundation and government grants the name of Roger Sessions was one to conjure with, and the number and combination of performers required for his symphonic works, as well as necessary rehearsal time, could indeed be expected to fit into the budgeted number of services per concert for the standard roster of players already under contract. Works that required mixed forces such as *Lilacs*, on the other hand, had to rely almost entirely on performances sponsored by universities and music schools. Much as Sessions had looked forward to *Lilacs*' performance under Solti, the result was a bitter disappointment to him—not because of either the orchestra as such or the conductor but simply because, like *Montezuma* in Berlin, the mixed forces required for *Lilacs* should have had the advantage of more combined rehearsal time. *Lucullus* and *Montezuma* have never been performed in a major American opera house. As opposed to a traditional repertory house in which the same roster of singers is responsible for an entire season's performances, and where preparation of new productions can be planned with forces constantly in residence, the star system of the large houses imposed an increasingly intricate patchwork of limited, interdependent availablities of internationally committed singers, which made the lengthy preparation time of a new opera prohibitively expensive.

Curiously, the situation was almost exactly reversed in Europe. The great radio networks supported world-class orchestras, whose box office receipts were not the immediate fiscal bottom line, although political considerations would be bound, very soon, to warrant results comparable to those in the United States. Similarly, opera was able to budget on sizable government grants, so that the unrecoverable costs of new productions could be factored into long-term planning. Conversely, however, European universities and conservatories had neither the resources nor the practical experience to mount performances on the level of their best American counterparts. Facing the historical truth that performance of the works of our Western musical heritage has never been self-supporting, an almost Darwinian principle evolved on both sides of the Atlantic, compensating in different but indigenous responses for the respective frailties of domestic musical life in crisis.

Meanwhile American academic honors for Sessions poured in. Rutgers University had been first to award him an honorary doctorate in 1962. In 1967, at the end of his year as Ernest Bloch Visiting Professor at Berkeley, the University of California granted him another—signed by Ronald Reagan, then governor of the state. Two more in 1971 were added respectively by Northwestern University and Williams. Princeton followed in 1972, Harvard and Cleveland in 1975, the University of Pennsylvania in 1976, and Rider in 1978.

Sessions' care for Lisl's comfort and ease on their shared journeys now reflected his prominent status abroad. In 1969 Glock—Sir William by that time—received a letter appealing for help with travel arrangements, a far cry from the days of finding overnight accommodations in farmhouses:

> Lisl and I will be in London from [illegible] to Sept. 10 and would like if possible to stay at the Connaught Hotel. We are told that it is almost obligatory to have a recommendation in order to get in there. We will be writing to the Hotel in a couple of days; but I wonder if I might ask you or Anne to phone them in the meantime and put in a word on our behalf. We would be tremendously grateful.[40]

I never asked him if his appeal was successful. At least he might have enjoyed a meal with Lisl in one of the Connaught's famous dining rooms, then as now so far above London's best as to justify the very steep cost.

After completing *Lilacs* Sessions continued from strength to strength. The Whitman cantata (1968–1970) was followed by a Rhapsody for Orchestra (also in 1970) and the Double Concerto for Violin, Cello, and Orchestra in 1971. His son, John, to whom the work is dedicated, was cello soloist at the premiere. In the summer of that year, Roger and Lisl took one last big trip together, to Norway from Oslo to Hammerfest and returning via London. The first indication of a problem with Lisl's health surfaced under mysterious circumstances: "We had taken a boat trip. Then, six miles from the Russian border or the Finnish border, Lisl had a little trouble—Lisl knew what it was—miles from anywhere. Past Hammerfest, at a place called Kirkenes, we called a doctor from the bus. A good doctor came with the right drugs and gave Lisl the right thing."[41]

"Lisl knew what it was." For some time she seems to have kept from her husband what she already feared. And with his determined optimism in situations outside his life as a composer, he was not inclined to probe. Certainly the episode did not cast a serious shadow over his happy memory of the trip when he returned:

> October 4, '71
>
> *Dear Fred*
>
> We only got back on the 30th (we had an absolutely *glorious* summer, first among the fjords and then up to the North Cape in Norway & along the coast of course—then for four days in Zürich, and then on Lake Como where I got a lot of work done). Otherwise I would have answered your letter sooner.
>
> Of course I am delighted to hear from you (from the horse's mouth, if you don't mind my saying so—at least I was brought up around horses, & developed both affection and respect for them, and also would not dream of riding you!) what I already had heard from David Drew, that the performances of the Rhapsody & the Eighth Symphony[42] went well. *Many* thanks!

In the following year Sessions added the Concertino for Small Orchestra, the Canon in Memory of Stravinsky, and Three Choruses on Biblical Texts for

Amherst to his rapidly growing list of works. In 1973, as music director of the Syracuse Symphony, I commissioned what would become Sessions' Symphony No. 9.

That was also the year, however, when Lisl's health became a dominant concern: fibrillations of the heart; a prolonged controversy over appropriate drugs and dosage; an incident of alarmingly depressed blood pressure but, just prior to the expected installation of a pacemaker, a sudden, unexplained improvement—it amounted to an uncertain prognosis and to periods of almost daily crises of confidence in a shared future.

When Lisl's condition had improved a little, later in the year, a trip to Amsterdam and London was to take the pressure off, but she suffered a bad fall and broke a bone in her pelvis. For nearly forty years Lisl's strength had supported her husband's work. Now, with uncertainties and misgivings over her condition constantly at the back of Roger's mind, his great flow of creative energy was suspended. As Lisl's condition stabilized, quiet holidays in Franconia, New Hampshire, or in the beautiful Alpine principality of Liechtenstein replaced journeys tacked onto either end of a hectic visit in pursuit of professional ends.

Outward strains and demands on a prominent composer's time and attention did not abate of course—performances promised, often canceled, and sometimes rescued by timely intervention; a change of publisher from his devoted advocate and friend Felix Greissle to the more efficient and much larger firm of Theodore Presser; a ragged correspondence that, even in Sessions' best times, had made him start most of his letters with an apology—in all this Lisl had been his fiercely loyal and energetic manager and conscience . To the great champion of contemporary composition and Sessions' particular friend philanthropist Paul Fromm of the Fromm Foundation she would send belated thanks for the long-unacknowledged present of a case of wine. Sessions was away to hear the first performance of his Third Piano Sonata, and she had just discovered the lapse: "If I weren't so mad at him I would say I hoped he had a good performance and still liked the piece."[43] But not all lapses of attention were as easily mended. Sessions' letter to Dallapiccola of December 8, 1974, accompanying recently published scores of Symphony No. 8, *Lilacs*, and the Concertino for Small Orchestra, began with customary apologies for his long silence. In a prompt and gracious reply, Dallapiccola declared himself "happy to see your handwriting again after five years." It was their last exchange of letters. Dallapiccola died on February 19, 1975.

Foremost among performance projects "promised, often canceled, and sometimes rescued" at that time, was Peter Mennin's plan for an American premiere of *Montezuma* in New York, as Juilliard's eightieth birthday present to the composer in 1976. But Boston's enterprising opera impresario and artistic director Sarah Caldwell had secured rights for an American premiere in 1969, chosen her cast, begun coaching and even sold tickets for the event, only to be forced, eventually, to cancel for lack of funds—I still have my tickets. Further postponements followed. When Juilliard approached the publishers, Sarah was in the last year of her contractual performance rights, and it was generally assumed that even that indomitable lady would not be able to raise the enormous funds required before that deadline. Instead, she confounded us all. Sessions wrote: "Sarah Caldwell suddenly appeared out of the blue, and had obviously gone even at that time—in May—full steam ahead with preparations, casting and all."[44] The prospect of losing the American premiere of *Montezuma* to Juilliard had galvanized her efforts and resulted in a performance that was superior in almost every way to the Berlin effort of 1964. The composer was thrilled: "Sarah worked her head off . . . I heard my music as I conceived it, for the first time, and was thoroughly convinced that it was all I had hoped."[45]

Paradoxically, one aspect of the Berlin perfomance—of increasingly bad memory, as far as Sessions was concerned—reassured him about what had not been solved in Boston nor would be at the Juilliard performance to come: "The voices, especially in the low register, were sometimes covered, though not everywhere in the hall, apparently. Since this problem was solved (and only in one instance, where the singer was placed much too high on the stage, were microphones necessary) in Berlin, that does not worry me in the slightest."[46]

The year 1976 also revived Sessions' creative powers, which had been dormant for three years. Major performances helped:

> For me this year has been, certainly, one of the best of my life. The performance [of *Lilacs*] was something of a disappointment . . . Five weeks later I had a really excellent performance, *much to my surprise*,[47] by none other than Pierre Boulez, of my 3rd Symphony; he really worked hard on it, listened to my comments, and gave every indication of understanding the music.—Of course the most important of all was Montezuma.[48]

And there was, ready to hand, the commission for what would become Symphony No. 9. As it happened, after an interval of three years since the composition of his most recent major work and, more important perhaps, of eight years since he had last written a symphony—the almost aphoristically condensed and concentrated No. 8—he found himself once again at a point of "new inner departure, & in which nothing one has done before seems to be any real help."[49] The commission, in fact, had not specified a "symphony," and, as often before, Sessions himself had to find out gradually what his new work wanted to be:

> I have made many sketches, and like them; and little by little the design of the whole has begun to clarify itself in my mind. *Quite between ourselves*, I haven't yet summoned up the effrontery to call it Symphony No. 9 though I might have to do so eventually. Forgive me for being so vague; but this is the way I work—I keep things "flexible" in my mind for a very long time whenever I am working on a long piece, and I am not yet ready to commit myself to anything more than to say it will definitely be a much bigger work than the Rhapsody and will probably contain more large contrasts ("movements," possibly) than my Eighth Symphony. A few things I must still keep under my hat—please forgive me. I <u>can</u> tell you however that it will definitely be a *major* work of mine, though not really a long one.[50]

Sessions' Ninth Symphony does indeed show large contrasts, not between its three movements as much as throughout the continuity of the musical narrative itself. As a conductor, I found it so difficult to approach that I had to ask for help. We had lunch at his favorite restaurant across the street from Juilliard—his choice. The name escapes me, but I remember waitresses with tall striped headdresses, something between a chef's hat and a bishop's mitre. I had prepared myself with a most careful analysis of the work—two tone rows for the first time in Sessions' oeuvre, which helped not at all, and a map of continuing contrasts that occur at consistently spaced time intervals, reflecting the numbers four and seven—which did not seem to help, either. He only smiled. Frustrated and bewildered, I found myself trying to prove that I had indeed done my homework on the score. When I brought forward my observation that the relative proportions of passages governed by either one or the other of two contrasting musical ideas remained in a ratio of 4:7 throughout—and to this day I can't help wondering whether or not this was, in fact, news to him—he smiled even more . Finally, in response to my exasperated (and uncalled-for) reminder that unlike the apparent state of affairs in *his* score, Beethoven's use of conflicting ideas served to effect interaction, change, and transformation, he asked in his best Zen manner, "do you read Blake?" I admitted as much. "Well then, think about the Tyger. " As he knew this baffled questioner so well, that reference was sufficient to suggest an innate coexistence of complementary opposites—a powerful musical matrix that informed the new work, as well as my required guide for performance. A year later, after hearing a tape of that performance with an English orchestra, he smiled the very un-Zen smile of a contented composer (it always seemed to split his face from ear to ear): "You see, they *did* come to an accommodation."

Opposing musical ideas that inform the substance of a symphony without interacting or transforming each other in the process but achieving an accommodation in the end—this was a remarkable departure from the adversarial nature of the development of themes or motifs in music of the nineteenth century or their entirely disconnected, isolated display during much of the twentieth. Defining and abiding opposites shape Sessions' Ninth Symphony in such a way that contrast itself becomes associative in the process, an extraordinary leap in articulating musical continuity. His earlier letter does not suggest that he found this new evidence of contrary but autonomous inner vision as disturbing as his erstwhile discovery of unexpected harmonic ambiguity in his First String Quartet. Forty years of putting his trust in the ultimate control of musical ideas would have taken the surprise out of "having to write music which was very different from my idea of myself at the time."[51] But even at this late stage in his creative life he was sufficiently puzzled to confess that "some things I must still keep under my hat."[52]

The way in which one musical idea may affect another in a piece of music, not by palpable modifications in shape or emphasis but simply by being heard repeatedly within the same incompatible context along the entire musical continuum, has not yet been explored by musical theory. In his Ninth Symphony, Sessions created such a continuity, opposing contrasting musical ideas that, absent any apparent impact on each other, might as well be passing *through* each other.

Was this new? Not really. Dialectical confrontations in music, even after Beethoven, inform a minority of musical works that feature contrasting thematic material. What *is* different in Sessions' Ninth Symphony is the unrelenting, short-term juxtaposition of disparities that do not seem ever to affect their respective identity. They have no "effect" on each other. Instead, and to a profound degree, they affect the listener's experience. Sessions was no minimalist, to be sure, but in his Ninth Symphony he was on to something.

In order to indicate the enormity of this departure to the reader who is not familiar with Sessions' Ninth Symphony, we shall once again resort to a metaphor borrowed from contemporary science. By way of illustrating ambiguity as a compositional environment, we related the story of Schrödinger's cat.[53] We shall now turn to another concept of subatomic theory, the wimp.

The term *wimp* is borrowed from the vocabulary of particle physics, according to which *WIMP* is the acronym for a Weakly Interacting Massive Particle. Because of their extremely weak capacity to interact, such particles may pass *through* other physical entities, rather like ghosts, leaving hardly a trace of their passage. In current cosmological theory, subatomic wimps are real enough. They may make up the 80 percent of the mysterious "dark matter" in the universe that accounts for antigravitational "dark energy" and accelerates its expansion begun by the big bang. According to Aristotle, earth, water, fire, and air were the four elements of our sublunar world, while for the moving heavenly spheres beyond the moon he allowed a "fifth essence." In a bow across the millennia, some cosmologists now refer to the force exerted by "dark matter" in the universe as the *quint*essence. Its mysterious existence in the universe is respectively hailed and disputed by astrophysicists.

The equally mysterious force with which one musical idea may affect another in the same piece of music, not by palpable modifications in shape or emphasis but simply by being heard repeatedly within the same musical continuum, has not yet been explored, let alone codified, by musical theory. In his Ninth Symphony, Sessions created such a continuity, in which opposing musical ideas "pass through each other" and, for the listener, seem to reach an accommodation in which neither is compromised.

"Who would dare to demand theory here!"[54] The closing sentence of Schoenberg's *Harmonielehre* revealed another great teacher's ultimate frustration with the limitations of analytical theory at the active cutting edge of new creation.

Roger Sessions, ever grateful to his own teacher Ernest Bloch for his solid grounding in musical analysis, insisted that his pupils gain a firm grasp on "how is *done*" but remained ever mindful of the fact that "the 'technique' of a piece of music is essentially the affair of the composer."[55] Only the composer, following the inner logic of his musical ideas, would know the evidence of things not seen, the quintessential "dark matter," which may exert such a powerful pull that he finds himself "surprised at writing the kind of music that I had to write."[56]

The musical terms in which Sessions increasingly preferred to discuss music in later life[57]—*continuity, association, contrast,* and *structural rhythms*—articulate his "long line" and inform musical "gestures." But underlying the contradiction of his insisting on informed understanding of evolving principles in Western musical tradition on the one hand and his equally strong belief in an open-ended composers' license for departure along uncharted roads of artistic creation on the other hand made him begin to distrust ultimate authority of analytical theory toward the end of his teaching career. To his former pupil and knowing colleague, Andrew Imbrie, he confided, "Andrew, there is too much analysis going on these days, and I'm afraid it's largely my fault."[58]

Sessions concluded his work as composer in 1981, with the Concerto for Orchestra, commissioned by the Boston Symphony and winner of a Pulitzer Prize. If the Ninth reveled in unforgiving contrasts, the Concerto for Orchestra made up for it. One of his most conciliatory compositions, it almost runs the risk of being claimed by contemporary advocates of "the new romanticism." It is, in any case, a beautiful, sweeping work. *New Yorker* critic Andrew Porter described it in one of his great lines: "One ascends it with animated tread, moves with slow wonder across its central reach, speeds again toward its close, and at the end pauses for a moment, quietly rapt, to consider both the journey made and the realms to which it may lead."[59]

But the journey was over. Unsuspected by him or anyone else at the time, the expansive realm of Sessions' work had reached its last frontier.

The year 1982 brought the third performance of *Montezuma.* I conducted that performance. Andrew Porter wrote in a five-page *New Yorker* review:

> The great American opera, Roger Sessions's *Montezuma*, comes closer to receiving the production it deserves; perhaps a full-scale presentation by the Metropolitan Opera will mark the composer's hundredth birthday, which falls on December 28, 1996. *Montezuma* was composed between 1941 and 1963, was first performed in Berlin in 1964. Sarah Caldwell gave the American première in Boston twelve years later. And now [February 1982] *Montezuma* has reached New York: the Juilliard American Opera Center mounted three sold-out performances of it last month.[60]

Press reaction on the whole was as negative as after the Berlin premiere, with a peculiar twist of damning the work while praising the performers—"the entire cast deserves credit for an impossible job well done."[61] One wonders how they knew. Porter's perceptive review, based not only on his having attended the earlier production in Boston as well as all three New York performances but also very clearly on close study of the score itself, celebrated the work: "Sessions's *Montezuma* captures the scale, the seriousness, and the romance of the subject in music that is powerful, splendid, colorful, and generous. But it is not an opera made for easy public success."[61] He found—rightly—that as in the Boston performance, the voices were often covered, "but even those who heard only sounds, not an interesting discourse, in, say, the long dialogue for Malinche and Cortes that ends Act I must have recognized that the Juilliard production was a stunning achievement."

The opening night of *Montezuma* in New York was the last time I saw Lisl. In my commemorative essay for Roger, which serves as the introduction for this book, I have described the unique and spontaneous public acclamation she shared with her husband after that first performance. In a life in which moments of celebration and triumph were more than commonly close-linked to her husband's public successes, it may have assuaged her lingering memory of the opera's premiere in Berlin. As it happened, it was their final moment of shared public celebration. Lisl died five months later, on July 9, 1982.

With Lisl's death, the great harvest of Sessions' life as composer came to an end. The sure touch of self-governing beginnings, of musical images to be recognized, apprehended, transformed, and developed in the ferment of "new inner departures," had left him. He was still Roger Sessions, and he would try to find his way once more through familiar interior paths to "new realms to be revealed." But the emperor had lost his Malinche.

In some ways Sessions' life as a composer bore striking resemblance to that of the emperor Montezuma, who never noticed that the vision that informed his glorious prime had become a matter of indifference to his people—until they killed him. In the long journey from his centuries-old, privileged background in the New World, Sessions came to believe in a musical future that recognized and subsumed deep roots in an ancient promise "from across the sea." He believed in a fusion of traditions that would transcend the limitations exacted by trendy "styles" of composition, and he made it work as he created his legacy—a difficult experience for composer, performer, listener—and for many years the musical life of his time cheered him on. He was not prepared to find himself, like the aging Aztec emperor, isolated at last from a musical world that had made him an icon and an honored prisoner of his past achievements.

Composers are rarely stoned to death, but covert sentence of "internal exile" may well be pronounced on their work while they are still alive. During his last years, Session suffered most keenly from thoughtless journalistic references to the "European affinities" of his music. He could not have been other than an American composer—as American as Aaron Copland, whose European family roots had been replanted in Brooklyn soil at about the same time that Sessions' parents moved there from Massachusetts. The fusion and confusion of roots embodied in Sessions' work owed nothing to national or ethnic identification. It was very much in the manner of America itself, as it defined itself during the years of Sessions' harvest—complex, vigorous, and difficult.

One could have wished that Sessions' last years might be summed up in Porter's words describing the final measures of the Concerto for Orchestra—

"quietly rapt, to consider both the journey made and the realms to which it may lead."[63] They were indeed quiet, but for the most part they were lonely. He did not lack friends, but he missed their casual companionship. Meetings with colleagues across the river in New York depended on special occasions. He thoroughly enjoyed a joint concert performance of Stravinsky's *Soldier's Tale* with a judiciously chosen cast of Aaron Copland as Narrator, himself as Soldier, and Virgil Thomson as the Devil. But younger friends and former pupils were busy with their own careers in far-off places. A cheerful Hispanic housekeeper looked after his daily wants but was not allowed to clean up his study. There he was plotting new works, a violin sonata for the Library of Congress and—in almost certainly unconscious irony—an operatic project on Hans Christian Anderson's tale "The Emperor's New Clothes."

Roger Sessions died on March 16, 1985. His daughter, Betsy, had moved to Princeton in order to be with him, and two of his oldest friends and colleagues, Milton Babbitt and Edward Cone, were at his bedside. His last words were, "What a damned nuisance!"

Headlines in the world press noted his passing in different ways: "SESSIONS' MUSIC WILL LIVE FOREVER," vowed the *Boston Globe*; "MR. ROGER SESSIONS, EMINENT AMERICAN COMPOSER," read the headline of his obituary in the *Times* of London. "ROGER SESSIONS, A COMPOSER AND PROFESSOR, IS DEAD AT 88," said the *New York Times*.

APPENDIX 1

Overview

Early in my research into the life of Roger Sessions, I provided him with "fact sheets" designed to list basic biographical information in chronological order. The results are incorporated in the table that follows. The selection of items and the wording, in italics, are Sessions' own. For a convenient general overview, additional information is listed in roman type. Apparent errors in Sessions' recollections are corrected in the notes.

Chronology

1896	*417 Washington Ave. Brooklyn, RS* *NY. Born December 28*	*Father: Archibald Lowery Sessions Mother: Ruth Huntington Sessions* *Sister: Hannah Sargent Sessions b. February 16, 1889*[1]
1897		
1898		
1899	*or 1900 First remembered events: Taken to Concert in Brooklyn or N.Y.—first signs of inclination for music*	*Brother: John Archibald S— born May 21*
1900	*Moved to Northampton, Mass. (23 Round Hill, later 109 Elm St.)* *Summers in old family houses, Hadley, Mass.*	
1901	*Moved to 109 Elm Street, Northampton, Mass.*	
1902	*Began taking piano lessons with Mr. Edwards, organist of the Episcopal Church in Northampton; later with Mr. Chase, who succeeded him; later with my mother*	
1903		
1904		*Death of Grandfather (Huntington) Episcopal Bishop of Central N.Y., residing in Syracuse, N.Y., except for summers in*

		Hadley; and on same day of his oldest son, my uncle —George Huntington, also a clergyman.	
1905			
1906	*Sept.–Dec.: Cloyne School, Newport, RI*		
1907	*January: Kingsley School, Essex Falls, NJ*		
1908	*Jan.–June Kingsley School; Sept.–Dec. Kent School, Kent, Conn.*	*Summer—first awareness that "I was singing (to myself) tunes of my own concoction instead of tunes I had played.*	
1909	*Kent School*		
1910	*Kent School*	*Performance of Meistersinger at Springfield(or Hartford) later of Carmen at Springfield.* *In vacations often visited father's sisters: Clara (Fischer), Grace (Hooper) and Adeline (Sessions).*	*Began to write an opera based on Tennyson's "dylls of the King" (Lancelot and Elaine).*
1911	*Jan.–June Kent School; Sept. Harvard. Apartment with sister at 41 Hawthorn St., Cambridge.*	*Talk with Mrs. Wilmerding (sister-in-law of Theodore Thomas)*	
1912	*Harvard—41 Hawthorn St.*		
1913	*Harvard* *from Sept.—Matheson Hall*		
1914	*Harvard*	Plan to study with Ravel after graduation foiled by outbreak of war in August.	
1915	*Harvard BA* *from Sept.—Yale Music School* *Composition with Horatio Parker*		
1916	*Yale Music School*		
1917	*June: Mus B at Yale* *Fall: Went to teach at Smith College, Northampton, Mass.*	*Won Steinert Prize for Symphonic movement.* *Northampton Music Dept. HD Spencer, Barbara Goode, Wilson [illegible], Miss Holmes; also Rafaello Piccoli (Ital. Dept.)*	

1918			
1919		*Began trips to New York for study with Ernest Bloch.* Met Roy Dickinson Welch, Bessie and Brenda Berenson, Barbara Foster at Smith.	
1920	*Still at Smith but going to N.Y.*	June: married Barbara Foster.	
1921	*Cleveland (asked by Bloch to teach at Cleveland Inst.*	*Cleveland*	
1922	*Teach at Cleveland Inst.*	*Friendship with Jean , Bineta Swiss pupil of Bloch, and his (JB's) wife Denise. (JB a very shy and modest, but very gifted young man, pupil of J. Dalcroze)*	
1923	*till June: Cleveland*		Incidental music for Andreyev's *The Black Maskers*
	from Fall: Florence, London, Paris, Geneva	*Met Nadia Boulanger in Paris, on Bloch recommendation*	
1924	*from fall: Cleveland*		
1925	*till June: Cleveland*	*Met Siegfried and Winifred Wagner at lunch with Bloch.*	Incidental Musik for Volksmueller's *Turandot*
	Fall—Europe: London, France, i.e., Paris (Dijon) Switzerland (Geneva), Italy (Florence)	*Occasionally saw N. Boulanger during all of those years on occasional visits to Paris, but never studied with her. Also at some points during those years was US representative at ISCM*	
1926	*Florence (Settignano c/o Berenson)*	*Berenson and various guests*	*Three Chorales for Organ*
1927	*Florence (Settignano c/o Berenson)*		*Symphony No. 1* Article: "Ernest Bloch"
1928	*till Sept.: Florence*		
	then Rome	*Prize at Am. Academy*	Article: "On Oedipus Rex"
1929	*Rome*	*Not at Am. Academy because of married status, but at Villa Sforza c/o "Russians"—Casella, G.F. Malipiero,*	Pastoral for Solo *Flute*
1930	*Rome*	*(1929–30) Met Otto Klemperer who was*	Piano Sonata No. 1, (final version) Song

		conducting in Rome—often walked with him—he urged me (& persuaded me)—to move to Berlin to live on basis of my First Sonata	(James Joyce): "On the Beach at Fontana," Orchestral Suite from *The Black Maskers*
1931	*till Sept. Rome* *Sept. moved to Berlin—Lützow Ufer*	*Met Schnabel, Stiedry, Strub,*[2] *Alfred Einstein, Krenek*	
1932	*Berlin*	*Continued friendship with Klemperer, also Alfred Einstein, Ernest Krenek, Artur Schnabel, Stephen Spender, Fritz Stiedry.*	
1933	*Leaving Berlin (Hitler in power since Feb.! [sic])* *From Florence returned to U.S.*	*Maggio Musicale in Florence—met Alban Berg (at Festival—Stiedry, Alfred Einstein*	
1934	*New York*	*Private teaching, first at Dalcroze School, then by mutual agreement at single apartment: 3rd Ave. and 61st Street (c/o Granberry Piano). Among first students: Hugo Weisgall.*[3]	Article: "Hindemith's Mathis Der Maler" Article: "Composer and Critic" Article: "New Vistas in Music Education"
1935	*Asked to teach music at Princeton & summer school at Berkeley, Calif.* (Faculty positions at Princeton and Berkeley summer school to continue until 1945)	*Among students: M. Babbit, E. Cone.* *Met Elizabeth Franck at Berkeley.* *Divorced first wife, Barbara, at Reno, Nevada.*	Violin Concerto Article: "Heinrich Schenker's Contribution"
1936		*Married Elizabeth Franck.* *Moved to New Jersey, first to Pennington, then to house on Carter Road, Princeton.*	String Quartet No. 1
1937		*John P(helps) S(essions) b. (May? born 5 1/2 mon. Premature)*	Article: "The New Musical Horizon" Article: "America Moves to the Avant Scene"

			Article: "Hindemith Theory"
1938		Student: A. Imbrie	Chorale for Organ Article: "To Revitalize Opera" Article: "Exposition by Krenek" Article: "Escape by Theory" Article: "The Function of Theory" Article: "Vienna—Vale, Ave"
1939			*Pages from a Diary* Article: "The Composer and his Message"
1940		*E(lizabeth) P(helps) S(essions) born September*	Article: "On the American Future"
1941			Article: "American Music and the Crisis"
1942			Article: "No More Business As Usual" Article: "Artists and the War"
1943			*Duo for V. & P.O.*
1944			*Turn O Libertad Chorus* (Princeton) *Symphony No. 2 begun* Article: "Schoenberg in the United States"
1945	*Move to Berkeley*	*Visit with Bloch, there on short visit*	Article: "Europe Comes to America"
1946		*Students: L(eon) Kirchner*	*Symphony No. 2* ended Second Piano Sonata
1947		*Henry and Lily Schnitzler . . . result–>*	Opera: *The Trial of Lucullus* Article: "The Scope of Music Criticism" Opera: *Montezuma* (sketches)
1948		*Arguments with Bukofzer*	Article: "Music in a Business Economy"
1949			Article: "The Composer in the University"

1950	till June: Berkeley		Books: *Harmonic Practice* *The Musical Experience*
	from Sept.: Florence,[4] Academia Luigi Cherubini, Florence	Leave of absence as Fulbright Scholar in Italy Friendship with Luigi Dallapiccola	Article: "How a Difficult Composer Gets That Way" Fulbright Lectures at Academia, published in United States in 1956
1951	from Sept.: U of Cal. Berkeley		*String Quartet No. 2*
1952			Article: "Some Notes on Schoenberg"
1953	from Sept.: William Shubael Professor, Princeton, 70 Alexander Street, Princeton		*Violin (Solo) Sonata* *Idyll of Theocritus*
1954			Brandeis lecture, "Music and the Crisis in the Arts."
1955			*Mass for Unison Chorus and Organ for Kent School*
1956			*Piano Concerto* Article: "Song and Pattern in Music Today" Italian lectures published in United States: Reflections on Music Life [*sic*] in the United States
1957			*Symphony No. 3 (commissioned by Boston S.O. 75th anniversary* *String Quintet (2 violas)* Article: "Contemporary Music in Our Concert Halls" Article: "Thoughts on Stravinsky"
1958		Russian trip (as much as eight months)—Leningrad, Moscow, Tiflis, Kiev	*Symphony No. 4* Article: "Music and the Crisis of the Arts"
1959			*Divertimento 1959* *Children's Pieces*

			work begun of Montezuma[5]
1960			*Work on Montezuma 1960–63* Article: "Problems and Issues Facing the Composer Today"
1961			Article: "Style and Styles in Music"
1962			
1963			*Montezuma completed 1963* (*sic*)[6] *Psalm 140*
1964		*Ginastera*	*Symphony No. 5*
1965	*Retired from Princeton*	*Trip to Argentina (also) Chile, Peru after two days in Rio di Janeiro)*	
1966	Moved to *63 Stanworth Lane, Princeton*		*Piano Sonata No. 3* *Symphony No. 6* *2 Cello Pieces (for JPS)*
1967			*Symphony No. 7* Article: "What Can Be Taught?"
1968		*Trip to Sicily: Syracusa, Palermo*	*Symphony No. 8*
		Commission from U. of Cal. received in Syracuse	*Began work on "Lilacs"*
1969			*Lilacs* continued
1970			*Lilacs* completed (on commission from U. of Cal.), performed Berkeley, Chicago, Boston (Cambridge) Rhapsody for Orchestra Double Concerto (V/Vc) begun
1971			Double Concerto completed Concertino begun Article: "In Memoriam Igor Stravinsky"
1972		Norway—Oslo to Russian border (Kirkenes), Ham-	*Concertino for Small Orch. (Chicago)*

		merfest & return via London	*Canon in Memory of Stravinsky* *3 Choruses on Biblical Texts —for Amherst & well performed there* Article: "Schoenberg in the United States" (revised)
1973			
1974			
1975		Luigi Dallapiccola died February 19	*Piano Pieces (dedicated to L.D.) (died on Feb. 19)* Article: "In Memoriam Luigi Dallapiccola"
1976			*Symphony No. 9* begun Waltz (Piano)
1977			*Symphony No. 9* continued
1978			*Symphony No. 9* completed
1980			
1981		*Pulitzer Prize* *Montezuma performed*[7]	*Concerto for Orchestra (Boston Symphony Orchestra)*
1982		*Lisl's death Princeton July 9, 1982*	
1983			
1984			
1985	Roger Sessions died March 16, Princeton		

APPENDIX 2

Musical Terms

Continuity "might almost be considered synonymous with time itself."

Articulation structure on various levels: smaller units combine into larger units and still larger ones until the overall design is complete.

Form not abstract patterns but living materials. Inner relationships and necessities that create "the basis of a living musical organism or train of thought:

- first of all the musical idea itself,
  and then the chain of acoustic and psychological necessities to which it gives rise."
- "There are very few basic patterns possible, but these are infinitely various in application."

Progression—Cumulation

maintenance of "the level of intensity or interest of movement" or raising of it.

Association

- "Through association musical ideas achieve their impact."
- The single impulse "is a gesture in the void. . . . Only through association can it really become effective."

Two kinds of association:

1. Music "in association with words"
2. Music in association with "music itself"

Contrast

The *large contrasts* contained in a work reveal its essential outlines and give it its largest rhythms, through alteration of musical ideas with their contrasting movement, emphasis, and dynamic intensity."

Technique

1. Mastery of musical language (craft)
2. Identical with musical thought
3. Problematic "in terms of substance rather than merely of execution"

APPENDIX 3

Ernest Bloch on Cleveland Dismissal in 1925

Ernest Bloch's own experience of his dismissal as head of the Cleveland Institute of Music is reflected in the following excerpts from his personal notes now part of the Bloch archive in the Library of Congress in Washington, D.C.:

May 12 After my lecture (master class) about 4 o'clock Dr. Briggs and Mr. Cary came—asked me to resign (after the end of September 1925). I said I wouldn't stand in the way, but would not resign:[1] "They can fire me!" "It would be more advantageous for me to resign." I asked to think about it. "Was it fair to kick me out in such a way, after 5 years of loyal services?" Cary: "I am not at liberty to answer, I am sorry."

The reason given: the secret meeting of the Executive Committee on Monday, May 11. "You are not popular among the community."

This was entirely new.

May 13 Went to see N. D. Baker.

In the afternoon, Mrs. Sanders, without telling me, rushed the teachers, like cattle, to sign their contracts. They came to my office, despaired—many crying—disgusted.

In the evening, I called Mrs. Sanders to ask her whether she thought that my resignation was to be immediate or for next season. She said "next season"; that my recital, May 29, with my Suite had to go on—

May 14 8:30 a.m. Called Cary by phone—for same question. Answer: no! you go ahead. Resignation for next season.

Went to see Dr. [name illegible] (as I am a nervous wreck, from exhaustion, sleeplessness and excitement) he was appalled.

May 15 After many thoughts I have made [up] my mind about the whole situation.

The following is the text from some pages of yellow foolscap on which Bloch tried to reconstruct the events that led up to his sudden dismissal and penciled some of his "many thoughts":

Last Board Meeting Monday, April 27:

(question of Brown House—changing the chart of I into corporation not for profit)

(I said: "Were we not always morally engaged?")

No question about me, nor my engagement for next year.

Attitude of *all people*, as if it were absolutely normal.

Contract postponed (till May 12) "not decisive factor"

Mrs. S. last budget (1925–26) error of $10,000.—for Board Meeting—she forgot two months [illegible]

In 1922 I saved her

Her intrigues, from the beginning
To resign? From what?
[illegible]
I am the goat—
I gave two more weeks than due this yr.
Lectures in 1921–22 (Jewish Women) I gave the $500 to the Institute Committee asked fee for [daughter] Susan in 1924–25
The Struggle of 2 Ideas Art and Honesty Society and "Business"
Institute? = EB (ask Cleveland!)
I made it. How [illegible] BR because he was a Jew.
The assertion that [they] cannot raise money because I am the head = a miserable lie
The real reason was this apathy (of the committee, on fund raising) and Dr. Briggs
Truth Victim of personal grudge

Bloch's own notes on the full board meeting of April 27, at which the attitude "was absolutely normal," should have indicated to him that whatever happened must have taken place between the date of that board meeting and the next. But the contrived nature of his alleged failings only made him examine the past for indications of "grudges" on the part of some board member(s). There is no evidence in these painful private musings that he looked for any other reasons to account for the suddenness of his dismissal.

Bloch's notes continue:

May 18 Call N. D. Baker. Tussle about premature talk to faculty (Cary: "talking would prevent settlement)

Later (4:30) Teachers saw Sanders.
Sanders' attitude changed—MIESS!! [Shabby!!].
"She is my friend! She has not known!" etc.

Situation on May 19th

1) I consider myself engaged for 1925–26, for 16 weeks at 15,000.—
However I decline responsibility—on account of their action on May 12, preventing my actions in Institute. Resignations of [illegible] & Sessions, etc.
2) They may want me to resign—all right. I am ready, but they owe me $15,000.- plus my attorney fees.
3) If they refuse, lawsuit.
4) They me (*sic*) let the Institute fail.
I propose them, if they really care for the Institute, to have the real causes of the difficulty to raise money removed. B-, Mrs. Sanders are the ones who have perpetuated this affair.
5) Arrangement as "Acting Director"—
In S.F. for 2 months I will receive a minimum of $8,000.
I might consider something of the kind, but not less than 12,000.—as I have been engaged for five years already, and my name is [illegible]—
I have made the I.

The reasons # Fundraising
(entirely new to me)
Not popular
of course, I am not a "Jazz" composer,
Nor was "Abraham Lincoln"

> Nor is Mrs. Sanders, nor Dr. Briggs as a man or a surgeon.

There follows some agonized speculation about possible negotiations behind his back . Is the board trying to replace him with George Enesco, Nadia Boulanger? The diary concludes:

> ***May 20*** They offer compensation for late notice of $5,000.—"I accept"—One does not argue with such people (N. D. Baker)
>
> Baker: Do I resign?
>
> No! I say it is an agreement that is all.
>
> ***May 22*** Press interview (saw them with Mrs. Sanders) bare statement:
>
> In 1920 a group of Cleveland citizens invited me to come to their city and assist in the foundation of a music conservatory, acting in the capacity of its director. In December of the same year the Cleveland Institute of Music opened its doors. Its beginnings were modest. Seven students were enrolled at the start. For five consecutive years, under my direction and with the devoted assistance of Mrs. Franklin B. Sanders, it has developed into one of the leading music schools of the country and has at present an enrollment of over five hundred students. The Executive Committee now feels that the Institute can progress without me . . . I have been engaged to supervise the San Francisco Conservatory of Music during January and February of 1926.
>
> Refused to answer details:
>
> "When did your contract expire" they ask—Sanders hastens "in June"—she lies, and knows it—poor slave—
>
> ***May 23*** Signed agreement at Baker
>
> ***May 27*** Cary: "The saddest thing in my life—But—it was a question of life or Death for the Institute!!!"

NOTES

CHAPTER 1 **The Matriarch**

1. Quoted passages in this chapter have been excerpted from Ruth Huntington Sessions' *Sixty Odd: A Personal History* (Brattleboro, Vermont: Stephen Haye, 1936).

CHAPTER 2 **The Consort**

1. Quoted passages in this chapter have been excerpted from Ruth Huntington Sessions' *Sixty Odd: A Personal History* (Brattleboro, Vermont: Stephen Haye, 1936).

CHAPTER 3 **Young Roger**

1. Ruth Huntington Sessions, *Sixty Odd: A Personal History* (Brattleboro, Vermont: Stephen Haye, 1936).
2. The family letters in this chapter and others to follow were generously placed at the author's disposal by Roger Sessions' daughter, Mrs. Elizabeth Pease.
3. FP interview.
4. Roger Sessions archive, Library of Congress, Washington, D.C.

CHAPTER 4 **Letters from Harvard**

1. From the penciled manuscript of Sessions' Fulbright Lectures in Florence. The manuscript draft of these lectures is in the Roger Sessions archive at the Library of Congress, Washington, D.C. It was later published in an unauthorized and bowdlerized version under the title *Music Life [sic] in the United States* (New York: Merlin, n.d.).
2. Ibid.
3. FP interview; Sessions was fond of this formulation of technical requirements needed to realize his musical ideas.
4. Edward T. Cone, *Conversations with Roger Sessions,* Perspectives on American Composers, edited by Benjamin Boretz and Edward T. Cone (New York: Norton), p. 91. Cone was one of Sessions' earliest pupils, became one of his most distinguished colleagues at Princeton and a lifelong friend.
5. Like those quoted in chapter 3, Sessions' letters in this chapter were placed at the author's disposal by his daughter, Mrs. Elizabeth Pease. Most of the letters are undated. Their likely sequence has been reconstructed through context and reference to verifiable events. For example, the second letter that follows was dated by noting that annual concerts would likely have taken place toward the end of semester, the only "Tuesday the 19th" to fit in 1911 or 1912 would be November 19, 1912, and hence the extant letters from Harvard appear to date from his sophomore year.
6. Walter Spalding (1865–1962), an American composer, taught at Harvard from 1895.
7. Edward Burligame Hill (1872–1960), an American composer, taught at Harvard from 1908 to 1940. Both his father and grandfather had been faculty members of Harvard, the latter also its president from 1862 to 1868. E. B. Hill's particular interest in

French impressionist music may have fostered Sessions' abiding love for that musical genre as a listener, even though there is no apparent reflection of it in his own music.

8. Carl Muck, chief conductor of the Boston Symphony Orchestra (1906–1908, 1912–1918), was not considered an advocate of contemporary music. In part, this reputation stemmed from his preference for stylistically homogeneous programs, i.e., all Classical-period music one week, all Romantic the next. Thus, absent all-contemporary programs, the inclusion of new works on many programs was not possible. Nevertheless, Muck conducted such Boston premieres of new European works as Schoenberg's Op. 16, as well as many works by regional composers.

9. See also the somewhat later undated letter to his mother, p. 49: "Most people think that you must be either radical or conservative; but I think he is often less sincere as there is a romance in iconoclasm which everybody experiences sooner or later."

10. See chapter 7 for a discussion of Sessions' Juilliard lectures of 1949, which were subsequently published as *The Musical Experience of Composer, Performer. Listener* (Princeton, New Jersey: Princeton University Press, 1950).

11. Johanna Gadski (1873–1932), an operatic soprano, was known especially for her roles in Wagner operas at the Metropolitan Opera in New York, Covent Garden in London, and the Bayreuth Festivals in Germany.

12. Isabella Stewart Gardner (1840–1924) was Boston's most flamboyant music patron. Her generous financial support helped Major Higginson found the Boston Symphony Orchestra, her patronage assisted the careers of numerous young composers and performers, and her Renaissance Palazzo in Boston—now the Isabella Stewart Gardner Museum—housed a great collection of musical instruments, paintings, and mementos of composers. Her musical receptions, legendary in her time, have continued as chamber music concerts and solo recitals in ours. Bostonians still refer to her by the affectionate nickname of "Mrs. Jack."

13. Jean De Reske (1850–1935), a Polish operatic singer, had gained renown, first, as a baritone in mostly French repertoire, then, from 1871, in made an international career as a dramatic tenor, including such roles as Tristan and Siegfried. After retirement he became a prominent teacher and coach.

14. The "song" is actually for chorus. The revision begins in the soprano in m. 16, in the lower voices in m. 13.

15. Cone, *Conversations with Roger Sessions,* p. 91.

CHAPTER 5 **Ernest Bloch**

1. As in the preceding chapters, the letters quoted here are addressed to Sessions' mother and, unless otherwise indicated, are excerpted from the collection of Sessions' daughter, Mrs. Elizabeth Pease.

2. The letter is undated but must have followed closely upon the one of November 17 with its reference to Parker's invitation to "drop in often." The description of Parker's family in this letter suggests a first visit.

Of some interest, furthermore, is a following brief reference to Sessions' recent trip to New York and to his concern about his father's poor health: "I felt that [Dad] was not at all well, and that something should be done about it. *He says it is only worry about the play business though*" (my emphasis). Archibald Sessions was a friend of David Belasco, playwright and celebrated Broadway producer. Concerning the elder Sessions' death, ten years later, Ruth Huntington Sessions claimed in *Sixty Odd: A Personal History* (Brattleboro, Vermont: Stephen Haye, 1936) that a "false friend . . . stole, and sold, my husband's play and broke his heart." (See chapter 6 of this book, p. 83.) Belasco had indeed stopped writing plays in 1916, concentrating entirely on the production on Broadway and in the early film industry of works by younger writers. Any connection, however, between "stealing" Archibald Sessions' play in 1915 and his death some ten years later may have existed only in Ruth Sessions' mind.

3. The letter is undated, but references in it to the imminent national elections of 1916 place it in the first semester of Sessions' second year at Yale. The projected symphony to which it refers is to become the "Symphonic Prelude," which would win him the Steinert Prize at graduation.

4. RS letter to his mother, February 11, 1917. Romain Rolland (1866–1944), a French writer and Nobel Laureate in 1916, was one of Europe's most prominent pacifists during the First World War.

5. RS letter to his mother, February 18, 1917.

6. Undated RS letter to his mother, likely to have been written after his graduation from Yale in 1917.

7. Ruth Sessions, *Sixty Odd.*

8. Roger Sessions, "Artists and This War," *Modern Music* 20, no. 1 (1942), reprinted in *Roger Sessions on Music: Collected Esssays*, edited by E. T. Cone (Princeton, New Jersey: Princeton University Press, 1979), p. 313. See also chapter 14, p. 196.

9. FP interview.

10. Ibid.

11. Ibid. This quote, as well as the two that follow, was in response to direct questions by the author: "Just what did Bloch say that clarified your musical thinking? How did he say it? How did it bear on your future work as a composer?" Sessions' responses here have been reduced to the relevant essentials of his replies. As usual, he enjoyed interlarding that information with a mass of anecdotal and personal reminiscence. In the interest of *How a "Difficult" Composer Got That Way,* this discursive material has been eliminated here.

12. Ibid.

13. Arnold Schoenberg, *Harmonielehre* (1911).

14. FP interview.

15. Roger Sessions, "Ernest Bloch," *Modern Music*, 5, no. 1 (1927), reprinted in *Roger Sessions on Music*, p. 338.

16. FP interview.

17. Ruth Sessions, *Sixty Odd.*

18. FP interview.

19. The following quotes are from correspondence now in the Ernest Bloch archive in the Library of Congress in Washington, D.C.

20. The excerpt of this letter and quotations from further correspondence and notes to follow were taken from the Ernest Bloch archive in the Library of Congress in Washington, D.C.

21. RS letter to Bloch, August 27, 1921.

22. Like most RS letters from Cleveland to his mother, this one is undated.

23. FP interview. The second half of this quote does not really relate to the anecdote, but I decided to leave it as a very characteristic example of Sessions' rhapsodic style of personal recollection.

24. The "Symphonic Prelude" he had first shown to Bloch was to have been part of a First Symphony. As we have seen, the project was abandoned on Bloch's advice.

25. Leonid Nikolayevich Andreyev (1871–1919) was a Russian writer and playwright. *The Black Maskers* was written in 1908.

26. FP interview.

27. Ibid.

28. Nicolai Sokoloff conducted the first concert of the Cleveland Orchestra (known

as Cleveland's Symphony Orchestra during its inaugural season in 1918) and remained its conductor until 1933, when Arthur Rodzinski became music director. Bloch and Sessions would have heard the orchestra in its temporary home, the Masonic Auditorium. Severance Hall, its famous permanent home, opened its doors in 1931.

29. See appendix 3.

30. FP interview.

31. FP interview.

32. See appendix 3.

CHAPTER 6 **Berenson**

1. Bernard Berenson, *Aesthetics and History* (Pantheon, 1948; reprinted, Garden City, New York: Doubleday, Anchor Books, 1954), p. 19.

2. Ibid. p. 18.

3. FP interview. It is likely that, with the hindsight of nearly sixty years Sessions simplified the respective motives of two young people whose personal relationship and professional orientation had long proven more suited to casual friendship than to marriage. Nevertheless, the fact remains that Barbara stayed in Paris while her husband established his base in Florence.

4. See chapter 4, p. 56.

5. Howard Hartog, ed., *European Music in the Twentieth Century* (London: Routledge and Paul, 1957), p. 252.

6. A play on words, popular at the time: *Boulangerie* could refer to Nadia Boulanger's teaching establishment as well as to a bakery.

7. FP interview.

8. Cyril Connolly (1903–1974), English writer and literary critic for the London *Sunday Times* and the *Observer*, was still a "gifted young man" when Sessions met him at I Tatti, later to be a very influential essayist.

9. Walter Lippmann (1889–1974), American journalist and influential political commentator and cofounder of the *New Republic* in 1914, he had been writing for the *New York World* since 1921 and later became its editorial page editor. From 1931 he was a syndicated columnist for the *New York Herald Tribune*. At the time when Sessions met him, he had authored two books: *A Preface to Politics* (1913) and *Public Opinion* (1922).

10. Ruth Draper (1884–1956) was an American actress celebrated for monodramas that she wrote and performed, often for private audiences. Sessions may well have seen one or more of her presentations at I Tatti.

11. FP interview; see also chapter 4, p. 37.

12. "Interview with Roger Sessions," *Boston Globe*, April 24, 1927 (on the occasion of the premiere of his First Symphony by the Boston Symphony under Serge Koussevitzky).

13. FP interview. Sessions repeated this statement often and always in the context of what he considered a basic characteristics not only of the newfound language of his First Symphony but also of his work to come: "instead of color—movement."

14. David Belasco (1853–1931) was an American playwright and Broadway producer. His plays included *Madame Butterfly* and *The Girl from the Golden West,* which were adapted as librettos for Puccini's operas. After the end of World War I Belasco devoted most of his time to producing plays in his Broadway theaters but also adapted and coauthored plays by younger writers whose work he encouraged and produced.

15. Ruth Huntington Sessions, *Sixty Odd: A Personal History* (Brattleboro, Vermont: Stephen Haye, 1936).

16. Ibid.

17. FP interview.

18. Roger Sessions, "An American Evening Abroad," review of a concert prresented by the Societé Musicale Independante of Paris, *New Music,* no. 4 (November 1926).

19. Ernest Samuels, *Bernard Berenson: The Making of a Legend* (Cambridge, Massachusetts: Belknap, 1987), p. 334.

20. Ibid., p. 306.

21. Ibid., p. 334.

22. The sentence is incomplete and quoted out of context. Parker wrote about "the fine tradition of these concerts. Seldom has it found truer expression than in the long and warm applause that on Saturday wreathed Mr. Chadwick of the departing generation, and the hearty clapping that saluted Mr. Sessions of the younger men uprising."

CHAPTER 7 **The Musical Idea I**

1. Roger Sessions' Juilliard lectures of 1949 were published by Princeton University Press (Princeton, New Jersey) under the title *The Musical Experience of Composer, Performer, Listener* in 1950. The following quotes were taken from a reprint edition by Atheneum (New York, 1962).

2. Ibid., p. 44.

3. Ibid., pp. 44–45.

4. Ibid., p. 50.

5. Ibid., p. 50.

6. Ibid., p. 50.

7. Ibid., pp. 50–51.

8. Ibid., pp. 51, 52, 53.

9. Sessions is mistaken about the date. From the context ("working in a cottage outside Florence") the events described must have taken place during his work on the sonata, at Settignano.

10. Roger Sessions, *Questions about Music,* published version of his Charles Eliot Norton Lectures at Harvard, 1968–1969 (New York: Norton, 1971), p. 29.

11. Ibid., p. 87. The quote is from Jacques Hadamard, *The Psychology of Invention in the Mathematical Field* (Princeton, New Jersey: Princeton University Press, 1945).

12. Sessions, *The Musical Experience*, p. 52.

13. See chapter 4, RS letter to his mother on the subject, p. 43.

14. Sessions, *Questions about Music*, p. 109.

15. Ibid., p. 110.

16. Ibid., p. 111.

17. Roger Sessions, "The Composer and His Craft," in *Roger Sessions on Music: Collected Essays,* edited by Edward T. Cone (Princeton, New Jersey: Princeton University Press, 1979, p. 4.

18. Chapter 3, p. 34.

19. Chapter 4, p. 55.

20. Chapter 5, p. 63.

21. Sessions, *Roger Sessions on Music*, p. 8.

22. Sessions, *The Musical Experience,* p. 108.

23. Sessions, *Questions about Music,* p. 104.

24. Sessions and Cone, *Roger Sessions on Music*, p. 90.

25. Sessions, *Questions about Music,* p. 106.

26. Ibid., p. 112.

27. Sessions and Cone, *Roger Sessions on Music*, pp. 190–191.

28. Sessions, *The Musical Experience,* p. 60.

29. Ibid., p. 60.

30. Ibid., p. 60.
31. Ibid., p. 61.
32. Ibid., p. 61.
33. Ibid., p. 112 (whence I have previously taken this same quote to amplify Articulation).
34. Sessions and Cone, *Roger Sessions on Music*, p. 25.
35. Sessions, *The Musical Experience*, p. 62.
36. Ibid., p. 63.
37. Ibid., p. 64.
38. For a painstaking and resourceful analysis see Michael Ian Crawford Campell, "The Piano Sonatas of Roger Sessions: Sequel to a Tradition," D.M.A. diss., Peabody Institute, Johns Hopkins University, 1982.
39. Sessions, *The Musical Experience*, p. 115.

CHAPTER 8 **Summer of 1929**

1. *Dictionnaire géographique de la Suisse* (Neufchâtel, France: Attinger, 1902), vol. 1, pp. 602–603.
2. RS letter to his mother, September 26, 1930.
3. The work referred to here remained an uncompleted sketch. The work now known as Sessions' Second Symphony was begun in 1944 and completed in 1946.
4. RS letter to his mother, July 13, 1929.
5. The International Society for Contemporary Music had been founded in Salzburg in 1922. Its American Section was organized in 1923.
6. RS, undated fragment of a letter (three last pages only), likely late 1928 or early 1929.
7. Ibid.
8. Paul Johnson, *A History of Christianity* (London: Weidenfeld and Nicolson, 1976), p. 466.
9. Ibid., p. 480.
10. RS letter to his mother, February 10, 1927.
11. FP interview: FP: "Have you any religious affiliation?" RS: "Well, I suppose we are all crypto-Catholics."
12. Paul Andrews, brother-in-law and judge in Syracuse, very active in Republican politics.
13. RS letter to his mother, Rome, March 9–11, 1928.
14. Jonathan and Catherine Guiness, *The House of Mitford* (New York: Penguin, 1984), p. 194.
15. RS letter to his mother, March 9–11, 1929.
16. RS letter to his mother, July 13, 1929.
17. Papal negotiator, 1929.
18. RS letter to his mother, July 27, 1929.
19. FP interview, January 1, 1983. In view of the letter of July 13, 1929, it is ironic that the following exchange took place in the same interview:

FP: "What did your brother do?"
RS: "He ran the family farm in Hadley."
FP: "Was he married?"
RS: "I don't remember now. But if he was it didn't amount to much."

20. Family nickname for Doheney Sessions (née Hackett).
21. RS letter to his mother, July 27, 1929.
22. RS letter to his mother, November 18, 1912 (chapter 4, p. 42).
23. Adolph Weissman, *Die Musik* 21, no. 9 (June 1929), p. 669.

24. Edwin Evans, *The Musical Courier,* May 1929.

25. Roger Sessions, "Composer and Critic," letter to the music editor of the *New York Times,* March 11, 1934, reprinted in *Roger Sessions on Music: Collected Essays,* edited by Edward T. Cone (Princeton, New Jersey: Princeton University Press, 1979), p. 121.

26. FP interview.

27. Ibid.

28. RS letter to his mother, July 13, 1929.

29. Ibid.

30. Jacques Barzun, "The State of Culture Today," 1975.

31. RS letter to his mother, July 13, 1929.

32. FP interview.

33. Roger Sessions, *Questions about Music,* published version of his Charles Eliot Norton Lectures at Harvard, 1968–69 (New York: Norton, 1971), p. 119.

34. RS letter to his mother, August 5, 1929.

35. RS letter to his mother, August 18–20, 1929.

CHAPTER 9 **Berlin Interlude**

1. RS letter to his mother, September 26, 1930.

2. Ibid.

3. Fifteen years later, Sessions tried once more to develop these sketches but found himself unable to get back into the workings of the old material.

4. RS letter to his mother, September 26, 1930.

5. FP interview. This anecdote, told gleefully more than once, was intended to support Sessions' lifelong contention that the autonomy of musical ideas determined how the composer "felt" about a work in progress as much as the intellectual and musical train of thought that marked its creation.

6. Susanne Everett, *Lost Berlin* (New York: Gallery Books, 1979), p. 110.

7. Ibid., p. 21.

8. Walter Lennig, *Benn* (Hamburg: Rowohlt, 1962), pp. 73–74.

9. Everett, *Lost Berlin,* p. 31.

10. Otto Friedrich, *Before the Deluge* (New York: Harper and Row, 1922), p. 34.

11. Ibid., p. 49.

12. Ibid., p. 70.

13. Ibid., p. 302.

14. FP interview.

15. The Kroll Opera House was named after Joseph Kroll, nineteenth-century architect of a cultural center in Berlin.

16. Peter Heyworth, *Otto Klemperer, His Life and Times,* vol. 1: *1885–1933* (Cambridge: Cambridge University Press, 1983), offers a fascinating portrait of the Kroll's cultural, social, and political history.

17. Gründgens was to be the central chracter in *Mephisto,* Klaus Mann's novel about the theater in Hitler's Third Reich.

18. Heyworth, *Otto Klemperer,* p. 249.

19. Ibid., p. 292. *Republik Zircus* refers to the location of the Kroll at Berlin's Republic Square and reflects Berg's disdain for what he considered a managerial and repertory "circus."

20. Ibid., p. 265.

21. "Das Unaufhörliche [*The never-ending*] suggests the apparently senseless repetition, the up and down of history, the fleeting quality of greatness and fame, the accidental transformations of our existence" (letter, July 29, 1930, from Benn to Hindemith, in

Lennig, *Benn*, p. 82). Hindemith's work was first performed by Klemperer and the Berlin Philharmonic on November 21, 1931.

22. H. H. Stuckenschmidt, *Schöpfer der Neuen Musik* (DTV, 1962), p. 175.

23. FP interview.

24. Ibid.

25. Ibid.

26. Ibid.

27. Ibid.

28. Ibid.

29. Roger Sessions, "Music and Nationalism," *Modern Music* 11, no. 1 (1933), reprinted in *Roger Sessions on Music: Collected Essays,* edited by Edward T. Cone (Princeton, New Jersey: Princeton University Press, 1979), p. 280.

30. FP interview.

31. Heyworth, *Otto Klemperer*, p. 346.

32. Roger Sessions, "Music in Crisis," *Modern Music* 10, no. 2 (1933), reprinted in *Roger Sessions on Music*, pp. 39–40.

33. Friedrich, *Before the Deluge*, p. 304.

34. FP interview.

35. "But they're not going to boycott me!" (FP interview).

36. Ernest Samuels, *Bernard Berenson: The Making of a Legend* (Cambridge, Massachusetts: Belknap, 1987), p. 334.

37. Klemperer, "Autobiographical Sketch," in Heyworth, *Otto Klemperer*, p. 414.

CHAPTER 10 **Home**

1. Joseph Mclellan, "Fast Forward: A Monthly Guide to Video, Music and Computers," *Washington Post*, July 1995, p. 22.

2. It may be worth noting that this was before our audiences expected to hear approved works from the canon of standard musical literature. Like their eighteenth-century European predecessors, the Thalbergs and Gottschalks, in their New York recitals, played mostly their own compositions.

3. FP interview; Sessions loved to tell this anecdote, and he assigned to it a number of different occasions. He also enjoyed recounting his independent vote as U.S. representative on the ISCM jury in 1930. While the gist of either tale never varied, the occasions were not always combined as in the story told here.

4. Wallingford Riegger, "To the New from the Old," quoted in Frank R. Rossiter, *Charles Ives and His America* (New York: Liveright, pp. 218–219).

5. In addition to the earlier performances of his First Symphony, the new version of the *Black Makers* Suite for full orchestra (1930) was performed by the BSO and the BBC in London.

6. Virgil Thomson, *Virgil Thomson* (New York: Da Capo Press, 1967), p. 207.

7. Ibid., p. 243.

8. Roger Sessions, "Music in Crisis," *Modern Music* 10, no. 2 (1933), reprinted in *Music: Collected Essays*, edited by Edward T. Cone (Princeton, New Jersey: Princeton University Press, 1979), p. 29.

9. Roger Sessions, draft for the last of his Fulbright Lectures, 1952, in *Reflections on the Music* [*sic*] *Life in the United States* (New York: Merlin, n.d.), pp. 162–163.

10. Roger Sessions, "Music and Nationalism," *Modern Music* 11, no. 1 (1933), reprinted in *Roger Sessions on Music*, p. 274.

11. An influential writer on music and music critic, Rosenfeld was a particular patron of Aaron Copland on his return from Europe.

12. Sessions, draft for the last of his Fulbright Lectures, pp. 153–157.

13. Ibid., p. 166.

14. Roger Sessions, "Composer and Critic," letter to the music editor of the *New York Times*, March 11, 1934.

15. Thomson, *Virgil Thomson*, p. 279.

16. RS letter to his mother, Fall 1935.

17. FP interview; this very harsh and strangely speculative recollection of the octogenarian composer in 1981 indicates the way he saw the relationship to his former teacher nearly a half-century before. It stands in contrast to the close friendship that developed between the two men in the years to follow.

18. FP interview.

19. FP interview with Milton Babbitt, Washington, D.C., 1997.

20. Marcel Dick, later violist in the Cleveland Orchestra, letter to RS, September 8/15, 1935.

21. Roger Sessions, "New Vistas in Musical Education," *New Music* 11, no. 2 (1934), reprinted in *Roger Sessions on Music*, p. 187.

22. Ibid., pp. 191–192.

CHAPTER 11 **Sea Change**

1. FP interview.

2. FP interview.

3. FP interview.

4. Hannah Sessions, letter to her brother, RS, April 17, 1935.

5. FP interview.

6. Hannah Sessions, letter to RS, November 26, 1934. The school to which Hannah sent the letter was most likely Dalcroze in New York City.

7. FP interview.

8. Hannah Sessions, undated letter to RS.

9. Catharine (daughter of Ruth's brother George), letter to RS, September 12, 1936.

10. Ibid.

11. See chapter 8, p. 111, RS letter to his mother, July 13, 1929.

12. Catharine to RS letter, undated.

13. Catharine to RS letter, October 8, 1935.

14. Aunt Addie to RS, letter, undated.

15. RS letter to his mother, Princeton, Saturday, undated but likely early October 1936 (cf. Hannah's reference in her letter of October 5: "I am so glad you had this good postcard, & really sorry I sent you the other letter. Don't pay any attention to it, for it was probably just a mood, and this represents the settled feeling. I wouldn't be surprised if she came to be perfectly devoted to Lisl.")

CHAPTER 12 **Something More**

1. Goethe, *Maximen* (FP translation).

2. "Right-wing" referred to composers committed to the establishment of an "American style of composition," as opposed to so-called internationalists, who associated themselves with Schoenberg and his "School." Juilliard, in midcentury, was very "right-wing."

3. Howard Taubman, *The Pleasure of Their Company: A Reminiscence* (Portland, Oregon: Amadeus Press, 1994).

4. FP interview.

5. FP interview, cf. introduction, p. 5.

6. Lewis Hyde, *The Gift: Imagination and the Erotic Life of Property* (New York: Vintage, 1983).

7. Roger Sessions, *Questions about Music*, published version of his Charles Eliot Norton lectures at Harvard, 1968–1969 (New York: Norton, 1971), p. 86.

8. Roger Sessions, "The Composer in the University," contribution to a symposium on the graduate study of music, joint session of the American Musicological Society and the Society for Music in the Liberal Arts College, New York City, 1940, quoted in *Roger Sessions on Music: Collected Essays*, edited by Edward T. Cone (Princeton, New Jersey: Princeton University Press, 1979), pp. 202, 203.

9. Ibid., pp. 194, 195.

10. Charles Rosen, *The Musical Languages of Elliott Carter* (Washington, D.C.: Library of Congress, 1984), p. 30

11. In the performance at the New England Conservatory as in various other performances, including the Columbia recording of the Double Concerto, Philharmonia Orchestra, London, Charles Rosen was always the solo pianist.

CHAPTER 13 **The Musical Idea II**

1. Martin F. Bukofzer (1910–1955) was a German musicologist whose studies in polyphony of the English Renaissance established him as a leading writer on the musical practices of the period. By no means as parochial as the anecdote suggests, he held strong views on the role of musicology, also in terms of interdisciplinary potentialities. His *Studies in Medieval and Renaissance Music* (1950) remains a standard reference on the subject.

2. FP interview.

3. Roger Sessions, *Harmonic Practice* (New York: Harcourt, Brace and World, 1951), p. ix.

4. Edward T. Cone, *Conversations with Roger Sessions*, Perspectives on American Composers, edited by Benjamin Boretz and Edward T. Cone (New York: Norton, 1971), p. 100.

5. Ibid.

6. Cf. Frederik Prausnitz, *Score and Podium* (New York: Norton, 1983), chapter 10.

7. FP interview with Milton Babbitt, Washington, D.C., 1997.

8. Roger Sessions, "Music in Crisis," *Modern Music* 10, no. 2, reprinted in *Roger Session on Music: Collected Essays*, edited by Edward T. Cone (Princeton, New Jersey: Princeton University Press, 1979), p. 33.

9. Ibid., p. 31.

10. Ibid., pp. 32–33.

11. Ibid., p. 33.

12. Cone, *Conversations with Roger Sessions*, p. 100.

13. See chapter 7, p. 99.

14. See chapter 7, p. 99.

15. Edward T. Cone, "Analysis Today," *Musical Quarterly*, April 1960.

16. FP interview.

17. Andrew Imbrie, *Roger Sessions: In Honor of His Sixty-fifth Birthday,* Perspectives on American Composers, edited by Benjamin Boretz and Edward T. Cone (New York: Norton, 1971), pp. 59–89.

18. Elliott Carter, *Musical Quarterly*, July 1959, pp. 376–377.

19. Erwin Schrödinger, *Naturwissenschaften*, vol. 23, p. 812.

20. Nick Herbert, *Quantum Reality* (Garden City, New York: Doubleday, Anchor Books, 1985).

21. Erwin Schrödinger, *Science and Humanism* (New York: Cambridge University Press, 1951).

22. Albert Einstein and Leopold Infeld, *The Evolution of Physics* (New York: Cambridge University Press, 1971).

23. Gary Zukav, *The Dancing Wu Li Masters: An Overview of the New Physics* (London: Fontana/Collins), p. 35.

24. Roger Sessions, "Escape by Theory," *Modern Music* 15, no. 3 (1938), reprinted in *Roger Sessions on Music*, p. 261.

25. Roger Sessions, *Questions about Music*, published version of his Charles Eliot Norton Lectures at Harvard, 1968–1969 (New York: Norton, 1971), p. 41.

26. Ibid., p. 257.

27. Leonardo Fibonacci, also known as Leonardo Pisano (c. 1170–1240), was a medieval mathematician whose name is associated with the discovery of a numerical sequence in which each term equals the sum of the two terms that immediately precede it, i.e., 1, 1, 2, 3, 5, 8, 13, 21, 34, 55, 89 . . . The Fibonacci series approximates to the irrational key-number of the Golden Section (the square of every number being equal to the product of the preceding and following numbers, plus or minus one). The division of any distance according to its Golden Section falls at a point where its total is multiplied by 0.618. The approximation of the Fibonacci series to the Golden Section is demonstrated in that the Golden Section of 55 is 34, that of 89 is 55, etc. Bartok was fascinated by the application of these mathematical relationships in nature and in art. The theoretical principles that support the structures of his own works have been demonstrated to reflect such relationships in astonishingly consistent detail. Cf. Ernö Lendvai, *Béla Bartók: An Analysis of His Music* (London: Kahn and Averill, 1971) and *The Workshop of Bartók and Kodaly* (Budapest: Edita Musica, 1983).

28. See chapter 7, p. 99.

29. Carter, *Musical Quarterly*, pp. 376–377.

30. See chapter 7, p. 100.

CHAPTER 14 **Teacher**

1. FP interview.

2. Cf. chapter 4, pp. 55–56.

3. Roger Sessions, Fulbright Lectures in Florence, published as *Reflections on the Music Life [sic] in the United States* (New York: Merlin, n.d.), chapter 10, n 14.

4. Alexander Leitch, *A Princeton Companion* (1978). www.princeton.edu

5. FP interview with Milton Babbitt, Washington, D.C., 1997.

6. See chapter 8, p. 116.

7. See chapter 12, p. 168.

8. FP interview with Milton Babbitt, Washington, D.C., 1997.

9. *Economist*, July 19–25, 1997.

10. Chapter 10, epigraph.

11. Roger Sessions, "Europe Comes to America," Address at Kenyon College, 1945, quoted in *Roger Sessions on Music: Collected Essays*, edited by Edward T. Cone (Princeton, New Jersey: Princeton University Press, 1979), p. 320.

12. Ibid., p. 322.

13. FP interview with Milton Babbitt, Washington, D.C., 1997.

14. Mark Schubart, "Roger Sessions: Portrait of an American Composer," *Musical Quarterly* 32 (1946), p. 198.

15. Miriam Gideon, *Perspectives of New Music* 23 (Spring/Summer 1985), "In Memoriam Roger Sessions," p. 147.

16. Andrew Imbrie, "Remembering Roger," *Perspectives of New Music* 23 (Spring/Summer 1985), p. 149.

17. Roger Sessions, "New Vistas in Musical Education," *Modern Music* 11, no. 2 (1934), reprinted in *Roger Sessions on Music*, pp. 190–191.

18. Ibid., p. 189.

19. Ibid., p. 190.
20. Ibid., p. 190.
21. Ibid., p. 191.
22. Ibid., p. 191.
23. Ibid., p. 192.
24. Roger Sessions, "To the Editor," *Perspectives of New Music* 5, no. 2 (Spring–Summer 1967), reprinted in *Perspectives on American Composers*, edited by Benjamin Boretz and Edward T. Cone (New York: Norton, 1971), p. 110. NB: This article was originally written in 1958 for the English periodical the *Score* and appeared in *Roger Sessions on Music,* under the title "What Can Be Taught?"
25. Ibid., p. 122.
26. Ibid., p. 108.
27. FP interview.
28. Ibid. (RS verbal exegesis of n. 24).
29. Ibid.
30. Imbrie, "Remembering Roger," p. 150.
31. Ibid.
32. FP interview with Milton Babbitt, Washington, D.C., 1997.
33. Ibid.
34. Roger Sessions, "The Composer in the University," contribution to a symposium on the graduate study of music, joint session of the American Musicological Society and the Society for Music in the Liberal Arts College, New York City, 1940, quoted in *Roger Sessions on Music*, pp. 199–200.
35. See chapter 5, p. 61.
36. Roger Sessions, "No More Business as Usual," *Modern Music* 19, no. 3 (1942), reprinted in *Roger Sessions on Music*, p. 306.
37. Ibid., p. 308.
38. Ibid., p. 309.
39. Ibid., p. 309.
40. Ibid., p. 310.
41. Ibid., p. 310.
42. Ibid., p. 312.
43. Ibid., p. 312.
44. See chapter 5, p. 61.
45. Roger Sessions, "Artists and This War, a Letter to an Imaginary Colleague," *Modern Music* 20, no. 1 (1942), reprinted in *Roger Sessions on Music*, p. 313.
46. Ibid., p. 315.
47. Roger Sessions, *Harmonic Practice* (New York: Harcourt, Brace and World, 1951), foreword, p. ix.
48. Schubart, "Roger Sessions."

CHAPTER 15 **Family, Friends, and Montezuma**

1. John Sessions letter to FP, March 15, 1998.
2. FP interview.
3. Elizabeth Pease letter to FP, undated (1998).
4. Urry was the childhood nickname for a grandmother who would delight in playing a bear or a big dog romping with her grandchildren, growling, "Urry, urry!"
5. Ibid.
6. John Sessions letter to FP, March 15, 1998.
7. Elizabeth Pease letter to FP, undated (1998).
8. John Sessions letter to FP, March 15, 1998.

9. Ibid.

10. FP interviews, September 1981.

11. Ernst Krenek, "Grundideen einer neuen Musik Ästhetic," in *Über neue Musik* (Vienna: Verlag der Ringbuchhandlung, 1937).

12. Roger Sessions, "Exposition by Krenek," *Modern Music* 15, no. 2.

13. Ibid., reprinted in *Roger Sessions on Music: Collected Essays*, edited by Edward T. Cone (Princeton, New Jersey: Princeton University Press, 1979), p. 249.

14. Krenek, "Grundideen einer Neuen Musikästhetik," in *Zur Sprache Gebracht: Essays über Musik* (Munich: Albert Langen, Georg Müller, 1958), p. 268.

15. See chapter 7.

16. Sessions, "Exposition by Krenek," in *Sessions on Music*, p. 253.

17. RS, Notes on *Montezuma*, Sessions archive in the Library of Congress, Washington, D.C.

18. See chapter 14, p. 189.

19. The reference to blood and soil was current at the time as a Nazi slogan (*Blut und Boden*) that informed much of the rhetoric of the regime and symbolized the values of a master race and its inherent rights of possession.

20. Roger Sessions, "Europe Comes to America," reprinted in *Roger Sessions on Music*, p. 323.

21. George Kubler, *The Shape of Time: Remarks on the History of Things* (New Haven, Connecticut: Yale University Press, 1962), p. 59.

22. Roger Sessions, talk on *Montezuma*, Boston, 1969, in lieu of scheduled American premiere, which had to be postponed for lack of money, Sessions archive in the Library of Congress, Washington, D.C.

23. Ibid.

24. Sessions, *The Musical Experience*, p. 64.

25. See chapter 18, p. 246.

26. Sessions, talk on *Montezuma*.

27. Ibid. NB: Extant sketches date back some *twenty* years.

28. Ibid.

CHAPTER 16 **Berkeley**

1. FP interview.

2. Gordon C. Cyr, "Roger Sessions at Berkeley: A Personal Reminiscence," *Perspectives of New Music* 23 (Spring–Summer 1985), "In Memoriam Roger Sessions," pp. 131–132.

3. See chapter 14, p. 185.

4. Chapter 14, p. 199.

5. John Sessions letter to FP, March 15, 1998.

6. Ibid.

7. *The History of Cal—Timeline: The First 150 years of Cal. UC*, Internet.

8. According to the *New Grove Dictionary of Music and Musicians*, Stravinsky did teach his first and only pupil in Hollywood, giving him some 215 lessons in two years.

9. Roger Sessions, "How a Difficult Composer Gets That Way," *New York Times*, January 8, 1950, reprinted in *Roger Sessions on Music: Collected Essays*, edited by Edward T. Cone (Princeton, New Jersey: Princeton University Press, 1979), p. 169.

10. Edward T. Cone, *Conversations with Roger Sessions*, Perspectives on American Composers, edited by Benjamin Boretz and Edward T. Cone (New York: Norton, 1971), p. 100. See also chapter 13.

11. See chapter 12, p. 168.

12. Gordon St. Cyr, "Roger Sessions at Berkeley."

13. Andrew Imbrie, "Remembering Roger," *Perspectives of New Music* 23 (Spring/Summer 1985), "In Memoriam Roger Sessions," p. 151.

14. Ibid., p. 151.

15. As a historical footnote, the further fate of the Dessau setting of Brecht's *Lucullus* is amusing. Composed in 1949 and first performed in East Berlin in a closed performance in 1951, it displeased the authorities, who insisted on a major rewrite of the libretto before it would be cleared for public performance. The inference that wars are not a good thing had to be amended to exclude defensive wars. Lucullus's private virtues, moreover, were irrelevant; hence *Das Verhör* [the trial; literally the hearing] *des Lucullus* became *Die Verurteilung* [The sentencing] *des Lucullus.*

16. S. Earl Saxton, *Perspectives of New Music* 23 (Spring/Summer 1985), "In Memoriam Roger Sessions," p. 161.

17. Ernst Krenek, "Darius Milhaud" (1930), in *Zur Sprache Gebracht: Essays über Musik*. Munich: Albert Langen, Georg Müller (1958), p. 86 (translated by FP).

18. Schoenberg letter to RS, Roger Sessions Archive, Library of Congress, Washington, D.C.

19. FP interview.

20. Ibid.

21. Cone, "Conversations with Roger Sessions," p. 107.

22. Roger Sessions, *The Musical Experience of Composer, Performer, Listener,* published version of his Juilliard Lectures, 1949 (Princeton, New Jersey: Princeton University Press, 1959; reprint, New York: Atheneum, 1962), p. 73.

23. Roger Sessions, *Questions about Music,* published version of his Charles Eliot Norton Lectures at Harvard, 1968–1969 (New York: Norton, 1971), p. 61.

24. Ibid., p. 158.

25. "Das Beste der Musik steht nicht in den Noten." *Gustav Mahler im Eigenen Wort—im Worte der Freunde* (Zürich: Peter Schifferli, 1958), p. 43.

26. Sessions, *The Musical Experience,* pp. 90–92.

27. Ibid, p. 75.

28. Sessions, *Questions about Music,* p. 42.

29. Roger Sessions, *Harmonic Practice* (New York: Harcourt, Brace & World, 1951).

30. Ibid., p. ix.

31. Ibid., pp. xiv–xv.

32. Sessions, "How A Difficult Composer Gets That Way."

33. J. William Fulbright (1905–1995) entered the House of Representatives (Democrat, Arkansas) in 1943, and was in the Senate from 1945 to 1974. He was Chairman of the Senate Committee on Foreign Relations from 1959 to 1974.

34. *University of California, Berkeley History II,* Internet.

35. FP interview.

36. See chapter 14, p. 197.

CHAPTER 17 **Dallapiccola**

1. Leslie Ayre, *The Proms: The Story of the Grandest Music Festival in the World* (London: Leslie Frewin, 1968), p. 108.

2. William F. Baker and George Dessart, *Down the Tube: An Inside Account of the Failure of American Television* (New York: Basic Books, 1998).

3. K. H. Ruppel, *Musica Viva 1945–1958* (Munich: Musica Viva, Nymphenburger, 1959), p. 44.

4. See chapter 16, p. 231.

5. Ibid., p. 232.

6. The Fulbright exchange program itself did not involve newly allocated U.S. public funds; rather, it authorized the use of foreign funds owed to the United States.

7. See chapter 16, p. 227.

8. Sessions, Fulbright Lectures (manuscript in the Library of Congress), published in an unauthorized translation as *Reflections on Music Life [sic] in the United States* (New York: Merlin, n.d.), pp. 107–108.

9. Roger Sessions, from his letter to Laura Dallapicola upon her husband's death in 1975, published in a collection of letters and recollections by the composer's colleagues and friends, *In ricordo di Luigi Dallapiccola* (Milan: Zuvini Zerboni, 1975), p. 52.

10. Ibid., p. 42.

11. Luigi Dallapiccola, *Dallapiccola on Opera: Selected Writings*, translated and edited by Rudy Shackelford (London: Toccata Press, 1987), p. 46.

12. Ibid., p. 47.

13. Ibid., p. 232, n. 1.

14. Edward T. Cone, *Conversations with Roger Sessions*, Perspectives on American Composers, edited by Benjamin Boretz and Edward T. Cone (New York: Norton, 1971), p. 104.

15. Michael Steinberg, "Roger Sessions, Symphony No. 2," *The Symphony: A Listener's Guide* (New York: Oxford University Press, 1995), p. 188.

16. Luigi Dallapiccola, "The Genesis of Canti di Prigionia and Il Prigioniero (*1950–1953*), an Autobiographical Fragment," in *Dallapiccola on Opera* (London: Toccata Press, 1987), pp. 41–42.

17. Ibid., p. 110.

18. Ibid., pp. 52–53.

19. Ibid., p. 55.

20. See chapter 8, p. 109.

21. Dallapiccola, *Dallapiccola on Opera*, p. 62.

22. Ibid., p. 91.

23. Frederik Prausnitz, *In ricordo di Luigi Dallapiccola*, pp. 36–37.

24. The letter, part of the Dallapiccola archive in Florence, is dated "5 sett. 1952." Unlike other letters in this collection, this one is not mimeographed but appears to be a typed copy. Its content and that of other 1952 letters that deal with a forthcoming visit by Dallapiccola to Berkeley that year suggest strongly that the date should read: September 5, 1951. NB: the translation from the Italian of all RS letters to LD is mine.

25. RS letter to Dallapiccola, Dallapiccola archive in Florence, 1952.

26. Dika Newlin, *Schoenberg Remembered* (New York: Pendragon Press, 1980), p. 333.

27. RS letter to Luigi Dallapiccola, Dallapiccola archive, Florence, dated Venerdi [Friday] 26 Settembre, 1952. NB: Unlike the earlier letter, the copy of this letter is a photostat of the original, clearly in Sessions' handwriting. Interestingly, however, the year "1952" appears to have been added by someone else's hand. If the year in both letters was added by the same person who typed the copy of the first letters, the apparent error in the first is easier to explain than the unlikely fact of Sessions himself postdating it by a year.

CHAPTER 18 **The Musical Idea III**

1. John Sessions letter to FP, March 15, 1998.

2. Franz Werfel, *Verdi* (New York: Simon and Schuster, 1925).

3. See chapter 7, p. 98.

4. Roger Sessions, *Questions about Music*, published version of his Charles Eliot Norton Lectures at Harvard, 1968–1969 (New York: Norton, 1971), p. 42.

5. See chapter 13, p. 180.

6. See chapter 6, p. 87, "Interview with Roger Sessions," *Boston Globe*, April 24, 1927.

7. Program book, San Francisco Symphony, January 1949.

8. See chapter 7, p. 97.

9. Schoenberg letter to RS, July 17, 1948, Library of Congress, Washington, D.C.

10. See chapter 12, p. 168.

11. See chapter 13, p. 174.

12. FP interview.

13. Michael Ian Crawford Campbell, "The Piano Sonatas of Roger Sessions: Sequel to a Tradition," DMA diss., Peabody Institute, Johns Hopkins University, 1982, chapter 4, pp. 140–141.

14. Frederik Prausnitz, *Score and Podium* (New York: Norton, 1983), chapters 6 and 8.

15. Andrew Imbrie, "The Symphonies of Roger Sessions" (except No. 9, which was not yet composed at the time), *Tempo: A Quarterly Review of Modern Music* 103 (1972), p. 27.

16. Roger Sessions, "Schenker's Contribution," *Modern Music* 12, no. 4, quoted in *Roger Sessions on Music: Collected Essays*, edited by Edward T. Cone (Princeton, New Jersey: Princeton University Press, 1979), pp. 231–240.

17. Ibid., p. 240.

18. Roger Sessions, "Schoenberg in the United States," *Tempo*, no. 9 (December 1944, old series).

19. Sessions, "Schoenberg in the United States," reprint of 1944 article, revised by author, *Tempo: A Quarterly Review of Modern Music* 103 (1972), p. 11.

20. Ibid., p. 16, n. 6.

21. See chapter 17, p. 240.

22. FP interview.

23. In the American premiere at Juilliard we performed the work both ways, in English before and in Italian after the intermission.

24. Hans Nathan, "The Twelve-Tone Compositions of Luidi Dallapiccola," *Musical Quarterly* 54, no. 3 (July 1958). (The letter, originally in Italian, was translated by Nathan.)

25. Ibid., p. 304.

26. Ibid., pp. 304–305.

27. See above, p. 260.

28. Edward T. Cone, *Conversations with Roger Sessions*, Perspectives on American Composers, edited by Benjamin Boretz and Edward T. Cone (New York: Norton, 1971), p. 104.

29. See p. 212.

30. See appendix 1, pp. 229–301.

31. See above, p. 264.

32. See p. 262.

33. See p. 263.

34. See p. 225.

35. *The New Grove Dictionary of Music and Musicians,* edited by Stanley Sadie, George Perle, and Paul Lansky, vol. 17; *Twelve-note composition* (London: Macmillan, 1880), pp. 287–297.

36. Campbell, "The Piano Sonatas of Roger Sessions," chapter 4.

37. Cone, *Conversations with Roger Sessions*, p. 303.

38. See chapter 5, p. 69.

39. Sessions, *Questions about Music*, pp. 116–117.

40. Sessions letter to FP, August 1, 1968.

41. Arnold Schoenberg, *Harmonielehre* ["Wer wagt hier Theorie zu fordern!"] (Universal Edition), p. 507.

CHAPTER 19 **Harvest**

1. FP interview.

2. RS letter to Glock, July 15, 1956.

3. Roger Sessions, "Song and Pattern in Music Today," *Score*, no. 17 (September 1956), pp. 73–84.

4. Roger Sessions, "To the Editor," in *Perspectives of New Music* 5, no. 2 (Spring–Summer 1967), pp. 81–97.

5. Sessions, "To the Editor," in *Conversations with Roger Sessions*, Perspectives on American Composers, edited by Benjamin Boretz and Edward T. Cone (New York: Norton, 1971), pp. 108–124.

6. Sessions, "What Can Be Taught?" in *Roger Sessions on Music: Collected Essays*, edited by Edward T. Cone (Princeton, New Jersey: Princeton University Press, 1979), pp. 204–227.

7. RS letter to Glock, May 24, 1958.

8. FP interview.

9. FP interview.

10. The expression was a favorite with Roberto Gerhard, Spanish composer, student of Schoenberg, and a protégé of William Glock. Sessions adopted it and used it frequently.

11. FP interview.

12. BSO program book, April 22, 1927.

13. See Schoenberg letter, chapter 16, p. 225.

14. RS letter to Glock, April 22, 1957.

15. The String Quintet was composed in 1957.

16. E. T. Cone, *Conversations with Roger Sessions*, Perspectives on American Composers, edited by Benjamin Boretz and Edward T. Cone (New York: Norton, 1971), p. 101.

17. FP interview.

18. FP interview with Earl Kim, 1986.

19. See p. 250.

20. Sessions letter to FP [undated].

21. RS letter to Dallapiccola, January 12, 1960.

22. Boris Blacher (1903–1975), a German composer and teacher of composition at the Dresden Conservatory from 1938 to 1939, was relieved of his post by the Nazi authorities. After the war, he was professor of composition at the Berlin Hochschule from 1948 to 1953, then director of the *Hochschule* until his retirement in 1970.

23. See p. 273.

24. FP interview.

25. The orchestral version of this work was first performed in 1966 by the Boston Symphony Orchestra under Erich Leinsdorf (Anne Elgar, soprano).

26. Now in the Library of Congress, Washington, D.C.

27. Heinrich Hollreiser (1913–   ) German conductor and principal conductor at the Deutsche Oper in Berlin from 1961 to 1964), was best known for his performances of Wagner and Strauss but also had a significant number of twentieth-century operas in his repertory, including Britten's *Peter Grimes*, Berg's *Wozzek*, Hindemith's *Mathis der Maler*, and Bartok's *Bluebeard's Castle*. From 1964 he worked as guest conductor in Bayreuth and at other major European opera houses.

28. "About Montezuma, what can I say?" RS letter to Dallapiccola, April 23, 1964.

29. Hans Werner Henze (1926–   ), a prolific German composer, had written five symphonies and a number of very successful operas by the time of the *Montezuma* premiere in Berlin. Living in Italy since 1953, he had turned to a Marxist worldview, re-

flecting in his work a perceived clash between militaristic or bourgeois existence and his aspirations to international socialism to come. *Versuch über Schweine* (Essay on pigs), *Das Floss der "Medusa"* (The raft of the "Medusa"), and a *Requiem for Che Guevara* were his musical challenge to a society he perceived as terminally corrupt.

30. Jannis Xenakis (1922–), is a French composer of Greek parentage. During the Second World War he served as secretary of the resistance against the Nazis at the Polytechnic Institute in Athens and was severely injured, captured, and sentenced to death but escaped and settled in Paris. Largely self-taught, he was encouraged by composer Oliver Messiaen and conductor Hermann Scherchen. As a trained engineer and deeply influenced by the work of architects, Xenakis also undertook several building assignments. Application of mathematical models in musical composition reflects his belief in a direct relation between architecture and musical forms.

31. Gilbert Amy (1939–), a French composer, had been a disciple of Pierre Boulez since 1959. He became a conductor notable for his championship of contemporary music.

32. RS letter to Luigi Dallapiccola, April 23, 1964 (FP translation).

33. See chapter 8, p. 115.

34. FP interview.

35. Ibid.

36. Michael Steinberg, "Sessions Cantata to Have East Coast Premiere Here Tomorrow," *Boston Globe*, March 21, 1975.

37. Chapter 6, p. 89.

38. FP interview.

39. Ibid.

40. RS letter to Glock, August 1969.

41. FP interview.

42. CBS recording with the New Philharmonia Orchestra of London.

43. Andrea Olmstead, *The Correspondence of Roger Sessions* (Boston: Northeastern University Press, 1992), p. 473.

44. RS letter to FP, August 6, 1975.

45. RS letter to FP, September 26/27, 1976.

46. Ibid.

47. The surprise referred back to an interview in the *New York Times*, in which, at the beginning of his tenure as music director of the New York Philharmonic (1971–1974), Pierre Boulez made derogatory reference to American "university composers." Himself a beneficiary of a more enlightened public musical life in Europe at the time, particularly the just-preceding William Glock period in England, Boulez was not yet aware of the situation that had driven almost all American composers into teaching positions.

48. Ibid.

49. See p. 278.

50. RS letter to FP, September 23, 1974.

51. Cone, *Conversations with Roger Sessions*, p. 100.

52. See RS letter p. 289.

53. See chapter 13, p. 180.

54. "*Wer wagt hier Theorie zu fordern!*", Arnold Schoenberg, *Harmonielehre* [Universal Edition], p. 507.

55. See chapter 7, p. 97.

56. See chapter 13, p. 174.

57. See chapter 7 and appendix 2.

58. Andrew Imbrie, "Remembering Roger," *Perspectives of New Music* 23 (Spring/Summer 1985), "In Memoriam Roger Sessions," p. 150.

59. Andrew Porter, *New Yorker*, November 9, 1981.
60. Andrew Porter, "A Magnificent Epic," *New Yorker* 58 (March 8, 1982).
61. *Time* magazine, March 8, 1982.
62. Porter, "A Magnificent Epic," *New Yorker* 58 (March 8, 1982).
63. See p. 292.

APPENDIX 1 **Overview**

1. Sessions' sister, Hannah, was born on February 16, 1888.
2. Max Strub, concertmaster of Klemperer's Kroll Oper, in whose apartment Roger Sessions rented a room.
3. Also among his private students in New York: Milton Babbitt, Marion Bauer.
4. Sessions is mistaken here: his Fulbright Lectures in Florence took place in 1951–52.
5. This refers to actual work on the opera's composition. Musical sketches were begun in 1947, work on libretto before that.
6. Should read: *1962.*
7. *Montezuma* was performed in February 1982.

APPENDIX 3

1. All emphases in Bloch's notes are his own.

SOURCES

In addition to my interviews with Roger Sessions (1981–1983), the principal sources for this book were his compositions and his writings, not only in their finished appearance but also in the available evidence of their genesis. Happily, Sessions did not destroy most of the sketches and preliminary versions of his major works and most of these are now accessible in the collections of the Library of Congress and in the Manuscript Division of the Princeton University Library.

The respective holdings of these two collections complement each other. At the time when this book went to press, plans to make these archives available for study in a combined version on microfilm were quite far advanced. Having made extensive use of the Sessions archive in the Library of Congress, I made my own index of its as yet uncataloged content, a copy of which follows. An index of the Princeton collection, Roger Sessions Scores, is available on the Internet at the Web site of Princeton University. At this time, both collections are housed in boxes, binders, and a large number of loose folders.

Sessions Archive, The Library of Congress

Box No. I

\# Notes on Sym. #4, 2 pp.
Notes (Fragment on *Lilacs*)
Outline for criteria: *Questions about Music*
Notes (Schwartz) Sym. #2—comp. in 1941 [? FP]
\# "Meine 2. Symphonie hatte ich im Jahre 1946 fertig gestellt . . . " in German, 3 pp.
Note on *Lucullus* (subtitle *Drama in Music*), 2 pp.
Notes on Andreyev's play (*The Black Maskers*)
Notes on Sym. #4, 2 pp./3 pp./4 pp. (typed 2pp.)
Program Notes on Sym. #8
Program Notes for *Psalm 140*, 12 pp.
\# Notes on *Montezuma* (complete)
\# Notes on Berlin perf. of *Montezuma*, 5 pp.
Musical Notes (sketches?) for *Montezuma*, 2 pp.
Montezuma Tempi (metronome)
Draft for *Montezuma* Preface
Notes on Borgese ms. for *Montezuma*, 4 pp.
Isolated pp.—draft of *Montezuma* lecture?
\# Notes for Schoenberg article (*Tempo* 1944, 1972)
Schoenberg in US (typed ms. of article)
(penciled ms.)
Folder: "Notes on Lectures" (various mss., pencil, not in order)
Folder: as above ("Writings not yet sorted")

Draft of *Talking and Thinking about Music* (publ. *Questions about Music*)
Outline for *"Criteria"* (#6 of *Questions about Music*)
ms. of *Criteria* (*Questions about Music)*
Draft of *Epilogue* (*Questions about Music*)
Introduction for *Questions about Music*

Box No. II

Notebook and sketches for *Concerto for Orchestra*

Box No. III

Notes on *Stravinsky's Oedipus*, pp. 2–8
Notes on *Schnabel's Second Symphony*
Lecture (?) pencil ms., starts with *E. Newman talk in Boston*, 20 yrs. earlier
typed ms *America moves to the Avant-Scene.*
Folder: *J.B. (Jean Binet)* "My memories of Jean Binet go back for forty years, to the time when we were both students of Ernest Bloch in New York [*sic*] . . . "
Folder: *"Notes on Lectures"* (2 pp. in German, e.g., "National Music?" etc.)
Folder: Sewannee, Tennessee, Oct. 1957 (Review), *Freedom and the Individual,* typed ms, complete
Folder: *Reflections, etc., Florence lectures 1951–52* and translation ("to be put in order") typed and penciled pp.
Florence lecture, Spring 1952 (in Italian)
Folder: *Reflections*, handwritten in Italian., handwritten and typed in
Folder: Comments on Music Appreciation text
Folder: Brandeis lecture Jan. 1954 (*Music and the Crisis in the Arts*).
Folder: Lecture—*Composing—I*, 74 pp. (?)
Folder: Notes on Andrew Imbrie
The Psychological Basis of Modern Dissonance (Harvard 1915)
Folder: *Style and Styles in Music*
Drafts for Norton Lectures

Box No. IV: *Montezuma* I

Text: *Montezuma* Text (with some musical sketches*) To be put in some kind of order* [Quote in RS handwriting]
Text, 3 folders + 2 loose pages, some musical sketches on typewritten pages
Folder: *Act II–III, reference copy* [in RS handwriting], handwritten revisions
Folder: Act III, handwritten revisions
Text revisions, some musical sketches
Text [far from final, some not known to me—FP], many musical sketches
Folder: *Act III, Miscellaneous sketches.* Actually much like the above
Folder: Outlines of distribution (measures?) of various characters over Acts, Scenes
Folder: Outlines of characterizations (by instruments) of protagonists, nationalities
Leitmotifs [RS term]
More numbers: e.g.,
landing
1—2—5 = 4 measure total
[measure numbers? FP]
Column is totaled (for each act—?)
[Act 29?—can't be measures . . . FP]

Box No. V: *Montezuma* II

Binder: Philosophical, technical, musical sketches—some numbered in red

Box No. VI: Symphony No. III

Folder: Particell sketches
Folder: Particell sketches
Folder: Particell sketches
Folder: Particell sketches (again additions)
Folder: Particell sketches
Folder: Particell sketches
loose pages: more advanced Particell sketches
loose score pages: advanced Particell sketches

Box No. VII

Folder: "Misc. Old Sketches" [RS handwriting]
Loose music paper: "Misc." [RS] 2 pp.
Misc. sketches, dated October 1, 1952
Single sheet of music ms.
Folder: "Foreign Relations" [RS], Musical sketches
Single sheet: "Scene 4, p. 2, "Whirling lines, unnatural patterns, phosphorous gloaming out of the dark" [sketch]
Single sheet: Sketch dated "Mon., Mar. 16, 1925" [RS] [26?]

Box No. VIII

9 pocket "composers' notebooks" (oblong, blue)
[1 dated July 3, 1955]
[1 dated July 14, 1955]
Several larger (quarto) notebooks (1 German)
Folder: "*Children's Pieces*" [RS]
Misc. ms. papers, 10 lines [include sketches 2nd Quartet?]

Box No. IX

Single sheet—Tristan Examples [for teaching or for *Questions about Music*]
Large score paper: Particell sketches
Folder: Songs [Sketches and engraved copy]
Folder: Sonata—Finale (complete or not quite, in detail?)
also contains: Fair Copy, RS ms. on oilskin of 3rd Symphony, beginning [23 pp.]

Box No. X

Folder: Sketches dated July 1, July 9, 1974
Folder: 7th Symphony Particell II
Folder: Unidentified sketches
Folder: 7th Symphony Particell III, pp. 13–18 missing
mixed with unidentified sketches, some for *Biblical Choruses*, "they have forsaken . . . ," including tone rows and transpositions
Folder "for sorting" [RS], June 1, 1979, tone row
Folder: "Misc." [RS], 2 pp. sketches
Folder: 7th Symphony, sketches

Box No. XI

Folder: 7th Symphony, pp. 18–25 missing, unsorted sketches
Folder: 3 pp. unsorted sketches
Folder: 7th Symphony, pp. missing: I, 1–18, 36; II, 37, 39–41, 43, 44; III 1, 2, 24, 25.
Folder: Sketches (*Choruses on Biblical Texts*)
Folder: 7th Symphony, pp. missing I, 10; III, 12, 19, 20.

Box No. XII

Folder, bound: *When Lilacs . . .* pencil draft, piano reduction
Folder: Opening of *Lilacs*, fair copy, pencil
Folder, bound: *Choruses on Biblical Texts*, pencil draft
Folder, bound: Double Concerto, pencil draft
Folder: *The Black Maskers*, No. III 2—piano arr.
Folder: *Pages from a Diary*, fair copy ('39/40)
Folder: Six Pieces for Cello, fair copy, 1966
Folder: *Lancelot & Elaine*, Act III, "Finished Dec. 23, 1910, at 12.28 AM"

Box Nos. XIII, XIV

Montezuma, particell

Not in Boxes

Binder: Sketches for Concerto for Orchestra, pencil and Xerox copy
2 pocket sketchbooks: *From My Diary*, String Quartet
Folder: 9th Symphony, sketches
Folder: Cello Pieces
Folder: Concerto for Orchestra, Canon for Igor Stravinsky
Folder: Piano Pieces, sketches
Folder: *Lilacs*, piano reduction
Offset score: *Lilacs*
Folder: 6th Symphony, particell
Folder, bound: 1936, '37, '39 sketches (including *Montezuma*)
Folder, bound: 1939 sketches (including *Montezuma*)
Folder: 9th Symphony, Concerto for Orchestra, sketches
Folder: 8th Symphony, particell
Folder: 7th Symphony, particell

Writings by Roger Sessions

Books

The Musical Experience of Composer, Performer, Listener. Published version of his Juilliard lectures, 1949. Princeton, New Jersey: Princeton University Press, 1950. Paperback edition, New York: Atheneum, 1962.

Questions about Music. Published version of his Charles Eliot Norton Lectures at Harvard, 1968–1969. New York, Norton, 1971.

Harmonic Practice. Harcourt, Brace and World, 1951.

Reflections on Music Life [sic] in the United States. New York: Merlin, n.d. Unauthorized and bowdlerized publication of ms. Sessions, *Musical Life in the United States*, six Italian Fulbright Lectures given in Florence, 1951–1952. The penciled English draft of these lectures is in the Roger Sessions archives of the Library of Congress in Washington, D.C.

Articles

The following articles, lectures, and essays were reprinted in an anthology edited by Edward T. Cone, *Roger Sessions on Music: Collected Essays* (Princeton, New Jersey: Princeton University Press, 1979):

"Artists and This War, a Letter to an Imaginary Colleague." *Modern Music* 20, no. 1 (1942).

"The Composer and his Message." Originally delivered as one of the Spencer Trask Lec-

tures at Princeton University, published in Augusto Centeno, ed., *The Intent of the Artist* (1941).
"The Composer in the University." Contribution to a symposium on the graduate study of music, joint session of the American Musicological Society and the Society for Music in the Liberal Arts College, New York City, 1940.
"Ernest Bloch." *Modern Music* 5, no. 1 (1927).
"Escape by Theory." *Modern Music* 15, no. 3 (1938).
"Europe Comes to America." Address at Kenyon College, 1945.
"Exposition by Krenek." *Modern Music* 15, no. 2 (1938).
"In Memoriam Igor Stravinsky." *Perspectives of New Music* 9, no. 2 (p. 12).
"Music and Nationalism." *Modern Music* 11, no. 1 (1933).
"Music in Crisis." *Modern Music* 10, no. 2 (1933).
"The New Musical Horizon." *Modern Music* 14, no. 2 (1937).
"New Vistas in Music Education." *New Music* 11, no. 2 (1934).
"No More Business As Usual." *Modern Music* 19, no. 3 (1942).
"On the American Future." *Modern Music* 17, no. 2 (1940).
"Schenker's Contribution." *Modern Music* 12, no. 4 (1934).
"Schoenberg in the United States." Reprint of 1944 article in *Tempo Magazine*, revised by author in *Tempo: A Quarterly Review of Modern Music* 103 (1972).
"Song and Pattern in Music Today." *Score* no. 17 (September 1956).
"Thoughts on Stravinsky." *Score* no. 20 (1957).
"Vienna—Vale, Ave." *Modern Music* 15, no. 4 (1938).
"What Can Be Taught?" Originally appeared under the title "To the Editor" in the English periodical the *Score* (1958), reprinted (still under that title) in *Perspectives of New Music* 5, no. 2 (Spring–Summer 1967), and in Perspectives on American Composers, edited by Benjamin Boretz and Edward T. Cone, New York: Norton, 1971. The new title, "What Can Be Taught?" appeared for the first time in the Cone anthology, *Roger Sessions on Music.*

Other Articles and Essays by Roger Sessions

"An American Evening Abroad." Review of a concert presented by the Societé Musicale Indépendante of Paris. *New Music* no. 4 (November 1926).
"Composer and Critic." Letter to the Music Editor of the *New York Times,* March 11, 1934.
"How a Difficult Composer Gets That Way." *New York Times*, January 8, 1950.
"How Far Will We Go with Popularization." *Saturday Review of Literature* 27 (1944).
In ricordo di Luigi Dallapiccola. Milan: Zuvini Zerboni, 1975.
"Musicology and the Composer." *Bulletin of the American Musicological Society* 5 (1941).
"Problems and Issues Facing the Composer Today." *Musical Quarterly* 46 (1960),
"The Scope of Music Criticism." In Richard F. French, ed., *Music and Criticism.* Cambridge, Massachusetts: Harvard University Press, 1948.
"Some Notes on Schoenberg and the Method of Composing with Twelve Tones." *Score* 6 (1952).
Thirteen articles, written as an undergraduate for the *Harvard Musical Review* 1–4 (1913–1915).

Writings about Roger Sessions

Books and Musical Dictionaries

Abruzzo, James, and Henry Weinberg. "Sessions, Roger (Huntington)." In *The New Grove Dictionary of Music and Musicians*. New York: Macmillan, 1978.

Gagne, C., and T. Caras. "Roger Sessions." In *Soundpieces: Interviews with American Composers*. Metuchen, 1982.

Harbison, John. "Sessions, Roger." In *The New Grove Dictionary of American Music*, vol. 4 (bibliography, Andrea Olmstead). New York: Macmillan, 1986.

Olmstead, Andrea. *The Correspondence of Roger Sessions*. Boston: Northeastern University Press, 1992.

———. *Roger Sessions and His Music*. Ann Arbor: University of Minnesota, 1985.

Sessions, Ruth Huntington. *Sixty Odd: A Personal History*. Brattleboro, Vermont: Stephen Haye, 1936.

Slonimsky, Nicolas. *Music since 1900*. New York: Scribners, 1971.

———. "Roger Sessions." Chapter 9 in Henry Cowell, ed., *American Composers on American Music*, vol. 1. Frederick Ungar, 1933.

Steinberg, Michael. "Roger Sessions, Symphony No. 2." In *The Symphony: A Listener's Guide*. New York: Oxford University Press, 1995.

Articles and Dissertations

Brunswick, Mark. "American Composers, Roger Huntington Sessions." *Modern Music* 10 (1932–33).

Campbell, Michael Ian Crawford. "The Piano Sonatas of Roger Sessions: Sequel to a Tradition." DMA diss. Peabody Institute, Johns Hopkins University, 1982.

Cogan, Robert. "Toward a Theory of Timbre, Verbal Timbre and Musical Line in Purcell, Sessions and Stravinsky." *Perspectives of New Music* 18 (1968).

Cone, Edward T. "Conversation with Roger Sessions." *Perspectives of New Music*, 1966.

———. "In Defense of Song: The Contribution of Roger Sessions." *Critical Inquiry* 2 (1975).

———. "In Honor of Roger Sessions." *Perspectives of New Music* 1972.

———. "Sessions: Second String Quartet." *Musical Quarterly* 43 (1957).

———. "Sessions's Concertino." *Tempo: A Quarterly Review of Modern Music* 115 (1976).

Copland, Aaron. "Contemporaries at Oxford." *Musical Quarterly* 9 (1931–1932).

Davies, P. M. "Montezuma." *New York Times*, April 21, 1964.

Hamilton, David. "The New Craft of the Contemporary Concerto: Carter and Sessions." *HiFi Magazine* 18 (1968).

Harbison, John. "Roger Sessions and Montezuma." *Tempo: A Quarterly Review of Modern Music* 121 (1977).

Hoberman, Jerome. "Idea and Style in Two Late Works of Roger Sessions." Diss., Peabody Institute, Johns Hopkins University. 1999.

Imbrie, Arthur. "Roger Sessions, in Honor of His Sixty-fifth Birthday." *Perspectives of New Music*, 1962.

———. "The Symphonies of Roger Sessions." *Tempo: A Quarterly Review of Modern Music* 103 (1972).

Keats, Sheila. "Reference Articles on American Composers: An Index." *Juilliard Review* no. 1 (1954).

Kress, S. "Roger Sessions, Composer and Teacher: A Comprehensive Analysis of Roger Sessions' Philosophy of Educating Composers and His Approach to Composition in Symphonies No. 2 and 8." Diss., University of Florida, 1982.

Laufer, E. C. "Montezuma." Perspectives of New Music 4 (1965).

Mason, C. "A Comprehensive Analysis of Roger Sessions' Opera Montezuma." Diss., University of Illinois at Urbana, 1982.

Merryman, M. "Aspects of Phrasing and Pitch Usage in Roger Sessions' Piano Sonata No. 3." Diss., Brandeis University, 1981.

Oja, C. J. "The Copland-Sessions Concerts and Their Reception in the Contemporary Press." *Musical Quarterly* 65 (1979).

Olmstead, Andrea. "The Plumed Serpent, Antonio Borgese's and Roger Sessions' Montezuma." *Tempo: A Quarterly Review of Modern Music* 152 (1985).

———. "Roger Sessions: A Personal Portrait." *Tempo: A Quarterly Review of Modern Music* no. 127 (1978).

———. "Roger Sessions and His Influence." *Essays on Modern Music* 2 (1985).

———. "Roger Sessions' Ninth Symphony." *Tempo: A Quarterly Review of Modern Music* 133 (1980).

Porter, Andrew. "An American Requiem." *New Yorker* 53 (1978).

———. "A Magnificent Epic." *New Yorker* 58 (March 8, 1982).

———. "The Matter of Mexico." *New Yorker* 52 (1977).

———. "Sessions of Strong-Sounding Thought." *New Yorker* 59 (1982).

———. "Sessions' Passionate and Profound Lilacs." *HiFi Magazine* 38 (1978). Andrew Porter, Celebration, *New Yorker* 57 (1981).

Schubart, Mark. "Roger Sessions: Portrait of an American Composer." *Musical Quarterly* 32 (1946).

Wheeler, S. "Harmonic Motion in the Music of Roger Sessions: An Examination of the Quintet, First Movement." Diss., Brandeis University, 1984.

"In Memoriam Roger Sessions," contributions by Milton Babbitt, Arthur Berger, Robert Black, Elliott Carter, Edward T. Cone, Gordon C. Cyr, David Diamond, Joel Feigin, Ross Lee Finney, Vivian Fine, Miriam Gideon, Andrew Imbrie, David Levin, Frederik Prausnitz, Harold Schiffman, S. Earl Saxton, William O. Smith, and Vincent Persichetti, *Perspectives of New Music* 23 (Spring/Summer 1985).

INDEX

Page numbers appearing in italics refer to illustrations.